The Topography of Baghdad in the Early Middle Ages

The Topography of Baghdad in the Early Middle Ages

TEXT AND STUDIES

by *Jacob Lassner*

WAYNE STATE UNIVERSITY

Wayne State University Press, Detroit, 1970

Published simultaneously in Canada
by The Copp Clark Publishing Company
517 Wellington Street, West
Toronto 2B, Canada.

Library of Congress Catalog Card Number: 69-11339
ISBN: 0-8143-1391-4

to my parents

Contents

Illustrations

Maps

Foreword

It has long been recognized that an urban order was, in the medieval Islamic world, both an ideal and a reality. Grammatical schools as well as fiction found their setting in cities and towns. Basrah or Kufah identify precise developments of early Muslim thought and it is around fifty cities that the twelfth-century best-seller known as the *Maqāmāt* wove the adventures of its linguistic genius and picaresque hero. It is in the city's citadel or palace rather than in the isolated *chateau-fort* that princes lived and that there grew a unique aristocractic imagery reflected in literature and in art. Pride in one's city or the mere cognizance of the city as the point around which life revolved appeared early and continued as late as in the local histories of the fifteenth and sixteenth centuries.

The character of the relationship between individual man and the urban order, or between social organisms and the city, varied considerably from century to century and from area to area. The antiquarian curiosity of a Maqrīzī listing and describing the monuments of Cairo in the fifteenth century differs from the painstaking, alphabetically ordained catalogues of great men made by the Khaṭīb al-Baghdādī or IbnʿAsākir for Baghdad and Damascus in the eleventh and twelfth centuries. It differs also from the panegyric of the Sāmānid dynasty and the nostalgic consciousness of a brilliant pre-Islamic past which appears in Narshakhī's tenth century *History of Bukhara*, just as it lacks the religious consciousness of the anonymous *Tarīkh-i Qumm* or of Mujīr al-Dīn's late descriptions of Jerusalem and Hebron. These variable attitudes, their relationship to each other, their history, and the influences which affected each and every one of them are still subjects of investigation for historiographers. Much in such eventual studies is bound to increase our appreciation and understanding of the many ways in which cities were seen by the people who lived in them.

But on a more practical and more specific side, there are other ways in which one can approach or imagine medieval cities. One such way centers on institutions, for, like any complex living organism, the Muslim city developed systems of authority and of legal or de facto rights and responsibilities. Some of these institutions met very practical needs, such as the control of weights and measures or taxation; others, like criminal or moral regulations or inheritance laws, expressed loftier aims and purposes, often independent from the character of any individual city and related to more universal Muslim concepts; some, finally, grew from the inner social or economic tensions of the organism itself and, like so many autovaccinations, served to solve individual problems, even when the titles by which they are called imply that they treat of a subject which is as wide as the Muslim world. Much in this institutional development is quite unknown, because scholarship has not yet been able, with very few exceptions, to penetrate completely into the inner workings of any one given city. Yet, in recent years, considerable progress has been made in defining the terms in which we should, at any one time, examine the evidence of our sources.

A second practical aspect of the city is its everyday life. Curiously enough, the daily problems and activities of towns have not only attracted little attention from contemporary scholars but are also very elusive in the better known medieval texts themselves, as though the medieval Islamic world was shy about its own life. Yet, here again, renewed interest in well-known sources such as Jāḥiẓ and Tanūkhī, as well as the recent publication of an eleventh century diary, and especially the amazingly rich Geniza documents are beginning to fill the gap. Consequently, men of old lose something of their abstract, shadowy character to acquire flesh and sentiments. Much remains to be done; in particular, archeological sources, ceramics, textiles, and miniatures have hardly been tapped at all, but with the planned publication of the Geniza fragments a great step forward will be accomplished in the proper direction.

The third facet of the Muslim city's specific character in the Middle Ages is its physical appearance. In a general sense everyone knows that there were mosques, palaces, baths, markets, rich and poor houses, cemeteries, shrines, walls, and gates in almost all cities. But did all these architectural features spring up suddenly and at the same time? How did a city grow? What were the universal components of its growth? What were purely local conditions? These questions are still, for the most part, unanswered. To be true, considerable work has been done on Cairo, probably the best documented in texts and monuments of all Near Eastern cities, but no single, complete account of the way in which the huge metropolis on the Nile became what it is today has been made available except in shortened form by Professor Wiet and from the point of view of a geographer by M. Clerget. Thanks to the late Jean Sauvaget and to Professor Le Tourneau, Aleppo and Fez are instances of towns whose full history has been scrutinized to the point where each individual period has been clarified to the limits of available evidence. For Mecca, Damascus, Jerusalem, Kufah, Basrah, Bukhara, Samarkand, and Merv, some preliminary work has been done, but the total picture is still far from being clear.

It is with these considerations in mind that one may perhaps best approach Dr. Lassner's work on Baghdad. Here was the "navel of the universe," consciously "molded and cast" into a perfect shape, the most superb creation of the Muslim empire at its highest moment of glory and unity, and so obviously economically and politically significant that it remained for over twelve hundred years as a major center, regardless of historical or natural accidents. It is quite obvious that a good understanding of the history and characteristics of such a city during the first few centuries of its creation has a double advantage. It permits us to define precisely the principal features of the avowed masterpiece of classical Islamic urban inventiveness and it sets the physical and ecological stage for the later history of Baghdad.

It is true, of course, that much has been written on the city of Baghdad. The fundamental text translated here into English for the first time has been known for many decades. The importance of a new translation and of new commentaries is that the progress otherwise attained in our understanding of Islamic cities permits Dr. Lassner to set more concretely the problems posed by this city which, unfortunately, is known through texts only. It is clear, for instance, from Dr. Lassner's work that the Khaṭīb's text, which has so often been used to define Baghdad at the time of the author's life, is only valid up to the middle of the preceding century.

One cannot sufficiently emphasize the importance of such precise dating, for still today the pernicious notion of a motionless Orient has tended to assume for all times what is only valid for a clearly identifiable moment of history. But, more importantly, the period which has preceded the foundation of Baghdad is so much better known archeologically than it was at the time of the first publication and utilization of the Khaṭīb's text that many features of Baghdad can now be much better understood. Contrary to what was written by ʿAbbāsid eulogists and accepted, in a modified form, by scholars of the early part of the century, Baghdad was not a creation ex nihilo, but a very logical continuation of architectural practices developed in the preceding century, although admittedly the scale and the symbolic and practical purposes of the new capital outweighed by far any of the preceding constructions.

There is yet another way in which a new translation of an old text is a step forward in our understanding of Baghdad. Old editions and old translations have a curious way of being known without being read any longer. While once again focusing scholarly attention on a fundamental text, a new edition or a new translation allows more easily for new or merely subtler interpretations. Thus several attempts have been made by Dr. Lassner to relate otherwise known events to the setting in which they were supposed to have taken place. These attempts have led him to a number of hypotheses or conclusions about actual functions and characteristics of individual parts of the Round City or about the central arteries of a traditional Near Eastern city: markets, mosques, canals, and changing urban and suburban centers. These hypotheses and conclusions help to explain why and how it was that the first city expanded so rapidly and transformed itself so completely a few years after its creation, a puzzling phenomenon if we consider the symbolic significance attributed to the shape of the imperial capital and the considerable thought that went into its planning.

For the full and complete understanding of Baghdad or of Islamic cities in general this is only the beginning. It will serve its purpose only if archeological investigations on the one hand and precise textual studies about this and other cities on the other are pursued in sufficient numbers to bring our knowledge of the medieval Islamic urban order from abstract consideration and theory down to a full reconstruction of its physical and human mechanisms.

Oleg Grabar
Ann Arbor, Michigan

Preface

Among the many cities that were part of the urban environment of the medieval Near East, Baghdad perhaps stands out above all others. The magnitude of its human and physical dimensions dwarfed all others in comparison. Its unique geographic position made it at the same time a major inland port, and a great center of overland trade. It was the administrative focal point of an empire, but also a great center of theological study, as well as more general learning. It was, in short, a city of no particular dimension, because it was a city of all dimensions, with life focusing on every aspect of human endeavor. What could have been more fitting than to call it the "navel of the universe," a city which was unlike all other cities, even in the years of its incipient decline.

Although it was the greatest city of the medieval Islamic world, the topographical setting of Baghdad is perhaps not as well known as some lesser sites owing to the absence of definitive archeological evidence. Nevertheless, the Islamic urbanist is fortunate to possess several detailed topographical accounts which set forth to describe the locations of the city in relation to one another as well as some incidental information relevant to the historical pattern of its growth. These literary sources form the basis of the modern studies, beginning with the books of G. LeStrange and M. Streck which appeared at the outset of this century and which remain standard works of reference even today.

In his ambitious book, which for technical reasons was, unfortunately, published without sufficient annotation, LeStrange, working largely from sources then found only in manuscript, attempted to reconstruct the city in various stages of historical development. The significance of this original contribution cannot be underestimated, but given the nature of the available sources, the plans of the city, by the author's own admission, "court criticism from anyone who will take the trouble of going through the evidence." It is, therefore, no suprise that the theoretical conclusions of LeStrange were soon challenged by L. Massignon. Although he recognized the obvious importance of literary sources, Massignon was led to disagree with LeStrange on methodological grounds. Unlike LeStrange who never studied the site, Massignon attempted a surface analysis of the general area in 1907–1908, and published the results of his findings some five years later. On the basis of certain fixed topographical points, he felt it necessary to disagree with some of the conclusions of LeStrange, not only with regard to the historical development of the city, but the actual position of various key locations. For Massignon, these fixed points are: various shrines which have remained at the same location since ʿAbbāsid times, and the markets of the city, which according to a rule formulated by him, are fixed from the time a city is created. This almost casual observation based largely on his experiences in Near Eastern cities around the turn of the century soon became a central concept in analyzing the medieval environment. Subsequent discussions on the topographical growth of the city generally reflect this difference of opinion between Massignon and LeStrange —between a method based essentially on a few scant physical remains, and one based entirely on a limited selection of literary sources.

However important these texts are for describing the physical layout of Baghdad, they are perhaps equally valuable to the historian of art; for the chapters of Yaʿqūbī and the Khaṭīb which deal with the city are the major documents from the early Middle Ages which describe in detail the monumental palace architecture of the Near East. E. Herzfeld, who visited the site somewhat later, not only added some pertinent remarks based on his personal observations, but undertook the tremendous task of reconstructing the architecture of the original city based on these literary descriptions, and his reconstructions were subsequently accepted, with some modification, by K. A. C. Creswell in his survey of early Muslim architecture. Like the work of LeStrange on topography, the significance of their contribution to an understanding of the early physical monuments is unquestioned; however, a more careful reading of the Arabic texts, and a more systematic attempt to relate architectural forms to changing historical conditions, will suggest further modifications of great importance. It is clear that these scholarly efforts raise many questions which will only be solved when and if systematic diggings are undertaken on the suspected site of the older city. For the present, the major source of information for the topography of Baghdad continues to be literary, and among the various descriptions of the city which are preserved, the most detailed account is the introduction of the Khaṭīb al-Baghdādī's *History* (*Taʾrīkh*) *of Baghdad.*

The publication of this critical text belongs to the earlier generation of scholarship. A partial edition based on some early manuscripts with a French translation and annotation was first published at Paris by G. Salmon in 1904; and an edition of the entire work (without translation or annotation) later appeared in Cairo. Although several new manuscripts have since come to light, they are all of a comparatively late date, and it is doubtful that they will provide many, if indeed any, emendations or corrections to the text, as works of this kind tend to be slavishly copied in subsequent generations. Since the text and French translation may be regarded as more or less reliable, one may ask what need there is for a new publication of the Khaṭīb in English. Without a new printing (and this seems unlikely), the Paris edition (already quite scarce) is becoming increasingly unavailable. What is more, there are serious limitations to the present edition of the work as it understandably does not take into consideration various important literary sources and materials which have appeared subsequently. Moreover, the existing annotation fails to cover systematically even the material which was then known in published historical and geographical texts. The problem becomes quite conspicuous when one takes into consideration that LeStrange evaluates material without annotation, and Streck simply catalogues places without giving an index. Scholars seeking the identification of specific localities have, therefore, to check the index of Salmon leading to the passages of the Khaṭīb, and then, more often than not, in the absence of a satisfactory entry, turn to the indices of various geographical and historical texts, a process which is, to say the least, rather time-consuming. The present work is thus intended to serve as a handy reference guide on the topography of the city, collecting, and unlike Streck, evaluating the information found in a variety of published texts.

Considering the importance of the Khaṭīb, the need for a new annotated translation would seem to be in order, although this in itself would not represent a strikingly original contribution. The present book is somewhat more ambitiously conceived. The text of the Khaṭīb is a convenient frame on which to add an introduction explaining how the work should be read; for a careful analysis of the sources used by the author will reveal that his description is not based, by and large, on contemporary observations, but reflects earlier conditions. Given such identifiable moments in the history of the city, it is possible to suggest various methods by which to evaluate topographical change. Such a study is only possible with the text of the Khaṭīb, since it alone among the extant works on Baghdad prefaces the varous accounts with full *isnād*. Yet no one has previously attempted to differentiate the chronological layers of the text. The Paris translation in fact omits any reference to the full chain of authorities, and any meaningful discussion of them. Moreover, there is a series of supplementary studies which will suggest a new pattern to the architectural and historical development of the ʿAbbāsid capital; and as a result of the recently published work by R. M. Adams on the hinterland of Baghdad, it has now also become possible for the first time to give some tangible analysis to the interrelationship of the regional and imperial environment. As a result, earlier concepts based on casual observations must now give way to newer hypotheses supported by some statistical data. If the general climate of historical investigations of the medieval Near East is slowly changing, then the study of Islamic urbanism, and of Baghdad in particular, must change with it.

Some may object because there are, to be sure, some periods and problems which are not directly covered by the format of the new edition. In particular, the events from late Būyid and Saljūq times on have been referred to only casually, if at all. This in spite of the fact that both the physical surface of the city and its institutions were then undergoing enormous changes in a period of decline, as can be seen from the studies of Makdisi on the topography of the eleventh century, and from his massive work on IbnʿAqīl.

Studies of Baghdad under the Būyids and Saljūqs were originally contemplated and various materials were collected; however, it soon became increasingly clear that these periods are already crowded with many eminent names and inaccessible manuscripts, unlike the earlier times which had been abandoned and left conceptually tidy by a previous generation of scholars, when the methods of rigorous historical investigation were somewhat less refined than they are today. There may be some bizarre attraction to studying a city beset by great turmoil in all spheres of life, but I hope it is still appropriate to turn once again to the early city; for the results are surely not without significance for the later periods as well. A further objection may be raised on the question of style. The book in its present format tends to be somewhat repetitious; but it is after all a composite work consisting of text and studies. Although some will hopefully read it from cover to cover, one should be able to examine the individual sections more or less independently of one another, and the general value of the work as a reference guide on the topography of the city should not be compromised by an overwhelming desire for structural conciseness.

The translation covers the chapters of Salmon's edition with the exception of the last chapter on al-Madā'in (Ctesiphon) which is an appendage to the material on Baghdad. In order to avoid the conjectural solutions which necessarily accompany attempts to fix a precise location, the present work restricts itself to identifying various places in relation to one another, within the confines of a general area; although it must be admitted that some of the conclusions reached are highly problematical. Topographical terms such as *ṭarīq* (road), etc., have as a rule been translated into English. However, it often happens that the name of a particular place will, in time, extend to the surrounding area, e.g., Bāb aṭ-Ṭāq (The Gate of the Archway) which refers not only to a given monument but to an entire quarter of the East Side. In such cases, the Arabic topographical terms have been retained and transliterated, so as to avoid the ambiguities involved in a translation, and the reader is referred to the glossary of Arabic terms in the appendices which follow the text. Maps of the city reproduced from LeStrange are also found in the appendices; but the reader is by now well aware that they are drawn almost entirely from literary sources, and as such are very much subject to question.

References to the K͟haṭīb are to the Cairo edition unless otherwise indicated. The figures in the margin which are set off by hyphens, and those which are in parentheses refer to the pagination of the Salmon and Cairo editions, respectively. The system of transliteration is the one commonly used in English publications dealing with Arabic subjects. The conventional Western spelling of Baghdad is retained throughout. The various formulas which indicate the reception of an account by the different links in the *isnād*, such as *ḥaddat͟hanā*, *ak͟hbaranā*, etc., although they differ in significance for the Muslim scholar, are all reduced to a single long line, e.g., "Abū Yaʿlā Muḥammad b. al-Ḥusayn———Abū Ṭāhir b. Abī Bakr," which thus stands for: "Abū Yaʿlā Muḥammad b. al-Ḥusayn related the following account to me on the authority of Abū Ṭāhir b. Abī Bakr." A more thorough search of the Arabic sources will, no doubt, yield information on some of the figures whom I have not, as yet, succeeded in identifying.

It is not unusual while a book is in press for new materials pertaining to the subject to come to light, and due to the advanced state of production, for it to be impossible to integrate these materials within the body of the text. In the long period the present book was in production, a number of such materials appeared. It is necessary to take notice of one very important work. I recently received a copy of a book written in Georgian (*On the History of the*

City of Baghdad) by Professor O. V. Tskitishvili. Aside from the author's analysis, this work contains photographs of the section on Baghdad in the Mashhad MS of Ibn al-Faqīh, *K. al-Buldān*, which I had spent five years attempting to obtain. More recently, I received photographs of a full copy of the latter from Paris. These materials will be dealt with in a separate publication.

A list of all those who helped in the preparation of this work would indeed be long. Special mention should, however, be made of Professor Franz Rosenthal who first brought the text of the Khaṭīb to my attention, and whose impeccable scholarly integrity and enormous learning forced upon me various crucial problems that I would have otherwise avoided. As a substantial portion of the text was written during a year-long stay in Ann Arbor, a word of thanks is in order to the entire Department of Near Eastern Languages and Literatures at the University of Michigan, and in particular to Professor Oleg Grabar, who graciously assented to write the foreword, and whose sympathetic ear and discerning mind have proved of incalculable assistance. I might mention as well my very dear friend and former classmate Professor Abraham Udovitch of Cornell University. The creation of so large a work regardless of its merits is due in no small part to individuals outside the immediate academic circles. The list here is also substantial. However, I call attention to Mr. Samuel Schnauser of New York, my secretary Mrs. Mary Anne Buchin who had to type so many strange names and symbols, and Miss Susan Coltharp of Flint, Michigan and Tanzania, Africa. The final stages of preparation were made possible with a faculty research fellowship from Wayne State University.

J.L.

Introduction

The Khaṭīb al-Baghdādī and the Descriptions of the City

Although all Muslims embraced one another within a single religious community, diverse forces of religious, ethnic, and geographic allegiance manifested themselves within the social structure of Islam. The Khaṭīb al-Baghdādī, in what may be regarded as a statement of cultural geography, not only divides the world into its seven inhabited climes, but describes the ethnic composition and inherent social characteristics of each particular sphere.[1] Thus the shortcomings of the Byzantines, the Slavs, the Turks and the Chinese, and of the Khurasanians, the Syrians, and the Negroes of Abyssinia, are all indicated by way of comparison with the author's native region; for at the center of this world of imperfection is the seventh clime, comprising the land of Iraq and its virtuous inhabitants. That the Khaṭīb should have included this geographical statement in the preface to his *History* (*Ta'rīkh*) *of Baghdad* is easily understood; for if Iraq was the "navel of the universe," Baghdad, its leading city, was the geographic center of the empire and capital of the dynasty. It is, therefore, with some justification that Baghdadis took pride in their city.

A particular characteristic of medieval Islam was the formation of great urban centers, of which Baghdad was the foremost, not only in the physical arrangement of its vast quarters and suburbs, but in the intellectual and religious climate created by its scholars and sainted individuals. The desire to express pride in one's city or region was a tangible outgrowth of this urban development, and gave rise in time to that diverse body of literature which is generally known as local history. The significance of this genre for the study of Islamic civilization cannot be overestimated; for the limited scope of local authors allowed them to focus on the important minutiae of economic and cultural life which are so frequently overlooked in the more comprehensive histories of the dynastic and world arrangment. Moreover, such works were not always conventional studies describing the events centered about a particular region, but like the Khaṭīb's history, often took the form of biographical dictionaries, listing the most important inhabitants according to alphabetical or chronological order. Occasionally, various local authors like the Khaṭīb prefaced their works with lengthy topographical introductions preserving a picture of the toponomy and physical arrangement of their surroundings, thereby adding yet another dimension to the study of the Near Eastern city.

It is fitting and understandable that the major work of this kind from the early Middle Ages, should be dedicated to its greatest city. For despite the shifting political fortunes of the Caliphate, Baghdad remained, from the time it was founded by al-Manṣūr (762) until the ascendency of the Būyids (ca. 945), the leading center of the Islamic world. Although many of its principal monuments still resisted decay in subsequent generations, the growing weakness of centralized authority led to the incipient decline which was to sap the city of its vitality and diminish its physical and human resources. But even then devoted Baghdadis could console themselves because the city in its declining imperial splendor remained different, and by implication superior to all other.[2]

If this imperial splendor is the physical image which the Khaṭīb wished to convey in his topographical introduction, the successive biographical volumes which comprise the remainder of the text are a proud reflection of Baghdad's intellectual climate. However, the biographical entries are not merely an expression of praise for local intellect; the survival of the Khaṭīb's work and those histories which were patterned after it is the result of comprehensive scholarship, and the educational need for these works at the various centers of theological study. But what of the introduction? Unlike the main body of the text which is treated with the judicious care that generally characterizes the religious sciences, the topographical introduction was more casually presented—its only purpose was to glorify the physical design of the city preliminary to the theological data that was more germane to the interest of the author. Yet, despite the haphazard arrangement, the introduction remains the major statement on the physical design of Baghdad, a fact of considerable importance when it is realized that no major excavations were ever undertaken on the presumed site of the medieval city. Any attempt to reconstruct the city according to the respective stages of its development is, therefore, dependent on an analysis of the specialized topographical information. In addition to establishing the reliability of certain statements, such a study may fix more precisely the date of various accounts, thereby providing the chronological framework upon which any topographical history of the city must be based. As the Khaṭīb's introduction is, for various reasons, the most detailed statement of this kind, it is the key to any such study.

Early Topographical Descriptions

In 145/762 al-Manṣūr built the circular city on the west bank of the Tigris that was to serve as his capital. Shortly after its completion, the city began to grow around the walled area and on the eastern side of the Tigris. The rapid growth of Baghdad which began in the lifetime of its founder presumably necessitated the collection of certain data for administrative purposes, including *systematic* descriptions of the physical layout. That is to say, a list of the various places which are situated adjacent to one another in a series of well defined areas, in contrast with incidental statements of topographical interest. It therefore seems likely that already beginning in the reign of al-Manṣūr, such descriptions were recorded in response to the administrative needs of the ʿAbbāsid regime.[3] The early accounts are not extant, but some information which they contained, in addition to more current data, was recorded in later geographical and historical works from the ninth to the eleventh centuries of which the last and most important is the Khaṭīb's history.

Since the systematic descriptions of Baghdad are generally arranged by quarters, and according to the major arteries of traffic, both roads and canals, it is understandable that the earliest extant sources of this information were descriptive geographical texts of the "road book" genre. Of these Yaʿqūbī's *K. al-buldān* (ca. 891) is the oldest surviving work.[4] The relevant section on the toponomy and the physical arrangement of the city is introduced by Yaʿqūbī with some historical observations, and general remarks of praise. Starting with the oldest area of major Islamic occupation, the author proceeds to describe the architectural elements of the Round City and its streets in detail, and then follows with a topographical account of the adjacent areas, beginning with West Baghdad and concluding with a much shorter description of the East Side. Not unlike similar works of this literary genre, Yaʿqūbī omits any mention of sources; but at the conclusion of his account he does indicate that his description is based on Baghdad as it existed in the time of al-Manṣūr (d. 775) and al-Mahdī (d. 783).[5] This statement is apparently confirmed by his limited description of the East Side; for while the left bank of the Tigris was completely built up in his own time, it first became an area of major occupation in the reign of al-Mahdī, the second ʿAbbāsid Caliph. The account is thus fixed on a particular moment in the topographical development of the city, and therefore can be most useful in charting the course of its growth.

Other preserved geographical works which contain such systematic descriptions are Suhrāb's *ʿAjā'ib al-aqālīm as-sabʿah* (ca. 925)[6] and the *K. al-buldān* of Ibn al-Faqīh (ca. 902).[7] The text of Suhrāb is considered to be a re-working of al-Khuwārizmī's scientific geography the *K. ṣūrat al-arḍ*;[8] however, unlike the other known scientific works, the format of the *ʿAjā'ib* contains some valuable topographical information on the rivers and waterways of Iraq. Most relevant to the present study is a systematic description of various places situated along the canals of Baghdad, which for the most part is arranged according to three large areas: the southwest suburb of al-Karkh, the northwest suburb of al-Ḥarbīyah, and the locations of the East Side. Suhrāb, like Ya'qūbī, gives no references to earlier authorities; but unlike the description in the *K. al-buldān* which is said to stem from a given period, i.e., that of al-Manṣūr and al-Mahdī, the account of the *'Ajā'ib* can be dated only on the basis of internal evidence. Nevertheless, it is abundantly clear from the content of the text that Suhrāb describes the hydrography of Baghdad as it existed in the time of al-Muqtadir (908–932), and thus is fixed on a second most important moment in the topographical development of the city. The account of Suhrāb is virtually identical with the Khaṭīb's chapter on the hydrography of the city, and it can be assumed that it was a source of information for the *Ta'rīkh Baghdād*,[9] a fact of considerable importance which will be treated more fully in a discussion of that chapter.

The published text of Ibn al-Faqīh does not contain a description of Baghdad;[10] however, it is believed to be an eleventh-century abridgement of a much larger work preserved[11] only in MS and found in Mashhad.[12] As access to this work is most difficult, I had not seen the MS, but it is described briefly by A. Z. Validi, P. Kahle, and V. Minorsky.[13] Some information in it is also discussed by Duri in his article on Baghdad in *Encyclopedia of Islam* (second edition). On the basis of these brief comments, it appeared that the original work of Ibn al-Faqīh contained the type of data on the architecture and physical arrangement of the city which is also found in the introduction of the Khaṭīb, and that it is therefore a major source of information on the topography of Baghdad; although with the MS unavailable it was impossible to determine what connection may exist between this text and other known descriptions of the city.

There were, to be sure, other attempts at describing the physical arrangement of Baghdad, and in literary sources other than geographical texts; but from what must have been a fairly substantial body of literature in the early Middle Ages only a few scattered fragments remain, in addition to the extant works previously mentioned. It is largely through the efforts of the Khaṭīb that these texts can be partially recovered. It is because he carefully prefaced accounts by citing the source of his authority (usually with a lengthy *isnād*) that we are able to glimpse the works of Aḥmad b. Abī Ṭāhir Ṭayfūr (d. 893),[14] Muḥammad b. Khalaf Wakī' (d. 918),[15] and Ibrāhīm b. Muḥammad b. 'Arafah al-Azdī Nifṭawayh (d. 935),[16] all of whom were, more or less, contemporaries of the same generation of scholarship.

Aḥmad b. Abī Ṭāhir Ṭayfūr's description of the city is found in the introduction to his partially preserved history (*ta'rīkh*) of Baghdad, an *adab* type work centered about the leading personalities of the times.[17] The introduction is not part of the preserved text, but is briefly mentioned in an Arabic source where it is reported that Aḥmad b. Muḥammad ar-Rāzī wrote "a description of Cordova dealing with the sections (*khiṭaṭ*) of the city and the residences of its distinguished inhabitants in the manner originated by Aḥmad b. Abī Ṭāhir Ṭayfūr in the *History* (*Akhbār*) *of Baghdad.*"[18] However, the exact arrangement of this description is not indicated, and the few fragments of a work by Ibn Ṭayfūr preserved by the Khaṭīb do not contain sufficient evidence to suggest what the exact nature of the original format may have been. This history was apparently used as a source of topographical information by Wakī', who cites Ibn Ṭayfūr without mentioning his work by title,[19] and thus fragments of it came to be preserved in the *Ta'rīkh Baghdād.*

Although Wakī' is known primarily for the *History of the Judges*, his biographical entry in the *Ta'rīkh Baghdād* also credits him with a work entitled the *K. aṭ-ṭarīq*.[20] As the title suggests, this book was, according to the *Fihrist*, a geographical text of the "road book" genre.[21] Since the early systematic descriptions of Baghdad are found in other works of this kind, i.e., Ya'qūbī and Ibn al-Faqīh, and since Wakī' is *the* major source of the Khaṭīb for his systematic description of the city, is it possible that this *K. aṭ-ṭarīq* contained such a description, and that it was subsequently quoted at length in the introduction to the *Ta'rīkh Baghdād*? The value of Wakī''s account goes beyond substantive statements of geographical interest; for of all the known descriptions of the city from the ninth and tenth centuries, only these fragments contain specific indications of earlier authorities. In addition to Aḥmad b. Abī Ṭāhir Ṭayfūr, they include: Muḥammad b. Mūsā al-Khuwārizmī

(d. 846),[22] al-Ḥārith b. Abī Usāmah (d. 896),[23] Aḥmad b. al-Haytham,[24] and Abū Zayd al-Khaṭīb.[25] There is no way of determining what the format of their works might have been, but it can be noted that al-Khuwārizmī, who was a famous mathematician, was the author of geographical and historical texts, and that al-Ḥārith b. Abī Usāmah was a scholar of wide general learning. Thus all or some of them may very well have been the authors of written sources on the topography of Baghdad.

The text of the Khaṭīb also contains several topographical accounts ultimately derived from Nifṭawayh,[26] who may be considered, next to Wakī', as his most important source for this type of information. The biographical entry on Nifṭawayh in the *Ta'rīkh Baghdād* indicates that he was the author of a history (*ta'rīkh*);[27] however, as there is no reference to it in the encyclopedic works, there is no evidence to suggest that it was a local history containing a topographical introduction similar to that of Ibn Ṭayfūr or the Khaṭīb. It is therefore possible that the fragments credited to Nifṭawayh are derived from a source other than this text, as the more conventional forms of historical writing do not seem to preserve information of this kind.

The Khaṭīb and the *Ta'rīkh Baghdād*[28]

Of the twenty-nine chapters which comprise the introduction to the *Ta'rīkh Baghdād*, only four contain detailed descriptions of the city: the chapter on the Round City, the chapters on the West and East Sides, and the chapter on hydrography. Some of the remaining sections also contain important topographical information, but it is mentioned by way of general comment and not in the form of systematic descriptions. An analysis as to the sources of these four chapters tends to confirm some of the statements made above.

The Round City:[29] The earliest established area of 'Abbāsid occupation was Madīnat as-Salām, the Round City completed by the Caliph al-Manṣūr on the western side of the Tigris in 149/766.

Various measurements for this construction are given by the Khaṭīb on the basis of five different *isnāds*.

1. On the authority of Aḥmad [b.] al-Barbarī.[30]
2. On the authority of Badr, the page of al-Muʿtaḍid (c. 892).[31]
3. On the authority of Rabāḥ, the architect (c. 764–765).[32]
4. On the authority of Muḥammad b. Khalaf Wakīʿ citing Yaḥyā b. al-Ḥasan b. ʿAbd al-Khāliq.[33]
5. On the authority of Muḥammad b. Khalaf Wakīʿ (d. 918).[34]

The authorities of *isnāds* 2, 3, and 4 are identifiable historical personalities who are not likely to have left written works on this subject. The first statement whose authority I have been unable to identify is a short comment, and is therefore not necessarily derived from a lengthy descriptive text. But the fifth account which contains the only detailed description of the Round City is that of Wakīʿ, who is the first link in the *isnād* on which most of the Khaṭīb's information for the systematic topography of Baghdad is based.[35] It has been noted that Yaʿqūbī also contains a description of the Round City and the adjacent areas, but the Khaṭīb, who, on one occasion, apparently quotes Yaʿqūbī as a source of historical information,[36] did not use him for his topographical description of Baghdad; although Yaʿqūbī's section on the city is quite detailed and invaluable as a supplement to the *Taʾrīkh Baghdād*, particularly his treatment of the Round City and its streets.

The West and East Sides:[37] The surburban areas which grew beyond the Round City were divided into sections on both sides of the Tigris and discussed by the Khaṭīb in a detailed manner, based largely on the account of Wakīʿ. However, the detailed topographical description is not consistently systematic as at times there is no apparent logical order in the sequence of localities. Whether this is characteristic of the original account, or the result of subsequent handling by the remaining links in the *isnād*, cannot be ascertained for certain, although one would suspect this haphazard arrangement could very well go back to the earlier recensions. It is clear, however, that the Khaṭīb's description of the East and

West Sides in its present form fails to take into consideration major changes in the development of the city during his lifetime and the century before, such as the disrepair of the canal system, and particularly the construction of the Būyid Dār al-Mamlakah[38] and the demolition of the riverside palaces in the period of the Saljūqs.[39] These last events not only altered the face of Baghdad in a marked way, but because of their significant political implications, could not have failed to impress even the most casual observer. It is, therefore, evident that he used earlier sources, and most important, his personal observations did not change the picture of the city which these earlier accounts set forth. This contention is made sufficiently clear by the Khaṭīb's treatment of the hydrography of the city.

The Hydrography of the City:[40] The Khaṭīb's information in this chapter, which is derived from one ʿAbdallāh b. Muḥammad b. ʿAlī al-Baghdādī, is virtually identical in content and language with an account preserved in the scientific geography of Suhrāb (ca. 925).[41] The report of the waterways includes a detailed description of the various places situated along the routes of the canals which is of particular importance since it fixes the position of many localities not mentioned in the other topographical descriptions of Baghdad and gives the most detailed information found on the economic infrastructure of the city. It is noteworthy that the Khaṭīb should rely entirely upon this account for his information on hydrography; possibly he had no access to more recent geographical information. However, it is significant that he failed to note the important changes in the canal system since 925,[42] although a casual observation in another chapter indicates that he was well aware of them and points out that many canals were no longer in existence.[43] The Khaṭīb thus produced an entire chapter on nonexistent places without critical comment. In failing to rework the topographical material at his disposal, the Khaṭīb seems to show a lack of scholarly concern for this type of information, as one might indeed expect of an authority whose particular competence and interest was not geography, but rather the religious sciences. This attitude is particularly important for examining the work of the Khaṭīb in relation to the other known histories of Baghdad, and for evaluating the *Ta'rīkh Baghdād* as a source for the topographical history of the city.

The Khaṭīb and Local History

The Khaṭīb's great reputation as a scholar in the religious sciences is acknowledged by his various biographers who credit him with having written at least fifty-six works,[44] of which forty-one are listed by Ibn al-Jawzī.[45] A number of these works are preserved, including the above-mentioned *History of Baghdad* (*Ta'rīkh Baghdād*) which prompted Ibn Khallikān to remark,[46] "Had he written nothing but his history, it would have been sufficient for his reputation." The printed edition of this work (Cairo, 1349/1931) consists of fourteen volumes of biographical entries arranged alphabetically, although this system was not consistently applied. There is a particular emphasis on jurists and *ḥadīth* scholars, indicating that the work was conceived as a handbook for those engaged in the religious sciences rather than a conventional secular history dealing with local events. However, it is noteworthy that the biographical section is preceded by a lengthy introduction containing cultural and historical information of general interest, and more relevant to the present study, juxtaposed accounts of topography and history which form one of the most important sources for the toponomy and physical arrangement of the city.

Although descriptive geographies are the sources of topographical material on Baghdad, they were not unique in presenting such information. In addition to the Khaṭīb, there is the missing introduction of Aḥmad b. Abī Ṭāhir Ṭayfūr whose *History* (*Ta'rīkh*) *of Baghdad* is reputed to have been the first work of its kind. Some statistical information ultimately derived from this work is cited by the Khaṭīb,[47] and it is possible that the missing introduction could have also contained such data thereby suggesting a direct link between the two texts. However, tempting as this may be, there is no indication that the Khaṭīb was in any way directly dependent on Aḥmad b. Abī Ṭāhir Ṭayfūr for his description of the city, although, as previously indicated, some data from the missing introduction reached the Khaṭīb through Wakīʿ who used Ibn Ṭayfūr as a source.[48] It is, of course, possible that the account of Wakīʿ which does not disclose earlier authorities was based in large part on Ibn Ṭayfūr, the reported prototype of such descriptions. However, one wonders why the Khaṭīb, who was familiar with this work and who quotes it elsewhere, nevertheless fails to mention it in this connection more often.

Unlike the history of the Khaṭīb, which is essentially a biographical dictionary, the main body (partially preserved) of Ibn Ṭayfūr's work is a detailed secular history reporting the events which centered about Baghdad, while following the accepted format of more general historical writing.[49] A transitional stage between Ibn Ṭayfūr and the religiously oriented *Ta'rīkh Baghdād* would seem to be Abū Zakarīyā's *History of Mawṣil.*[50] Quotations in other authors indicate this to be a biographical work on the *ḥadīth* scholars of that city arranged according to the *ṭabaqāt* division;[51] however, fragments of the text preserved in MS contain elements of an annalistic history (*akhbār*) covering the years 101–224 A.H.[52] It has been conjectured that, "this may have constituted a separate part, or even a different work to which the *Ṭabaqāt* of *ḥadīth* scholars was the biographical companion volume." This conjecture takes on added weight if one can assume that the Abū Dhkw(r)h al-Mawṣilī, who is mentioned by Masʿūdī as the author of a *K. at-ta'rīkh wa-akhbār al-Mawṣil*, is to be identified with the Abū Zakarīyā' mentioned above.[53] Even if such were the case, there is no indication that this particular format was used in any of the known histories of Baghdad, although it appears to be a logical step in the formation of this literature.

The contribution of the Khaṭīb to the development of this genre of literature was in the arrangement of the biographical entries which follow the introduction to his text. In the second century of Islam, the necessity of biographical information for the science of traditions led to the systematic arrangement of this material accord- to chronological layers (*ṭabaqāt*).[54] Each *ṭabaqah* signified a generation, but since there was no general agreement as to the length of a *ṭabaqah* in actual years, estimates varied from ten to forty. It has been pointed out that the use of the *ṭabaqāt* arrangement for a given locality began early in the more general biographical books, and that the oldest preserved work of this type for a specific location is Aslam b. Sahl Baḥshāl's *History of Wāsiṭ* (ca. 900).[55] In the tenth century, theologically oriented local histories had a wide geographical distribution, and in addition to increasing the number of biographical entries, some of these works abandoned the *ṭabaqāt* division for an alphabetical arrangement.[56] The obvious advantage to the new arrangement is that it made for an easier system of reference, requiring only the full name, and not the details of the subject's life. Unlike the secular local histories, these works were conceived as handbooks for scholars of the religious sciences, in particular the students at the various local centers of theological learning.

Although the Khaṭīb retained the lengthy type of topographical introduction which is found in Ibn Ṭayfūr's history of Baghdad, he replaced the secular accounts with biographical entries arranged according to alphabetical order—a task presumably more germane to his interests as a religious scholar. However, these entries are preceded by a section listing the Companions of the Prophet (*Ṣaḥābah*) who are reported to have settled in the general area where the city of al-Manṣūr was later built.[57] It has been pointed out "this was actually a relic of the *ṭabaqāt* arrangement, but was reinterpreted by the authors of the alphabetically arranged works as a sign of the importance of the *Ṣaḥābah*, and as a means to facilitate the knowledge of their names."[58] The *Ta'rīkh Baghdād* served as the model for subsequent histories of the city, which generally adopted the alphabetical arrangement in preference to the *ṭabaqāt* division;[59] but, unlike the Khaṭīb, these authors failed to demonstrate any interest in detailed topographical information, since accounts of this type were not really an integral part of their works. The introductions to religiously-oriented histories are subsequently shortened to some incidental remarks and expressions of praise. It is, therefore, clear that the work of the Khaṭīb represents a transitional stage between the type of history composed by Aḥmad b. Abī Ṭahīr Ṭayfūr, and the theologically colored alphabetical histories subsequent to the *Ta'rīkh Baghdād*, and thus came to preserve elements of a topographical description.

Other Sources of Topographical Descriptions

Because of the thorough and comprehensive scholarship which was required by the secular and religious histories of Baghdad, there was no real need for a second *magnum opus* in any given generation. Moreover, authors in subsequent generations tended to imitate rather than experiment with new forms of their own. Upon the death of Ibn Ṭayfūr, the chronicles of Baghdad were not re-written but brought up to date by his son ʿUbaydallāh in a manner similar to the continuation of Ṭabarī's universal history.[60] Changes in form only resulted from the changes in function attending the development of the theologically oriented works; but once composed, the biographical format of the Khaṭīb's history was very much like the secular history of Ibn Ṭayfūr, slavishly copied by later authorities. The number of these works in circulation was therefore limited at all times. Moreover, since the followers of the Khaṭīb no longer prefaced their texts with lengthy introductions, the topographical descriptions preserved in this literature were presumably few in number. There existed, however, another type of local history which was not so circumscribed by the weight of its own scholarship, and as such could have developed at the outset into a variegated and large body of literature.

Technically within the limits of local historiography were the pseudohistorical works in praise of a city or region.[61] Generally distinguished by the words *khawāṣṣ* or *faḍāʾil* in their title, such works usually contained some historical and geographical data in dealing with the praiseworthy characteristics of a particular locality and its inhabitants. From the eleventh century, such titles more generally denoted monographs containing quotations from the *Qurʾān*, *ḥadīth*, and related sources to the exclusion of any historical information. Because the function of the *faḍāʾil* works was to express pride in one's city or region, the composition of these texts was not necessarily the exclusive province of the leading historian or jurist of his generation, but could have been written by numerous scholars of lesser stature. The number of *faḍāʾil* works in circulation was therefore most likely to have been greater than that of the more comprehensive secular and religious histories. The size of these works no doubt varied, but even the largest must have appeared most insignificant when contrasted with works like that of the Khaṭīb or Ibn ʿAsākir's multi-volume *History* (*Ta'rikh*) *of Damascus*.

Although the older *faḍā'il* works of Baghdad are not preserved, evidence of their composition is conveyed by several statements in later literature. As a source for some short historical fragments dealing with pre-Islamic times, Yāqūt[62] mentions a treatise (*risālah*) on the *faḍā'il* of Baghdad which he attributes to a certain Mahbundādh al-Kisrawī.[63] In connection with this work, the following account is related by the literateur al-Muḥassin b. ʿAlī at-Tanūkhī:[64]

> I (at-Tanūkhī) mentioned a book by a certain Yazdjard b. Mahbundādh al-Kisrawī who lived in the time of al-Muqtadir. I had seen the book in the house of Abū Muḥammad al-Muhallabī. He had given some folios of this book to me and some others who were present, in order to have them copied for Prince Rukn ad-Dawlah; for he wanted a description of Baghdad and a census of the baths there. Yazdjard mentioned that they numbered 10,000, and many officials arrive at that number. He also was to give the number of people living in that place, the boats and sailors, and the amount of wheat, barley, and foodstuffs required daily. He mentioned that the daily income of the ferry men selling ice was thirty or forty thousand (dirhams). Another person mentioned a book composed by Aḥmad b. aṭ-Ṭayyib on a similar subject.

The picture of these *faḍā'il* books obtained from the account of Tanūkhī could very well describe the particular section in the Khaṭīb's introduction which deals with statistics on the city.[65] Moreover, a different version of this story reported in that section of the Khaṭīb on the authority of Hilāl b. al-Muḥassin aṣ-Ṣābi' parallels an account found in Hilāl's *Rusūm Dār al-Khilāfah*.[66] The recent publication of that very important text reveals that Hilāl's census report, which is part of a much larger account estimating the population of the city, is taken from the *K. faḍā'il Baghdād al-ʿIrāq* of Yazdjard b. Mahamandār al-Fārisī, thus confirming the statement of Tanūkhī mentioned above. It is, therefore, to be assumed that certain information was common to both the *faḍā'il* works and the introductions to the larger histories. In fact, the Khaṭīb also devotes an entire chapter to the praiseworthy characteristics of the city;[67] and other chapters, such as those on the cemeteries and the mosques,[68] contain the type of information which is known to have existed in the *faḍā'il* works of other regions.[69] Might the shorter works have then contained, in addition to some incidental topographical information, elements of a systematic description, possibly truncated versions of a more comprehensive account? It may be noted that reference to a work by Yazdjard al-Kisrawī is also obtained from Ḥajjī Khalīfah who classifies it among the local histories of Baghdad;[70] it can be assumed that this text and the book described by Tanūkhī and Hilāl aṣ-Ṣābi' are one and the same. In addition to preserving statistical data of the type mentioned above, Ḥajjī Khalīfah adds that it also contained a description of the city; but there is no hint as to the length and arrangement of this description, or whether it was based on the personal observations of the author, or some written sources which may have been available to him. Unfortunately, these scattered fragments and references were the only remaining indications of this work known to me; the structure of Kisrawī's description as well as the rest of the *Risālah* was therefore still subject to speculation.[70a]

There is reason to suggest that some kind of topographical description was also an important element in other works of this kind. The book of Aḥmad b. aṭ-Ṭayyib[71] which is mentioned in the account of Tanūkhī is perhaps the lost *Faḍā'il Baghdād wa-akhbāruhā*. Although it is listed in various encyclopedic works under the author's name, there was no indication, other than the previous statement, as to its form and content.[72] Since Sarakhsī was the author of several treatises on scientific and descriptive geography, including a text of the "road book" genre,[73] it is quite possible that this work, like that of Kisrawī, could have contained a description of the city. One can probably assume that such descriptions which may have been preserved in this truncated form of local history were, as a rule, quite limited, and that more complete information was generally reserved for the larger works such as that of the Khaṭīb and Ibn Ṭayfūr. However, if the *Faḍā'il* of Sarakhsī did, in fact, contain some description of the city, the early composition of the text and the author's particular competence in geography may serve to indicate that it was a most important source on the topography of Baghdad, and, therefore, may have been more detailed than similar *faḍā'il* texts from later periods.

From this literature, at least one text is preserved containing a description of the city. The account is found in the *Virtues* (*Manāqib*) *of Baghdad*,[74] a short treatise which has been atrributed to Ibn al-Jawzī (d. 1200),[75] and which consists for the most part of several abbreviated accounts culled from the introduction to the *Ta'rīkh Baghdād*, with only a very few incidental comments relating to more recent times. However, the work also includes a lengthy statement of Abū-l-Wafā' b. ʿAqīl, a younger contemporary of the Khaṭīb.[76] In response to an inquiry about Baghdad, Ibn ʿAqīl sets forth to describe the outstanding monuments and places of his own quarter, the section called Bāb aṭ-Ṭāq; but he includes, as well, some general information about other sections of the city. However informative, the account of Ibn ʿAqīl is rather limited and is in itself not part of a larger systematic description. According to Makdisi, it is the type of passage one could expect to find in Ibn ʿAqīl's encyclopedic work, the *K. al-funūn*, an edition of which is to be released soon.[77] But it is not likely that a text of this kind would have originated in the restricted format of an encyclopedic work. In some remarks preliminary to the translation of this passage, Makdisi points out the great sense of pride that is evident in the style of Ibn ʿAqīl's statement. Although this does not necessarily indicate that the source of this account was a *faḍā'il* text, it does suggest that short, but most useful, topographical statements of this kind could have been preserved in other works similar to the *Manāqib*.

Conclusions

While perhaps not as detailed as the larger systematic accounts, reports like that of Ibn ʿAqīl are quite important; for they are based on the personal observations of the author and thus can be dated from a particular generation. These accounts may be regarded as the direct expression of an identifiable moment in the topographical development of Baghdad. Given the availability of similar statements from other periods, it is possible to suggest a basic developmental pattern to the growth of the city.

The standard works on Baghdad, all of which were written some fifty years ago, were based on a limited selection of sources. Moreover, no attempt was made to differentiate the reports in the topographical accounts with regard to chronology. Consequently, the description of Baghdad which is obtained from such authors as Reitemeyer[78] and Streck[79] is largely a catalogue of various locations. Although the more imaginative books of LeStrange[80] and Massignon[81] are very much concerned with the historical development of the city, they are not directed to the critical problem of dating the individual reports which make up the systematic descriptions. A given account which is preserved in ninth-century text does not necessarily describe that particular moment in the history of the city—witness Ya'qūbī's report on Baghdad which is to be dated on internal evidence from the reign of al-Manṣūr, and that of al-Mahdī.[82]

The great value of the Khaṭīb's description is not only its detailed presentation; it is the only systematic account which gives specific indications of earlier authorities. Since the Khaṭīb made no effort to interpolate more current information, it is evident that his systematic description of the city generally predates the death of Wakī' (918), his primary source. The *Ta'rīkh Baghdād* does contain some incidental information of topographical importance, but no effort is made to work this material into his comprehensive description of the city. If the Khaṭīb therefore has certain limitations as a topographical source of his own times, it is not because of his protracted absence from Baghdad as suggested by Makdisi,[83] but rather his heavy reliance on older materials from the preceding century.

It appears self-evident that the growth of an urban center must be measured according to some quantitative yardstick. When undertaken in a city circumscribed by its walls, archeological excavation may yield, in addition to the exact plan of its physical arrangement, relevant data as to the size and density of occupation. No such major excavations have been undertaken at Baghdad, although the area presumed to have been occupied by the original city and the suburbs of the West Side has not been resettled in modern times. In the absence of definitive archeological evidence, it has become necessary to turn to the above-mentioned literary sources for a description of the city as it existed in the time of the ʿAbbāsid Caliphs.

In the successive periods which elapsed between the death of Wakīʿ and that of the Khaṭīb in 1071, Baghdad was ruled *de facto* by the Amīr al-Umarāʾ, the Būyids and the Saljūq sultans. During the course of this time there were significant changes in the topography of the city as a result of construction, demolition, fires and floods. The sources indicate a general decline;[84] but since these changes are not recorded in any of the known systematic descriptions of Baghdad, there is no comprehensive picture of the physical arrangement of the city for this period. However, in addition to the statement of Ibn ʿAqīl, which is a useful supplement to the older descriptions found in the Khaṭīb, the chroniclers who describe the events of the later periods report much incidental information about the changing face of the city, particularly Ibn al-Jawzī whose shortcomings as an historian unfortunately obscure the real value of the *Muntaẓam* as a work rich in information on the more prosaic aspects of life. A chronological survey of the major changes which are described in these sources permits a more current description and also brings to light important material for reconstructing the history of the Būyid period and that of the Saljūqs which followed,[85] although such a complete study is reserved for some future publication. It is hoped that the new annotated translation will not only present additional information on the physical arrangement of Baghdad, but will, in view of the previous remarks, also make it a more usable source for charting the growth of the city according to the respective stages of its topographical development.

Manuscripts, published editions, and sources of the Khaṭīb's *Taʾrīkh Baghdād* (*TB*) are given in Appendix H.

I

The Topography of Baghdad according to the Khaṭīb al-Baghdādī

A Translation

1

The Building of Madīnat as-Salām[1]

The Qāḍī, ʿAlī b. Abī ʿAlī al-Muʿaddil at-Tanūkhī———Talḥah b. Muḥammad b. Jaʿfar———Muḥammad b. Jarīr, who gave license to transmit this information:[2] The oath of allegiance was rendered to Abū Jaʿfar al-Manṣūr in the year 136/754. He laid the foundations of the city in the year 145/762, completed construction in 146/763, and named the city Madīnat as-Salām.[3]

The Shaykh, al-Khaṭīb: I received an account that when he decided to build the city, al-Manṣūr summoned the engineers,
)* architects, and experts in measuring, surveying, and the division of plots. He showed them the plan which he had in mind, and then brought in ordinary laborers, and skilled personnel including carpenters, diggers, blacksmiths, and others. The Caliph allotted

* The paginations of the two editions of the Arabic text used for this translation are given in the margins and are differentiated as follows:

Numbers set off by hyphens—G. Salmon, *L'Introduction topographique à l'histoire de Baghdadh d'Abou Bakr Aḥmad Ibn Thābit al-Khaṭīb al-Baghdādhī*, Paris, 1904, pp. 1–87. Cited as *S*.

Numbers enclosed in parentheses—al-Khaṭīb al-Baghdādī, *Ta'rīkh Baghdād*, Cairo, 1931, 1:66–127, Topographical Introduction. Unless otherwise indicated, citations are to this volume (*C*). *TB* refers to the entire Cairo edition (14 vols.). Khaṭīb refers to the present translation according to pagination *C* (numbers in parentheses).

them their salaries, and then wrote to every town asking them to send inhabitants with some knowledge of the building trade. But he did not begin construction until the number of craftsmen and skilled laborers in his presence reached many thousands.[4] Then he traced the city plan, making the city round.[5] They say that no other round city is known in all the regions of the world.[6] The foundations were laid at a time chosen for al-Manṣūr by Nawbakht, the astrologer.[7]

Muḥammad b. ʿAlī al-Warrāq and Aḥmad b. ʿAlī al-Muḥtasib
-2- ———Muḥammad b. Jaʿfar an-Naḥwī———al-Ḥasan b. Muḥammad as-Sakūnī: Muḥammad b. Khalaf: Muḥammad b. Mūsā al-Qaysī———Muḥammad b. Mūsā al-Khuwārizmī, the mathematician:[8] Abū Jaʿfar went from al-Hāshimīyah to Baghdad, ordered the construction of the city, and then returned to al-Kūfah one hundred forty-four years, four months, and five days after the Hijrah. He continued: Abū Jaʿfar finished building the city, settled in it with his troops, and named it Madīnat as-Salām one hundred forty-five years, four months, and eight days after the Hijrah. Muḥammad b. Khalaf: Al-Khuwārizmī: The enclosure wall of Baghdad and all the work connected with the city were completed one hundred forty-eight years, six months, and four days after the Hijrah.[9]

Muḥammad b. al-Ḥusayn b. al-Faḍl al-Qaṭṭān———ʿAbdallāh b. Jaʿfar b. Durustawayh an-Naḥwī———Yaʿqūb b. Sufyān:[10] In the year 146/763 Abū Jaʿfar completed the construction of Madīnat as-Salām, settled in it, and had the royal coffers, state treasuries, and the *dīwāns* transferred there. In the year 149/766 he completed the construction of the moat wall and everything connected with the city.[11]

-3- Abū-l-Qāsim al-Azharī———Aḥmad b. Ibrāhīm b. al-Ḥasan ———Abū ʿAbdallāh Ibrāhīm b. Muḥammad b. ʿArafah al-Azdī:[12] A story is told on the authority of one of the astrologers: When he completed Madīnat as-Salām, al-Manṣūr said to me, "Take the horoscope!" Thereupon I looked into the horoscope of the city
(68) which was for Jupiter in Sagittarius. I told him what the stars indicated about the city's duration, the greatness of its civilization, how the world would gravitate to it, and the desire of people for

that which it would offer. Then I said to him, "May God honour you, O Commander of the Faithful. I bring you good tidings of yet another gift indicated by the stars. No Caliph shall ever die in the city." I saw him smile upon hearing these words. Then he said, "Praise unto God, for that is the grace of God. He shows favor to whom He wishes. He is the possessor of all mighty grace."[13] Hence, ʿUmārah b. ʿAqīl b. Bilāl b. Jarīr b. al-Khaṭafī said when the Caliphs shifted their capital from Baghdad,[14]

Have you seen in all the length and breadth of the earth
  A city such as Baghdad? Indeed it is paradise on earth.
Life in Baghdad is pure; its wood becomes verdant,
  While life outside of it is without purity or freshness.
The lifespan in it is long; its food
  Is healthful; for some parts of the earth are more healthful
    than others.
Its Lord has decided that no Caliph shall die
  In it; indeed he determines what he wishes for his creatures.
There the eye of a stranger closes in sleep, but you will not see
  A stranger coveting sleep in the land of Syria.
4- If Baghdad fails to receive its due reward from them,
  It has previously given only good rewards.
If it is accused of rancor and hatred,
  It merits neither rancor nor hatred.

These verses have also been attributed to Manṣūr an-Namarī,[15] and God knows better.

Abū ʿAbdallah Aḥmad b. Muḥammad b. ʿAbdallāh al-Kātib ———Abū Jaʿfar Muḥammad b. Aḥmad b. Muḥammad, a client of the Banū Hāshim, known as Ibn Mutayyam———Aḥmad b. ʿUbayadallāh b. ʿAmmār: Abū ʿAbdallāh Muḥammad b. Dāwūd b. al-Jarrāḥ:[16] No Caliph has died in Madīnat as-Salām from the time it was founded except Muḥammad al-Amīn. He was killed on the Bāb al-Anbār Road, and his head was carried to Ṭāhir b. al-Ḥusayn who was at his camp between Baṭāṭiyā and the Bāb al-Anbār. Al-Manṣūr, the Caliph who built Madīnat as-Salām, died a pilgrim, having already entered the holy territory. Al-Mahdī died in Māsabadhān, al-Hādī in ʿĪsābādh, Hārūn in Ṭūs, and al-Ma'mūn in al-Badhandūn which is in the Byzantine Territory. His body is said to have been transported to Ṭarsūs where it was buried.

(69) Al-Muʿtasim and his sons and grandsons that ascended to the Caliphate after him, all died in Sāmarrā except al-Muʿtamid, al-Muʿtaḍid, and al-Muktafī; they died in the castles at az-Zandaward. Al-Muʿtamid's body was transported to Sāmarrā, al-Muʿtaḍid was buried in a place at the Palace of Muḥammad b. ʿAbdallāh b. Ṭāhir, and al-Muktafī at the Palace of Ibn Ṭāhir.

The Shaykh al-Ḥāfiẓ Abū Bakr: I mentioned this account to the
-5- Qāḍī, Abū-l-Qāsim ʿAlī b. al-Muḥassin at-Tanūkhī and he said: Muḥammad al-Amīn also was not killed in the city, but having boarded a boat on the Tigris in order to divert himself, he was seized in mid-river and killed there.[17] Aṣ-Ṣūlī and others mentioned this, but Aḥmad b. Abī Yaʿqūb al-Kātib stated:[18] Al-Amīn was killed outside the Bāb al-Anbār near the Garden of Ṭāhir.[19]

Let us return to the account of the building of Madīnat as-Salām.

2

Tracing the Plan of Madīnat al-Manṣūr, Fixing the Limits of the City, and Those Responsible for its Arrangement

Abū ʿUmar Ḥasan b. ʿUthmān b. Aḥmad b. al-Falw al-Wāʿiẓ———Jaʿfar b. Muḥammad b. Aḥmad b. al-Ḥakam al-Wāsiṭī———Abū-l-Faḍl al-ʿAbbās b. Aḥmad al-Ḥaddād———Aḥmad [Ibn] al-Barbarī:[1] The city of Abū Jaʿfar occupied an area of 130 *jarīb*; and the area of its moats and walls was thirty *jarīb*. Eighteen million [dirhams] were spent on the construction of the city, and it was built in the year 145/762.[2]

Abū-l-Faḍl———Abū-ṭ-Ṭayyib al-Bazzār[3]———his maternal uncle, an official in the service of Badr———Badr, the page of al-Muʿtaḍid: The Commander of the Faithful said, "Find out the area of Abū Jaʿfar's city." We calculated and found that the city was two *mīl* by two *mīl*.

Ash-Shaykh Abū Bakr:[4] I noticed in some books that Abū Jaʿfar
5- al-Manṣūr spent 4,000,833 dirhams upon his city, its mosque, the Gold Palace [Qaṣr adh-Dhahab], and the gates and markets until construction was completed. That sum in terms of *fals* comes to
0) 100,023,000. A work-foreman earned a daily wage ranging from one *qirāṭ* to five *ḥabbah*, and a laborer received two to three *ḥabbah*. Abū Bakr al-Khaṭīb: This sum conflicts with that previously mentioned as the sum of the expenditures for the construction of the city. I therefore observe a large discrepancy between the two accounts, and God knows better.[5]

Abū-l-Ḥasan Mūḥammad b. Aḥmad b. Rizq al-Bazzār——— Ja'far al-Khuldī———al-Faḍl b. Makhlad ad-Daqqāq——— Dāwūd b. Ṣaghīr b. Shabīb b. Rustam al-Bukhārī:[6] I observed in the time of Abū Ja'far that a sheep sold for a dirham, a lamb for four *dāniq*, dates at sixty *raṭl* a dirham, oil at sixteen *raṭl* a dirham, and butter at eight *raṭl* a dirham. That was when a man worked as a mason on the walls at five *ḥabbah* a day.[7] Ash-Shaykh Abū Bakr: Similar to this account is the one we received on the authority of al-Ḥasan b. Abī Bakr———'Uthmān b. Aḥmad ad-Daqqāq ———al-Ḥasan b. Salām as-Sawwāq———Abū Nu'aym al-Faḍl
-7- b. Dukayn:[8] The price of beef in Jabbānat Kindah was announced at ninety *raṭl* a dirham, and the price of lamb at sixty *raṭl* a dirham. Then Abu Nu'aym mentioned honey and said it sold at ten *raṭl* a dirham while butter sold at twelve *raṭl* a dirham.[9] Al-Ḥasan b. Salām: I entered Baghdad and related this to 'Affān, who said, "There was a *qiṭ'ah* in my belt which fell down upon the back of my foot, and thus I perceived it and then bought six *makkūk* of rice flour with it.[10]

Muḥammad b. 'Alī al-Warrāq and Aḥmad b. 'Alī al-Muḥtasib ———Muḥammad b. Ja'far an-Naḥwī———al-Ḥasan b. Muḥammad as-Sukūnī———Muḥammad b. Khalaf———Yaḥyā b. al-Ḥasan b. 'Abd al-Khāliq: The area of Madīnat al-Manṣūr was 1 *mīl* by 1 *mīl*, and the bricks used in its construction 1 square cubit. Muḥammad b. Khalaf: Aḥmad b. Maḥmūd ash-Sharawī related that the task of tracing the city of Baghdad was entrusted to al-Ḥajjāj b. Arṭāt and a group of men from al-Kūfah.[11]

(71) Abū-n-Naṣr al-Marwazī———Aḥmad b. Ḥanbal:[12] Baghdad comprises everything from the Ṣarāt Canal to Bāb at-Tibn. Al-Khaṭīb al-Ḥāfiẓ: Aḥmad [b. Ḥanbal] in that statement, meant Madīnat al-Manṣūr and what is adjacent to it, since the upper part of the city is the Fief of Umm Ja'far, below which is the trench that divides this fief from the buildings connected with the city [proper]. Similarly, the lower part of the city, consisting of al-Karkh and what is adjacent to it, is separated from the city [proper] by the Ṣarāt Canal. That is the boundary of the city and what is adjacent to it measured by its length.[13] As for the boundary of the city according to its width, it extends from the bank of the Tigris to a

place called the Kabsh wa-l-Asad. All these places were completely built up with palaces and dwellings. Today, the Kabsh wa-l-Asad is a sown field some distance from the city. I once saw that place while visiting the grave of Ibrāhīm al-Ḥarbī, who is buried there, and I noticed houses which gave it the appearance of a village in which farmers and woodcutters dwell. Later I returned to that place and saw no trace of any dwellings.[14]

Abū-l-Ḥusayn Hilāl b. al-Muḥassin al-Kātib———Abū-l-Ḥasan Bishr b. ʿAlī b. ʿUbayd an-Naṣrānī al-Kātib:[15] When I used to pass through the Kabsh wa-l-Asad with my father, I could not force myself free of the surging crowd in the markets.

A report reached me by way of Muḥammad d. Khalaf, i.e., Wakīʿ, that Abū Ḥanīfah an-Nuʿmān b. Thābit was appointed to supervise brick-making for the city, and to count them until the construction of the city wall adjacent to the moat was completed. Abū Ḥanīfah used to count them with a cane, and was the first to do so; others then made use of his practice.[16]

Muḥammad b. Isḥāq al-Baghawī mentioned that Rabāḥ the architect, who was entrusted with the task of constructing the wall of al-Manṣūr's city, related to him, "The distance between each of the city's gates was one *mīl*." In each of the brick courses there were 162,000 Jaʿfarī bricks. When we had built a third of the wall we made it thinner and laid only 150,000 to a course, and when we had completed two thirds, we made it thinner again and laid 140,000 bricks to the course until the top.[17]

Muḥammad b. ʿAlī al-Warrāq and Aḥmad b. ʿAlī al-Muḥtasib———Muḥammad b. Jaʿfar an-Naḥwī———al-Ḥasan b. Muḥammad as-Sakūnī———Muḥammad b. Khalaf———Ibn ash-Sharawī: We demolished part of the wall adjacent to Bāb al-Muḥawwal and found a mud-brick with red incription indicating its weight as 117 *raṭl*. We then weighed it and found this to be so.[18]

Muḥammad b. Khalaf: They say, when al-Manṣūr built his city he constructed four gates, so that if one came from al-Ḥijāz, he entered by way of the Kūfah Gate; if he came from al-Maghrib, he entered by way of the Damascus Gate; if he came from al-Ahwāz, al-Baṣrah, Wāsiṭ, al-Yamāmah and al-Baḥrayn he entered through the Baṣrah Gate; and if he arrived from the east he entered through the K͟hurāsān Gate. The reference to the K͟hurāsān Gate was omitted from the text, and was not mentioned by Muḥammad b. Ja'far on the authority of as-Sakūnī; but we corrected the text from a different account. He, that is to say, al-Manṣūr, placed every gate opposite the palace. He capped each gate with a dome, and erected eighteen towers between each gate, with the exception of the wall between the Baṣrah and Kūfah Gates where he added an additional tower. He fixed the length between the K͟hurāsān Gate and the

-10- Kūfah Gate at 800 cubits, and from the Damascus Gate to the Baṣrah Gate at 600 cubits. There were five iron gates between the main entrance to the city and the gate which led to the courtyard.

Wakī' related in the account which I have on his authority, that Abū Ja'far built the city in a circular form because a circular city has advantages over the square city, in that if the monarch were to be in the center of the square city, some parts would be closer to him than others, while, regardless of the divisions, the sections of the Round City are equidistant from him when he is in the center.[19] Al-Manṣūr then built four main gates, dug moats,

(73) and erected two walls and two *faṣīls*.[20] Between each main gate were two *faṣīls*, and the inner wall was higher than the outer wall. He commanded that no one be allowed to dwell at the foot of the higher inner walls or build any dwelling there; but ordered construction along the wall in the second *faṣīl* because it was better for the fortification of the wall. Then he built the palace and mosque.[21] In back of al-Manṣūr's palace was a reception hall [*iwān*] thirty by twenty cubits and in back of this hall was an audience room twenty by twenty by twenty cubits, whose ceiling ended in a dome. Above this audience room was a similar chamber, above which rested the green dome. The chamber stood twenty cubits high until the point where the vaulting of the dome begins. The distance between the ground line and the top of the green dome was eighty cubits, and surmounting the green dome, which could be seen from the outskirts of Baghdad, was the figure of a mounted horseman.

Al-Qāḍī Abū-l-Qāsim at-Tanūk͟hī: I heard a group of scholars

-11- mention that the green dome was surmounted by the figure of a horseman holding a lance in his hand. If the Sultan saw that figure with its lance pointing to a given direction, he knew that some rebels would make their appearance from there; and before long word would reach him that a rebel had appeared in that direction, or something to that effect.[22]

Ibrāhīm b. Makhlad al-Qāḍī———Ismā'īl b. 'Alī al-Khuṭabī:[23] The top of the green dome which surmounted the palace of Abū Ja'far's city fell on Tuesday, the 7th of Jumādā II, 329/941, during a night of torrential rain, awesome thunder, and terrible lightning. Indeed, that dome was the crown of Baghdad, a guidepost for the region, and one of the memorable things that one associates with the 'Abbāsids. It was built at the beginning of their rule and remained intact until this time. Over 180 years elapsed between its construction and fall.

Wakī' related in the account, which I have received on his authority, that the city was round, and encompassed by round walls. The diameter measured from the Khurāsān Gate to the Kūfah Gate was 1,200 cubits; and the diameter measured from the Baṣrah Gate to the Damascus Gate was 1,200 cubits. The height of the interior wall, which was the wall of the city, was thirty-five cubits. On the wall were towers, each rising to a height of five cubits above it, and battlements.[24] The thickness of the wall at its base was approximately twenty cubits.[25] Then came the *faṣīl*, 60 cubits wide between the inner and outer walls, followed by the outer wall which protected the *faṣīl*,[26] and beyond which the moat was situated. The city had four gates: east, west, south and north, and each gate in turn was made up of two gates, one in front of the other, separated by a corridor [*dihlīz*] and a court [*raḥbah*] opening unto the *faṣīl* which turned between the two walls. The first gate was that of the *faṣīl*, the second that of the city. When one entered the Khurāsān Gate, one first turned to the left in a vaulted corridor constructed of burnt brick cemented by gypsum. The corridor was twenty cubits wide by thirty cubits long. The entrance was in the width, and the exit, which was in the length, led to a court sixty cubits by forty cubits.[27] This court extended to the second gate,[28] and was walled on both sides from the first to the second wall. In back of the court was the second gate which was the gate of the city; flanking to the right and left of the court were two doors

leading to the two *faṣīls*. The one to the right led to the *faṣīl* of the Damascus Gate; the left door led to the *faṣīl* of the Baṣrah Gate, which then turned from the Baṣrah Gate to the Kūfah Gate. The *faṣīl* which led to the Damascus Gate turned to the Kūfah Gate in exactly the same fashion, since the four gateways were identical in regard to gates, *faṣīls*, courts, and arcades.[29] The second gate was the gate of the city and was protected by the large wall which we have described. The main gate gave access to a vaulted passage, constructed of burnt brick cemented by gypsym, which was
-13- twenty cubits long and twelve cubits wide. This was true as well for the other of the four gates. Above the vaulted passage of each gate was an audience room with a staircase against the wall by which means one ascended to it.[30] Crowning this audience room was a great dome which reached a height of fifty cubits.[31] Each dome was surmounted by a figure different from those of the other
(75) domes, which turned with the wind. This dome served as the audience room of al-Manṣūr when he desired to look at the river or see whoever approached from the direction of Khurāsān. The dome of the Damascus Gate served as the audience room when he desired to look at the suburbs and the countryside surrounding them. When he wished to look at al-Karkh and whoever might approach from that direction, the dome of the Baṣrah Gate served as his audience room; and the dome of the Kūfah Gate served this function when al-Manṣūr desired to view the gardens and the estates. The gateways in both the city's walls were protected by a heavy iron double door of large dimensions.[32]

Muḥammad b. ʿAlī al-Warrāq and Aḥmad b. ʿAlī al-Muḥtasib ———Muḥammad b. Jaʿfar———al-Ḥasan b. Muḥammad as-Sakūnī———Muḥammad b. Khalaf: Aḥmad b. al-Ḥārith reported on the authority of al-ʿAttābī[33] that Abū Jaʿfar transferred the gates from Wāsiṭ where they had been the gates of al-Ḥajjāj. Al-Ḥajjāj found them at the site of a city opposite Wāsiṭ, which was built by Sulaymān b. Dāwūd, and which was known as az-Zanda-
-14- ward; these gates were five in number. Al-Manṣūr, also, erected a gate in the Khurāsān Gateway, which he brought from Syria and which was made by the Pharaohs. In the exterior Kūfah Gateway he erected a gate made by al-Qaṣrī, which he brought from al-

Kūfah. The Caliph also constructed a gate for the Damascus Gateway, but it was weaker than the others.[34] Then al-Manṣūr built his castle which he named al-Khuld on the Tigris, entrusting this task to Abān b. Ṣadaqah and ar-Rabīʿ.[35] He ordered a bridge constructed near the Bāb ash-Shaʿīr, and distributed fiefs among his companions, consisting of plots fifty cubits square.[36]

Ash-Shaykh Abū Bakr: The palace of al-Manṣūr was named al-Khuld because of its likeness to *Jannat al-Khuld*, "the Garden of Eternity,"[37] and because it commanded a remarkable view, and revealed superior planning, and magnificent architectural construction. It was situated beyond the Khurāsān Gate, but it was demolished, and no trace of it remains now.

Al-Qāḍī Abū-l-Qāsim ʿAlī b. Al-Muḥassin at-Tanūkhī——— Abū-l-Ḥasan ʿAlī b. ʿUbayd az-Zajjāj ash-Shāhid, who was born in the month of Ramaḍān, 294/907: I mention in the account of the year 307/919–920: The populace had smashed the prisons of Madīnat al-Manṣūr, allowing the inmates to escape. However, the iron gates of the city were still intact and were shut. The police pursued those who had broken out of prison until they captured all the prisoners without letting one escape.[38]

Ash-Shaykh Abū Bakr: Let us return to the previous statement of Wakīʿ.

He said: Then one enters from the second corridor into a court twenty cubits square. On entering the court, one is confronted with a path to the right and another to the left. The path to the right leads to the Damascus Gate, while the one to the left leads to the Baṣrah Gate; the court is like the one we described. The *faṣīl* then turns past the other gates in this fashion; the gates of the streets open from this *faṣīl*, which extends completely around the wall. The width of each *faṣīl* from the wall to the entrance to the streets is twenty-five cubits. From the court which we have described, one enters the arcades which are fifty-three in number, not counting the arcade of the court entrance which is protected by a large double door of teakwood.

The arcades are fifteen cubits in width and 200 cubits in length, from the beginning of the arcade to the court which separates these arcades from the small arcades. There are rooms for the guard between each of the arcades on both sides.[39] The same is true for the other remaining gates. Past the arcades, one enters a court twenty cubits square. To the right is a path which leads to the corresponding court of the Damascus Gate, and then turns towards the corresponding courts of the Kūfah and Baṣrah Gates.

Let us return to our description of the Khurāsān Gate, for each one of these gates is alike. The gates of some streets open into this *faṣīl*. One is then confronted by the little arcades which are adjacent to the corridor of the city[40] and from which one enters into the court that extends around the palace and mosque.[41]

-16- ʿAlī b. al-Muḥassin———al-Qāḍī Abū Bakr b. ʿAbī Mūsā al-Hāshimī:[42] The dams burst at Qubbīn, and the black waters came, destroyed the arcades of the Kūfah Gate, and entered the city destroying our dwellings. We then left for al-Mawṣil. This event took place sometime in the 330's. We remained in al-Mawṣil several years and then returned to Baghdad where we dwelled in the Ṭāqāt al-ʿAkkī.[43]

(77) Al-Khaṭīb al-Ḥāfiẓ: I received the following account of Abū ʿUthmān ʿAmr b. Baḥr al-Jāḥiẓ:[44] I have seen the great cities, including those noted for their durable construction. I have seen such cities in the districts of Syria, in Byzantine territory, and in other provinces, but I have never seen a city of greater height, more perfect circularity, more endowed with superior merits or possessing more spacious gates, or more perfect *faṣīls* than az-Zawrā', that is to say, the city of Abū Jaʿfar al-Manṣūr. It is as though it is poured into a mold and cast. The proof that Baghdad was named az-Zawrā' is found in the words of Salm al-Khāsir,

> Where is the lord of az-Zawrā' since you invested him with sovereignty for twenty-two years.[45]

Al-Ḥusayn b. Muḥammad al-Mu'addib———Ibrāhīm b. ʿAbdallāh ash-Shaṭṭī———Abū Isḥāq al-Ḥujaymī———Muḥammad b. al-Qāsim Abū-l-ʿAynā':[46] Ar-Rabīʿ: Al-Manṣūr asked me,

-17- "O Rabīʿ, should I be besieged, do you know of a place in my city from which I can leave and emerge a distance of two parasangs from it?" I said, "No!" Al-Manṣūr then said, "There is such a place from which I can leave the city."

Abū 'Ubaydallāh Muḥammad b. 'Imrān b. Mūsā al-Marzubānī: Al-'Abbās b. al-'Abbas b. Muḥammad b. 'Abdallāh b. Mughayrah al-Jawharī delivered a book to me which he indicated was written by 'Abdallāh b. Abī Sa'd al-Warrāq.[47] In it the following was stated: 'Abdallāh b. Muḥammad b. 'Ayyāsh at-Tamīmī al-Marwarūdhī related the following account to us: I heard my grandfather 'Ayyāsh b. al-Qāsim say:[48] Stationed on the city gates, adjacent to the courts, were guards and chamberlains, with a military commandant to supervise each gate. The commandant of the Damascus Gate was Sulaymān b. Mujālid, commanding the Baṣrah Gate was Abū-l-Azhar at-Tamīmī, the Kūfah Gate was supervised by Khālid al-'Akkī, and the Khurāsān Gate by Maslamah b. Ṣuhayb al-Ghassānī; each commanded 1,000 men. Neither al-Manṣūr's uncles nor anyone else could enter the city except on foot, save his uncle Dāwūd b. 'Alī who suffered from the gout, and, therefore, was carried in a litter, and his son Muḥammad al-Mahdī. The courts were swept everyday by servants and the dirt was transported outside the city. 'Abd aṣ-Ṣamad, the Caliph's uncle, said to him, "O Commander of the Faithful, I am a very old man. Would you not permit me to dismount inside the gates." The Caliph, however, did not grant him permission. Thereupon his uncle said, "O Commander of the Faithful, grant [?] me one of the water-carrying mules which enter the courts." The Caliph then asked ar-Rabī', "Mules that carry water enter my courts?" Whereupon ar-Rabī' said, "Yes!" Then the Caliph said, "Begin construction immediately of teakwood conduits to extend from the Khurāsān Gate until they reach my palace." And this was carried out.[49]

Al-Ḥusayn b. Muḥammad b. al-Ḥasan al-Mu'addib——— Ibrāhīm b. 'Abdallah b. Ibrāhīm ash-Shaṭṭī who related to us in Jurjān———Abū Isḥāq al-Ḥujaymī: Abū-l-'Aynā': I have heard it said that al-Manṣūr, who was giving an audience one day, said to ar-Rabī', "See which one of the ambassadors is at the gate and invite him in." Ar-Rabī' related: I said, "There is an ambassador from the Byzantine Emperor." "Invite him," said al-Manṣūr, and the Byzantine then entered. The ambassador was sitting in the presence of the Commander of the Faithful, when al-Manṣūr heard a shriek which just about made the palace tremble. "Ar-Rabī'!

Have this investigated!" said the Caliph. Then he heard a shriek more penetrating than the first, and al-Manṣūr said, "Ar-Rabīʿ! Have this investigated!" and then he heard a shriek which was more penetrating than the first two. Whereupon he said, "Ar-Rabīʿ! Go out yourself!" Ar-Rabīʿ left, then returned and said, "O Commander of the Faithful, a cow was being brought to be slaughtered, but it overcame the butcher and bolted, running about amidst the markets." The Byzantine listened to ar-Rabīʿ trying to understand what he was saying. As al-Manṣūr perceived that the Byzantine was listening attentively, he said, "Ar-Rabīʿ, explain the incident to him." And ar-Rabīʿ did so.

-19- Thereupon the Byzantine remarked, "O Commander of the Faithful, indeed you have erected an edifice such as no one before you; yet it has three shortcomings." "What are they?" asked the Caliph. "The first shortcoming," said the Byzantine, "is the distance of the palace from water which is necessary for the lips of the populace. As for the second shortcoming, indeed the eye is green and yearns for green foliage, yet there is no garden in this palace of yours. Now, as for the third shortcoming, your subjects are with you at your palace, and when subjects are with the King in his palace, his secrets are disclosed."

Al-Manṣūr stiffened in his attitude toward the ambassador and said, "As for your statement concerning the water, we have calculated the amount of water necessary to moisten our lips. With regard to the second shortcoming, indeed we were not created for frivolity and play; and as for your remarks concerning my secrets, I hold no secrets from my subjects." But the Caliph then understood what had to be done; he sent for Shamīs and Khallād, who was the grandfather of Abū-l-ʿAynāʾ, and said,
(79) "Dig two canals leading from the Tigris, landscape al-ʿAbbāsīyah, and transfer the populace to al-Karkh."[50]

Ash-Shaykh Abū Bakr: Al-Manṣūr had a canal dug from the Dujayl which is a tributary of the Tigris, and from the Karkhāyā which is a tributary of the Euphrates. He brought these canals into his city via vaulted structures whose foundations were firm, and whose superstructure was solidly made of burnt brick cemented by quicklime [*ṣārūj*]. Each of these canals entered the city and passed through the streets, side streets, and suburbs, flowing without any interruption in summer and winter. For the population of al-Karkh and its environs, al-Manṣūr dug a canal known as Nahr ad-Dajāj. This canal was so named because the poultrymen [*asḥāb ad-dajāj*] used to stop there. He also dug a canal known as Nahr al-Qallā'īn. Someone told us that he saw it empty into the Tigris below the harbor [*furḍah*]. There was also a canal named Nahr Ṭābaq, and one called Nahr al-Bazzāzīn concerning which I heard someone say that he obtained water for ablutions from it———also, a canal in the Anbārite Mosque Quarter which I saw after it had dried up. These canals have fallen into disrepair, and most of them have disappeared so that no trace of them can be found.[51]

3

The Development of al-Karkh[1]

Muḥammad b. al-Ḥusayn b. al-Faḍl al-Qaṭṭān ——— ʿAbdallāh b. Jaʿfar b. Durustawayh an-Naḥwī ——— Yaʿqūb b. Sufyān: In the year 157/774 Abū Jaʿfar moved the markets from Madīnat al-Manṣūr and Madīnat ash-Sharqīyah to Bāb al-Karkh, Bāb ash-Shaʿīr and Bāb al-Muḥawwal.[2] Using his own funds, al-Manṣūr ordered ar-Rabīʿ, his client, to build this market which is known as al-Karkh.[3] In the same year, al-Manṣūr also widened the roads of the city and its suburbs so they were forty cubits wide, and ordered the destruction of all those dwellings which would project upon the roads intended for widening.

Abū-l-Qāsim al-Azharī ——— Aḥmad b. Ibrāhīm b. al-Ḥasan ——— Ibrāhīm b. Muḥammad b. ʿArafah al-Azdī: Then in the year [1]57/774 Abū Jaʿfar appointed Yaḥyā b. ʿAbdallāh to the office of Muḥtasib, but since he incited the populace to revolt,
(80) Abū Jaʿfar had him executed at Bāb adh-Dhahab, and shifted the markets of the city to Bāb al-Karkh, Bāb ash-Shaʿīr and Bāb al-Muḥawwal.[4] He ordered that ar-Rabīʿ build the new markets, and
-21- widened the roads of Madīnat as-Salām to forty cubits, ordering the destruction of those dwellings which would project upon the roads intended for widening. In the year [1]58/774 al-Manṣūr built his castle on the Tigris and named it al-Khuld.

Muḥammad b. ʿAlī al-Warrāq and Aḥmad b. ʿAlī al-Muḥtasib ———Muḥammad b. Jaʿfar an-Naḥwī———al-Ḥasan b. Muḥammad as-Sakūnī: Muḥammad b. Khalaf: Al-Khuwārizmī, i.e., Muḥammad b. Mūsā: Using his own funds, Abū Jaʿfar shifted the markets to al-Karkh one hundred and fifty six years, five months, and twenty days after the Hijrah. He began the construction of Qaṣr al-Khuld on the bank of the Tigris one month and ten days later.

Muḥammad b. Khalaf: Al-Ḥārith b. Abī Usāmah related the following account to me:[5] When Abū Jaʿfar al-Manṣūr completed Madīnat as-Salām, establishing the markets in the arcades on each side of the city, a delegation from the Byzantine Emperor visited him. At his command, they were taken on a tour of the city, and then invited to an audience with him at which time the Caliph asked the Patrikios, "What do you think of this city?" He answered, "I found it perfect but for one shortcoming." "What is that?" asked the Caliph. He answered, "Unknown to you, your enemies can penetrate the city anytime they wish. Furthermore, you are unable to conceal vital information about yourself from being spread to the various regions." "How?" asked the Caliph. "The markets are in the city," said the Patrikios. "As no one can be denied access to them, the enemy can enter under the guise of someone who wishes to carry on trade. And the merchants, in turn, can travel everywhere passing on information about you." It has been suggested that, at that time, al-Manṣūr ordered moving the markets out of the city to al-Karkh, and ordered the development of the area between the Ṣarāt and the ʿĪsā Canal.[6] This task was entrusted to Muḥammad b. Ḥubaysh[7] al-Kātib. Al-Manṣūr called for a wide garment, and traced the plan of the markets on it, arranging each type of market in its proper place. He said, "Place the Butcher's Market (Sūq al-Qaṣṣābīn) at the end because their wits are dull, and they have sharp cutting tools. Then he ordered that a mosque be built for the people of the markets so that they may assemble there on Friday without having to enter the city. This task, undertaken especially for them, was entrusted to a man called al-Waḍḍāḥ b. Shabā who then built the palace known as Qaṣr al-Waḍḍāḥ, and the adjoining mosque. Because it was situated east [*sharq*] of the Ṣarāt, this section was called ash-Sharqīyah.[8] Al-Manṣūr did not fix any rents on the markets as long as he lived, but when al-Mahdī became Caliph, Abū ʿUbaydallāh advised him to do this. At the Caliph's command, a tax [*kharaj*] was levied on the shops, and Saʿīd al-Ḥarrashī was appointed to supervise this in the year 167/783–784.[9]

Muḥammad b. ʿAlī and Aḥmad b. ʿAlī———Muḥammad b. Jaʿfar an-Naḥwī———al-Ḥasan b. Muḥammad as-Sakūnī: Muḥammad b. Khalaf: Before being transfered to al-Karkh, the Dār al-Baṭṭīkh Market was situated on the streets known as Darb al-Asākifah, Darb az-Zayt, and Darb al-ʿĀj. The market was then moved to the interior of al-Karkh in the reign of al-Mahdī. Most of the streets touched upon the dwellings which Aḥmad b. Muḥammad aṭ-Ṭāʾī bought.[10] The estates adjacent to the Ṣarāt near Bāb al-Muḥawwal were granted by al-Manṣūr as fiefs to ʿUqbah b. Jaʿfar b. Muḥammad b. al-Ashʿath, a descendent of Uhbān b.
-23- Ṣayfī Mukallam adh-Dhiʾb. However, when ʿUqbah opposed al-Maʾmūn, his residence was plundered. Al-Maʾmūn then granted these estates to the descendents of ʿĪsā b. Jaʿfar.[11] The residences adjacent to the Baṣrah Gate between the moat and the bank of the Ṣarāt, and opposite the Residences of the Companions [Dār aṣ-Ṣaḥābah] belonged to the Ashā ʿithah. Today, they are owned by the family of Ḥammād b. Zayd. The residence of Jaʿfar b. Muḥammad b. al-Ashʿath al-Kindī was adjacent to Bāb al-Muḥawwal; it later passed into the possession of al-ʿAbbās, his son.

Al-Ḥasan b. Abī Ṭālib———Abū ʿUmar Muḥammad b. al-ʿAbbās al-Khazzāz———Abū ʿUbayd an-Nāqid———Muḥammad b. Ghālib: I heard Abū Muslim ʿAbd ar-Raḥmān b. Yūnus mention a statement credited to al-Wāqidī:[12] Al-Kharkh is infested with the lowest rabble. Ash-Shaykh al-Khaṭīb: Al-Wāqidī meant by his statement certain sections of al-Karkh inhabited only by Rāfiḍites.[13] He did not mean the other sections of al-Karkh, and God knows better. The following poem was recited to us by al-Ḥasan b. Abī Bakr b. Shādhān———his father[14]———Abū ʿAbdallāh Ibrāhīm b. Muḥammad b. ʿArafah Nifṭawayh who composed it:

Let the morning clouds shower
  The dwellings of al-Karkh with
Continuous rain and every
  Sort of steady sprinkle,
Mansions that contain every
  Beauty and splendor:
They are superior to every [other] mansion.

4

The Development of ar-Ruṣāfah[1]

Muḥammad b. ʿAlī b. Makhlad al-Warrāq and Aḥmad b. ʿAlī b. al-Ḥusayn at-Tawwazī———Muḥammad b. Jaʿfar an-Naḥwī at-Tamīmī———al-Ḥasan b. Muḥammad as-Sakūnī———Muḥammad b. Khalaf: Aḥmad b. Muḥammad ash-Sharawī———his father: Delegations were sent to al-Mahdī upon his return from al-Muḥammadīyah in ar-Rayy in Shawwāl
-24- of 151/769. Al-Manṣūr then built him ar-Ruṣāfah with a wall, moat, park, and garden; and provided, as well, for running water.[2]

Muḥammad b. Khalaf: Yaḥyā b. al-Ḥasan: Except for the residences which he occupied himself, al-Mahdī used mud-bricks [*rahṣ*] for construction. The building of ar-Ruṣāfah and everything there was completed in the year 159/775–776. This is the account reported by Yaḥyā b. al-Ḥasan.

Ibn Makhlad and Ibn at-Tawwazī———Muḥammad b. Jaʿfar ———as-Sakūnī———Muḥammad b. Khalaf: Al-Ḥārith b. Abī Usāmah: The building of ar-Ruṣāfah was completed in the year 154/770–771.

I studied with al-Ḥasan b. Abī Bakr the following report on the authority of Aḥmad b. Kāmil al-Qāḍī———Muḥammad b. Mūsā ———Muḥammad b. Abī-s-Sarī———al-Haytham b. ʿAdī:[3] Entering the palace which he had built at ar-Ruṣāfah, al-Mahdī walked about accompanied by Abū-l-Bakhtarī Wahb b. Wahb. The Caliph then asked him, "Can you recite a tradition for this occasion?" Abū-l-Bakhtari answered—Yes! Ja'far b. Muḥammad related to me on the authority of his father that the Prophet said, "The best courtyards are those in which your eyes have wandered."[4]

Abū-l-Ḥusayn 'Alī b. Muḥammad b. 'Abdallāh al-Mu'addil ———'Uthmān b. Aḥmad ad-Daqqāq———Muḥammad b. Aḥmad b. al-Barrā'———'Alī b. Yaqtīn:[5] We had gone out with al-Mahdī when he said to us one day, "I'm entering this veranda in order to sleep. Let no one rouse me till I awaken." The Caliph then went to sleep, and we slept as well, only to be awakened by his crying. Frightened, we got up and asked, "What is the matter, O Commander of the Faithful?" "Just now, a visitor came to me in my sleep," he exclaimed, "an old man whom I swear I would recognize, even if he were one in a hundred thousand. He seized the door posts and called out,

> I have the impression here that the people of this palace are gone
> and its pillars and chambers are deserted of them.
> The master after times of joy and rule
> winds up in the grave covered by stones."

Al-Qāḍī, Abū 'Abdallāh al-Ḥusayn b. 'Alī aṣ-Ṣaymarī——— Muḥammad b. 'Imrān al-Marzubānī———Muḥammad b. Yaḥyā ———Muḥammad b. Mūsā al-Munajjim:[6] Al-Mu'taṣim and Ibn Abī Du'ād disagreed as to whether the city of Abū Ja'far or ar-Ruṣāfah was situated at a higher elevation. The Caliph ordered me to take levels, and in doing so I found the city to be situated approximately two and two-thirds cubits above ar-Ruṣāfah.

Ash-Shaykh Abū Bakr: Ar-Ruṣāfah was named 'Askar al-Mahdī because al-Mahdī camped ['*askara*] there while journeying to ar-Rayy.[7]

٢

The Quarters, Arcades, Side Streets [Sikkah], *Streets* [Darb], *and Estates* [Rabaḍ] *of Madīnat as-Salām; and after whom they Were Named. The West Side*

Muḥammad b. ʿAlī b. Makhlad and Aḥmad b. ʿAlī b. al-Ḥusayn at-Tawwazī———Muḥammad b. Jaʿfar at-Tamīmī an-Naḥwī———al-Ḥasan b. Muḥammad as-Sakūnī———Muḥammad b. Khalaf, Wakīʿ: The Ṭāqāt al-ʿAkkī was named after Muqātil b. Ḥākim, who originated from Syria.

The Ṭāqāt al-Ghiṭrīf after al-Ghiṭrīf Ibn ʿAṭā', the brother of al-Khayzurān, and maternal uncle of al-Hādī and ar-Rashīd, who was governor of Yemen. He is said to have been a descendent of al-Ḥārith b. Kaʿb, and that al-Khayzurān belonged to Salamah
-26- b. Saʿīd. He bought her from people of Jurash who had raised her as an Arab.

The Ṭāqāt of Abū-Suwayd, whose name was al-Jārūd, were contiguous to the Cemetery of the Damascus Gate.[1]

The Estate [*Rabaḍ*] of al-ʿAlā' b. Mūsā near the Street of Abū
(84) Ḥayyah.[2] The estate of Abū Nuʿaym Mūsā b. Ṣubayḥ, who is from the people of Merv, near [a street] called Shīrawayh.[3] It is said Abū Nuʿaym was the maternal uncle of al-Faḍl b. ar-Rabīʿ.

Ash-Shaykh Abū Bakr al-Ḥāfiẓ: [The street] called Shīrawayh is the name of a place on this estate.

The Estate of Abū ʿAwn ʿAbd al-Malik b. Yazīd on the street which reaches the Palace of Ṭāhir.[4]

The Estates of Abū Ayyūb al-Khūzī and at-Turjumān, who is at-Turjumān b. Balkh, are connected with the Suburb of Harb.[5]
The Square [*Murabba'ah*] of Shabīb b. Rūḥ al-Marwarrūdhī. That is the way it was reported to be by Ibn Makhlad and Ibn at-Tawwazī. But he is Shabīb b. Wa'j according to Aḥmad b. Abī Ṭāhir, Ibrāhīm b. Muḥammad b. 'Arafah al-Azdī, and Muḥammad b. 'Umar al-Ji'ābī.[6]
The Square of Abū-l-'Abbās, i.e., al-Faḍl b. Sulaymān aṭ-Ṭūsī from the people of Abīward.[7]

Muḥammad b. Khalaf: Aḥmad b. Abī Ṭāhir———Abū Ja'far Muḥammad b. Mūsā b. al-Furāt al-Kātib:[8] The village which was situated on the Square of Abū-l-'Abbās was before him that of his maternal grandfather, one of the *dihqāns* known as the Banū Zarārī.[9] The village called al-Wardanīyah and another village remain standing until this day, adjacent to the Square of Abū Qurrah.[10]
Muḥammad b. Khalaf: The Square of Abū Qurrah is named after 'Ubayd b. Hilal al-Ghassānī, one of the followers of the 'Abbāsid dynasty.

Aḥmad b. al-Ḥārith expressed the following opinion on the authority of Ibrāhīm b. 'Īsā:[11] There existed at the place known presently as Dār Sa'īd al-Khaṭīb, a village called Sharqanīyah.[12] It was marked by a palm grove which is still standing today next to the Bridge [*Qanṭarah*] of Abū-l-Jawn.[13] He was one of the *dihqāns* of Baghdad residing among the people of that village.

Muḥammad b. Khalaf: The Estate of Sulaymān b. Mujālid.[14]
The Estate of Ibrāhīm b. Ḥumayd.
The Estate of Ḥamzah b. Malik al-Khuzā'ī.[15]
The Estate of Raddād b. Sinān, a general.[16]
The Estate of Ḥumayd b. Qaḥṭabah b. Shabīb b. Khālid b. Ma'dan b. Shams aṭ-Ṭā'ī. The village of Ma'dan, which is known as Būs, is in 'Umān on the coast.[17]
5) The Estate of Naṣr b. 'Abdallāh is on the Dujayl Road and is known as an-Naṣrīyah.[18]
The Estate of 'Abd al-Malik b. Ḥumayd, the Secretary of al-Manṣūr before Abū Ayyūb.
The Estate of 'Amr b. al-Muhallab.

The Estate of Ḥumayd b. Abī-l-Ḥāriṯ, a general.
The Estate of Ibrāhīm b. Uṯmān b. Nuhayk near the Quraysh Cemetery.[19]
The Estate of Zuhayr b. al-Musayyab.[20]
The Suburb, and the Square of the Persians which al-Manṣūr granted to them as fiefs.[21]
    Muḥammad b. Ḵẖalaf: Al-Firāsẖī Aḥmad b. al-Hayṯam: the Fiefs of al-Musayyab b. Zuhayr on the Kūfah Gate Road are bounded by the Residence of al-Kindī, the Suwayqah of ʿAbd al-Wahhāb, and the entrance to the cemetery.[22]
-28- The Fiefs of the Qaḥāṭibah extend from the Kūfah Gate Road to the Damascus Gate.[23]
    Abū-l-Qāsim al-Azharī———Aḥmad b. Ibrāhīm———Ibrāhīm b. Muḥammad b. ʿArafah: The Street of the Qaḥāṭibah is named after al-Ḥasan b. Qaḥṭabah, whose dwelling was situated there. Al-Ḥasan, one of the great men of the dynasty, died in the year 181/797–798.
    Ibn Maḵẖlad and Ibn at-Tawwazī———Muḥammad b. Jaʿfar as-Sakūnī: Muḥammad b. Ḵẖalaf: Al-Maʾmūn granted Ṭāhir b. al-Ḥusayn his palace as a fief. Before him it belonged to ʿUbayd al-Ḵẖādim, a client of al-Manṣūr. Al-Baghayīn, fiefs granted by al-Manṣūr to these people extending from Darb Sawār to the end of Rabaḍ al-Burjulānīyah, where the dwellings of Ḥamzah b. Malik are located.[24]
Al-Ḵẖuwārizmīyah, one of al-Manṣūr's military colonies.[25]
Al-Ḥarbīyah is named after Ḥarb b. ʿAbdallāh, the chief of al-Manṣūr's guard.[26]
Az-Zuhayrīyah is named after Zuhayr b. Muḥammad, a general from the people of Abīward.[27]
The Tower of Ḥumayd aṭ-Ṭūsī.
    Muḥammad b. Ḵẖalaf: Abū Zayd al-Ḵẖaṭīb: I heard my father say: Shahār Sūj al-Hayṯam is named after al-Hayṯam b. Muʿāwiyah, the general.[28]
Abū Zayd al-Ḵẖaṭīb: The tower on the Anbār Road was constructed by Ṭāhir at the time he entered the city.
Muḥammad b. Ḵẖalaf: The Garden of the Priest [*al-Quss*] was so named because of a priest who lived there before Baghdad was

built.[29] The Suwayqah of ʿAbd al-Wahhāb b. Muḥammad b. Ibrāhīm al-Imām.[30]

Muḥammad b. Aḥmad b. Rizq———ʿUthman b. Aḥmad ad-Daqqāq———Muḥammad b. Aḥmad b. al-Barrā'———ʿAli b. Abī Maryam: I passed by the Suwayqah of ʿAbd al-Wahhāb and its dwellings were in ruin. On one of the walls was written:

> There are the dwellings of people whom I
> observed living the ample and carefree life that is desired.
> The fortunes of fate cried out to them and they
> were turned toward the grave without leaving any trace.

Ibn Makhlad and Ibn at-Tawwazī———Muḥammad b. Jaʿfar ———as-Sakūnī: Muḥammad b. Khalaf: As for the Dwellings of the Companions [*Ṣaḥābah*],[31] Abū Bakr al-Hudhalī has a mosque and street. Muḥammad b. Yazīd, Shabbah b. ʿAqqāl and Ḥanẓalah b. ʿAqqāl have a street known today as al-Istikhrājī. ʿAbdallāh b. ʿAyyāsh has a dwelling on the bank of the Ṣarāt Canal.[32] ʿAbdallāh b. ar-Rabīʿ al-Ḥāṛithī has a dwelling which is situated among those of the Companions.

Ibn Abī Saʿlā, the poet, and Abū Dulāmah Zayd b. Jawn have fiefs. Zayd is written with the letter *yā* in the account of Muḥammad b. Jaʿfar on the authority of as-Sakūnī.

Muḥammad b. al-Ḥasan b. Aḥmad al-Ahwāzī———Abū Aḥmad al-Ḥasan b. Abdallāh b. Saʿīd al-ʿAskarī———Abū-l-ʿAbbās b. ʿAmmār———Ibn Abī Saʿd: Aḥmad b. Kulthūm: I saw Abū ʿUthmān al-Māzinī and al-Jammāz in the presence of my grandfather Muḥammad b. Abī Rajā'. He asked them. "What is Abū Dulāmah's proper name?" They were not able to reply; whereupon my grandfather said, "It is Zand. Beware of misspelling it and saying Zayd."[33]

Abū Aḥmad al-ʿAskarī: Abū Dulāmah is Zand b. al-Jawn, the client of Qusāqis al-Asadī, and companion of as-Saffāḥ, and al-Manṣūr whom he praised. Among the ancestors of the prophet descended from Ismāʿīl is Zand b. Iʿrāq ath-Tharī.

ʿUbaydallāh b. Aḥmad b. ʿUthmān aṣ-Ṣayrafī———Muḥammad b. ʿAbdallāh b. Ayyūb———Abū-l-ʿAbbās Aḥmad b. ʿUbaydallāh b. ʿAmmār ath-Thaqafī: Abū Ayyūb, that is to say Sulaymān b. Abī Shaykh: Abū Jaʿfar al-Manṣūr ordered a number of the

Companions' houses to be destroyed or confiscated. Included among these was the house of Abū Dulāmah, who then said:[34]

Ye children of the heirs of the Prophet in whose palms
his wealth and landed estates have come to rest.
The entire earth is yours; so lend your slave what is
contained within the walls of his dwelling.

It is as if he has gone and left
among you what you lend out,
But has dissolved whatever
is not lent out.

Ibn Makhlad and Ibn at-Tawwazī———Muḥammad b. Ja'far ———as-Sukūni———Muḥammad b. Khalaf: The spot now occupied by the New Prison was a fief granted to 'Abdallāh b. Malik, and Muḥammad b. Yaḥyā b. Khālid b. Barmak made his residence there. During the reign of Muḥammad, it became part of the building which Umm Ja'far erected, and which she called al-Qarār.[35]

The Residence of Sulymān b. Abī Ja'far is situated on a fief originally granted to Hishām b. 'Amr al-Fazārī.[36]

The Residence of 'Amr b. Mas'adah is situated on a fief granted to al-'Abbās b. 'Ubaydallāh b. Ja'far b. al-Manṣūr.

-31- The Residence of Ṣāliḥ al-Miskīn was a fief granted to him by Abū Ja'far.

The Suwayqah of al-Haytham b. Shu'bah b. Zuhayr, the client of al-Manṣūr who died in the year 156/772–773 while lying with a slave girl.[37]

The Residence of 'Umārah b. Ḥamzah, one of the most eloquent and illustrious scribes. He is said to have been a descendant of the Prophet's client Abū Umāmah, or a descendant of 'Ikrimah.[38]

The Palace (*Qaṣr*) of 'Abdawayh from al-Azd, one of the notables of the dynasty, who undertook its construction during the reign of al-Manṣūr.[39]

The Dwelling of Abū Yazīd ash-Sharawī, the client of 'Alī b. 'Abdallāh b. 'Abbās.[40]

The Street (*Sikkah*) of Muhalhil b. Ṣafwān, the client of 'Alī b. 'Abdallāh.

The Field of Abū-s-Sarī al-Ḥakam b. Yūsuf, a general who was the client of the Banū Ḍabbah.
Ar-Rahīnah, belonged to a group of people who were taken as hostages [*rahīnah*] during the reign of al-Manṣūr. It is adjacent to the Estate of Nūḥ b. Farqad, a general.
The Field of Qīrāṭ, the client of Ṭāhir, and of his son ʿĪsā b. Qīrāṭ.[41]
Dār Isḥāq which was an island granted by al-Manṣūr to Isḥāq b. Ibrāhīm.[42]
The Suwayqah of Abū-l-Ward, that is, ʿUmar b. Muṭarrif al-Marwazī, who presided over the Maẓālim Courts for al-Mahdī. Adjacent to it is the Fief of Isḥāq al-Azraq ash-Sharawī, a confidant of al-Manṣūr.[43]

Abū ʿUbaydallāh al-Marzubānī———ʿAbd al-Bāqi' b. Qāniʿ: The Suwayqah of Abū-l-Ward was so named because ʿĪsā b. ʿAbd ar-Raḥmān used to be called Abū-l-Ward while he served al-Manṣūr. The suwayqah was named after him.

Ibn Makhlad and Ibn at-Tawwazī———Muḥammad b. Jaʿfar———as-Sakūnī———Muḥammad b. Khalaf: The Pond [*Birkah*] of Zalzal, the lute-player. He was a page of ʿĪsā b. Jaʿfar; he had it dug to serve as a public fountain.[44]

Al-Ḥasan b. Abī Bakr———his father———Ibrāhīm b. Muḥammad b. ʿArafah Niftawayh, who composed the following verse:

> If Zuhayr and Imrū'-l-Qays could have seen
> the lovely surroundings of Birkat Zalzal,
> They would not have described Salmā
> and Umm Sālim
> And would not have mentioned
> "Ad-Dakhūl and Ḥawmal" so often.[45]

Ibn Makhlad and Ibn at-Tawwazī———Muḥammad b. Jaʿfar as-Sakūnī———Muḥammad b. Khalaf———Aḥmad b. Abī Ṭāhir———Aḥmad b. Mūsā one of the *dihqāns* of Bādurāyā: The Fief of ar-Rabīʿ originally consisted of fields occupied by people from a village called Banāwarī in the district [*rustāq*] of al-Farawsyaj in Bādūrayā. The village is still registered in the dīwān under that name.[46]

Muḥammad b. Khalaf: They say that al-Manṣūr granted ar-
-33- Rabīʿ his outer fief, and another fief [at] Bayn as-Sūrayn in back of the Street [*Darb*] of Jamīl. The merchants and occupants of his fief, however, gained possession of it from his son. Previously, the Fief of ar-Rabīʿ and the Suwayqah of Ghālib were called Warthāl. It is said that al-Mahdī granted ar-Rabīʿ his outer fief, and that al-Manṣūr granted him the inner fief.[47]

Abū-l-Qāsim al-Azharī——Aḥmad b. Ibrāhīm——Ibrāhīm b. Muḥammad b. ʿArafah: The Fief of ar-Rabīʿ is named after ar-Rabīʿ, the client of al-Manṣūr.

As for the Fief of the Supporters [*Anṣār*], al-Mahdī preferred them to swell the ranks of his supporters and thus distinguish himself with their presence. Therefore, he granted them this fief, which
(89) was near the Dwellings of the Barmakids.[48]

Ibn ʿArafah continued: As for the Fief of the Dogs [*Kilāb*], a shaykh reported to me on the authority of one of its inhabitants, that his father said: When Abū Jaʿfar was granting fiefs, this area remained unassigned. Since there were many dogs [*kilāb*] there, some of the inhabitants commented that this is the Fief of the Dogs, thus giving the area its name.[49]

The streets [*sikkah*] of the city are named after the clients and generals of Abū Jaʿfar. Among them is the Street of Shaykh b. ʿAmīrah, a general who succeeded the Barmakids as commander of the guards.[50]

The Dwelling of Khāzim is named after Khāzim b. Khuzaymah an-Nahshalī, who was a giant. During one battle in Khurāsān he killed 70,000 men and captured some 10,000 others whom he subsequently had beheaded.

The Street [*Darb*] of al-Abrad is named after al-Abrad b. ʿAbdallāh,
-34- one of ar-Rashīd's generals, and the governor of Hamadhān.

The Street of Sulaymān is named after Sulaymān b. Abī Jaʿfar al-Manṣūr.[51]

The Street [*Sikkah*] of the Police in the city was settled by members of al-Manṣūr's police force.[52]

The Street [*Sikkah*] of Sayyābah is named after one of al-Manṣūr's companions.

Az-Zubaydīyah which is between the Khurāsān Gate and Shāriʿ

Dār ar-Raqīq is named after Zubaydah, the daughter of Ja'far b. Abī Ja'far al-Manṣūr. The same is true for az-Zubaydīyah, the section of the West Side below Madīnat as-Salām.[53]
The Palace [*Qaṣr*] of Waḍḍāḥ is named after Waḍḍāḥ ash-Sharawī, the client of al-Manṣūr.
The Banū Nuhayk whose dwellings are near Bāb al-Muḥawwal belonged to a distinguished family from Simmar[54] who were scribes and public officials in the service of 'Abdallāh b. Ṭāhir.
As for the Street [*Darb*] of Jamīl, it is named after Jamīl b. Muḥammad, one of the scribes.
The Anbārite Mosque Quarter is so called because of the vast number of these people who lived there.[55] The first was one Ziyād al-Qandī, who was active during the reign of ar-Rashīd. The Caliph appointed Abū Wakī' al-Jarrāḥ b. Malīḥ as Director of the Public Treasury [*Bayt al-Māl*] and Ibn Malīḥ, in turn, nominated Ziyād as his successor. Ziyād, who was a staunch Shī'ite, embezzled funds from the public treasury in league with a group of scribes. When ar-Rashīd received proof of this action he ordered that Ziyād's hand be cut off. The accused then cried out, "O Commander of the Faithful, it is not necessary to cut my hand off, for I am but an entrusted official whose only guilt is a breach of trust." Ar-Rashīd then desisted from cutting off his hand.

Ibn 'Arafah: Among the great men who settled in the Anbārite Mosque Quarter were Aḥmad b. Isrā'īl, whose dwelling was on the Street of Jamīl, and Dulayl b. Ya'qūb, whose dwelling was situated among the residences of the Banū Nuhayk. Also situated there was the Dwelling of Abū-ṣ-Ṣaqr Ismā'īl b. Bulbul. Abū Aḥmad al-Qāsim b. Sa'īd, a cultured scribe, was among these Anbārite notables who were our contemporaries.

Ibn Makhlad and Ibn at-Tawwazī———Muḥammad b. Ja'far ———as-Sakūnī———Muḥammad b. Khalaf: After the Archway [*Ṭāq*] of al-Ḥarrānī Ibrāhīm b. Dhakwān comes the Old Market [*as-Sūq al-'Atīqah*], which continues to Bāb ash-Sha'īr.[56]

Al-Khaṭīb: In the Old Market there is a mosque which the Shī'ites frequent and venerate, for they claim that the Caliph 'Alī b. Abī Ṭālib prayed at that spot. However, I have not seen a single scholar confirm that ʿAlī entered Baghdad, and the only account that we have received to this effect is that of al-Qāḍī Abū ʿAbdallāh al-Ḥusayn b. ʿAlī aṣ-Ṣaymarī———Aḥmad b. Muḥammad b. ʿAlī aṣ-Ṣayrafī———al-Qāḍī Abū Bakr Muḥammad b. ʿUmar al-Jiʿābī al-Ḥāfiẓ. Mentioning Baghdad, he said: The Caliph ʿAlī b. Abī Ṭālib is said to have passed through Baghdad on his way to and from an-Nahrawān, and to have prayed at certain places while at Baghdad. If this is correct, those companions who were with him also entered Baghdad.

Al-Khaṭīb Abū-Bakr: It is generally accepted that ʿAlī traveled by way of al-Madā'in while going to and coming from an-Nahrawān, but God knows better.

Abū-l-Faḍl ʿĪsā b. Aḥmad b. ʿUthmān al-Hamadhānī———
-36- Abū-l-Ḥasan b. Rizqawayh:[57] One day, while I was in the presence of Abū Bakr al-Jiʿābī, a group of Shīʿites came to him, greeted him, and presented him with a purse full of dirhams, saying, "O Qāḍī, indeed you have collected the names of Baghdad's tradition-scholars, and mentioned those people who came to the city. Since the Commander of the Faithful ʿAlī b. Abī Ṭālib came there, we are asking you to mention him in your book." Abū Bakr replied, "Yes—Boy! Bring the book!" The slave brought the book, and Abū Bakr wrote in it: And the Commander of the Faithful ʿAli b. Abī Ṭālib: It is said that he came to Baghdad. Ibn Rizqawayh: When the group departed, I asked Abū Bakr, "Who mentioned the statement that you added to the book!" He replied, "The people you just observed," or something to that effect.

(91) Ibn Makhlad and Ibn at-Tawwazī [al-Qāḍī]———Muḥammad b. Jaʿfar———as-Sakūnī———Muḥammad b. Khalaf: The Mosque of Ibn Raghbān is that of ʿAbd ar-Raḥmān b. Raghbān, the client of Ḥabīb b. Maslamah.[58]

The Ṭābaq Canal is none other than the Canal of Bābāk b. Bahrām b. Bābāk, who dug it and chose the foundations [*ʿaqr*] where the Palace [*Qaṣr*] of ʿĪsā b. ʿAlī is found.[59]

In the west, Nahr ʿĪsā runs in al-Farawsyaj; in the east, it runs in the district [*rustāq*] of al-Karkh until the Thorn Bridge [Qanṭarat ash-Shawk]. In this district are the dwellings of the Maʿbadites, the Banū Zurayq Bridge, Dār al-Baṭṭīkh, Dār al-Quṭn, and the

Fief of the Christians. To the east in al-Kar<u>kh</u> is the Nahr Tābaq Quarter, and to the west is the village of Banāwarī.⁶⁰
The section of the Wāsiṭ Mosque, with the Colonnade of May<u>sh</u>awayh, who was a Christian *dihqān*, extends until the Ṣīnīyāt [?] Trench [*K̲h̲andaq*].⁶¹ [. . .] until al-Yāsirīyah. West of this quarter [*shāri'*] are the villages called Barā<u>th</u>ā, to the east is the district [*rustāq*] of al-Farawsyaj.⁶²
East and west of the Darb al-Ḥijārah, and the al-'Abbās Bridge [*Qanṭarah*] is the Nahr Kar<u>kh</u>āyā Quarter and part of Barā<u>th</u>ā.⁶³
The Kar<u>kh</u>āyā Canal was so named because it brought water to the districts [*rustāq*] of al-Farawsyaj and al-Kar<u>kh</u>. When 'Īsā built the Abū Ja'far Mill, he bisected the Kar<u>kh</u>āyā Canal and diverted drinking water to the district [*rustāq*] of al-Kar<u>kh</u> by way of the Rufayl Canal.⁶⁴
Al-'Abbāsīyah is a fief named after al-'Abbās b. Muḥammad.⁶⁵
Al-Yāsirīyah is a fief named after Yāsir, the client of Zubaydah.
The Banū Zurayq Bridge [*Qanṭarah*] is named after *dihqāns* from the people of Bādūrayā.
The Bridge of the Ma'badite is named after 'Abdallāh b. Ma'bad al-Ma'badī.
The Mills of the Patrikios, Ṭārāth b. al-Lay<u>th</u> b. al-'Ayzār b. Ṭarīf b. Fūq b. Mawriq, Ambassador from the Byzantine Emperor. He built this source of income but it was seized from his estate when he died.⁶⁶
Abū 'Abdallāh al-Ḥusayn b. Muḥammad b. Ja'far al-<u>Kh</u>ālī' ———'Alī b. Muḥammad b. as-Sarī al-Hama<u>dh</u>ānī———al-Qāḍī Abū Bakr Muḥammad b. <u>Kh</u>alaf———Isḥāq b. Muḥammad b. Isḥāq: I was told that Ya'qūb b. al-Mahdī asked al-Faḍl b. ar-Rabī' about the Mills of the Patrikios:⁶⁷ "Who is the Patrikios that these mills are named after?" Al-Faḍl replied: When your father became Caliph, an Ambassador from Byzantium came to congratulate him. The Caliph, having invited the Ambassador to his presence, addressed him with the aid of an interpreter. The Byzantine then remarked, "I have not come to the Commander of the Faithful for the sake of wealth or any ulterior motive, but have come yearning to meet him and thereby see his face, for, indeed, we have found written in our books that the third person of the

house of the Prophet of this nation will fill the earth with justice, just as in the past it had been filled with tyranny." Al-Mahdī replied, "Your words cause me to rejoice; and we will fulfill any wish that you may have." Then the Caliph ordered ar-Rabīʿ to settle the Ambassador in his quarters and to honor him with gifts. After having remained there sometime, he left his quarters to take a walk, and passed by the future location of the mills. Looking at this spot, he said to ar-Rabīʿ, "Lend me 500,000 dirhams so that I may build an establishment that will bring in 500,000 dirhams every year." Ar-Rabīʿ indicated he would do so, and brought the matter to the attention of al-Mahdī, who then commanded, "Give him 500,000 dirhams, and 500,000 better; also pay him whatever income the property may yield, and should he leave for his native land, send it to him yearly."[68] Ar-Rabīʿ acted accordingly, and the mills were built. The Byzantine returned to his native land, and they forwarded the income to him until the time of his death. Al-Mahdī then ordered the mills annexed to his own property. The name of the Patrikios was Ṭārāth b. al-Layth b. al-ʿAyzār b. Ṭarīf. His father was one of the Byzantine Kings in the days of Muʿāwiyah b. Abī Sufyān.

Abū-l-Qāsim al-Azharī——Aḥmad b. Ibrāhīm——Ibrāhīm b. Muḥammad b. ʿArafah: The Fief of Khuzaymah is named after Khuzaymah b. Khāzim, one of ar-Rashīd's generals. He lived until the reign of al-Amīn and became blind late in his life.[69]

The section of the Tigris' bank [*shāṭi' Dijlah*] which runs from the
-39- Palace of ʿĪsā to the dwelling at Qarn aṣ-Ṣarāt presently occupied by Ibrāhīm b. Aḥmad was granted as a fief to ʿĪsā b. ʿAlī, that is to say, b. ʿAbdallāh b. ʿAbbās, after whom the ʿĪsā Canal and the Palace of ʿĪsā are named.[70] ʿĪsā b. Jaʿfar.[71] The Harbor [*Furḍah*] of Jaʿfar and the Fief of Jaʿfar are named after Jaʿfar b. Abī Jaʿfar. The Palace of Ḥumayd was built at a later time.[72]

The section of the Tigris' bank which runs from Qarn aṣ-Ṣarāt to the bridge, and from the limits of the dwelling which belonged to Najāḥ b. Salamah—it then passed into the hands of Aḥmad b. Isrā'īl, and is presently in the possession of Khāqān al-Mufliḥī—until the Khurāsān Gate, that section is called al-Khuld. What extends beyond until the Main Bridge is al-Qarār. Al-Manṣūr settled there toward the end of his reign, and al-Amīn later took up residence there.

ʿAlī b. Muḥammad b. ʿAbdallāh al-Muʿaddil———Al-Ḥusayn b. Ṣafwān al-Bardhaʿī———Abū Bakr ʿAbdallāh b. Muḥammad b. Abī-d-Dunyā———al-Ḥasan b. Jahwar: I passed by al-Khuld and al-Qarār with ʿAlī b. Abī Hāshim al-Kūfī. When he gazed upon the ruins, he paused reflectively and said:[73]

> They built and said, "We shall not die,"
> But the builders built for destruction.
> From what I have seen, there is no wise man
> Who trusts in what life holds in store.

Abū-l-Qāsim al-Azharī———Aḥmad b. Ibrāhīm———Ibn ʿArafah: The Palace [*Dār*] of Isḥāq is named after Isḥāq b. Ibrāhīm al-Muṣʿabī who continuously directed the police from the reign of al-Maʾmūn to that of al-Mutawakkil. He died in the year 235/849–850 at the age of fifty-eight years, eight months, and eleven days.[74] The Fief of Umm Jaʿfar is named after her.

6

The East Side[1]

Muḥammad b. ʿAlī b. Makhlad and Aḥmad b. ʿAlī at-Tawwazī———Muḥammad b. Jaʿfar at-Tamīmī———al-Ḥasan b. Muḥammad as-Sakūnī———Muḥammad b. Khalaf: The Street [*Darb*] of Khuzaymah b. Khāzim was granted to him as a fief.[2]

The Archway [*Ṭāq*] of Asmā', the daughter of al-Manṣūr, which passed into the possession of ʿAlī b. Jahshiyār. It is situated between the two palaces [*bayn al-qaṣrayn*], the Palace of Asmā', and that of ʿUbaydallāh b. al-Mahdī.[3]

The Suwayqah of Khuḍayr, the client of Ṣāliḥ Ṣāḥib al-Muṣallā, who sold jars [*jirar*] there.[4]

The Suwayqah of Yaḥyā b. Khālid was granted to him as a fief, but then passed into the possession of Umm Jaʿfar. Al-Ma'mūn then granted it as a fief to Ṭāhir.[5]

The Suwayqah of Abū ʿUbaydallāh Muʿāwiyah b. ʿUbaydallāh b. Yāsar al-Ashʿarī, the Wazīr.[6]

The Palace of Umm Ḥabīb was a fief granted by al-Mahdī to ʿUmārah b. Abī-l-Khaṣīb.[7]

The Suwayqah of Naṣr b. Mālik b. Al-Haytham al-Khuzāʿī. A mosque stood there that passed out of use in the reign of al-Mustaʿīn.[8]

Sūq al-ʿAṭash was built by Saʿīd al-Ḥarrashī for al-Mahdī. Saʿīd then transferred every kind of merchant to this market, which was likened to al-Karkh. He named it the Market of Satiety [*Sūq ar-Riyy*], but this name was superseded by the Market of Thirst [*Sūq al-ʿAṭash*].[9]

The area between the Baradān Bridge [*Qanṭarah*] and the Main Bridge [*al-Jisr*] belongs to as-Sarī b. al-Ḥuṭam. They said: Abū-n-Naḍr[10] Hāshim b. al-Qāsim bought the place of his residence from as-Sarī b. al-Ḥuṭam. They used to say: There is not a better dwelling in this entire quarter [*shāriʿ*] than that of Abū-n-Naḍr.[11]

Abū ʿAbdallāh al-Ḥusayn b. Muḥammad b. Jaʿfar al-Khāliʿ ———ʿAlī b. Muḥammad b. as-Sarī al-Hamadhānī———al-Qāḍī Abū Bakr Muḥammad b. Khalaf———Aḥmad b. al-Ḥārith:[12] Baghdad's land, markets, thoroughfares [*shāriʿ*], palaces, and canals of both the East and West Sides were illustrated for the Byzantine Emperor. The illustration included the thoroughfares and palaces of the East Side extending from Bāb-al-Jisr to the three gates [*thalāthat al-abwāb*]. Among the thoroughfares of the East Side were the Shāriʿ al-Maydān and Shāriʿ Suwayqat Naṣr b. Mālik.[13] The markets and thoroughfares from the Suwayqah of Khuḍayr until the Baradān Bridge [*Qanṭarah*] were also illustrated. When the king was drinking, he would call for the illustration and drink a toast, looking at the drawing of the Shāriʿ Suwayqat Naṣr. He used to say: I have never seen an illustration of a better built place.

Ibn Makhlad and Ibn at-Tawwazī———Muḥammad b. Jaʿfar ———as-Sakūnī———Muḥammad b. Khalaf: The Square [*Murabbaʿah*] of al-Ḥarrashī is named after Saʿīd al-Ḥarrashī.[14] The Palace of Faraj ar-Rukhkhajī, a slave of Ḥamdūnah, the daughter of Ghaḍīḍ who was an *umm al-walad* of ar-Rashīd.[15]

Al-Azharī———Aḥmad b. Ibrāhīm———Ibrāhīm b. Muḥammad b. ʿArafah: The Palace of Faraj is named after Faraj ar-Rukhkhajī whose son ʿUmar was appointed in charge of the *dīwān*, but was later punished by al-Mutawakkil.

The Thoroughfare [*Shāriʿ*] of ʿAbd aṣ-Ṣamad is named after ʿAbd aṣ-Ṣamad b. ʿAlī b. ʿAbdallāh b. al-ʿAbbās who had the shortest pedigree of any man of his time, since his ancestors traced back to

ʿAbd Manāf are identical in number with those of Yazīd b. Muʿāwiyah although 121 years separated the death of ʿAbd aṣ-Ṣamād from that of Yazīd. Muḥammad b. ʿAlī died in the year [1]18/736–737. Sixty-five years separated his death from that of ʿAbd aṣ-Ṣamad, and fifty-two years separated the death of ʿAbd aṣ-Ṣamad from that of Dāwūd b. ʿAlī. ʿAbd aṣ-Ṣamad who died during the reign of ar-Rashīd, was the paternal uncle of his grandfather, and is the subject of numerous accounts. His front teeth and molars were connected without leaving any space. Ar-Rashīd imprisoned him, but then consented to release him.[16]

(95) Ibn Makhlad and Ibn at-Tawwazī———Muḥammad b. Jaʿfar ———as-Sakūnī———Muḥammad b. Khalaf: The Street [*Darb*] of al-Mufaḍḍal b. Zimām, the client of al-Mahdī, was granted to him as a fief.[17]

The Court [*Raḥbah*] of Yaʿqūb b. Dāwūd al-Kātib, the client of the Banū Sulaym.[18]

The Khan of Abū Ziyād, who was one of the Nabataeans that al-Ḥajjāj branded. He came from the lowlands of al-Kūfah where he lived until the reign of al-Manṣūr, at which time he moved, settling in this place. Though his *kunyah* was Abū Zaynab, he was generally called Abū Ziyād. A son born to him was given a gentleman's education, and was eloquent in his speech.

The Palace of al-Banūqah, the daughter of al-Madhī.[19]

The Suwayqah of al-ʿAbbāsah, and the Palace of al-ʿAbbāsah which is in al-Mukharrim. The Fief of al-ʿAbbās which is at Bāb al-Mukharrim is named after al-ʿAbbās b. Muḥammad b. ʿAlī b.
-43- ʿAbdallāh b. ʿAbbās, the brother of Abū Jaʿfar.[20]

Abū-l-Qāsim al-Azharī———Aḥmad b. Ibrāhīm———Ibn ʿArafah: The Fief of al-ʿAbbās on the East Side is named after al-ʿAbbās b. Muḥammad b. ʿAlī b. ʿAbdallāh b. al-ʿAbbās, the brother of al-Manṣūr. Although he was Abū-l-ʿAbbās' brother, al-ʿAbbās, who was governor of al-Jazīrah, died fifty years after him, as Abū-l-ʿAbbās passed away in the year 136/754, while al-ʿAbbās died in the year 186/802. His family was suspicious of ar-Rashīd, and claimed that the Caliph had poisoned him, causing al-ʿAbbās to suffer from dropsy, the disease which killed him. Al-ʿAbbāsīyah is named after him.

Al-Khaṭīb Abū Bakr: Meaning al-ʿAbbāsīyah, the Fief of al-ʿAbbās that is situated on the West Side, as we have previously mentioned.

ʿUbaydallāh b. Aḥmad b. ʿUthmān aṣ-Ṣayrafī———Abū-l-Ḥasan ʿAlī b. ʿUmar al-Ḥāfiẓ———Ibn Durayd:[21] Yazīd b. Badr b. Mukharrim al-Ḥārithī was a descendant of the master [*ṣāḥib*] of al-Mukharrim in Baghdad.

Abū-l-Ḥasan Muḥammad b. Aḥmad b. Rizq———Abū ʿUmar az-Zāhid———Abū ʿAlī al-Kharaqī———ʿAbdallāh b. Aḥmad b. Ḥanbal———his father:[22] Al-Mukharrim is the stronghold of the Sunnites.

Ibn Makhlad and Ibn at-Tawwazī———Muḥammad b. Jaʿfar at-Tamīmī an-Naḥwī———al-Ḥasan b. Muḥammad as-Sakūnī———Muḥammad b. Khalaf———Muḥammad b. Abī ʿAlī———Muḥammad b. ʿAbd al-Munʿim b. Idrīs———Hishām b. Muḥammad:[23] I heard the Banū-l-Ḥārith b. Kaʿb saying that al-Mukharrim in Baghdad was named after Mukharrim b. Shurayḥ b. Mukharrim b. Ziyād b. al-Ḥārith b. Malik b. Rabīʿah b. Kaʿb b. al-Ḥārith b. Kaʿb b. ʿAmr. The fiefs of al-Mukharrim were granted to him at the time the Arabs settled there in the reign of ʿUmar b. al-Khaṭṭāb.[24]

Ibn Makhlad and Ibn at-Tawwazī———Muḥammad b. Jaʿfar———as-Sakūnī———Muḥammad b. Khalaf———Yaḥyā b. al-Ḥasan b. ʿAbd al-Khāliq: The Dwelling of Abū ʿAbbād Thābit b. Yaḥyā was a fief granted by al-Mahdī to Shabīb b. Shaybah al-Khaṭīb. Abū ʿAbbād bought it from the heirs in the reign of al-Ma'mūn.

Muḥammad b. Khalaf: The Tuesday Market (*Sūq ath-Thalāthā'*) belonged to a group from the people of Kalwādhā and Baghdad.[25]
The Suwayqah of Ḥajjāj al-Waṣīf, the client of al-Mahdī.[26]
The Dwelling of ʿUmārah b. Abī Khuṣayb, the client of Rūḥ b. Ḥāṭim.[27] It has been said that he was the client of al-Manṣūr.
The Canal of Muʿallā b. Ṭarīf, the client of al-Mahdī, whose brother was al-Layth b. Ṭarīf.

Al-Azharī———Aḥmad b. Ibrāhīm———Ibrāhīm b. ʿArafah: The Mahdī Canal was named after the Caliph. His official residence was situated along the canal, but his pleasure palace was at ʿĪsābādh.[28] As for the Muʿallā Canal, al-Muʿallā was one of ar-Rashīd's great generals. The Caliph gave him authority over as many provinces at one time as no other great man ever held. He was governor of al-Baṣrah, Fārs, al-Ahwāz, al-Yamāmah, al-Baḥrayn, and al-Ghawṣ. These provinces were also held together by Muḥammad b. Sulaymān b. ʿAlī b. ʿAbdallāh b. al-ʿAbbās b. ʿAbd al-Muṭṭalib, and by ʿUmārah b. Ḥamzah,[29] after whom the Palace of ʿUmārah is named. The latter was a client of the Banū Hāshim and a descendant of ʿIkrimah, the client of Ibn ʿAbbās, as his mother was the daughter of ʿIkrimah. He was the haughtiest of men and the expression, "More haughty than ʿUmārah" was frequently used. It is claimed that one of his companions entered into his presence. Beneath his seat was a magnificent jewel which he wished to bestow upon this companion. However, too proud to extend his hand in order to reach it, he called to his companion, "Lift the seat and take what is underneath it."

-45- Ibn Makhlad and Ibn at-Tawwazī———Muḥammad b.
(97) Jaʿfar———as-Sakūnī———Muḥammad b. Khalaf: The Street [*Darb*] of al-Aghlab which is in the vicinity of the Madhī Canal is named after al-Aghlab b. Sālim b. Sawādah, father of the ruler of the Maghrib and a descendant of the Banū Saʿd b. Zayd Manāt b. Tamīm. Harthamah had his son Ibrāhīm b. Al-Aghlab, made a governor.[30] Aṣ-Ṣāliḥīyah belongs to Ṣāliḥ al-Miskīn.[31]

The Domes [*Qibāb*] of al-Ḥusayn on the road to Khurāsān are those of al-Ḥusayn b. Qurrah al-Fazārī.[32]

ʿĪsābādh is named after ʿĪsā b. al-Mahdī whose mother was al-Khayzurān.

Ibrāhīm b. Makhlad———Ismāʿīl b. ʿAlī al-Khuṭabī: In the year 64, that is to say 164/780–781, al-Mahdī built his palace at ʿĪsābādh, which he named Qaṣr as-Salām.

Al-Azharī———Aḥmad b. Ibrāhīm———Ibn ʿArafah: The Tank [*Ḥawḍ*] of Dāwūd is named after Dāwūd b. ʿAlī.[33]

Ibn Makhlad and Ibn at-Tawwazī———Muḥammad b. Jaʿfar as-Sakūnī———Muḥammad b. Khalaf: The Tank of Dāwūd b. al-Hindī, the client of al-Mahdī. Some say that he is Dāwūd, the client of Nuṣayr, and that it was Nuṣayr who is the client of al-Mahdī.

The Tank of Haylānah. She is said to have been a stewardess

[*qayyimah*] of al-Manṣūr, and to have dug this pool. There is an estate between al-Karkh and Bāb al-Muḥawwal which bears her name. However, there are people who say that Haylānah was the servant of ar-Rashīd about whom he said:[34]

> Shame upon the world, its pleasures
> and material things.
> Since someone has scattered dust
> upon Haylānah in the grave.

Al-Ḥasan b. ʿAlī al-Jawharī———Muḥammad b. ʿImrān b. ʿUbaydallāh al-Marzubānī———Aḥmad b. Muḥammad b. ʿĪsā al-Makkī———Muḥammad b. al-Qāsim b. Khallād———al-Asmaʿī:[35] Haylānah, whom ar-Rashīd loved very much, belonged to Yaḥyā b. Khālid before him. One day, previous to his becoming Caliph, ar-Rashīd came to Yaḥyā where al-Haylānah encountered him in a hallway. She grabbed the sleeves of his garment and asked, "Why don't you spend a day with me sometime?" He said, "Yes—but how is that possible?" "Take me from this aged man," she said. Then the Caliph said to Yaḥyā, "I should like you to present me with so and so," and Yaḥyā presented him with Haylānah, who then became the Caliph's favorite. As she often said, "Let's go now" [*Hayya-l-ānah*?], he called her Haylānah.[36] She stayed with the Caliph three years and then died. Ar-Rashīd, who was overcome with great grief, recited the following verse:

> I say as they bury you and sadness is in my bosom,
> Be off, for nothing will ever make me happy after you.

Muḥammad b. Abī ʿAlī al-Iṣbahāni———Abū Aḥmad al-Ḥasan b. ʿAbdallāh b. Saʿīd al-ʿAskarī———Muḥammad b. Yaḥyā aṣ-Sūlī———al-Ghallābī———Muḥammad b. ʿAbd ar-Raḥmān: When Haylānah, the slave girl of ar-Rashīd, died, al-ʿAbbās b. al-Aḥnaf was ordered by ar-Rashīd to eulogize her and recited:[37]

> Ye whose death was good news for graves to tell each other,
> Time intended for you to hurt me and thus smote you.
> I desire a companion and do not see one except when I
> return to such a place where I used to see you.

-47- A king has wept over you and grieved long after you.
If he could, he would have ransomed you with his kingdom.
He makes his heart inaccessible to women lest some woman
other than you profane the sanctuary of his heart.

The Caliph ordered that the poet be rewarded with 40,000 dirhams, 10,000 for each verse and then added, "Had you given us more, we would have given you more."

Al-Azharī———Aḥmad b. Ibrāhīm———Ibn ʿArafah: The section of the Tigris' bank on the East Side begins with the building of al-Ḥasan b. Sahl which is presently the Caliphal Palace.[38] Extending to the Dwellings of Dīnār, and Rajā' b. Abī-ḍ-Ḍaḥḥāk, it then reaches the Dwellings of the Hāshimites and continues to the Palaces of al-Muʿtaṣim and al-Ma'mūn. Next, are the dwellings of the family of Wahb which reach the bridge [*al-jisr*]. These were fiefs granted to certain Hāshimites and followers of the Caliphs.[39]

In Madīnat as-Salām there are streets and places whose names are derived from districts [*kūrah*] in Khurāsān. Many places are named after people who did not receive them as fiefs. It is said that the streets [*darb*] and side streets [*sikkah*] of Baghdad have been counted, and total 6,000 on the West Side and 4,000 on the East Side.[40]

7

The Dār al-Khalīfah [Khilāfah], al-Qaṣr al-Ḥasanī, and at-Tāj[1]

Abū-l-Ḥusayn Hilāl b. al-Muḥassin : The Caliphal Residence situated on the bank of the Tigris below Nahr al-Muʿallā, previously belonged to al-Ḥasan b. Sahl and was named al-Qaṣr al-Ḥasanī. After his death it passed on to Būrān, his daughter. Al-Muʿtaḍid bi-llāh, however, claimed it for himself. She asked for a delay of several days so that she could move out and turn it over to him. She then repaired the palace, plastered and white-washed it, and decorated it with the best and most exquisite furnishings, hanging all sorts of curtains on its portals. She filled the cupboards with everything that might prove serviceable to the Caliphs, and arranged for men servants and slave girls to answer whatever need should arise. Having accomplished this, she moved and sent word to the Caliph that he could go ahead with the transfer of his residence. When al-Muʿtaḍid moved into his residence, he found that it exceeded his expectations, and it pleased him. The Caliph then appropriated the areas adjacent to the palace in order to widen and enlarge it, and he built a connecting wall around the area which he fortified.[2]

After him, al-Muktafī bi-llāh began the construction of at-Tāj on the Tigris, erecting to the rear of the structure domes and audience rooms of the greatest possible width and length.

Al-Muqtadir bi-llāh then expanded the area of at-Tāj and completed what al-Muktafī had begun.[3] The hippodrome [*maydān*], and the Thurayyā [Palace], and zoological garden were connected with the palace precinct.[4]

Ash-Shaykh al-Ḥāfiẓ: Hilāl b. al-Muḥassin told me that Būrān turned the palace over to al-Muʿtaḍid; but this account is incorrect since Būrān died before the reign of al-Muʿtaḍid. However, Muḥammad b. Aḥmad b. Mahdī al-Iskāfī mentions in his history that she died in the year 271/884–885 at the age of eighty, so that it is possible that she could have turned the residence over to al-Muʿtamid ʿalā-l-llāh—but God knows better.[5]

Al-Qāḍī Abū-l-Qāsim ʿAlī b. al-Muḥassin at-Tanūkhī——— Abū-l-Fatḥ Aḥmad b. ʿAlī b. Hārūn al-Munajjim———his father ———Abū-l-Qāsim ʿAlī b. Muḥammad al-Ḥawārī:[6] During a period in the reign of al-Muqtadir bi-llāh when his fame was wide-
-49- spread, and his power firmly established, there were numerous
(100) servants at his residence; there were on the payroll 11,000 eunuchs, Slavs, Byzantines, and Negroes. ʿAlī added: This refers to a single category of slaves gathered at his residence; in addition, there was the Ḥujarite guard numbering many thousands, and the male attendants.[7]

ʿAlī also said: Abū-l-Fatḥ———his father, and paternal uncle ———their father, Abū-l-Ḥasan ʿAlī b. Yaḥyā:[8] Each shift of servants at the court of al-Mutawakkil ʿala-l-llāh numbered 4,000 men. However, we neglected to ask how many shifts there were.

Abū-l-Ḥusayn Hilāl b. al-Muḥassin: Abū Naṣr Khawāshādhah, the treasurer of ʿAḍūd ad-Dawlah: I was walking about the Dār al-Khilāfah—the areas which were occupied and those which were destroyed. I passed by the *ḥarīm* area, and the places in the general and immediate vicinity. It was like the city of Shīrāz.[9]

Hilāl: I heard the following account from another group of scholars expert in such matters: Ambassadors of the Byzantine Emperor had arrived in the region of al-Muqtadir bi-llāh.[10] The palace was furnished with beautiful carpets and magnificent furniture. The Chamberlains, their subordinates, and the servants were arranged according to rank along the gates, corridors, passageways, courts, and audience rooms. In a formation of two lines the mounted troops sat smartly dressed on horses wearing saddles of gold and silver. In front of them were parade horses similarly outfitted. Displaying considerable military equipment and diverse weapons, the troops ranged from above Bāb ash-Shammāsīyah to the area near the Dār al-Khilāfah. After the troops, and leading to the very presence of the Caliph, stood the Ḥujarite pages, and the servants attached to the building and the palace grounds, garbed in elegant attire with swords and ornamented girdles.

The markets of the East Side, together with its thoroughfares, rooftops, and roads [*maslak*], were filled with peering people as every shop and room which faced the street was rented for many dirhams. On the Tigris the *shadhā'ah*, *ṭayyārah*, *zabzab*, *zallālah*, and *sumayrīyah* boats were beautifully ornamented, and arranged according to proper order. The Ambassador and his retinue passed by until they reached the palace. After entering a passageway, he came to the Palace of Naṣr al-Qushūrī, the Chamberlain. Observing so large a party and so marvellous a sight, he thought Naṣr al-Qushūrī to be the Caliph, and was seized by awe and fear until he was told that this was the Chamberlain. The Ambassador was then conducted to the Palace assigned to the Wazīr which contained the audience room of Abū-l-Ḥasan ʿAlī b. Muḥammad b. al-Furāt. Seeing greater splendor than that which was shown him in the Palace of Naṣr al-Qushūrī, he did not doubt that Ibn al-Furāt was the Caliph until he was told that this is the Wazīr. He was then seated in an audience room which was situated between the Tigris and the gardens, and in which the curtains had been hung, the carpets spread about, and seats arranged. About him stood servants armed with maces and swords. Then, after touring the palace, he was brought into the presence of al-Muqtadir bi-llāh who was sitting flanked by his children. The Ambassador was awed by the sight he witnessed, and then departed for the palace that had been prepared for him.[11]

The Wazīr, Abū-l-Qāsim ʿAlī b. al-Ḥusayn, Ibn al-Muslimah ———the Commander of the Faithful, al-Qā'im bi-amr Allāh ———the Commander of the Faithful, al-Qādir bi-llāh———his grandmother Umm Abī Isḥāq b. al-Muqtadir bi-llāh: When the Byzantine Ambassador arrived at Takrīt, the Caliph al-Muqtadir gave orders for him to be detained there for two months. Later, upon arriving at Baghdad, the Ambassador was lodged at the Palace of Ṣāʿid. He remained there two months, unable to reach the Caliph until al-Muqtadir completed the decoration of his palace and the arranging of the furniture therein. Then the Caliph had his troops lined up, comprising 160,000 cavalry and infantry, from the Palace of Ṣāʿid until the Dār al-Khilāfah. The Ambassador passed between them until he reached the palace, and then was conducted through a vaulted underground passage. After passing through this passage, he appeared before al-Muqtadir and communicated the message of his master.[12] The order was then given to conduct the Ambassador about the palace which was staffed by eunuchs, chamberlains, and Negro pages—but in which no troops were stationed. The eunuchs numbered 7,000, of whom 4,000 were white and 3,000 Negro. There were 700 chamberlains, and the number of Negro pages other than the eunuchs totaled 4,000. They were stationed along the rooftops and in the upper chambers.

(102) The coffers were then thrown open and the jewels arranged
-52- therein as is done with bridal chests. The tapestries were hung and the Caliphal jewels arranged in cubicles on chests covered with black brocade. The amazement of the Ambassador grew even greater upon entering the Tree Room [*Dār ash-Shajarah*]; for there he gazed upon birds fashioned out of silver and whistling with every motion, while perched on a tree of silver weighing 500 dirhams. The Ambassador's astonishment at seeing this was greater than at everything he had witnessed.

Hilāl b. al-Muḥassin al-Kātib: I found an explanation of this in the account of an author who indicated that he copied it from the handwriting of al-Qāḍī Abī-l-Ḥusayn b. Umm Shaybān al-Hāshimī who indicated that he copied it from the Amīr—I think it was the Amīr Abū Muḥammad al-Ḥasan b. ʿĪsā b. al-Muqtadir bi-llāh. The number of curtains which hung in the palaces of the Caliph al-Muqtadir totaled 38,000. These consisted of gold brocade curtains embroidered with gold, and magnificently adorned with representations of goblets, elephants, horses and camels, lions, and birds. The curtains included large drapes of single and variegated colors from Baṣinnā, Armenia, Wāsiṭ, and Bahnasā, as well as embroidered drapes from Dabīq. Included in the total of 38,000 curtains were 12,500 brocade curtains embroidered with gold as previously described. There were 22,000 rugs and carpets from Jahram, Dārābjird, and Dawraq. They were placed in the corridors and courtyards where the generals and the Ambassadors of the Byzantine Emperor passed. These extended from the new Bāb al-ʿĀmmah to the very presence of the Caliph al-Muqtadir. However, this total did not include the carpets from Ṭabaristān and Dabīq in the alcoves and audience halls which were to be seen and not walked upon.[13]

The Ambassadors were then conducted from the corridor of the great Bāb al-ʿĀmmah to a palace called the Khān of the Cavalry [*Khān al-Khayl*] which was largely a peristyle court with marble columns. On the right side of the court were five hundred horses girded with gold and silver saddles, but without saddlecloths, and to the left were five hundred horses with brocade saddlecloths and long blinders. Each horse was entrusted to a groom attired in beautiful garb. The Ambassadors were then conducted from this palace through corridors and passageways which connected to the zoological garden. In this palace [*dār*] there were herds of wild animals, which were brought there from the garden, and which drew near to the people, sniffing them, and eating from their hands. They were then brought to a court where there were four elephants adorned with brocade and cloth marked by figure work. Mounted on each elephant were eight men from Sind and fire hurlers. The sight of this filled the Ambassadors with awe.

They were then led to a court containing one hundred lions—fifty to the right and fifty to the left, each handled by a keeper, and collared and muzzled with chains of iron. Next, they were taken to the New Kiosk [*al-Jawsaq al-Muḥdith*], a building situated amidst two gardens. In the center was an artificial pond of white lead surrounded by a stream of white lead more lustrous than polished silver. The pond was thirty by twenty cubits and contained four fine *ṭayyārah* boats with gilt seats adorned with brocade work of Dabīq and covered with gold work of Dabīq. Surrounding this lake was a

lawn area (maydān) in which there was a garden containing, it is said, four hundred palm trees, each five cubits high. Dressed in a
-54- sculptured teakwood, each tree was covered from top to bottom with rings of gilt copper, and each branch bore marvelous dates which were not quite ripe. On the sides of the garden were citrons, *dastanbūy*, *muqaffa'a*, and other kinds of fruit.

From this place, they were conducted to the Tree Room [*Dār ash-Shajarah*] where a tree stood in the center of a large round pond of limpid water. The tree had eighteen boughs, each containing numerous twigs on which were perched gold and silver birds of many species. The boughs, most of which were made of silver, though some were of gold, swayed at given times, rustling their leaves of various colors, the way the wind rustles the leaves of trees; and each of the birds would whistle and sing.[14] On one side of the palace to the right of the tank, are the figures of fifteen mounted horsemen dressed in brocade and similar finery, and hold-
(104) ing long lances. They all turn on a single line in battle formation [so that one gets the impression that each horseman is pointed towards his companion on the left side]; for on the left is a similar row of horsemen.[15]

They were then led to a palace called Qaṣr al-Firdaws which contained rugs and ornaments of such number that they could not be counted. Here 10,000 gold breastplates were hung in the corridors. Next, they were taken to a passageway 300 cubits long, on
-55- either side of which there hung some 10,000 pieces of armor consisting of leather shields, helmets, casques, cuirasses, coats of mail, ornamented quivers, and bows. Stationed in rows to the right and left were 2,000 white and Negro servants. After touring twenty-three palaces, they were conducted to the Court of the Ninety [*as-Ṣaḥn at-Tis'īnī*]. Here were the Ḥujarite pages fully armed, holding swords, axes, and maces, and excellently attired, thus giving an elegant appearance.[16]

The Ambassadors next passed by lines formed by persons dressed in black including deputy chamberlains, troops, footmen, and the young sons of generals. Then they entered the Dār as-Salām. In all the palaces, a great number of eunuchs and slaves were providing ice water, sherbet, and fruit drinks to the people; others escorted the Ambassadors. Because it was such a long tour, they sat down and rested at seven particular places, and were given water when they so desired it. Accompanying the Ambassadors at all times, and dressed in a black tunic with sword and girdle, was Abū ʿUmar ʿAdī b. Aḥmad b. ʿAbd al-Bāqi' aṭ-Ṭarsūsī, Ṣāḥib as-Sultān, and Commander of the Syrian Frontier.

They arrived at the presence of al-Muqtadir while he was seated in [*Qaṣr*] at-Tāj, which was adjacent to the Tigris. He was wearing a long cap [*ṭawīlah*] on his head, and was attired in garments from Dabīq, embroidered with gold. He was seated upon an ebony throne, covered with Dabīq cloth embroidered in gold. Suspended on the right of the throne were nine necklaces, like prayer beads, while on the left were seven others containing the most splendid jewels, the largest of which eclipsed the daylight with its brightness. Before the Caliph sat five of his sons, three to the right and two to the left. The Ambassador then appeared with his interpreter before al-Muqtadir and bowed before him. Addressing Mū'nis al-Khādim, and Naṣr al-Qushūrī, who served as interpreters on behalf of the Caliph, he proclaimed: Were I not afraid that one of your ambassadors might be required to kiss the rug [when he comes to Byzantium as an ambassador], indeed I would have kissed it. But I have done what your ambassador will not be required to do, since bowing is required by our protocol.[17]

For an hour, the two Ambassadors stood, a youth and an old man. The youth was the chief Ambassador, and the old man was his interpreter. In the event of the younger man's death, the Byzantine Emperor had empowered the older man with the responsibility for the embassy. Then al-Muqtadir bi-llāh personally handed him his detailed and long answer to the Byzantine Emperor. The Ambassador took the message and kissed it as a sign of honor. They were then led from the Private Gate [*Bāb al Khāṣṣah*] to the Tigris, where they and the rest of their companions were seated in one of the special vessels. The ambassadors travelled upstream to the palace where they were lodged, which was known as the Palace of Ṣāʿid. Fifty purses, each containing 5,000 dirhams, were then brought to them. ʿAlī b. Abī ʿUmar ʿAdī was honored with official robes and given a horse to ride on, which he mounted. This took place in the year 305/917.[18]

8

The Dār al-Mamlakah which is situated in the Upper Part of al-Mukharrim

-57- Abū-l-Ḥusayn Hilāl b. al-Muḥassin al-Kātib: The Dār al-Mamlakah in the upper part of al-Mukharrim, opposite the harbor, belonged previously to Subuktakīn, the page of Muʿizz ad-Dawlah. However, ʿAḍud ad-Dawlah demolished most of it so that nothing remained except the Bayt as-Sittīnī, which was situated amidst colonnades, in back of which were other colonnades ending in vaulted domes. Its western doors opened out to the Tigris, and the eastern doors led to a court. In back of the court, there was a garden with palm trees and other kinds of trees. The palace, in which the Bayt as-Sittīnī was located, was converted by ʿAḍud ad-Dawlah into the Public Building [*Dār al-ʿĀmmah*]. The Bayt as-Sittīnī was made into an audience room assigned to the wazīrs, the colonnades and domes adjacent to it into government offices, and the court [*ṣaḥn*] into a sleeping place for the Daylamite guards during the summer nights.[1]

Hilāl continued: This palace with the above-mentioned Bayt as-Sittīnī and the colonnades is presently in ruin. I saw the audience room of the wazīrs which was located in that building as well as the waiting-room for those seeking audience with them. Jalāl ad-Dawlah had converted this place into a stable in which he kept his horses and grooms. The buildings which were built by ʿAḍud ad-Dawlah and his son[s] after him still resist decay.

Ash-Shaykh Abū Bakr: When Ṭughril Bak al-Ghuzzī entered Baghdad and became its master, he repaired this palace, restoring many of the dilapidated structures. This took place in the year 448/1056–1057.[2] The palace remained this way until 450/1058–1059, when it was set on fire, and looted of most of its furnishings. However, it was later repaired, and the furnishings restored.[3]

Al Qāḍī Abū-l-Qāsim ʿAlī b. al-Muḥassin at-Tanūkhī: I heard my father saying: I was walking with al-Malik ʿAḍud ad-Dawlah in the Dār al-Mamlakah which was located in al-Mukharrim, and which previously had been the residence of Subuktakīn, the chamberlain of Muʿizz ad-Dawlah. He was looking carefully at what was built up and what was demolished. He had wanted to leave some space in the parade ground [*maydān*] of Subuktakīn in order to remake it into a garden by replacing the earth with sand. The earth was to be deposited under the balcony facing the Tigris. He had purchased numerous buildings, large and small, and demolished them, using elephants to batter down their walls so as to save on the expenditures for provisions. He then annexed the area on which these houses stood—which was twice the size of the parade ground—to the area of the parade ground itself, and built a dam for the entire area.

He saw what had already been constructed, and estimated the cost of what was still to be built, when he said to me that day, "Do you know, O Qāḍī, what it cost to move the earth this far, and build this trifling dam, combined with the cost of the houses purchased and that of annexing the area to the parade ground?" I replied, "I should think it cost a great deal." He said, "Until now, it has cost 900,000 dirhams of good quality;[4] and a similar sum, or perhaps twice that, will be necessary until the removal of the earth is completed, and the area is entirely refilled with sand to surface the garden." When that task was completed, and the garden became an expanse of white earth devoid of trees and plants, he said, "Until this point, upwards of 2,000,000 dirhams of good quality have been spent on this project."

ʿAḍud ad-Dawlah then considered irrigating the garden with the aid of water wheels which he could construct along the Tigris; but realizing these would not be sufficient, he dispatched engineers

-59- to the canals outside the East Side of Madīnat as-Salām in order to divert a canal which would water his palace. Only the Khāliṣ Canal met their requirements. ʿAḍud ad-Dawlah then raised the ground between the city and the canal to a height which would allow for the flow of water without causing damage [to the surrounding area].
(107) He constructed two great hillocks equal in height to the level of the Khāliṣ, thereby rising several cubits above the plain. Between the hillocks, he dug a canal with an embankment on both sides, using elephants to trample the entire area so thoroughly as to render its surface compact. When the canal, which he wished to connect with his palace, reached the city dwellings, he decided to run it through the Street of the Chain [*Dārb as-Silsilah*]. He had the earth firmly pounded down there, raised the thresholds of the entrances to the houses, and reinforced them. Along both sides of the canal where it flowed in the city, until reaching his palace, and irrigating the garden, he constructed embankments of burnt brick cemented by lime [*kils*] and tar.[5]

My father: According to a report which I heard from some retainers of ʿAḍud ad-Dawlah, the expenditures for constructing the garden and supplying its water amounted to 5,000,000 dirhams. I believe he spent a sum perhaps equal to this in building the palace, and intended to tear down the dwellings between his palace and az-Zāhir in order to extend it that far. However, he died before that.

9

The Enumeration of the Mosques on Both Sides of the City in which Friday Services Were Held and the Two Festivals Were Celebrated

Abū Jaʿfar al-Manṣūr established the city's principal mosque contiguous to his palace which was known as the Gold Palace [*Qaṣr adh-Dhahab*]. He constructed this mosque, which became the old court [*aṣ-ṣaḥn al-ʿatīq*], from mud brick cemented with clay. Its dimensions have been reported to us by Muḥammad b. ʿAlī al-Warrāq and Aḥmad b. ʿAlī al-Muḥtasib ———Muḥammad b. Jaʿfar an-Naḥwī———Al-Ḥasan b. Muḥammad as-Sakūnī———Muḥammad b. Khalaf:

The dimensions of al-Manṣūr's palace were 400 cubits by 400 cubits and those of the first mosque 200 cubits by 200 cubits. The wooden columns of the mosque were each of two pieces fastened together by bolts, glue, and clamps of iron, except for five or six columns near the minaret. Each of the columns supported a round composite capital, made of wood like the shaft.[1]

Muḥammad b. Khalaf———Ibn al-Aʿrābī: The *qiblah* needs turning slightly toward the Baṣrah Gate; the qiblah at ar-Ruṣāfah is more correct.[2] The principal mosque of the city continued as it was until the reign of Hārūn ar-Rashīd, who ordered its demolition and restoration with burnt brick cemented with gypsum. This task was accomplished, and ar-Rashīd's name was inscribed on the mosque, together with his order for its construction, the name of the architect and carpenter, and the date. This inscription is still visible on the outer wall of the mosque on the side of the Khurāsān Gate.[3]

Ibrāhīm b. Makhlad———Ismā'īl b. 'Alī al-Khuṭabī: The mosque of Abū Ja'far al-Manṣūr was demolished, enlarged, and solidly reconstructed; this task was begun in the year [1]92/808, and was completed in [1]93/808–809.[4] Prayers were conducted in the old court [*ṣaḥn al-'atīq*] which served as the principal mosque until it was enlarged with the addition of the building known as the Dār al-Qaṭṭān which previously had been a *dīwān* of al-Manṣūr. The Dār al-Qaṭṭān was built on the order of Mufliḥ the Turk by
-61- his companion al-Qaṭṭān, after whom it is named, and it became a place of worship [*muṣallā*] for the populace in the year 260/873–874 or 261/874–75. Al-Mu'taḍid then added the first court [*aṣ-ṣaḥn al-awwal*], which was part of al-Manṣūr's palace. He connected it to the mosque by opening seventeen arches along the wall between the palace and the old mosque. Of these, thirteen opened into the court and four opened into the side arcades. He then transferred the *minbar*, *miḥrab*, and *maqṣūrah* to the new mosque.[5]

Ibrāhīm b. Makhlad———Ismā'īl b. 'Alī: The Commander of the Faithful, al-Mu'taḍid bi-llāh was informed that there was not sufficient room for worship in the principal mosque of the West Side which was situated in Madīnat al-Manṣūr. This lack of room compelled the populace to pray in places in which prayer was not permissible. Therefore, the Caliph ordered that the prayer area be enlarged by adding to it a section of al-Manṣūr's palace. A mosque was therefore built of approximately the same dimensions as the First Court [*ṣaḥn al-awwal*]. This new court was opened along the axis [*fī ṣadr*] of the old mosque, connecting it to the palace and allowing sufficient room for the populace. Construction was completed, and services were held there in the year 280/893–894.[6]

Ash-Shaykh Abū Bakr: At that time Badr, the client of al-Mu'taḍid added the *msqṭt* known as al-Badrīyah from the palace of al-Manṣūr.[7] As for the principal mosque at ar-Ruṣāfah, al-Mahdī built it at the beginning of his reign.

(109) Muḥammad b. al-Ḥusayn [b. al-Faḍl] al-Qaṭṭān———'Abdallāh b. Ja'far b. Durustuwayh———Ya'qūb b. Sufyān: In the year

159/775–776 al-Mahdī built the principal mosque at ar-Ruṣāfah. In the city, Friday prayers were held only at the two principal mosques of Madīnat as-Salām, and that of ar-Ruṣāfah until the reign of al-Muʿtaḍid. In the year 280/893–894, after he had become Caliph, al-Muʿtaḍid gave orders to occupy the palace known as al-Ḥasanī on the Tigris. He expended considerable funds on this palace, which is designated as the Dār al-Khilāfah. The Caliph also gave orders to construct dungeons in the palace, according to plans which he personally drew up for the builders. They were built in a manner never before seen for sturdiness of construction and narrowness. These dungeons were made a prison for the enemies of the state. However, the populace also used the building for Friday prayers, although it was not intended to be a mosque. They were allowed to enter only at the time of prayer, and were to leave upon completing their devotions.

When al-Muktafī became Caliph in 289/902, he left[8] the palace and ordered the dungeons which al-Muʿtaḍid had built to be demolished. In their place he ordered the construction of a principal mosque in which the people might pray. When this was completed, the people came in the morning to recite their Friday prayers at the palace mosque. They were not prevented from entering and remaining there until sundown. This practice continues until today. At Baghdad, the Friday prayers were always conducted in the three mosques which we have mentioned, until the reign of al-Muttaqī.[9]

At the place known as Barāthā there was a mosque frequented by the Shīʿites, who said their prayers and held meetings there. When it was called to the attention of al-Muqtadir that the Rāfiḍites assembled at that mosque in order to slander the Companions [of the Prophet] and rebel against the state, he ordered the mosque surrounded on a Friday during the time of prayer. It was, therefore, surrounded and everyone found there was seized, punished, and sentenced to a lengthy prison term. The mosque was razed to the ground and all traces of it were erased as the area became part of the adjoining burial ground. It remained this way until 328/940, when the Amīr Bajkam ordered it solidly reconstructed, over an enlarged area. It was built of burnt brick cemented by gypsum, and was roofed with carved teakwood. The area was enlarged with addition of some adjacent property which had been purchased from its owners. On an upper part of the building was inscribed the name of ar-Rāḍī bi-llāh. The people went there to recite their prayers and receive blessings.[10]

(110) Afterwards, al-Muttaqī li-llāh gave orders to set up a *minbar* which had been in the mosque of Madīnat al-Manṣūr. This *minbar* which was not being used, was hidden in the mosque's storage room, and was inscribed with the name of Hārūn ar-Rashīd. It was set up at the *qiblah* [wall] of the new mosque. Aḥmad b. al-Faḍl b. ʿAbd al-Malik al-Hāshimī, the Imām at the mosque in ar-Ruṣāfah, was asked to go there and conduct Friday prayers. He left for the mosque accompanied by people from both sides of Madīnat as-Salām. At the mosque they assembled in great numbers, and the prefect of the police was also present. The Friday prayers were then begun on the 12th of Jumādā I, 329/941 and continued on consecutive Fridays so that this place of prayer became one of the principal mosques of the capital. Abū-l-Ḥasan Aḥmad b. al-Faḍl al-Hāshimī was appointed to the position of Imām and was consequently relieved of his responsibilities at the Ruṣāfah mosque.[11]

Ash-Shaykh Abū Bakr al-Khaṭīb: Everything that I have reported is derived from an account of Ismāʿīl b. ʿAlī al-Khuṭabī which I received from Ibrāhīm b. Makhlad who heard it from him.

-64- Abū-l-Ḥusayn Hilāl b. al-Muḥassin al-Kātib: The people speak of a woman from the East Side who had a dream in Dhū-l-Ḥijjah, 379/990. She dreamt she saw the Prophet who told her that she would die the following day, at the time of the ʿAṣr prayer. He was praying at a mosque in the Fief of Umm Jaʿfar which was situated on the West Side in the vicinity of al-Qallā'īn,[12] and placed the palm of his hand against the *qiblah* wall. Upon wakening she interpreted this vision and was directed to that place where the imprint of a palm was discovered—the woman then died at the designated time. Abū Aḥmad al-Mūsawī then repaired and enlarged the mosque, and asked aṭ-Ṭā'iʿ li-llāh to establish it as a mosque for the Friday prayers. This request was based on the assertion that the mosque was situated beyond a moat which divided it from the town [*balad*], thus making the area in which the mosque was situated a town in its own right. The Caliph granted permission, and the mosque, thereby, became a place of assembly for the Friday prayers.

Hilāl b. al-Muḥassin also related that Abū Bakr Muḥammad b. al-Ḥasan b. ʿAbd al-ʿAzīz al-Hāshimī had built a mosque in al-Ḥarbīyah during the reign of al-Muṭīʿ li-llāh which was to have been a principal mosque in which the Khuṭbah was recited. However, al-Muṭīʿ prohibited this, so that the mosque remained in this state until al-Qādir bi-llāh became Caliph, and asked the jurists for a legal opinion on this matter. Since they agreed that it was necessary to conduct prayers there, the Caliph ordered that the mosque be repaired and furnished and a *minbar* be erected. He appointed an Imām to lead the Friday prayers. This took place in the month of Rabīʿ II, 383/993.

I witnessed Friday prayer services in Baghdad held in the mosque of the city, the Ruṣāfah mosque, the mosque of the Caliphal Palace, and that of Barāthā, the mosque of Umm Jaʿfar's Fief, which was also known as Qaṭīʿat ar-Raqīq, and the Ḥarbīyah mosque. The Friday services continued to be held at these mosques until I left Baghdad in 451/1059–1060. Then the Barāthā mosque fell into disrepair and was no longer used.

10

The Canals of Baghdad which Flow among the Palaces and Residences. An Enumeration of the Places where They Flow[1]

As for the canals which flow in Madīnat al-Manṣūr and al-Karkh on the West Side, passing through the quarters and among the dwellings: Most of these waterways are branch canals of the Canal [*Nahr*] of ʿĪsā b. ʿAlī which is a tributary of the Euphrates. At the mouth of Nahr ʿĪsā there is a bridge called Qanṭarat Dimimmā. Watering the district [*ṭassūj*] of FīrūzSābūr the canal flows by the villages and domains which were situated on both its banks until it reaches al-Muḥawwal where the canals that pass through Madīnat as-Salām branch off.[2] It continues until the village of al-Yāsirīyah where it is spanned by a bridge, and on to ar-Rūmīyah where it is spanned by a bridge which was called Qanṭarat ar-Rūmīyah. The canal then flows on until az-Zayyātin where there is a bridge called Qanṭarat az-Zayyātīn
(112) and continues until a place where potash [*ushnān*] is sold and where is is spanned by a bridge called Qanṭarat al-Ushnān. Then it reaches a place where thorns [*shawk*] are sold and where it is spanned by a bridge called Qanṭarat ash-Shawk. Flowing on it comes to a place where pomegranates [*rummān*] are sold and where it is spanned by a bridge called Qanṭarat ar-Rummān. Next it comes to Qanṭarat al-Maghīd; a pool [*maghīd*], near which mills are situated, is located there. The canal then flows by Qanṭarat al-Bustān and Qanṭarat

al-Maʿbadī until reaching Qanṭarat Banī Zurayq. It then empties into the Tigris below the Palace of ʿĪsā.[3]

On the authority of some eminent scholars, ʿAbdallāh b. Muḥammad b. ʿAlī al-Baghdādī mentioned an account to me in Tripolis concerning the Canals of Baghdad: Among the canals of Baghdad is the Ṣarāt.[4] Connecting with the ʿĪsā Canal above al-Muḥawwal it waters the domains and gardens of Bādūrayā and numerous canals branch off from it until it reaches Baghdad. It flows by Qanṭarat al-ʿAbbās and Qanṭarat aṣ-Ṣīniyāt until it reaches the Bridge [*Qanṭarah*] of the Patrikios' Mill which is Qanṭarat az-Zabad.[5] It then flows until reaching the Old Bridge [*al-Qanṭarah al-ʿAtīqah*], continues by the New Bridge [*al-Qanṭarah al-Jadīdah*], and empties into the Tigris.[6]

A canal called Khandaq Ṭāhir is a tributary of the Ṣarāt. Beginning a parasang from the mouth of the Ṣarāt, it waters the domains and then turns around the walls of Madīnat as-Salām which are adjacent to al-Ḥarbīyah. It continues until reaching Bāb al-Anbār, where it is spanned by a bridge and then on to Bāb al-Ḥadīd where it is again spanned by a bridge. The canal flows on until Bāb al-Ḥarb where there is a bridge, and continues to Bāb Qaṭrabbul where there is also a bridge. Passing through the Fief of Umm Jaʿfar, it finally empties into the Tigris above the Palace of Ibrāhīm b. Isḥāq b. Ibrāhīm aṭ-Ṭāhirī.[7]

A canal called Karkhāyā is a branch canal of the ʿĪsā. Beginning below al-Muḥawwal it passes through the district [*ṭassūj*] of Bādūrayā where canals branch out spreading into the domains which are situated on both its banks. It continues until entering Baghdad at a place called Bāb Abī Qabīṣah. It then passes by the Bridge [*Qanṭarah*] of the Fief of the Jews, and continues by Qanṭarat Darb al-Ḥijārah, Qanṭarat al-Bīmāristān, and Bāb al-Muḥawwal. All the canals watering al-Karkh branch off from this waterway. Among them is a canal called Nahr Razīn which connects with the Karkhāyā on the Estate of Ḥumayd where it turns. It then comes to the Suwayqah of Abū-l-Ward and flows on until Birkat Zalzal where it curves, and after coming to Bāb Ṭāq al-Ḥarrānī, it empties into the Ṣarāt below the New Bridge.[8]

When the Razīn Canal passes the gate of the Suwayqah of

Abū-l-Ward, a channel branches off and its waters are carried over the Old Bridge by way of an aqueduct. It then continues until the road of the Kūfah Gate from where it enters Madīnat al-Manṣūr. The main canal passes by the Kūfah Gate until reaching the Road of the Qaḥāṭibah and then passes the Damascus Gate, and the Bridge Road until it comes to az-Zubaydīyah where it disappears.

The Karkhāyā then passes the Bridge of the Hospital [*al-Bīmāristān*],[9] and when it reaches ad-Darrābāt, it is called al-ʿAmūd. Branching out from this stream are the canals running through the inner section of al-Karkh. The canal now continues to a place called al-Wāsiṭiyīn and then on until a place called al-Khafqah, from where its branch canal the Nahr al-Bazzāzīn originates. This canal veers from the Road of al-Muṣawwir, passes the residence of Kaʿb, and reaches Bāb al-Karkh and from there it enters the Markets of the Clothesmakers [*Bazzāzīn*], Cobblers [*Kharrāzīn*], and Soap Boilers [*Asḥāb aṣ-Ṣābūn*] before emptying into the Tigris. The main canal then flows from al-Khafqah to the edge of the Oil Merchants Square [*Zayyātīn*]. At this point a canal called Nahr ad-Dajāj veers from it and passes by the Market of the Reed-weavers [*Aṣḥāb al-Qaṣab*] and the Road of Pitchworkers [*Qayyārīn*]; and then it empties into the Tigris by the Food Market [*aṭ-Ṭaʿām*].[10] The Karkhāyā flows from the Oil Merchants Square to the Mound of the Ass, at which point a canal called Nahr al-Kilāb veers from
-68- it, and continues until emptying in the ʿĪsā below Qanṭarat ash-Shawk. The main canal then continues from the Mound of the Ass to a place called Murabbaʿat Ṣāliḥ at which point a canal called Nahr al-Qallā'īn veers from it, and passes by the Markets of the Flour Merchants [*Sawwāqīn*] and the Reed-weavers, before emptying into the Dajāj Canal. They then flow together forming a single canal. The Karkhāyā continues from Murabbaʿat Ṣāliḥ to a place known as Nahr Ṭābaq, and then empties into the ʿĪsā Canal in the vicinity of the Dār al-Baṭṭīkh. These are the canals of al-Karkh.

As for the canals of al-Ḥarbīyah: Among them is a canal called Nahr Baṭāṭiyā which is a branch canal of the Dujayl. It originates six parasangs below the mouth of the Dujayl and waters numerous domains and villages amidst the district of Maskin where it disappears.[11] There is a branch canal of the Dujayl which begins somewhat below the Baṭāṭiyā Bridge [*Jisr*] and flows toward Madīnat as-Salām. Passing over the aqueduct of Qanṭarat Bāb al-Anbār, it enters Baghdad. From there, the canal flows by the Bāb al-Anbār Road and the Kabsh Road where it disappears. There is a branch canal of the Baṭāṭiyā below the first canal, which approaches Baghdad, passing over an aqueduct called ʿAbbārat al-Kūkh,[12] between Bāb Ḥarb and Bāb al-Ḥadīd.[13] It then enters Baghdad from there, passing the Dujayl Road, and continuing to the Square of the Persians. A canal called Nahr Dukkān al-Abnā',[14] which is a branch canal of the Baṭāṭiyā, originates and ends there.

The main canal then continues from the Square of the Persians to Qanṭarat Abī-l-Jawn. At this spot a branch canal flows from it, reaching the Orphans School and the Square of Shabīb, before emptying into a canal in the Shāriʿ Quarter. Nahr Baṭāṭiyā then flows from Qanṭarat Abī-l-Jawn until the Road of Qaṣr Hāni' and Bustān al-Quss, and then empties into the canal that flows by the Road of the Qaḥāṭibah. A branch canal of the Baṭāṭiyā begins below ʿAbbārat al-Kūkh and flows in the direction of Baghdad crossing over the aqueduct of Qanṭarat Bāb Ḥarb. From here it enters into the middle of the Bāb Ḥarb Road and then comes to the Square of Abū-l-ʿAbbās, and the Square of Shabīb before emptying into the canal which we have mentioned. This canal then flows to the Damascus Gate where it empties into the canal of that gate. These canals are all open with the exception of the canals in al-Ḥarbīyah which flow in underground conduits, although they begin above ground.

On the East Side, Nahr Mūsā branches from Nahr Bīn and continues until the Palace of al-Muʿtaḍid bi-llāh which is called Qaṣr ath-Thurayyā. It enters the palace area and flows about the palace grounds. Then it comes to a place called the Water Divide [*Maqsim al-Mā'*] where it is divided into three canals, the first of which continues to the Gate of the Market of the Pack Animals and then it flows on until the Palace of al-Bānūqah[15] where it disappears.[16] A branch of the Mūsā enters the Market of the Pack Animals and continues to the Market of the Fodder-Sellers [*ʿAllāfīn*] before entering into the canal which was dug by al-Muʿtaḍid. Another branch flows to the Gate of the Lamb Market, continues

on to Khandaq al-ʿAbbās[17] in Bāb al-Mukharrim, and then flows
-70- into the Tigris. The Mūsā Canal also passes Qanṭarat al-Anṣār at which point it has three tributaries. The first empties into the Tank of the Anṣār, the second into the Tank of Haylānah, and the third into the Tank of Dāwūd. The Mūsā Canal then passes the palace of al-Muʿtaṣim bi-llāh. At this point a tributary branches
(115) off and flows in the middle of Shāriʿ Karm al-ʿArsh[18] to Sūq al-ʿAṭash, before it disappears after flowing into the residence of ʿAlī b. Muḥammad b. al-Furāt, the wazīr. The Mūsā Canal flows adjacent to al-Muʿtaṣim's palace until reaching the Road of ʿAmr ar-Rūmī, and then enters and waters the Bustān az-Zāhir before emptying into the Tigris below that place.

The second canal, which leads from the Water Divide, is called the Nahr al-Muʿallā.[19] It flows until Bāb al-Abraz[20] where it enters al-Mukharrim, continuing amid the dwellings until it reaches Sūq ath-Thalāthā'. The canal now enters and flows about the grounds of the Caliphal residence known as al-Firdaws before emptying into the Tigris. The third canal which leads from the Water Divide continues to the Gate of the Fief of Mūshajīr[21] and then enters the grounds of the Qaṣr al-Ḥasanī before emptying into the Tigris.

A canal called the Nahr al-Faḍl is a branch canal of the Khāliṣ.
-71- It flows until the Bāb ash-Shammāsīyah where the Nahr al-Mahdī branches off from it. This canal [Nahr al-Mahdī] enters the city at a road called the Mahdī Road and then comes to Qanṭarat al-Baradān. It enters Dār ar-Rūmiyīn from where it continues to the Suwayqah of Naṣr b. Mālik. Entering ar-Ruṣāfah, it passes the principal mosque and continues until it reaches the Garden of Ḥafṣ before emptying into a spring on the grounds of the Ruṣāfah Palace.[22] There is a tributary of this canal which begins at the Suwayqah of Naṣr, and flows down the middle of the Khurāsān Gate Road, before emptying into Nahr as-Sūr[23] at the Khurāsān Gate. These are the canals of the East Side.

11

The Number of Bridges [Jisr] which Existed in Previous Times at Madīnat as-Salām

Muḥammad b. al-Ḥusayn b. al-Faḍl al-Qaṭṭān ———ʿAbdallāh b. Jaʿfar b. Durustuwayh———Yaʿqūb b. Sufyān: In the year 157/774 Abu Jaʿfar built his palace which is called al-Khuld, and the bridge near Bāb ash-Shaʿīr.[1]

Muḥammad b. ʿAlī al-Warrāq and Aḥmad b. ʿAlī al-Muḥtasib ———Muḥammad b. Jaʿfar an-Naḥwī———al-Ḥasan b. Muḥammad as-Sakūnī———Muḥammad b. Khalaf———Aḥmad b. al-Khalīl b. Malik———his father: Al-Manṣūr had given orders to erect three bridges; one for the women, and two others at Bāb al-Bustān for his personal use and that of his household retinue.[2] At az-Zandaward there were two bridges which Muḥammad (al-Amīn) had erected.[3] Ar-Rashīd had erected two bridges at Bab ash-Shammāsīyah, and Abū Jaʿfar a bridge at Suwayqat Qaṭūṭā. These bridges stood until the death of Muḥammad (al-Amīn) when they fell into disrepair. However, three bridges remained in use during the reign of al-Maʾmūn; then another one fell into disrepair.[4]

Abū ʿAlī b. Shādhān: I saw three bridges at Baghdad: one was situated opposite Sūq ath-Thalāthāʾ, another was at Bāb aṭ-Ṭāq, and the third was in the upper part of the city near the Dār al-ʿIzzīyah opposite the parade ground [*maydān*].[5]

A scholar, other than Ibn Sh̲ādh̲ān, informed me that the bridge opposite the parade ground was moved to the harbor at Bāb aṭ-Ṭāq, so that there were two bridges—one for the people coming, the other for those going.[6]

Hilāl b. al-Muḥassin: In the year 383/993 a bridge was erected at the Wharf of the Cotton Merchants [Mas̲h̲ra'at al-Qaṭṭānin], which remained in use for some time before falling into disrepair. After that the only bridge remaining in Baghdad was situated at Bāb aṭ-Ṭāq, until it was moved in the year 448/1056, and erected between the Wharf of the Water Jars [Rawāyā] on the West Side, and the Woodcutters' Wharf [Ḥaṭṭābin] on the East Side. It fell into disrepair in the year 450/1059–1060, but was later erected at the Wharf of the Cotton Merchants.[7]

As̲h̲-S̲h̲ayk̲h̲ Abū Bakr: I have always heard it said that the bridge of Baghdad is the embroidered border of the city.

Abū-l-Ḥasan 'Alī b. al-Ḥasan b. aṣ-Ṣaqr————'Alī b. al-Faraj, the S̲h̲āfi'ite jurist who composed the following verse:

-73-
> O what a bridge across the Tigris
> Well constructed and beautifully shaped.
> It is the majesty and glory of Iraq,
> A place for one to find relief of past longing.
> If you come in contemplation you will see it as if it were
> A line of black perfume drawn on the [white] parting [mafriq] of the hair, or
> Like ivory which is ornamented with ebony, cut in the shape of
> Elephants beneath which there is a ground of mercury.

(117)   Abū-l-Qāsim 'Alī b. al-Muḥassin at-Tanūk̲h̲ī————his father who composed the following verses:

> One day while we stole a joyous moment of life
> In an isolated meeting-place along the Tigris shore,
> The wind was gently blowing [raqqa] in front of that place and
> I became a slave [riqq] to the joyous time;
> It was as though the Tigris was a white robe [ṭaylasān] and
> The bridge which spanned it was the black embroidered border.

Hilāl b. al-Muḥassin: It is reported that in the time of Nāṣir li-dīn Allāh, i.e., Abū Aḥmad Ṭalhah al-Muwaffaq, a count was taken of the sumayrīyah and ma'baranīyah vessels in the Tigris. The total came to 30,000 vessels and the combined daily wage of the sailors was estimated at 90,000 dirhams.

12

The Length and Width of the Two Sides of Baghdad, the Total Area, and the Number of Mosques and Bathhouses

Muḥammad b. ʿAlī al-Warrāq———Abū-l-Ḥasan Aḥmad b. Muḥammad b. ʿImrān———Abū Bakr Muḥammad b. Yaḥyā an-Nadīm: Aḥmad b. Abī Ṭāhir mentioned in the *Kitāb Baghdād* that the area of Baghdad's two sides comprised 53,750 *jarīb*. The area of the East Side comprised 26,750 *jarīb*, and that of the West Side 27,000 *jarīb*.[1]

Abū-l-Ḥasan: I saw in a copy, other than that of Muḥammad b. Yaḥyā, that the area of Baghdad comprised 43,750 *jarīb*. The area of the East Side comprised 16,750 *jarīb*, and that of the West Side 27,000 *jarīb*.[2]

Returning to the account of Muḥammad b. Yaḥyā: At that time, the public baths in Baghdad numbered 60,000. The minimum number of servants attending each bathhouse was five: a bath attendant, a steward, a sweeper, a stoker, and a water carrier. The total number of attendants was, therefore, at least 300,000. For each bathhouse there were five mosques, making a total of 300,000. Since the minimum number of men serving each mosque was five, the total number of men was at least 1,500,000.[3] Each of these men required a *raṭl* of soap for the night of the ʿĪd festivals, making a total of 1,500,000 *raṭl*. Since each jar contained 130 *raṭl*, there were $11,538\frac{1}{2}$ jars. Each oil jar contained sixty *raṭl*, so that the equivalent number of oil jars would have contained a total of 692,310 *raṭl*.[4]

Hilāl b. al-Muḥassin: One day in the year 383/993–994, when I was in the presence of my grandfather, Abū Isḥāq Ibrāhīm b. Hilāl aṣ-Ṣābi',[5] one of the merchants who used to come to him entered. While conversing with my grandfather, he remarked, "One of the merchants told me that there are presently 3,000 bathhouses in Baghdad." Grandfather exclaimed, "That is only a sixth of the bathhouses which we counted and listed!" The merchant asked, "How can that be?" And my grandfather said, "I remember that Rukn ad-Dawlah Abū-l-Ḥasan b. Buwayh wrote to the Wazīr Abū-Muḥammad al-Muhallabī: We have been informed about the great number of mosques and baths in Baghdad. However, we have found that the reports concerning this matter conflict with one another, and since we desire to know the exact number, inform us of the exact details." Grandfather continued, "Abū Muḥammad then gave me the letter and said, 'Go to the Amīr Muʿizz ad-Dawlah, show him the letter, and ask him for permission to proceed with this task.' This I did."

The Amīr then said to Abū Muḥammad, "Gather the information and make it known to me." Abū Muḥammad al-Muhallabī then ordered Abū-l-Ḥasan al-Bāzighjī, who was in charge of the police [*sāḥib al-maʿūnah*], to count the bathhouses and mosques. I do not recall what was said about the number of mosques, but there
-76- were some 10,000 bathhouses. Returning to Muʿizz ad-Dawlah, I informed him of this, whereupon he ordered, "Make a note on the subject of bathhouses, and indicate that they number 4,000." From his remarks, we sensed that he was being cautious for fear that he might incite the envy of his brother [Rukn ad-Dawlah] because he possessed so great a city. Abū Muḥammad was startled, as we were, at the then current number of bathhouses. For they were counted
(119) during the reign of al-Muqtadir, and totaled 27,000, and the time which had elapsed between these two periods was not long enough to account for this difference.

Hilāl: It is said that during the reign of ʿAḍud ad-Dawlah there were more than 5,000 bathhouses.[6]

Al-Khaṭīb: In the entire world, there has not been a city which could compare with Baghdad in size and splendor, or in the number of scholars and great personalities. The distinction of the notables and general populace serves to distinguish Baghdad from other cities, as does the vastness of its districts, the extent of its borders, and the great number of residences and palaces. Consider the numerous roads [*darb*], thoroughfares [*shāri'*], and localities, the markets and streets [*sikkah*], the lanes [*aziqqah*], mosques and bathhouses, and the high roads [*ṭarīq*][7] and shops———all of these distinguish this city from all others, as does the pure air, the sweet water, and the cool shade. There is no place which is as temperate in summer and winter, and as salubrious in spring and autumn. The very great population also distinguishes it from all other cities.

It reached its highest point in buildings and population during the reign of ar-Rashīd, since there reigned quiet and the utmost prosperity in the world. Then came the civil war and continuous tribulations. The city decayed and the population departed. However even with the general decline, Baghdad in the period before our own time was different from all other cities and urban centers.[8]

Al-Qāḍī Abū-l-Qāsim 'Alī b. al-Muḥassin at-Tanūkhī——— his father———Abū-l-Ḥasan Muḥammad b. Ṣāliḥ al-Hāshimī who stated in the year 360/970–971;[9] A man who only sold gruel made with chick peas—he gave me his name, but I forgot it—told me that every year he measured the amount of gruel made at his market. The chick peas made up 280 *kurr*, and the final product was 140 *kurr*. This amount was set aside every year until nothing remained, at which point, he made preparations for the next year. The gruel was tasteless and only eaten by patients and the feeble for a period of two or three months when fruits were lacking; the majority of people, however, did not eat it.

Al-Khaṭīb: If someone were to request this gruel today, not a single *makkūk* could be found on either side of Baghdad.

Muḥammad b. 'Alī al-Warrāq and Aḥmad b. 'Alī al-Muḥtasib ———Muḥammad b. Ja'far an-Naḥwī———al-Ḥasan b. Muḥammad as-Sakūnī———Muḥammad b. Khalaf———Abū-l-Faḍl Aḥmad b. Abī Ṭāhir: The length of East Baghdad was measured for Abū Aḥmad, i.e., al-Muwaffaq bi-llāh, when he entered Madīnat as-Salām. It was found to be 250 *ḥabl* in length; the width was

105 *ḥabl*, making a total area of 26,250 *jarīb*. The West Side was also found to be 250 *ḥabl* in length, but its width was 70 *ḥabl*, making a total area of 17,500 *jarīb*. The entire area of all Baghdad then totaled 43,750 *jarīb*, of which the cemeteries occupied 74 *jarīb*.[10]

13

The Cemeteries of Baghdad where Scholars and Ascetics are Buried

The Cemetery of the Quraysh is located on the West Side in the upper part of the city. Buried there are Mūsā b. Ja'far b. Muḥammad b. 'Alī b. al-Ḥusayn b. 'Alī b. Abī Ṭālib and a group of distinguished men.[1]

Al-Qāḍī Abū Muḥammad al-Ḥasan b. al-Ḥusayn b. Muḥammad b. Rāmīn al-Astarābādhī———Aḥmad b. Ja'far b. Ḥamdān al-Qaṭī'ī———Abū 'Alī al-Ḥasan b. Ibrāhīm al-Khallāl:[2] Whenever I am worried about some matter, and go to the grave of Mūsā b. Ja'far to communicate with him, God makes possible for me what I desire.

Muḥammad b. 'Alī al-Warrāq and Aḥmad b. 'Alī al-Muḥtasib———Muḥammad b. Ja'far———as-Sakūnī———Muḥammad b. Khalaf: The first person to be buried in the Cemetery of the Quraysh was Ja'far al-Akbar b. al-Manṣūr, and the first to be buried in the Cemetery of the Damascus Gate was 'Abdallāh b. 'Alī, who was buried there at the age of fifty-two in the year 147/764–765. The Cemetery of the Damascus Gate is the oldest graveyard in Baghdad. Buried there is a group of learned men, tradition-scholars, and jurists, and the same is true of the Bāb at-Tibn Cemetery, which is situated along the trench opposite the Fief of Umm Ja'far.

Abū Ya'lā Muḥammad b. Al-Ḥusayn b. al-Farrā' al-Ḥanbalī ———Abū Ṭāhir b. Abī Bakr:[3] My father told me about a man who used to come to Abū Bakr b. Malik. He [Abū Bakr] was asked, "Where would you like to be buried when you die?" He replied, "In al-Qaṭī'ah; for indeed 'Abdallāh b. Aḥmad b. Ḥanbal is buried there." 'Abdallāh had been questioned about [his wanting to be buried in al-Qaṭī'ah]—I believe he had stipulated in his last will that he be buried there—and had said, "I am certain that a prophet is buried in al-Qaṭī'ah, and I find it more desirable to be buried near a prophet, than near my father." The Cemetery of the Ḥarb Gate is situated outside the city beyond the trench, and is adjacent to the Qaṭrabbul Road. It is known as a cemetery of the people of goodness and virtue, and contains the graves of Aḥmad b. Muḥammad b. Ḥanbal and Bishr b. al-Ḥārith. The Ḥarb Gate [*Bāb*] is named after Ḥarb b. 'Abdallāh, one of the companions of Abū Ja'far al-Manṣūr. The section called al-Ḥarbīyah is also named after him.[4]

Abū 'Abd ar-Raḥmān Isma'īl b. Aḥmad al-Ḥayrī aḍ-Ḍarīr ———Abū 'Abd ar-Raḥmān Muḥammad b. al-Ḥusayn as-Sulamī in Naysābūr———Abū Bakr ar-Rāzī———'Abdallāh b. Mūsā aṭ-Ṭalḥī———Aḥmad b. al-'Abbās:[5] Upon leaving Baghdad, I was approached by a person who bore the mark of a devout man. He inquired, "Where are you coming from?" "From Baghdad," I said. "I fled the city, for at seeing the corruption there, I feared it might be swallowed up with its populace." He said, "Return and do not
-80- fear. For there, indeed, are the graves of four saints of God. They are a fortress for the people of Baghdad against every misfortune." "Who are they?" I inquired. "Buried there are the Imām Aḥmad b. Ḥanbal, Ma'rūf al-Karkhī, Bishr al-Ḥāfī, and Manṣūr b. 'Ammār." I did not leave the city that year, but returned and visited the graves.

Al-Khaṭīb: The grave of Ma'rūf is in the Bāb ad-Dayr Cemetery; the other three are buried in the Cemetery of the Ḥarb Gate.[6]

(122) Al-Ḥasan b. Abī Ṭālib———Yūsuf b. 'Umar al-Qawwās——— Abū Muqātil Muḥammad b. Shujā'———Abū Bakr b. Abī-d-Dunyā———Abū Yūsuf b. Bakhtān, who was one of the most virtuous Muslims:[7] When Aḥmad b. Ḥanbal died, a man dreamt that

he saw a lamp on each grave. "What's this?" he asked. "Don't you know," came a reply, "that the graves of the dead were illuminated when this man descended among them? There were those among the dead who were tormented, but now they have received compassion."

Abu-l-Faraj al-Ḥusayn b. ʿAlī b. ʿUbaydallāh at-Ṭanājirī——— Muḥammad b. ʿAlī b. Suwayd al-Mu'addib———ʿUthmān b. Ismāʿīl b. Bakr as-Sukkarī———his father———Aḥmad b. ad-Dawraqī:[8] I had a dream about a neighbor of mine who died. He was wearing two shrouds. I asked, "What's your story?—What is this?" "Bishr b. al-Ḥārith is buried in our cemetery," he said; "therefore the dead each wear two shrouds."

Al-Khaṭīb: There are several cemeteries in the vicinity of al-Karkh. Among them is the Bāb al-Kunās Cemetery which is adjacent to Barāthā, and in which a group of the greatest ḥadīth scholars are buried. The Shūnīzī Cemetery, which contains the graves of Sarī as-Saqaṭī and other ascetics, is situated behind a place known as at-Tūthah which is close to the canal of ʿĪsā b. ʿAlī al-Hāshimī. I heard some scholars say: The Cemetery of the Quraysh was previously known as the Cemetery of ash-Shūnīzī the Younger, while the graveyard behind at-Tūthah was known as the Cemetery of ash-Shūnīzī the Elder. There were two brothers called Shūnīzī; it is said each was buried in one of these two cemeteries, thereby giving it its name. The grave of Maʿrūf al-Karkhī is found in the Bāb ad-Dayr Cemetery.[9]

Ismāʿīl b. Aḥmad al-Ḥayrī———Muḥammad b. al-Ḥusayn as-Sulamī———Abū-l-Ḥasan b. Miqsam———Abū ʿAlī aṣ-Ṣaffār ———Ibrāhīm al-Ḥarbī:[10] The grave of Maʿrūf is the proven theriac [for all ailments].

Abū Isḥāq Ibrāhīm b. ʿUmar al-Barmakī———Abū-l-Faḍl ʿUbaydallāh b. ʿAbd ar-Raḥmān b. Muḥammad az-Zuhrī: I heard my father say:[11] The grave of Maʿrūf al-Karkhī has a proven effect in enabling one to fulfill his needs. It is said that God grants the needs of that man who asks Him when he recites "Say: He is Allah, One" one hundred times at the grave of Maʿrūf al-Karkhī.[12]

Abū ʿAbdallāh Muḥammad b. ʿAlī b. ʿAbdallāh aṣ-Ṣūrī——— Abū-l-Ḥusayn Muḥammad b. Aḥmad b. Jumayʿ———Abū

ʿAbdallāh b. al-Maḥāmilī:[13] I have been familiar with the grave of
-82- Maʿrūf al-Karkhī for seventy years; and God has dispelled the anxieties of every troubled person who has visited there.

The Khayzurān Cemetery is on the East Side. The graves of Muḥammad b. Isḥāq b. Yāsar, author of the *Sīrah*, and Abū Ḥanīfah an-Nuʿmān b. Thābit, the jurist, and Imām of the school of independent reasoning are found there.[14]

Al-Qāḍī Abū ʿAbdallāh al-Ḥusayn b. ʿAlī b. Muḥammad aṣ-Ṣaymarī———ʿUmar b. Ibrāhīm al-Muqrī'———Mukram B. Aḥmad———ʿUmar b. Isḥāq b. Ibrāhīm———ʿAlī b. Maymūn: I heard ash-Shāfiʿī say:[15] Indeed I go, that is to say as a visitor, to the grave of Abū Ḥanīfah every day to derive blessings from it. If I should have some need, I perform two genuflexions [*rakʿah*], and then go to his grave to ask God to satisfy this need. The need is then satisfied shortly thereafter.

Buried in the Cemetery of ʿAbdallāh b. Mālik are numerous jurists, tradition-scholars, ascetics, and virtuous people. It is known as al-Mālikīyah. The Bāb al-Baradān Cemetery also contains the graves of distinguished people.[16]

At the place [*al-muṣallā*] which is designated for saying the ʿĪd prayers, there is a grave called the Grave of the Vows [*Qabr an-Nudhūr*]. It is said that a descendant of ʿAlī b. Abī Ṭālib is buried there, and that people derive blessings from visiting his grave. Those who have needs go there to have them fulfilled.[17]

Al-Qāḍī Abū-l-Qāsim ʿAlī b. al-Muḥassin at-Tanūkhī———his father:[18] I was sitting in the presence of ʿAḍud ad-Dawlah. We were encamped close to the *muṣallā* of the festivals on the East Side
-83- of Madīnat as-Salām, and wanted to leave with him for Hamadhān the first day he came to the encampment. However, his eyes fell upon the building which housed the Grave of the Vows, and he asked me, "What is this building?" I answered, "That is the Shrine [*Mashhad*] of the Vows," but did not use the word grave [*qabr*] because I knew he would regard this an evil omen. He was satisfied with my answer and said, "I know that it is the Grave of the Vows. Only I wanted an explanation of the name." I replied, "It is
(124) said this is the grave of ʿUbaydallāh b. Muḥammad b. ʿUmar b. ʿAlī b. al-Ḥusayn b. ʿAli b. Abī Ṭālib.[19] One of the Caliphs was

anxious to kill him in secret. He therefore prepared a trap [*zubyah*] at this place and covered it. The latter, unaware, fell in it and was buried alive as the earth collapsed about him. The grave became famous as the Grave of the Vows because whoever takes a vow there will have his wish fulfilled, and thereby, will be bound to fulfill his vow. I was one of those who offered vows there several times when confronted with difficult problems. Then I surmounted these problems and as I was obligated by my vow, I fulfilled it." He did not accept this explanation, and indicated this happens to occur only rarely and that the common people try to exaggerate such occurrences and spread fictitious stories about them. I thereby desisted from saying anything further.

One morning, several days later, as we were encamped at our position, he summoned me and said, "Ride with me to the Shrine of the Vows." I rode with him and some of his retainers until we reached that place. He entered the building and visited the grave, performing two genuflexions followed by a full prostration. He remained in that state speaking silently to God and no one could hear him. We then rode with him to his tent where we remained several days. After that we left with him for Hamadhān, and upon arriving there camped with him for several months. Some time later he summoned me and said, "Do you not remember what you told me concerning the Shrine of the Vows in Baghdad?" I said, "Surely." Then he said, "Indeed I lectured you concerning the meaning of its name without speaking my mind out of consideration for the goodness of your friendship. In reality, my heart told me that everything which had been said about this place was false. However, a short time later, I was beset by the fear of something that might occur. I searched my mind for a way to solve this difficulty, even if I had to utilize all the resources of my treasuries and my armies; however, I could not find a way to overcome this problem. But I recalled what you told me about a vow which is taken at the Grave of the Vows, and said,'—Why don't I try?' So I vowed, '—Should God enable me to overcome this problem, I will fill the chest of this tomb with 10,000 dirhams of good quality.' When the day came bringing news of my triumph over this difficulty, I ordered Abū-l-Qāsim ʿAbd al-ʿAzīz Ibn Yūsuf—i.e., ʿAḍud

ad-Dawlah's secretary—to write to Abū-r-Rayyān—his lieutenant
(125) at Baghdad—entrusting him to deliver the dirhams to the shrine." He then turned to ʿAbd al-ʿAzīz, who was present and ʿAbd al-ʿAzīz said, "I have already composed a letter concerning this matter and it has been dispatched."

ʿAlī b. Abī ʿAlī al-Muʿaddil———Abū Bakr Aḥmad b. ʿAbdallāh ad-Dūrī al-Warrāq———Abū ʿAlī Muḥammad b. Hammām b. Suhayl, the Shiʿite scribe———Muḥammad b. Mūsā b. Ḥammād al-Barbarī———Sulaymān b. Abī Shaykh:[20] I said to him: Concerning the person who is buried in the Grave of the Vows, it is said that he is ʿUbaydallāh b. Muḥammad b. ʿUmar b. ʿAlī b. Abī
-85- Ṭālib. He retorted, "That is not so. The person buried there is ʿUbaydallāh b. Muḥammad b. ʿUmar b. ʿAlī b. al-Ḥusayn b. Alī b. Abī Tālib. ʿUbaydallāh b. Muḥammad b. ʿUmar b. Abī Ṭālib is buried on an estate [*dayʿah*] of his near al-Kūfah called Lubayyā."

Abū Bakr ad-Dūrī———Abū Muḥammad al-Ḥasan b. Aḥmad b. Akhi Ṭāhir al-ʿAlawī: ʿUbaydallāh b. Muḥammad b. ʿUmar b. ʿAlī b. Abī Ṭālib is buried in an estate of his near al-Kūfah called al-Bayy. The Grave of the Vows is the burial place of ʿUbaydallāh b. Muḥammad b. ʿUmar b. ʿAlī b. al-Ḥusayn[21] b. ʿAlī b. Abī Ṭālib.

Al-Khaṭīb al-Ḥāfiẓ: The oldest cemetery on the East Side is the Khayzurān Cemetery. Abū-l-Qāsim al-Azharī———Aḥmad b. Ibrāhīm———Ibrāhīm b. Muḥammad b. ʿArafah: The Khayzurān Cemetery is named after al-Khayzurān, mother of Mūsā and Hārūn, that is to say the sons of al-Mahdī. It is the oldest of the cemeteries [of the East Side] and contains the graves of Abū Ḥanīfah, and Muḥammad b. Isḥāq, the author of the *Maghāzī*.

Muḥammad b. ʿAlī al-Warrāq and Aḥmad b. ʿAlī al-Muḥtasib———Muḥammad b. Jaʿfar an-Naḥwī———al-Ḥasan b. Muḥammad as-Sakūnī———Muḥammad b. Khalaf: Some people say that the spot where the Khayzurān Cemetery is situated was, before the building of Baghdad, the place of the Magian Cemetery; and that the first person to be buried there was al-Bānūqah, the daughter of al-Mahdī; al-Khayzurān was buried there later. Muḥammad b. Isḥāq, the author of the *Maghāzī*, al-Ḥasan b. Zayd,

and an-Nu'mān b. T͟hābit are buried there. It is said His͟hām b.
'Urwah is also buried there.[22]

As͟h-S͟hayk͟h Abū Bakr: It is known among us that the burial
place of His͟hām b. 'Urwah is on the West Side beyond the Trench
above the Cemetery of the Ḥarb Gate. The grave is conspicuous
and well known there. It bears an engraved tombstone indicating
it to be the burial place of His͟hām.

In connection with this: Abū Muḥammad al-Ḥasan b. 'Alī al-
Jawharī———Muḥammad b. al-'Abbās al-K͟hazzāz, and Abū-l-
Qāsim al-Azharī———Aḥmad b. Muḥammad b. Mūsā———Abū-
l-Ḥusayn b. al-Munādī:[23] Abū-l-Mund͟hir His͟hām b. 'Urwah b.
az-Zubayr b. al-'Awwām al-Quras͟hī died during the reign of Abū
Ja'far in the year 146/763–764, and was buried on the West Side
outside the wall near Bāb Qaṭrabbul.

Abū Ṭāhir Ḥamzah b. Muḥammad b. Ṭāhir ad-Daqqāq, who
was an intelligent man and a ranking scholar, heard Abū-l-Ḥusayn
Aḥmad b. 'Abdallāh b. al-K͟haḍir deny that the grave of His͟hām
b. 'Urwah b. az-Zubayr is the famous one on the West Side. That
famous grave is the burial place of His͟hām b. 'Urwah al-Marwazī,
the companion of Ibn al-Mubārak. The grave of His͟hām b. 'Urwah
b. az-Zubayr is in al-K͟hayzurānīyah on the East Side.[24]

Abū Bakr al-Barqānī———'Abd ar-Raḥmān b. 'Umar al-
K͟hallāl———Muḥammad b. Aḥmad b. Ya'qūb b. S͟haybah———
his grandfather:[25] His͟hām b. 'Urwah, whose *kunyah* was Abū-l-
Mund͟hir, died in Baghdad in the year 146/763–764. It has been
said that his grave is in the K͟hayzurān Cemetery.

Al-Ḥasan b. al-Ḥusayn b. al-'Abbās———his maternal grandfather, Isḥāq b. Muḥammad an-Ni'ālī———'Abdallāh b. Isḥāq
al-Madā'inī———Qa'nab b. al-Muḥarraz Abū 'Amr al-Bāhilī:
'Abd al-Malik b. Abī Sulaymān[26] and His͟hām b. 'Urwah died in
Baghdad in the year 145/762–763, and were buried in Sūq Yaḥyā,
which is near the K͟hayzurān Cemetery. Although Qa'nab b.
al-Muḥarraz has indicated this to be the burial place of His͟hām, we
regard the account of Aḥmad b. 'Abdallāh b. al-K͟haḍir as correct;
however, we do not know of anyone named His͟hām b. 'Urwah
among the companions of Ibn al-Mubārak. Furthermore, we are
not acquainted with any scholarly tradition concerning a His͟hām

whose father's name is ʿUrwah, with the exception of Hishām b. ʿUrwah b. az-Zubayr b. al-ʿAwwām, and God knows better.

Near the grave attributed to Hishām on the West Side are the burial places of a group of people, which is known as the Cemetery of the Martyrs [*Shuhadā'*].[27] I constantly hear the populace say that they are the graves of a group of companions of the Commander of the Faithful, ʿAlī b. Abī Ṭālib. They were present together
(127) with the Caliph at the battle against the Khārijites at an-Nahrawān. They were taken out of the battle wounded, and returning from the conflict they died at that spot, and ʿAlī buried them there. It is said that among these martyrs were those who were companions of the Prophet.

However, Ḥamzah b. Muḥammad b. Ṭāhir has likewise denied this story which is widely held among the populace, as I heard him contend it is without foundation—and God knows better.

II

The Topographical Growth of an Imperial City

Studies and Appendices

4

The Search for an ʿAbbāsid Capital

When the Caliph ʿAlī b. Abī Ṭālib left the holy city for al-Kūfah to do battle with Muʿāwiyah, he initiated a series of events which were to have a profound effect on the course of the next century. In abandoning al-Madīnah for Iraq, he formally shifted the capital of the Muslim world eastward, thus marking an end to the pre-eminence of the Ḥijāz. Although his decision was born of necessity and later proved to be historically logical, it was at this time ill-fated and premature. The inconclusive battle with the Syrians followed by a series of diplomatic fiascos seriously compromised the moral and political status of the Caliph. With the subsequent deterioration of his position, and finally his death at the hands of an assassin, Damascus became the new center of gravity of the Muslim world, and as the official capital of the Umayyads, it retained this pre-eminence until the fall of that regime. Despite this, the orientation of the later Umayyads gradually turned eastward to Iraq, Persia, and the newly acquired territories beyond the Oxus.

The assimilation of the eastern provinces could have firmly established Umayyad rule over a wide geographical area. However, the social and economic abuses levied by the ruling Arab aristocracy on the Muslim clients of Iraq and the newly acquired

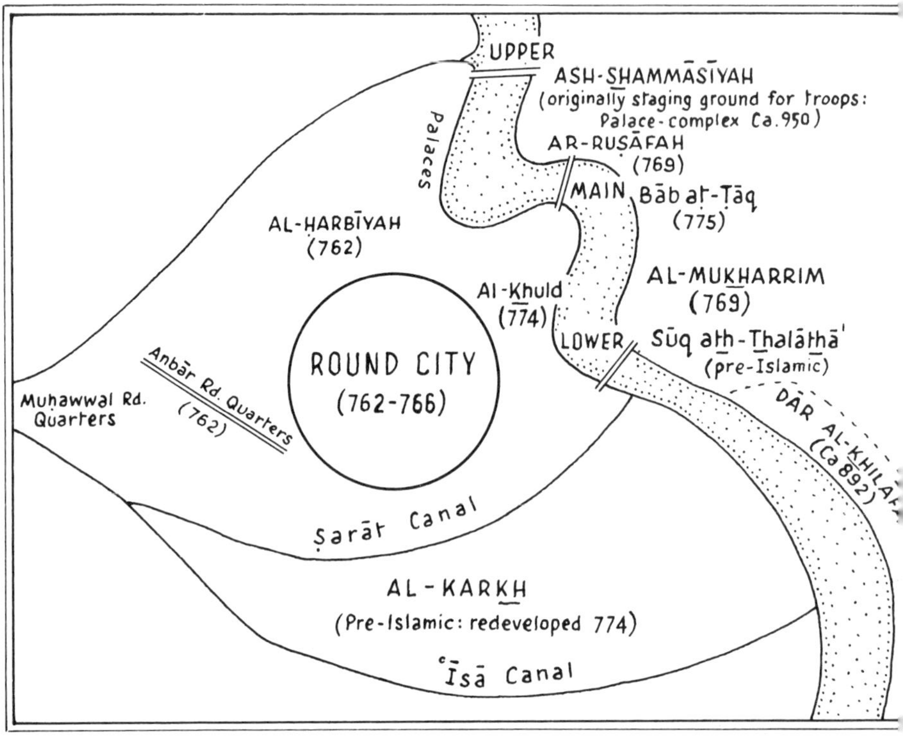

Chronological Map

territories precluded any such success. Owing to serious shortages of revenue, attempts to redress certain economic grievances failed, thereby intensifying the alienation of the inhabitants, and giving rise to the coalition of forces both Arab and Persian which ultimately dislodged the Umayyads from power. The final defeat of the Caliph's armies on the river Zāb was more than a military catastrophe; it marked the complete destruction of the existing ruling institution, predicated as it was on a ruling Arab aristocracy, and paved the way for redefining the Islamic community on a much wider basis, an undertaking of magnitude requiring conspicuous changes in the very nature of the Islamic Empire. Foremost among these was the transfer of the government from Syria to Iraq, a step which signified not only the formal change of dynasty, but a profound understanding of the commercial and political importance of the eastern provinces which spawned and nurtured the 'Abbāsid revolution.

During the formative years of 'Abbāsid rule, the center of government in Iraq was shifted from location to location as the Caliph searched for a place at which to establish a permanent capital. This quest came to an end when al-Manṣūr built an administrative center near the confluence of the Tigris and Ṣarāt, and named it Madīnat as-Salām. Shortly thereafter, it grew into a sprawling city which retained the name of the Persian hamlet that had previously occupied the site—Baghdad.

The administrative capital of the 'Abbāsids before the building of Baghdad was called al-Hāshimīyah. This does not refer to a single place but to wherever the Caliph chose to establish his residence. The confusion as to the location of al-Hāshimīyah stems from the existence of more than one place of that name as each in turn was occupied for a period of time as the official residence of the 'Abbāsid Caliph. As-Saffāḥ, after leaving al-Kūfah, settled at a site opposite Qaṣr b. Hubayrah,[1] where he built a city and named it al-Hāshimīyah. Previously, the Caliph had begun construction at Qaṣr b. Hubayrah itself, but he abandoned this location when the populace, in preference to al-Hāshimīyah, persisted in referring to the town by the name of its founder, the last Umayyad governor of Iraq, Yazīd b. 'Umar b. Hubayrah. This same Yazīd originally built a city on the Euphrates near al-Kūfah,[2] but was forced to abandon this site by order of the Umayyad Caliph Marwān II.[3] In 134/752, as-Saffāḥ moved once again and established his capital near al-Anbār,[4] formerly the Persian city Fīrūz Sābūr, but he died before completing it in 136/754.[5]

The authorities report that al-Manṣūr, who now became Caliph, established his residence at a new location in the general vicinity of al-Kūfah.[6] According to Ṭabarī, this location was adjacent to Madīnat b. Hubayrah.[7] This site is not to be confused with Qaṣr b. Hubayrah, which was situated, as previously noted, midway between al-Kūfah and Baghdad. These accounts seem to suggest that the center of al-Manṣūr's administration was the city near al-Kūfah which was first built and later abandoned by the governor of Marwān II. There were, therefore, no less than four ʿAbbāsid capitals: the capitals of as-Saffāḥ at Qaṣr b. Hubayrah, the site opposite that town, and at al-Anbār; and the city of al-Manṣūr at Madīnat b. Hubayrah. This proclivity of the ʿAbbāsid Caliphs for this constant moving is still unexplained; but it does suggest that they were searching for a site which could satisfy certain particular needs.

Al-Manṣūr's decision to move the government to Baghdad is reportedly the result of several factors. The Caliph's current residence was near the turbulent Shīʿite stronghold of al-Kūfah, a source of potential danger to his rule. His uneasiness as to possible intrigues was heightened in the year 141/758 by the riot of some Rāwandīyah extremists within the very court of his palace.[8] There are indications that the Caliph then was compelled to personally undertake the journey in search of another location for his capital.[9] Following the course of the Tigris upstream, he passed through Baghdad and Jarjarāyā,[10] and then continued on to al-Mawṣil. During the journey, al-Manṣūr dispatched troops in advance of his party to seek an advantageous location.[11] The returning scouts described a place to him which was close to Bārrimā, a village situated near al-Mawṣil on the left bank of the Tigris.[12] The Caliph, after spending the night there, consulted with his advisors and agreed that the climate was desirable, but logistically the area could not sustain the required military and civil population.[13] He then returned to Baghdad and traced the city plan,[14] although actual construction did not begin until 145/762.[15]

The Arabic accounts which discuss al-Manṣūr's decision to build a city at Baghdad are an interlacing of various reports from which two distinct traditions emerge: the first is somewhat apocryphal, the second gives some evidence of historicity.

1. The Story of Miqlāṣ[16]

Reported with some variation, the story indicates that al-Manṣūr was informed of an old tradition in which a king named Miqlāṣ[17] was destined to build a city between the Tigris and the

Ṣarāt. Upon hearing this, the Caliph revealed that he had been nicknamed Miqlāṣ in his youth, so that no obstacle remained in his path to establish the new ʿAbbāsid capital. A version of this story which is preserved in Ṭabarī reports that one of the Muslims who accompanied the Caliph was being treated by a Christian doctor.[18] When the doctor ascertained that the Caliph was seeking to build a city, he related the following:

> We find it written in one of our books that a man called Miqlāṣ will build a city called az-Zawrā'[19] between the Tigris and the Ṣarāt. When he has laid the foundation and constructed a part of the wall, it will be breached from the Ḥijāz, thereby interrupting the building of the city. The king will undertake to repair the breach, and when he is at the point of repairing it, the wall will be breached again from al-Baṣrah to a greater degree of damage than before. But it will not be long before he repairs the breaches and returns to building the city; then he will complete it....

There can be no doubt that these breaches are an allusion to the ʿAlid uprising of Muḥammad b. ʿAbdallāh in al-Madīnah and that of his brother Ibrāhīm in al-Baṣrah. In order to meet this threat, al-Manṣūr was compelled to take the field against them in 145/762, although the city had not yet been completed. Construction was, therefore, halted during the duration of the Caliph's military campaign, and he did not return until the rebels had been successfully disposed of later that year.[20] Only then were the state offices and treasuries moved from al-Hāshimīyah to Baghdad signifying the formal change of capital.[21]

It is therefore clear that the author of this account, in order to promote its authenticity and add to the Caliph's stature, employed the ancient literary technique of describing a recent historical event by projecting it back into the remote past, in a tale deliberately vague and prophetic. The story of Miqlāṣ is similarly reported for the building of ar-Rāfiqah, a city which was founded by al-Manṣūr in 155/772, thereby indicating that this motif may have become a cliché which Muslim authors used to glorify the building programs of the Caliph.[22] The tale itself was probably suggested by the account of the Manichaean Imām, Miqlāṣ, who, in accordance with the tradition of his faith, had to reside in Babylonia, and therefore assumed the headship of his community at the monastery which was near Ctesiphon.[23]

2. Climatic Conditions and Strategic Considerations

Expressions in praise of Baghdad frequently extol the invigorating climate.[24] Accordingly, the Caliph, in choosing Baghdad as the site of his city, was influenced by climatic conditions there which were conducive to year-round occupation, as well as by the relative lack of mosquitoes, an explanation also reported in the building of al-Kūfah.[25] To these accounts we can add the report of the Khaṭīb that al-Manṣūr favored Baghdad after testing the soils of various regions, and that this choice was subsequently reinforced by a visit to the site.[26] However, judging by modern conditions, there is little to suggest that Baghdad offered any climatic advantages that might not have been available at numerous other locations.

The sources also indicate that the Caliph's choice was determined by strategic considerations;[27] and this has been the explanation most generally accepted by Western scholars.[28] The description of al-Manṣūr's expedition in search of a site indicates that he followed the course of the Tigris rather than that of the Euphrates. It has been pointed out that the advantages of a site on the Tigris were conspicuous.[29] Not only was the land fertile on both sides of the river, but by means of various channels, the Tigris was navigable until the Persian Gulf. However, the Euphrates was the major waterway linking Iraq with Syria and the western trade route to Egypt. Moreover, it connected the important cities of ar-Raqqah, al-Anbār, and al-Kūfah, and gave access to the Arabian peninsula along the pilgrimage routes to the Ḥijāz. Control of the far-flung Islamic Empire, therefore, required access to both of these waterways, as well as the great highways connecting the Eastern provinces with Iraq.

The location of Baghdad was particularly well-suited for the tasks of the ʿAbbāsid administration. It was situated along the Tigris, but it also connected with the Euphrates by way of the Ṣarāt Canal, a major commercial artery dating back to Sassanian times.[30] These considerations are reported with some variation in several Arabic sources—among them Yaʿqūbī, who credits al-Manṣūr with the following statement:[31]

> Indeed, this island between the Tigris in the East and the Euphrates in the West is the harbor of the world. All the ships that sail up the Tigris from Wāsiṭ, al-Baṣrah, al-Ubullah, al-Ahwāz, Fārs, ʿUmān, al-Yamāmah, al-Baḥrayn, and the adjacent areas will anchor here. Similarly, goods brought on ships sailing down the Tigris from al-Mawṣil, Diyār Rabīʿah, Adharbayjān and Armenia, and down the Euphrates from Diyār Muḍar, ar-Raqqah, Syria, the border regions, Egypt and al-Maghrib, these goods will be brought and unloaded here. It will be a stopping place for the people of al-Jabal, Iṣfahān, and the districts of Khurāsān. Praise God who preserved it for me and caused all those who preceded me to neglect it. By God I will build it. I will dwell in it as long as I live and my descendants will live there after me. It will indeed be the most flourishing city in the world.

There is no reason to deny that this account and similar variants are an echo of the Caliph's desire for a centrally located site. Nevertheless, if the favorable geographic location of Baghdad was so apparent, it is surprising that none of the settlements which dotted the general vicinity in early Islamic times attained any political or commercial importance.[32] Ctesiphon,[33] which was situated along the Tigris some thirty kilometres downstream, had been a capital of the Sassanid Dynasty and the site of an important city dating back at least to the fourth century B.C. However, it declined rapidly after the Islamic conquest when the Arabs established the garrison cities (*amṣār*) of al-Kūfah and al-Baṣrah along the Euphrates. Although Wāsiṭ which later became the Umayyad Capital of Iraq was situated along the Tigris, its strategic importance was conceived in terms of its position between the rebellious cities of the *amṣār*. Whereas the Sassanid capital was the gateway to an empire in the East, the *amṣār* were administrative centers of an empire whose focal point was situated originally in the Ḥijāz, and later under the Umayyads in Syria. However, unlike their predecessors, the ʿAbbāsids who swept to power from Khurāsān more fully recognized the political and economic importance of the eastern provinces and significantly they were able to effect action in recognition of these facts. If the choice of Baghdad was characteristic of their thinking in general, the ʿAbbāsids would seem to have emphasized that a necessary condition for rule was the true integration of those disparate elements which before Islam were the great empires of Persia and Byzantium. The choice of Baghdad, therefore, seems to have been a logical one based on presumed political unity of the entire Islamic realm. In order to promote this unity it was necessary to destroy the existing divisive structure of an Arab aristocracy which was the foundation of Umayyad society although it had become an anachronism and perhaps its greatest weakness, and to substitute for it an Islamic Empire which took into consideration the aspirations and needs of its non-Arab subjects—particularly the powerful Persian allies of the ʿAbbāsids in Khurāsān. It is this changing relationship of subject to sovereign which brings to mind some additional questions concerning the founding of Madīnat al-Manṣūr.

Some Speculative Thoughts

The proximity of the ʿAbbāsid capital to Ctesiphon may be coincidental, but this fact leads to more speculative thoughts. It is noteworthy that the Khaṭīb al-Baghdādī concludes his introduction to *The History of Baghdad* with a chapter on al-Madā'in (Ctesiphon), and preserves in that chapter an historical tradition about the building of al-Manṣūr's city.[34] In order to obtain building materials for the construction at Baghdad, al-Manṣūr is reported to have ordered the demolition of the palace of Khusraw (Īwān Kisrā) at al-Madā'in. This step was undertaken despite the counsel of a non-Arab advisor who argued that the ruined palace was a monument to the Arab victory over the Sassanid Dynasty, and, as such, should not be destroyed. This advice was rejected because the advisor was suspected of pro-Persian sentiments. However, when the undertaking proved unmanageable, al-Manṣūr was forced to halt the demolition. According to a variant in Ṭabarī, the advisor, who is identified as Khālid b. Barmak, now argued against terminating the project, since this would be an admission of the Caliph's inability to destroy this vestige of Sassanian rule thus implying that it would reduce his stature in the eyes of the Persians.

While there is no way of determining any historical basis for this tradition from internal evidence, it is clear that al-Manṣūr was beset at the outset of his reign by the opposition of various dissident groups particularly in those territories formerly held by the Sassanian dynasty, and which in Islamic times became the breeding ground of the ʿAbbāsid revolution. To this one can add al-Manṣūr's difficulties with the caliphal pretensions of his uncle ʿAbdallāh b. ʿAlī,[35] and the imagined or real disaffection of his previous ally, Abū Muslim, the former leader of the ʿAbbāsid revolutionary movement in Khurāsān.[36] Although the ambitions laid to this convert may be largely the invention of later heresiographers,[37] a real distinction can be drawn between his personal ambitions and the aspirations of others which were apparently invoked in his name. There is no reason to doubt that his continued power and great prestige among the Persians in Khurāsān was a source of great concern to the Caliph. Because of the potential danger of a full-scale revolt in the East, al-Manṣūr was determined to remove him, and after failing to transfer Abū Muslim to another province, he lured him to a spot near Ctesiphon, and had him executed in 137/755.[38] Ironically, the elimination of Abū Muslim did not resolve these difficulties, but led to a series of wide-spread revolts which were invoked in his name.[39] If these last events are not mentioned prominently by the chroniclers, it is in all likelihood because they were relatively minor affairs. However, the revolts of Sunbādh, Isḥāq the Turk, and Ustādhsīs are not without importance in that they represent a type of opposition which plagued the ʿAbbāsids in the early years of their rule and which was to reappear in the revolt of Bābāk the following century. The activities of Sunbādh, because he is better known than the others, may serve to illustrate the ideological grounds on which al-Manṣūr's claims to rule were challenged.[40]

Immediately following the death of Abū Muslim, Sunbādh led a revolt in Khurāsān which extended from Naysābūr to Qūmis and ar-Rayy. Reportedly a former aid of Abū Muslim seeking to avenge him, he took the field against a royal army of 10,000 troops and was defeated as 60,000 of his followers were slain. The extent of this uprising which is preserved in the short account of Ṭabarī may be exaggerated; but two central facts remain clear: Sunbādh pressed the legitimacy of his claim on the authority of Abū Muslim and his revolt was sufficiently important to force a cancellation of the scheduled summer expedition for that year.[41] The nature of this revolt is more carefully delineated in the *Siyāsat Nameh* of Niẓām al-Mulk, although his account is no doubt marked by considerable shaping.[42] If it can be assumed, however, that the Persian account is not entirely the invention of later times, then the author's description may serve to indicate another important dimension to the uprising which is not explicitly stated by Ṭabarī: its ideological pretensions and their particular appeal to the national consciousness of the Iranian peoples. In effect, the ambitions attributed to Sunbādh are not compromised by a desire for regional independence but are nothing short of a claim for the restoration of an Iranian Empire, and the substitution of a syncretistic national religion for that of Islam: The substantive expression of these claims was framed by familiar eschatological conceptions. The death of Abū Muslim, like that of various Shīʿite imāms, therefore comes to be regarded as an ophthalmic illusion. In reality he was able to turn himself into a white pigeon and thus miraculously escape death at the hands of al-Manṣūr's executioners. Presently in hiding, his imminent return as the forerunner of the *Mahdī* and the subsequent collapse of Arab rule was eagerly anticipated.

As a serious challenge to the Caliph's authority, the powers exercised by such dissident groups were probably more apparent than real. But the struggle for rule in a dynastic society extends beyond the formal elements of power to touch upon the fundamental question of legitimacy. It is the historic need of every sovereign, particularly the founder of a newly established dynasty, to announce himself as an authentic successor of the great family of kings which preceded him. This particular need was, no doubt, even more pressing for the early ʿAbbāsids since the basis of their power was to a significant extent dependent on the continued cooperation of their Persian supporters.

If there is any historicity to the accounts reported in Ṭabarī and the Khaṭīb concerning the demolition of Īwān Kisrā and the subsequent use of the building materials for the Caliph's palace at

Baghdad, then the manner in which the ʿAbbāsid capital was founded at that site may have been more than the logical consequence of certain geographic considerations. It may have the additional nuance of demonstrating that the Caliph was anxious to promote himself as an heir to the defunct Sassanian Empire, and as such, could claim the allegiance of those subjects who dwelled on its former territories, the followers of Abū Muslim notwithstanding. This is not to say that the Caliph consciously attempted to emulate a given Sassanian monarch but rather that he attempted to associate himself with that particular style of grand rule which characterized the great empires before him, and from which lingering Sassanian forms provided his most convenient models. It is true that Ctesiphon and its magnificent palaces had become, in the eyes of the Arabs, synonymous with Sassanian rule, but more generally it was also considered as a city where great kings came to establish their realm. Yāqūt,[43] in an attempt to explain the name al-Madā'in (pl. *Madīnah* meaning city), mentions an account indicating that it was so named because each of the Sassanian monarchs and the rulers that preceded them there built a city adjacent to that of his predecessor. The chain of worthy figures includes Alexander the Great and goes back to Zāb who ruled in the era following that of Moses.

A new capital is therefore not merely the choice of a new city—witness the unsuccessful attempts at al-Hāshimīyah—it carries with it the prestige and authority of the Caliphate itself. The search for legitimacy is concerned with the tangible expressions of that authority. Evidence from archeological and literary sources suggests that from a period as early as that of the Umayyad ʿAbd al-Malik, the sovereigns of the Islamic realm were becoming extremely conscious of the visible symbols of their office.[44] The growth of an elaborate court ceremonial based, to a large extent, on Persian models may be interpreted as a direct reflection of this concern. The ascendance of the ʿAbbāsids brought about significant innovations in the general style of rule and changes in ceremonial usage and forms borrowed with some modification from earlier standards. However, whereas the royal image of the Umayyad Caliphs was generally restricted to the confines of their distant chateaux and palaces, their successors and their courtiers were portrayed in full regalia before the multitude of their subjects in a manner consistent with the formal usage that a Persian might understand. These are not spontaneous developments but the outgrowth of those historical conditions which are operative in a society that looks upon its sovereign and the symbols of his office as the ultimate in human authority. The needs resulting from the challenge to al-Manṣūr's claims of legitimacy could only have served as a direct stimulus to the development of those forms.

Such symbols of authority that were developed could also be expressed through architectural forms and decorative motif. It is therefore pertinent to ask whether the curious architectural arrangement of al-Manṣūr's city could have been a conscious attempt to recapture the grandeur of his imperial predecessors in a physically striking manner. Although there have been no excavations of the Round City, detailed descriptions have been preserved by both Ya'qūbī and the Khaṭīb.[45] The picture obtained from these sources is that of a perfectly circular city with two concentric defending walls separated by an *intervallum* (*faṣīl*) and surrounded by a moat. Beyond the inner wall which is flanked by roundels is a residential area, and extending from the outer fortifications which are entered through a bent entrance are four elaborate gate complexes and arcades each equidistant from one another thereby forming the quadrants of the city. The center of the city is formed by a large enclosed court which surrounds the principal mosque and the residence of the Caliph, a palace in back of which there was an audience-hall surmounted by a green dome that could be seen from the outskirts of the city.[46]

Although many general features of the Round City are prominently displayed at several known pre-Islamic sites in Iran and Mesopotamia—namely, Hatra, Dārābjird, Gūr, and Ctesiphon—the available archeological and literary evidence does not suggest any direct prototype for the city as a whole. Creswell's suggestion[47] that it was probably the plan of Dārābjird which directly inspired the creation of al-Manṣūr's edifice does not seem likely, since it is difficult to believe, on historical ground alone, that this inconspicuous provincial town should have served as a direct prototype to the great ʿAbbāsid capital. The same objection would seem to apply to Gūr; for although it was the original capital of Ardashīr, the first Sassanian monarch, it was Ctesiphon which soon became the leading city of the realm. It is rather Ctesiphon with its tradition as a city of great kings and its palace architecture which could have inspired the Arabs to direct imitation when constructing a city of their own just thirty kilometers away. However, the limited excavations of the German expedition at that site did not uncover sufficient evidence to justify such a conclusion.[48]

Yet if there is no direct parallel to Madīnat al-Manṣūr there is a definite relationship between the general features and the style of architecture that characterize that city and the other known pre-Islamic sites. These features have already been described earlier; the style is summarized by O. Reuther in his description of Sassanian city planning:[49] "In any society organized into a hierarchy of classes under an autocracy, symmetry and axial plans predominate not only in the design of individual buildings but in the arrangement of groups of buildings, and finally in the layout of the inclusive group, in the city." Reuther's broad statement does more than describe a mode of city planning; it is an indication of how architectural concepts and forms are a reflection of a more general idea—the mode of rule conceived of the formal relationship between sovereign and subject. The grand style of rule that characterized the government of the Khusraw and the grand style of architecture that characterized his city are functions of the same attitude.

If the founding of Baghdad is a reflection of an evolving style of government which would have aided the Caliph to command the allegiance of the eastern provinces, then presumably measures were also taken to gain the recognition of those Arabs living in the former strongholds of Iraq and Syria. Significant archeological diggings since the last war have uncovered data which have an important bearing on this very problem. They indicate that it is in the personal domain of the sovereign that the most striking parallels to the Round City have been discovered. However, these are not examples of the pre-Islamic architecture of the region as one might expect, but are rather the Umayyad government palaces of al-Kūfah and Wāsiṭ.[50] The feature common to all these constructions is the relationship of a square palace to an adjoining mosque of smaller dimensions in accordance with the Sassanian architectural principle of constructing a religious edifice along an axis running through the iwan of a royal palace.

The palace-mosque complex apparently became an accepted feature of Islamic architecture dating from the period of the conquests since it is indicated that already in the reign of ʿUmar, Saʿd b. Abī Waqqās shifted the mosque of al-Baṣrah so that it lay adjacent to his government palace.[51] This arrangement is, however, unknown in the western architecture of the Umayyads with the notable exception of Muʿāwiyah's Khaḍrā', which is reported to have been situated along the south wall of the mosque in Damascus.[52] It is possible that because the arrangement is more common to Sassanian concepts, it never did become a prominent feature of the Umayyad architecture of Syria and Palestine. The existence of Muʿāwiyah's Khaḍrā' in Damascus, however, necessitates a more convincing explanation. This explanation is perhaps to be found in the respective functions of the buildings.

The Umayyad chateaux of Syria and Palestine were located some distance from the great urban centers. On the other hand, the palaces of Iraq were erected at al-Kūfah, Wāsiṭ, and al-Baṣrah, and the Dār al-Imārah of Abū Muslim, a similar structure dating from ca. 750 was constructed at Merv.[53] Although the buildings of Iraq prominently display features which are common to Sassanian royal architecture, they are like Abū Muslim's Dār al-Imārah, palaces of provincial governors. Even Muʿāwiyah's Khaḍrā' in Damascus, the official capital of the Umayyad realm, was constructed while he was still the governor of Syria during the reign of ʿUthmān b. ʿAffān. It is therefore clear that the palace-mosque complex consisted of a large ensemble of units including treasuries, storage rooms, registries, and similar elements. It was the administrative center at which the daily business of government was conducted, and the visible expression of the authority of the state. It is in this tradition that the Round City was constructed, publicly demonstrating the unique power of the monarch, and thereby distinguishing it from the so-called royal Umayyad architecture of Syria and Palestine.

In Iraq the governors were synonymous with Umayyad rule, and in particular al-Ḥajjāj b. Yūsuf. It was al-Ḥajjāj who put an end to the caliphal pretensions of ʿAbdallāh b. az-Zubayr, and pacified the province. He improved the lands of the region by digging new canals and repairing the old, and he was granted the great honor of issuing coinage. From the capital which he built at Wāsiṭ, he subjected the rebellious cities of al-Kūfah and al-Baṣrah thus solidifying the Umayyad hold on this turbulent province. Any great similarity between the palace-mosque of al-Ḥajjāj at Wāsiṭ and that of al-Manṣūr at Baghdad is, therefore, to be treated with some consideration.

Although the archeological evidence from Wāsiṭ is still incomplete,[54] descriptions of both these buildings are known from literary sources.[55] The dimensions of the palace and mosque as indicated by Yāqūt coincide with those mentioned by the Khaṭīb for the palace and mosque of al-Manṣūr at Baghdad. What is more remarkable is that these figures of 200 cubits square for the mosque and 400 cubits square for the palace are apparently confirmed by the diggings of the Iraqi expedition to that site. Both palaces are reported to have been surmounted by the green dome (*al-qubbat al-khaḍrā'*) of remarkable height which could be seen at a great distance from the city and which served as a characteristic landmark for the surrounding region.[56] Moreover, ar-Ruṣāfah, which was the functioning capital of the Umayyads during the reign of Hishām (724–743) also featured a green dome serving as an audience-hall and Muʿāwiyah is reported to have given receptions under the *khaḍrā'* of his palace in Damascus.[57] The question raised by Grabar in his treatment of this material is therefore incisive: "Is there a Syrian Umayyad tradition of such domes, perhaps going back to Muʿāwiyah's Khaḍrā' in Damascus (the official capital of the dynasty) which would have been imitated by al-Ḥajjāj."[58] If such tradition did in fact exist, it would seemingly represent more than an architectural curiosity; for the green dome would then seem to be symbolic of the authority of the realm. It is not likely that al-Manṣūr's dome was an historic accident since Ṭabarī in his description of the revolt of the Rāwandīyah at the Caliph's former palace indicates that several of the rioters ascended the Khaḍrā' and jumped as if to fly.[59] If the account describing this event at al-Hāshimīyah does not confuse both palaces, then the Caliph was apparently quite conscious of the symbolic meaning of the green dome.

Furthermore, there is the tradition that the iron gates of the palace at Wāsiṭ were brought to Baghdad and placed in the palace of al-Manṣūr[60]—a tradition which brings to mind the Caliph's attempt to demolish the Palace of Khusraw at al-Madā'in in order to supply building materials for Baghdad. In the medieval Near East the transfer of gates from one city to another is believed to be a symbolic act indicating an expression of authority. After conquering Ctesiphon, Sa'd b. Abī Waqqāṣ settled at al-Kūfah, modeled his palace after the Īwān Kisrā, and removed the iron gates from that building for his own use. Similarly, when al-Ḥajjāj built Wāsiṭ he brought the gates of his city from nearby az-Zandaward, a town which tradition ascribes to Sulaymān b. Dāwūd. It is noteworthy that Wāsiṭ was the Umayyad capital of Iraq, and that its populace continued to resist the 'Abbāsids, even after the fall of the Umayyad Dynasty.[61] Presumably, it was necessary that Baghdad assume the symbolic trappings of authority which had previously accrued to Wāsiṭ and the capitals of the Umayyad realm.

The building of Baghdad may therefore be seen as an attempt to unify politically and geographically the widespread regions of the Islamic Empire under the aegis of the 'Abbāsid Caliphate. The only means by which the Caliph could effect this union was that of appealing to the native populations in the visual language which they understood—as a successor of the great traditional emperors of the Near East. Implicit in this contention is the notion that these peoples would have accepted a ruling monarch of a different national origin provided that he could show himself to be a worthy successor to that great family of kings which preceded him. The Umayyads surely made attempts at gaining such stature. The more traditional picture of the Umayyad Caliph living on the periphery of the desert indulging in the romantic pursuits of bedouin life hardly does justice to their real outlook. It is not a love for the *bādiyah*, but the inflexible structure of Umayyad society which prevented their Caliphs from achieving a true unity of the realm and forestalling the eventual demise of their regime. They may therefore be regarded as having begun the transition from the Arab-centered "primitive Islam" to the more universal empire which was symbolized by its great capital at Baghdad. The building of Baghdad did, however, signify great innovations in city planning —changes that were to have a marked effect on the topographical and economic growth of the capital.

13

The Caliph's Personal Domain: The City Plan of Baghdad Re-examined

Islamic urbanists recognize the existence of two distinct places of major occupation by distinguishing between the created and spontaneous cities of the Islamic realm—between cities built according to a preconceived plan, and those such as the garrison towns of the *amṣār*, whose development was stimulated by response to the particular needs of the Islamic conquest.[1] The early pattern of growth which was characteristic of such military colonies as al-Baṣrah and al-Kūfah was rapid and without real awareness of the formal elements of city planning. However, the original military camps soon gave way to permanent installations. Extended routes of supply were replaced by fixed markets and an incipient industrial organization, as an outer town of artisans and merchants grew around the original military settlement. The growth of the *amṣār* town was therefore directed from the center out, giving the impression that these urban areas were not so much the execution of an orderly plan, but the product of several stages of spontaneous generation.

The historical growth of Baghdad, beginning with the magnificent Round City constructed by al-Manṣūr in 145/762, suggests a rather different type of urban development. The Round City, or Madīnat as-Salām as it was also called, was not a prefabricated military camp given permanence by a growing sedentary environment, but rather the creation of that consummate planning and execution which caused the essayist, al-Jāḥiẓ, to remark: "It is as though it was poured into a mold and cast"—clearly a major undertaking based on a preconceived plan of the Caliph's own choosing.[2] What then was the design and function of the original Islamic structure, and what was the pattern of its early development?

Public Works and City Planning

The successful completion of so vast a project presupposes not only a predetermined architectural design, but a highly organized and efficient set of work procedures. It was not until a large labor force had been assembled that construction was actually begun, and it was not until four years later that all the major elements of the Round City were completed, allowing for the year in which construction was halted while the Caliph was busy with Shīʿite revolts in al-Baṣrah and the Ḥijāz. The essential feature of this public works program was the recruiting of skilled and unskilled labor from the outlying regions of present day Syria and Iraq, including such places as al-Mawṣil, al-Jabal, al-Kūfah, Wāsiṭ, and al-Baṣrah. Salaries were fixed according to the division of labor and were apparently paid out at set intervals giving the impression of an emerging boom-town. The total number of workers is reported by Yaʿqūbī to have exceeded 100,000, a figure which reflects the magnitude of construction, though perhaps exaggerated. Each quarter was under the general supervision of a military commander whose troops provided for security, while technical affairs were entrusted to individuals who were experts in such matters.[3]

With thousands of workers assembling from the outlying districts, the skilled and unskilled labor, the artisans, and the military would have all required adequate housing and access to established markets for services, as well as an incipient industrial plant for the production of building materials.[4] All these factors tend to indicate that Baghdad was assuming a quality of permanence even before the Round City was completed. In time the urban area grew around the original walls of Madīnat as-Salām, and developed into a sprawling complex of interdependent elements, each containing its own markets, mosques, and cemeteries, and giving rise as well to its own autonomous institutions. Judging from the description of the fiefs situated there, the northwest suburb of al-Ḥarbīyah was heavily populated with al-Manṣūr's generals and military personnel.[5] From what has been said, it is likely that the earliest grants were issued concurrent with the growth of the original city and were situated in or adjacent to the various military colonies (*jund*) established in that sector according to tribal or ethnic grouping. The civilian laborers and artisans no doubt took up residence in the old inhabited market areas of al-Karkh to the south of the emerging city well before the completion of the original structure.[6] Therefore, contrary to popular belief, the growth of the suburbs on the West Side of the Tigris must have preceded rather than followed the construction of Madīnat as-Salām, although there are statements which perhaps suggest otherwise. To be sure there was an expansion of the outlying areas, however, the textual evidence which indicates the subsequent development of these suburbs (157/774) after the completion of the Round City, presumably refers then to the needs created by a natural increase in the population of these districts over a period of twelve years.[7] Such being the case, Baghdad, unlike the cities of the *amṣār*, did not at first develop from the inside-out, but rather from the outside-in.

This unique pattern of growth is to a large extent determined by the pre-Islamic character of the site, a factor which until now has been almost entirely neglected. Although the strategic situation of the west bank was ideal for a major urban center, the Sassanid monarchs chose to establish their capital somewhat downstream at Ctesiphon (al-Madā'in). However, the major market areas servicing Ctesiphon as well as the hinterland were situated across the river at Seleucia, thereby resulting in the curious arrangement of a capital some short distance from its main commercial center. The decline of Ctesiphon in the early Islamic period must have seriously affected the old market areas, but they no doubt continued to service the remaining agriculturists from the surrounding region. It is this type of arrangement which the Caliph seems to have desired at Baghdad; but rather than move to Ctesiphon, he established an administrative center at the confluence of the Tigris and the Ṣarāt. It was, therefore, not the location but the architectural arrangement of the Round City which enabled the Caliph to emulate his Persian predecessors in withdrawing his administration from the immediate presence of the general population. This contention is fully supported by the available historical and architectural evidence, and suggests the need of defining still another type of urban occupation, that of the administrative center.

Architectural Aspects of the Administrative Center

As previously indicated, excavations have never been undertaken on the presumed site of the Round City; information on the architecture and physical layout is therefore derived from literary sources, of which the two most significant accounts are the section on Baghdad in Yaʿqūbī's *K. al-Buldān*, and those chapters in the Khaṭīb's history which deal with the construction of Madīnat as-Salām and its mosques.[8] The Khaṭīb and Yaʿqūbī appear to use independent authorities. Yaʿqūbī's source is not given, but it is indicated that the description is based on the city as it existed in the time of al-Manṣūr. The report of the Khaṭīb is derived essentially from an account of the jurist Wakīʿ (d. 918), which is in turn based on various older authorities. The two sources complement each other with regard to detail, the account of the Khaṭīb being the more extended description. Occasionally there are conflicting figures suggesting perhaps that the authors refer to different metrological systems.

Certain general characteristics of these works raise serious problems as to their value for any proposed reconstruction of the city. Yaʿqūbī's report is terse with little, if any, pretense at a critical handling of the material. On the other hand, the Khaṭīb, whose forte was the religious sciences, indicates perhaps by force of habit several reports for various accounts, usually with a complete *isnād*. However, when taken as a whole, his account describing the plan of the Round City is quite fragmentary, and details are often lacking for certain major structures. Since numbers are easily confused in an Arabic text, the statistical evidence which is the basis of any architectural reconstruction is not above suspicion. In general, the Khaṭīb was probably a reliable transmitter of the information which he possessed; but lacking an inclination for technical problems, and without professional knowledge of architecture and topography, he seems to have been somewhat arbitrary in his choice of accounts, and not too concerned with the critical problems to be found in the original texts. The task of reconstructing the Round City is, therefore, highly theoretical and very speculative. The major architectural work on this subject is that of E. Herzfeld, whose reconstructions were subsequently accepted with some modification by K. A. C. Creswell in his monumental survey, *Early Muslim Architecture.*[9] It is clear that their efforts raise many questions which will only be solved if and when systematic diggings are undertaken on the suspected site of the Round City. However, on the basis of the literary evidence alone, it is possible to offer some divergent views which represent a new concept of the city plan, and a different thesis as to its architectural function and historical development in the earliest period.

When completed, the city of al-Manṣūr consisted of three architectural elements: the outer fortifications, an inner residential area of symmetrically arranged streets, and the vast inner courtyard where the Caliph's mosque and residence were situated. The outer fortifications took the shape of two concentric walls separated by an *intervallum* (*faṣīl*) and surrounded by a moat. The inner wall, since it was the protective wall of the city, was the larger of the two, and was flanked by roundels. Access to the residential area and the central court was gained through four elaborate gateways and arcades beginning at the outer wall and ending at the great circular courtyard. Situated equidistant from one another along the axis of the Caliph's residence, four gate complexes centered the northeast, northwest, southeast, and southwest quadrants of the residential area. A second *intervallum* separated the houses from the outer fortifications, and a third separated them from the enclosure wall of the great central court where the palace-mosque was situated.[10]

The sources conflict in reporting the total area which was circumscribed by the walls of the structure as there are no less than seven *isnāds*, giving figures ranging from 576,000 to 64,000,000 square cubits. Within this wide range, Herzfeld and Creswell were inclined to accept the report which is attributed to Rabāḥ, the architect of the city walls, and accordingly obtained a figure of approximately 20,000,000 square cubits by calculating the distance between each of the symmetrically arranged gateways (1 *mīl*).[11] Allowing even for the largest measurements, and keeping the city plan in mind, the area circumscribed by the walls of al-Mansur's city was too small for the major urban center of the ʿAbbāsid Empire. Moreover, certain architectural features of the Round City give the impression that it was constructed as a governmental complex that retained some of the outward features of an integrated city, but which was more correctly a palace precinct of which the Caliph's residence-mosque in the central court was the major element.[11a]

The Khaṭīb does not indicate whether any other structures occupied this court; however, Yaʿqūbī mentions two additional buildings. One adjacent to the Damascus Gate housed the chief of the guard (*ḥaras*) and his troops; the other, the location of which is not indicated, was a large portico (*saqīfah*) raised on columns of burnt brick cemented with gypsum. This portico contained the apartment (*dār*) of the chief of police (*shurṭah*) and presumably room for his men, thereby providing maximum security for the Caliph's personal domain. These buildings were probably intended for those men who were actually on duty in the central courtyard,[12] the remainder of the contingent was no doubt quartered in those streets designated for the police and the guards, which were situated in the residential area flanking the arcades of the Baṣrah Gate.[13] According to Yaʿqūbī, these were the only buildings in the central court other than the palace and principal mosque. The text also indicates that surrounding the court[14] were the residences of al-Manṣūr's younger children, his servants in attendance, the slaves, and in addition, the treasury (*bayt al-māl*), the arsenal (*khizānat as-silāḥ*), the *dīwān* of the palace personnel (*al-aḥshām*), the public kitchen, and various other government agencies.

Despite these explicit statements in Yaʿqūbī, and although it can be assumed that these buildings were an important element in the original city plan, there is no provision for these structures in the diagram of the Round City as reconstructed by Herzfeld and Creswell.[15] LeStrange, who is somewhat more faithful to the Arabic text, included these buildings in his plans, but lacking any clear picture as to their arrangement he arbitrarily placed them at various points around the palace of the Caliph.[16] The text of Yaʿqūbī is, however, explicit. Aside from the palace-mosque, there were only two buildings in the court itself: the structure designated for the guards, and the portico of the police. It is therefore clear that the various *dīwāns* and the residences of al-Manṣūr's children and servants were not situated in the courtyard but surrounded it, thus forming a ring of buildings between the third *intervallum* which marked the limits of the residential area, and the central court itself. As for the city plan *in toto*, this ringed structure must be regarded as having originally been an integral element of the architecture of the central court, i.e., the Caliph's personal domain, comprising the area, his residence, and the governmental machinery.[17]

Incidental evidence from an historical source not only supports this contention, but also solves a number of difficulties arising from the text of the Khaṭīb.[18] Among the statements which he preserves on the building of the city, Ṭabarī mentions that the gates of the chambers (*maqāṣir*) of a group of al-Manṣūr's generals and scribes opened onto the court (*raḥbah*) of the mosque. Since the court is expressed here by the term *raḥbah*, and not *ṣaḥn*, it is clear that the account refers not to the internal court of the mosque, but the great central yard which surrounded it and the adjoining residence. These chambers cannot be accounted for in the plans of Herzfeld and Creswell; but the statement is consistent with the description of Yaʿqūbī, as well as the reconstruction of the ringed area suggested above. Moreover, following this report, Ṭabarī continues with a discussion of the central courtyard. He cites an account, which is also reported in the Khaṭīb, that ʿĪsā b. ʿAlī (*the Caliph's uncle*) complained about having to walk from the gate of the (*central*) court to the palace, and suggested that he might instead hitch a ride on one of the beasts that entered the courtyard.[19] The Caliph was astonished to find out that such traffic was entering his personal domain, and gave orders for the people (*residing in the ringed area*) to shift the gates (*which opened onto the court*) so that they faced the *intervalla* of the arcades (*ṭāqāt*).[20] No one was permitted to enter the courtyard except on foot. Markets were then transferred to each of the four arcades (*previously occupied by guards*) and remained there until the Caliph, fearful of the security problem which they posed, removed them from the Round City when the matter was brought to his attention by a visiting Byzantine Ambassador.[21]

The story of 'Īsā b. 'Alī's attempt to ride into the court and thus overcome the pain of his gout not only confirms the existence of the presumed ringed area, but in doing so provides a plausible explanation of the structure and function of the arcades which covered each gateway leading to the central court. These were flanked by rooms for the guards, who numbered 1,000 at each gate under the command of a hand-picked general; various ceremonial functionaries were also attached to the staff of the gate complex. The (*large*) arcades, which consisted of 54 arches, are reported to have been 15 cubits in width and 200 in length from the first arch to the court which separated these structures from the small arcades.[22] According to the Khaṭīb, there was a second series of arcades, but there is no indication as to the number or arrangement of the arches.[23]

Because Herzfeld and Creswell made no provision for the ringed structure, they assumed that the great inner court was circumscribed by an enclosure wall only five cubits thick, which separated it from the third *intervallum* of the residential area.[24] Since the large arcades ended at this *intervallum*, the vagueness of the Arabic text left them with the problem of providing a suitable position for the small arcades. Herzfeld allowed for a series of free standing arches which connected to the enclosure wall. The total width of the arcade was estimated at five cubits so as to correspond with the assumed projection of the corridor leading to the central court.[25] However, this reconstruction does not provide sufficient abutment for the thrust of the vaulting, assuming that analogous to the larger arcades, they supported a roof of burnt brick and not wood.[26] Moreover, Herzfeld's reconstruction is also marked by certain functional difficulties. If one can assume a thickness of one cubit for each arch, then the total width of the passageway was only four cubits, thereby indicating a narrow walk, unconnected to any rooms, and leading nowhere along a very wide circumference.

Since Herzfeld's city plan just does not allow for an acceptable reconstruction of the small arcades, Creswell is forced to conclude that this structure was not an arcade at all, but a series of blind arches resting on half round piers along the enclosure wall, with the exception of the four entrances to the main court which were flanked by quarter round piers of the same projection. This plan which is based on the analogy of the Court of Honor at Ukhayḍir and the walls of the *ziyādah*s at the great mosque in Sāmarrā gives the small arcades a decorative rather than structural function.[27] Creswell's reconstruction, although theoretically possible, is not convincing. The textual evidence of a sizeable ringed structure between the *intervallum* of the residential area and the central court, is obviously more plausible than the enclosure wall invented by Herzfeld. Moreover, the existence of a ringed structure provides for a lengthening of the main gateways leading to the Caliph's palace, thereby leaving sufficient space for the second series of arcades. The small arcades which framed the inner ring are presumably identical in structure with the larger unit that framed the residential quadrants; both are situated along the same access leading to the great central court. The distinction between the two arcades is then in the number of arches, rather than the position or function.[28]

Assuming the existence of this inner ring and its components, the architectural evidence tends to indicate that the Round City was, in fact, an administrative center, and not at all a city in the conventional sense of the term. What is more, this view is consistent with the historical evidence and points to the need of re-evaluating the historical development of Madīnat al-Manṣūr in the formative period.

The Changing Function of the Round City

The relocation of the gates in the inner ring, and the subsequent shift of certain markets to the four arcades is apparently an indication of the changing function of the Round City. The inner ring, as originally conceived, housed the machinery of government and certain elements of the Caliph's household, and comprised along with al-Manṣūr's residence and mosque, a single unit representing his personal domain. In order to insure maximum security, and no doubt avoid a repetition of the events at al-Hāshimīyah, access to the central area was limited to four main passages, each at the termination of an elaborate gateway protected by military personnel. The gate-complex must be considered as an extension of the palace area to which it led, thereby explaining the required presence of various ceremonial functionaries, and more particularly, the existence of a royal audience-hall (*majlis*) surmounting each of the city's outer gates.[29] Thus the visiting dignitary, from the moment he stepped into the outer gateway, was made to feel as if he were in the presence of the Caliph's palace.

When al-Manṣūr shifted the entrances of the inner ring so that they opened onto the third *intervallum*, he connected the administrative agencies that were formerly part of the Caliph's domain with the residential area of the quadrants, thus limiting his personal domain to the structures actually situated in the great central court, his residence, mosque, and the security buildings. It was now possible to move various markets into the rooms flanking the arcades since the gate-complex was no longer an integral element of the palace precinct, and therefore did not require the presence of the guard, whose duties were no doubt ceremonial as well as military. The new markets made it possible for the residents of the Round City to receive their provisions without leaving the walled area.[30] However, the limited space in the arcades for these markets is an indication that the great commercial center of the city still remained in the suburb of al-Karkh where it had been situated since pre-Islamic times.[31] When the Caliph later decided to redevelop the suburbs and, for security reasons, to remove the markets from the arcades, he understandably chose to relocate them in the general area of al-Karkh, and provided for improved transportation in the commercial districts, and in the city itself.[32]

As previously reported, the Caliph's decision to relocate the markets and return the guard to the arcades, was determined by security problems which were brought to his attention by a visiting

Byzantine ambassador. As no one was denied access to the markets, the Patrikios pointed out that the enemy may enter the city under the guise of carrying out trade, and that the merchants in turn could pass on vital information concerning the Caliph's activities. Al-Manṣūr then transferred the markets to al-Karkh, and ordered the general redevelopment of the area between the Ṣarāt and the ʿĪsā Canal, according to a plan which he had himself conceived. This intensive development of the suburban districts in 157/774 was probably due, in part, to the natural growth of Baghdad since the time the foundations of the Round City were laid twelve years earlier. With the presumed increase in population, it was also necessary to build a second principal mosque for the inhabitants of al-Karkh, who had previously recited their Friday prayers in the Round City. The existence of a second building would not only have relieved the congestion at the mosque of the central court, but would have made it unnecessary for the people of the markets to enter the walled city for their prayers, thereby further tightening the security of the Caliph's domain.

In later times al-Karkh, which was heavily populated by Shīʿites, was the scene of frequent religious disturbances.[33] The historian al-Wāqidī (d. 207), a Shīʿite of modest persuasion, is credited with having said that it is infested with the lowest rabble, to which the Khaṭīb added by way of clarification: al-Wāqidī meant by this statement certain sections of al-Karkh inhabited only by the Rāfiḍites (i.e., Shīʿites).[34] Whatever historicity there may be to the account of the Byzantine ambassador, there is still further reason to believe that the Caliph was troubled by the presence of a seditious element in the arcades of the Round City, if we are to believe a second explanation for the transfer of the markets as preserved by Ṭabarī and the Khaṭīb.[35] It is reported that in the year 157/774, Abū Zakarīyā' Yaḥyā b. ʿAbdallāh, who had been appointed supervisor (*muḥtasib*) of the city's markets, made cause with Shīʿite followers of Muḥammad and Ibrāhīm b. ʿAbdallāh by inducing the rabble to revolt; the implication being that he used his position as market supervisor to carry on subversive activities against the state.[36] The abortive revolt ended when the seditious *muḥtasib* was executed and his body was hung for all to see in the great central court, a public demonstration of the authority of the government and its swift justice. The subsequent transfer of the arcade markets to redeveloped districts outside the walled city, and the return of the guard to the flanking rooms seems therefore to have served two purposes: it relieved the increasing pressures of urban growth, while at the same time providing for increased security in the governmental machinery of the state.

In the wake of these developments, the original concept of the palace precinct was temporarily abandoned. Although the Round City continued to function as an administrative center, the Caliph now moved to a newly built residence (al-Khuld), which was situated along the Tigris above the Khurāsān Gate,[37] and which became the first of a series of estates extending along the shore road.[38] The idea of combining the administrative agencies and the Caliphal residence within a self-contained unit, nevertheless remained a desideratum of various ʿAbbāsid rulers. Implicit in this notion was the desire to direct all the affairs of government from a central location, at some distance from the general populace, so as to demonstrate the unity and authority of the state.

Why Did al-Manṣūr Build ar-Ruṣāfah?

The position of al-Khuld in relation to the newly developed East Side enabled the Caliph to retain some of the outward features of the administrative complex. Al-Manṣūr's change of residence and the expansion of the western suburbs was preceded by major construction on the other side of the river. When his son, al-Mahdī, now the heir apparent, returned from ar-Rayy in Shawwāl of 151/769, al-Manṣūr began to build him ar-Ruṣāfah, a palace complex, directly opposite al-Khuld on the eastern bank of the Tigris.[39] This construction, which apparently took eight years to complete, was an undertaking of great magnitude. It was surrounded by a protective wall and moat, and contained a military review ground (*maydān*) in addition to the garden areas. All the structures, with the exception of al-Mahdī's palace, were built of mud brick (*rahṣ*).[40] As was true of the Round City, the palace at ar-Ruṣāfah was situated adjoining a principal mosque; and it is said to have been even

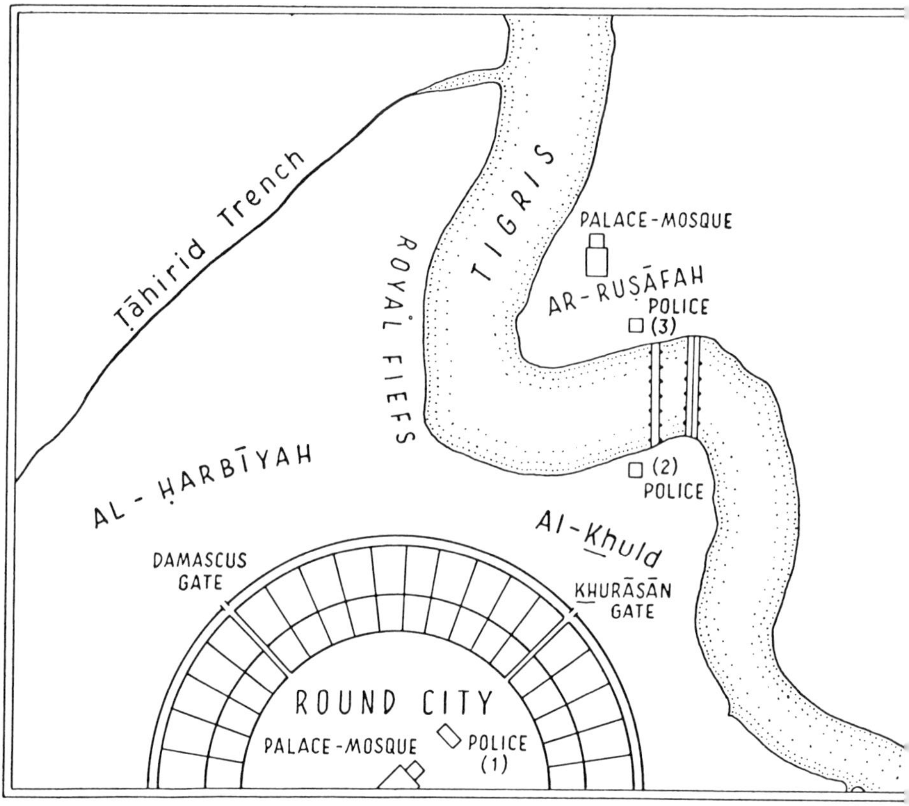

Ar-Ruṣāfah and the Upper West Side

larger and more splendid than that of al-Manṣūr.[41] Unfortunately, there is no information on ar-Ruṣāfah that is comparable to the descriptions of the Round City. It is, however, evident that the entire complex covered considerable real estate and was somewhat similar in function to the original Madīnat al-Manṣūr.

What could have prompted the Caliph to erect a palace complex much like his own on the other side of the Tigris? It is reported that ar-Ruṣāfah was originally called ʿAskar (Military Encampment of) al-Mahdī, and was so named because al-Mahdī camped (*ʿaskara*) there while journeying to ar-Rayy.[42] More persuasive, however, is the explanation of Ṭabarī,[43] who indicates that at the suggestion of Quṯham b. al-ʿAbbās, the Caliph divided his troops according to regional and tribal groupings after skillfully kindling the traditional enmity between the Muḍar and Yaman. One detachment then encamped on the East Side, the other remained on the right side of the city; so that the Caliph could now play one faction against the other. Should an insurrection break out on the left side of the river, the Caliph then would have access to military support and provisions on the opposite shore; the reverse would of course be true for the right bank. Al-Mahdī then took charge of the eastern area, settling in the palace which was built expressly for him.[44]

When al-Manṣūr later constructed his palace at al-Khuld, he connected the lower East Side with al-Karkh (west bank) by spanning the river with a pontoon bridge that subsequently became a major artery of traffic.[45] The Khaṭīb indicates that the Caliph also ordered the erection of three additional bridges: one for the women, and two others at Bab al-Bustān for his personal use and that of his household retinue.[46] Al-Jisr, the main public bridge which spanned the river at this point, was presumably erected as a result of these developments. In light of the account cited by Ṭabarī, the new Caliphal residence bisected the entire northern section of the city, and therefore was strategically situated between the major areas of military settlement. The western approach to the main public bridge was guarded by the headquarters (and men) of the Sāḥib ash-Shurṭah, while private and rapid movement across the river was easily available to the Caliph and his household. Similarly, the western extremities of his estate gave access to the suburb of al-Ḥarbīyah, the royal stables, and the administrative agencies of the Round City.[47] Although al-Manṣūr no longer enjoyed the security of an elaborate protective wall, he was still situated near the pulse of the government, at some distance from the general populace, with large and accessible security forces nearby. The Caliph's new residence may have been more vulnerable to frontal assault, but it afforded him better protection against the more subtle danger of a possible coup. In any event, he still had access to the walled fortress of the Round City, and al-Mahdī's palace at ar-Ruṣāfah.

Ṭabarī's account, which is also consistent with what is known of the organizational structure of the early ʿAbbāsid armies, is to some extent substantiated by reports on the distribution of fiefs in Baghdad. In effect, the construction of ʿAskar al-Mahdī created two distinct centers of military occupation: The northwest suburb of al-Ḥarbīyah, which was heavily populated by the Persian clients of the ʿAbbāsids, and the elaborate installations on the East Side, which continued to be a staging ground for troops in the following centuries.

This arrangement is also reflected in the social organization of the suburb, as Yaʿqūbī[48] indicates, that each regional group in al-Ḥarbīyah was governed by two distinct officials—a *qā'id* (usually an officer commanding a large body of men) and a *ra'īs*, who was presumably in charge of affairs that were not of a technical military nature. The sum effect of the system of military settlements, as well as the division of the market areas according to industry,[49] was to create certain interdependent but self-contained units which could give rise in time to quasi-autonomous organizations within the larger city structure. The advice of Qutham b. al-ʿAbbās suggests a lingering echo of the great tribal rifts which helped precipitate the downfall of the Umayyad regime. The extent to which this echo was still heard in ʿAbbāsid Baghdad, and the effect of similar self-contained settlements according to regional and industrial groups on the social organization of the city, is a subject deserving of serious attention.

While this evidence serves to indicate the reason for a military establishment on the left bank of the Tigris, it does not entirely explain the necessity for the magnificent palace architecture. What need (other than perhaps the desire to have a fortress on each side of the city) was there for al-Manṣūr to undertake the construction of a second major ediface while he was still situated in the Round City?

It is of particular importance that the account of al-Mahdī's triumphal return from the east[50] is directly followed in Ṭabarī by a second report on his status as the heir apparent.[51] It is indicated that in that same year, al-Manṣūr convened the ʿAbbāsid dignitaries in his audience hall, and had them renew pledges of allegiance (*bay'ah*) to himself, his son and heir apparent, al-Mahdī, and his nephew, 'Īsā b. Mūsā, who stood second in line for the Caliphate. Each dignitary taking the pledge is reported to have kissed the hand of al-Manṣūr and that of al-Mahdī; but they only touched the hand of 'Īsā b. Mūsā.

When as-Saffāḥ was Caliph, and al-Manṣūr the heir apparent, 'Īsā b. Mūsā was made, according to the Caliph's desire, second in line; and oaths were taken to insure this arrangement. Upon assuming the role of Caliph, al-Manṣūr recognized the position of his nephew and placed al-Mahdī behind him in the line of succession. However, fearful that 'Īsā might eventually favor his own son, and thus deprive al-Mahdī of his rightful place, al-Manṣūr became determined to remove him from his position as immediate successor. 'Īsā b. Mūsā was, however, obdurate in refusing to relinquish his position, and only did so after strong and extended coercion. Even then he was not entirely eliminated from the line of succession but only changed places with al-Mahdī, for which he received considerable financial compensation.[52] The sources describing these events tend to indicate that al-Manṣūr's difficulties with his nephew stemmed from his inability to goad 'Īsā into open rebellion. It must be assumed, however, that 'Īsā, who was governor of al-Kūfah, had sufficient support within the 'Abbāsid hierarchy to thwart the Caliph from taking immediate and open action.

Since the apparent snub of 'Īsā b. Mūsā took place in the audience-hall of the Caliph,[53] it is quite obvious that it occurred subsequent to al-Mahdī's return from Khurāsān. It is safe to assume that this was no ordinary visit on his part, for upon returning from the east, al-Mahdī was met by delegations from Syria, al-Baṣrah, al-Kūfah, and other regions. Some among these visitors were designated by the Caliph to be his son's companions. They were all honored with raiment and given gifts by al-Mahdī; the Caliph did likewise, presenting each man with a sum of 500 dirhams.

The triumphal nature of al-Mahdī's return, the renewal of the pledge and snub of 'Īsā, as well as the construction of the great palace complex at ar-Ruṣāfah, were therefore all concurrent, and apparently related events. They tend to illustrate not only the

Caliph's wish to insure the succession of his son, but more particularly, his intense desire to give that wish public expression. The construction of a second great palace on the East Side for al-Mahdī left no doubt as to the Caliph's determination in this matter, and thus authenticated the claims of his chosen successor. With the death of al-Manṣūr, al-Mahdī's palace in ar-Ruṣāfah became the official residence of the ʿAbbāsid house. ʿĪsā b. Mūsā was once again passed over, and was forced to give up his position in favor of al-Madhī's son Mūsā, the future Caliph al-Hādī. Twice spurned, he retired from the active political arena to live out his life in relative seclusion.

However, ar-Ruṣāfah failed to fully satisfy the new Caliph's needs. Towards the end of his reign al-Mahdī spent a good deal of his time at a pleasure palace in ʿĪsābādh, a place located somewhere on the East Side of the city. Al-Hādī also lived there briefly, but ar-Rashīd returned to al-Khuld where his son al-Amīn also came to reside. Al-Ma'mūn, following the great civil war, remained distant from the hostile populace, spending most of his reign away from Baghdad, and his successor al-Muʿtasim made the break completely by transferring the capital of the realm some sixty miles up the Tigris to Sāmarrā. After the Sāmarrā interlude, the Caliphs returned to Baghdad and once again set about the task of constructing a major palace complex, this time further to the south near the old Tuesday Market. Their frequent moves from place to place in an effort to create a viable administrative center had a profound effect on the growth of the city. This must be fully understood in any attempt to trace the pattern of its topographical development, and in particular the evolution of its economic infrastructure.

C

The Complexities of Growth in an Imperial Center: Massignon and the Markets of Baghdad

For more than half a century, one of the most distinguished contributors to the understanding of the Islamic city and its institutions was the late L. Massignon, whose topographical studies covered such diverse locations as Fās, al-Kūfah, al-Baṣrah, Ukhayḍir, and most relevant to the present study, Baghdad.[1] Guided largely by his experiences in cities of the Near East around the turn of the century, Massignon based his methodology from the outset on "un fait constant et général, la fixité de la reparition topographique des corps de métiers dans un cité islamique determinée à partir du moment de sa fondation." It is, of course, true that the topography of a city may be altered by given historical circumstances; but this will reflect only the changing surface of the city—its monuments rather than its geographical setting. As this position was rigidly held for *all* Islamic cities, regardless of their historical development, the picture of Baghdad, implicit in Massignon's view, is that of an integrated city covering a land surface which must, of necessity, be limited by the distance of any populated location from the services of its single set of markets; for there can be no large urban occupation in the absence of these institutions.[2]

It is this particular position which is the basis of Massignon's controversial views on Baghdad, leading him to disagree with LeStrange on such fundamental questions as the location of certain markets, the disposition of the city bridges, and supposed shift of the East Side in the eleventh century.[3] Subsequent remarks on the history of the city generally reflect this difference of opinion. Thus Herzfeld agrees with Massignon on the shift and presumably the fixity of the markets.[4] Canard favors LeStrange on the shift but Massignon on the markets,[5] and Makdisi follows LeStrange on the shift—but for reasons other than those cited by him—and Massignon on the markets with certain reservations.[6] The city plan, as rendered in the maps of Duri[7] and Aḥmad Sūsah, more or less follows the plans of LeStrange.[8]

In the absence of extensive archeological investigations, the present physical evidence is not sufficient as to allow for a decisive judgment. The proof of Massignon's theory is therefore dependent on the validity of two implicit and related assumptions: the limited size of the city and the centrality of its institutions. Neither seems relevant to the situation at Baghdad; for Massignon allowed himself to be guided by theoretical considerations against the established literary evidence, and more particularly, he apparently did not fully grasp the unique historical development of the city, its royal foundation, and subsequent growth as an imperial center. For three interlaced factors distinguish the capital of the ʿAbbāsids from most other cities of the realm: the enormous surface area, the dominant relationship to the land behind it, and the desire to separate the agencies of government from the general populace.

Baghdad was not an integrated city, that is to say, a city built around a single set of municipal institutions over a circumscribed land surface. It was a sprawling urban center of enormous size and population, consisting of smaller interdependent elements each containing to some extent its own institutions, and each the creation of specific historical circumstances related to the development of the administrative agencies of the government. The incipient decline of this great urban center can be noticed as early as the tenth century. For official purposes, the passing of the ʿAbbāsid dynasty in 1258 marks an end to the pre-eminence of their capital, although in reality it had at various moments been eclipsed by other major cities. By the time of Massignon's travels, the land surface had contracted around the old caliphal quarter of the East Side, and a truncated section of al-Karkh across the river.[9]

It is, therefore, clear that the city of Massignon's *Mission* in 1907–1908 was not the great ʿAbbāsid capital of the Middle Ages, a significant though obvious distinction which must serve as the focal point of any study on the growth of the city and the surrounding region.

Assumption I (A City of Limited Size or a Major Urban Center?)

The physical arrangement of Sāmarrā, which is partially known from excavations, is an indication of the enormous land surface that the great administrative centers of the realm came to occupy. Although Baghdad is generally known only from literary sources, there is reason to believe that the statements preserved by the Khaṭīb (d. 1071) on the dimensions of the city are, more or less, accurate thus justifying the claims of native Baghdadis that their city was more spacious than all others.[10] One account gives a figure of 53,750 *jarīb*; two others indicate 43,750 *jarīb*—the lower estimate apparently having been obtained from a survey undertaken in the time of al-Muwaffaq (ca. 890). It is significant that the figures cited in this account are not only expressed in terms of *jarīb* but in linear measurement as well. The West Side was found to be 250 *ḥabl* in length and 105 in width making for a total of 26,250 *jarīb*. The East Side was 250 *ḥabl* in length and 70 in width making for a total of 17,500 *jarīb*, and for the entire city 43,750 *jarīb*. Simple arithmetic computation reveals that the figures correspond, and one square *ḥabl* = one *jarīb*.

Since the known value of the *jarīb* is 1,592 square meters, one *ḥabl* should equal the square root of 1,592, or approximately forty meters. This figure and the entire equation is confirmed by the account of Iṣṭakhrī-Ibn Ḥawqal[11] which indicates the length of the city, as measured along the Tigris, was five *mīl*., that is to say, 10,000 meters. Accordingly, one *ḥabl* equals forty meters or 10,000 divided by 250 *ḥabl*, the figures given by the Khaṭīb for the length of the city. It does not appear likely that the scholars, who were responsible for the transmission of these accounts, would have adjusted them to make the figures consistent. The fact that the dimensions of the city, as obtained in three different accounts and according to three different metrological systems (*ḥabl*, *jarīb*, *mīl*), are in agreement may be taken as an indication of their accuracy. If one, therefore, accepts the lower estimate (43,750 *jarīb*) as being more correct, Baghdad still would have covered almost 7,000 hectares, thus making it five times larger than tenth-century Constantinople, and thirteen times the size of Ctesiphon, the great capital of the Sassanian Empire.[12]

There is, admittedly, a serious methodological question to be considered. Impressive as they are, the figures for Baghdad reflect total land surface and not the real size of the city, which is to be determined by correlating the area contained within the geographic limits with the character of occupation. The total land surface of tenth century Constantinople was only about 1,400 hectares, but these were largely circumscribed by the city walls, ordinarily indicating a higher density of occupation than one would expect in a location like Baghdad which was covered by extensive suburbs. One should, however, not be misled into thinking that all the so-called suburban areas were characterized by gardens, parks, and small holdings and were of necessity sparsely populated. To the contrary, the large southern suburb of al-Karkh, which was also the major market area of the city, became congested within the first decade of its existence, and was thus subject to extensive redevelopment, including the construction of new commercial facilities, and the widening and expansion of the major arteries of traffic.[13] Moreover, the Khaṭīb indicates that the area to the north comprising the Round City and suburb of al-Ḥarbīyah had been completely built up from the Ṣarāt Canal to Bāb at-Tibn, which marked the northern limit of the city.[14] While much of al-Ḥarbīyah had fallen into ruin by the eleventh century, Yaʿqūbī (ca. 891) could still report that there was not a larger or more important section in Baghdad, and that it contained markets and streets equal to any in the city.[15] Although it seems that this statement refers specifically to the suburb of Ḥarb (= al-Ḥarbīyah), and not the entire NW quarter which came to be known by that name, the description of the general area leaves no doubt that other sections of al-Ḥarbīyah were similarly inhabited with splendid streets and markets.

West of the Round City, between the Kūfah and Damascus Gates, were a series of smaller quarters bounded by the Anbār Gate Road.[16] The last of these was a place known as the Kabsh wa-l-Asad, which was at one time considered the western limit of the city (Madīnat al-Manṣūr).[17] The Khaṭīb recalls having passed through that location and having come across a village of the type in which farmers and woodcutters dwell. Upon a subsequent visit, he found it to be a sown field some distance from the city without any trace of human habitation. However, Bishr b. ʿAlī, an authority who lived two generations earlier, used to pass through the Kabsh wa-l-Asad with his father, and remembers being unable to free himself of the surging crowd in the markets.[18] It appears that aside from the royal holdings on the narrow strip along this Tigris only the quarters leading to al-Muḥawwal were sparsely populated, as they, unlike the above mentioned areas, are characterized by various domains with almost no mention of commercial enterprises.[19]

It is, therefore, understandable that when the city was extended to the left bank of the Tigris, various building regulations were put into effect to restrict construction in the exclusive new sections and thus avoid the congestion that was said to be characteristic of the areas across the river.[20] The general impression given by the literary sources therefore serves to indicate that the West Side, which comprised some 60 per cent of the total land surface of Baghdad (4,000+ hectares), was well populated. The left bank, though somewhat more spacious at the outset, must have also grown in population as the administrative agencies of the government were moved—first to ar-Ruṣāfah and then to the Dār al-Khilāfah further downstream. Nevertheless, the tenth-century geographers still report that the West Side was the more populous of the two. The physical and human resources of Baghdad were indeed vast by any standard of measurement.[21]

To what extent the human resources can be expressed in real figures is another matter. Some local histories contain chapters dealing with the statistics of the city.[22] While there is no hint of any census, various crude efforts were attempted to calculate the population, usually by the use of multipliers based on such factors as the consumption of foodstuffs, men of specialized occupations, and the number of houses and baths. Such isolated statistics as the number of licensed doctors (860) reported in Ibn Abī Uṣaybiʿah[23] might prove of some value; but the figures generally cited, although consistently high, are quite unreliable, and give rise to population estimates ranging from 1.5 million (based on bathhouses)[24] to 96 million (based on the number of residences).[25] The latter total is by the author's admission a modest one, as his scholarly nature prevented him from indulging in the exaggerated speculations of the uninformed. There is apparently no way of giving such statistical data more tangible expression. But does it seem unreasonable that if the land surface of fifth century Constantinople (about 700 hectares) supported a population which according to most recent and extremely conservative estimates was about 150,000, then Baghdad, considering the nature of its suburbs and the fact that it was ten times that size, could have supported a population twice that if not more? Accepting the lower estimates, the density of occupation in Constantinople was approximately 200 per hectare. Even if one were to divide this by five (a most conservative assumption which is not necessarily warranted), then the total population of Baghdad still would have reached 280,000. A figure twice that does not seem altogether impossible.[26]

The Land behind the Imperial Center

Is it really conceivable that Near Eastern cities of such staggering dimensions existed in the Middle Ages? Given the enormous size of Baghdad and later Sāmarrā, the growth of the imperial center unlike all other cities presupposes the existence of truly vast human and physical resources, and raises the question as to how such an urban complex managed to sustain itself. Where did the populace come from and how were they fed? Since the character of a city is defined not only by its own physiognomy but by that of the surrounding areas, the tremendous development of Baghdad is inextricably tied to that of its regional environment, and to the extent that the city was the center of ʿAbbāsid rule, to the condition of the empire as a whole.

The recent study by R. M. Adams[27] on the hinterland of Baghdad indicates that the trend toward the creation of great urban centers in Iraq is already observable in pre-Islamic times although it was only the later period that provided the necessary context for the remarkable growth of the Islamic capitals. Based on archeological surveys undertaken by the University of Chicago in 1936–1937 and then again after the war, almost nine hundred sites were registered for the area of the lower Diyala Plains in an attempt to retrace the previous pattern of occupation. As the surveys were confined largely to surface reconnaissance, chronological indicators were generally limited to ceramic materials; and although the typology tends to break down in Sassanian, and more particularly Islamic times, the general outlines of occupation seem abundantly clear even though some doubts may persist on the applicability of modern data with regard to basic patterns of agricultural subsistence and the density of population.

Using various criteria arbitrarily chosen to distinguish the different types of settlement, the figures below indicate increasing urban development under the Sassanids.

Settlements	
Cities:	over 100 hectares
Small urban centers:	over 30 hectares
Large towns:	over 10 hectares
Towns:	over 4 hectares
Village or hamlet:	less than 4 hectares

Seleucid–Parthian (based on Adams, p. 62)	
Total:	199 recorded sites, aggregating
Approximately:	1500 ha. of settlement including:
Cities:	4 (430 ha.)
Small urban centers:	5 (255 ha.)
Large towns:	24 (345 ha.)
Towns:	50 (285 ha.)
Villages:	116 (172 ha.)

Sassanian (based on Adams, p. 72)

Total:	437 recorded sites, aggregating
Approximately:	3,500 ha. of built up area including:
Cities:	9 (1834 ha.)
Small urban centers:	4 (188 ha.)
Large towns:	35 (600 ha.)
Towns:	59 (356 ha.)
Villages:	308 (439 ha.)
Non-residential:	22 sites (72 ha.)

There was therefore under the Sassanids an increase of some 130 per cent in the total area of settlement and presumably a substantial increase in population as well as the areas under cultivation. On the basis of the figures cited above, there are indications that all the irrigable lands of the region (8,000 square kilometers) were under cultivation in Sassanian times as compared with possibly 4,500 square kilometers for the preceding period.[28] Aside from a seeming decline in small urban centers (actually the result of the changing status of certain sites), there is a general if uneven increase in all types of settlement with regard to both the number of sites and the average area which they comprise. Cities are up 125 per cent, large towns 50 per cent, towns 20 per cent, and significantly, villages 160 per cent.

Settlement	*Number of Sites*		*Increase*	*Average Area of Settlement*	
	P	S		P	S
Cities:	4	9	+125%	110 ha.	205 ha.
Small urban centers:	5	4	−20%	51 ha.	47 ha.
Large towns:	24	35	+50%	14.3 ha.	17.1 ha.
Towns:	50	59	+20%	5.7 ha.	6.0 ha.
Villages:	116	308	+160%	1.5 ha.	1.4 ha.

	Parthian Sites (continuing into or re-occupied during the S Period—at times with different classification of settlement)	*Sassanian Sites* (newly founded—based on Adams, p. 72)
Cities:	6	3 (4: one unlocated but known)
Small urban centers:	2	2
Large towns:	19	16 (22: six additional known)
Towns:	18	41
Villages:	62	246

The growth of Sassanian settlement which appears striking is even more substantial than the figures indicate. A more realistic appraisal is possible when one takes into consideration the general decline that was presumably characteristic of the later Parthian period, and the extent to which the Sassanids founded new sites. Although the total increase in the number of towns for the later period is 20 per cent (50–59), 70 per cent of these were new foundations; moreover, only 20 per cent of the villages and hamlets survived from the previous period.[29] The larger towns and small urban centers appear to be somewhat more stable as greater numbers of Parthian sites continue to be inhabited. As is true of the towns and villages, the increase or decrease in the average area of settlement is modest. It is in the cities that the most pronounced changes can be observed, and most particularly in the imperial center of Ctesiphon. These include, in addition to the existing Parthian cities, all of which survived in the later period save one, two large towns and one small urban center grown in size and now reclassified, and four new cities founded by the Sassanids.

Whereas Parthian cities occupied 28.5 per cent of the total settled area (430 hectares) those of Sassanian times represent 52 per cent of the total settlement (1,834 hectares) when all the irrigable lands of the region, some 8,000 square kilometers, were under cultivation. On the other hand, the Sassanian town, that is to say the smaller unit of urban occupation, included only 33 per cent of all settlement in contrast with 59 per cent of the earlier period, apparently showing that the increased urbanization was accomplished at the expense of the towns and small urban centers rather than by concentrating the dispersed rural population in the newly founded cities.[30] The average area comprised by these settlements excluding Ctesiphon is 162 hectares, a marked increase over the average of 110 hectares (including Ctesiphon) that characterized the Parthian city. This is explained primarily by the most striking development of the imperial center which grew to perhaps five times its previous size. Ctesiphon itself may have been larger by 25 per cent than the entire urban settlement of the previous period.

Conclusion: The change of rule from the Parthians to the Sassanians resulted in a marked change of the pattern of occupation. The disruption was most severely felt in the smaller units of occupation: the villages and towns. With the strengthening of Sassanian authority there was a large increase in the total area of settlement with regard to all types of sites. There must have been a concurrent increase in population and the lands under cultivation. The increase was most pronounced in the cities. Ctesiphon in particular seems to have grown to several times its previous size thus dominating the entire area of the Diyala Plains and distinguishing itself from the other urban settlements of the region.

The Islamic Occupation

Although well situated geographically, the enormous growth of Ctesiphon seems explicable only as a consequence of wider considerations derived from its status as the capital of the Sassanid realm. At a later time, in the very same region, much larger Islamic cities serving as the capitals of a vast empire would dominate the lands of the Diyala Plains to an even greater extent. Even without Baghdad and Sāmarrā, Islamic cities represent 33 per cent of the total settled area; the capitals in turn were seven times the total including the other cities, and four times larger than the combined area of settlement under the Sassanids. Since apparently only five to six thousand square kilometers were then under cultivation, in contrast with eight thousand square kilometers for the preceding period (234 villages in contrast to 308),[31] the tremendous growth of the Islamic cities—described by the study as the greatest degree of urbanization prior to modern times—was not concomitant with the greatest intensity of land usage but was seemingly a sequel to a decline in provincial settlement.

It would be difficult to explain this situation as arising entirely from a major transfer of the indigenous population from the town and rural areas; for the breakdown of Sassanid rule, unlike that of the Parthians before them, was marked by a corresponding decline in *all* types of sites, with the urban areas the most severely disturbed.

Almost 60 per cent of the settlement was abandoned or partly abandoned during or some time after the Sassanian period regardless of classification. Cities are reduced approximately 78 per cent, small urban centers 25 per cent, large towns 70 per cent, and the remaining settlements 67 per cent. Most of these sites were never resettled.

As during the time of the early Sassanian period, the Islamic conquest led eventually to the founding of many new sites although the full recovery of the region was only possible with the restoration of political and economic power at the newly built ʿAbbāsid capital: Baghdad. The manner in which the city was constructed—ex nihilo by imported labor—also suggests that the source for the rapidly growing population of the urban areas was not primarily a movement from village to city but the colonization of non-indigenous elements originally consisting of artisans, laborers, military personnel, and the like who with their families soon became a permanent feature of the urban scene. This is most clearly reflected by the toponymy of Baghdad as pictured in the literary sources.[32] There is no doubt that the geographical center of a newly created empire of such dimensions should have stimulated a movement of people and wealth from the various outlying provinces. The resurgence of the Diyala Plains must in part reflect such an increase in population, and more particularly such a redistribution of political and economic power.

Considering only non-Islamic foundations in an attempt to measure the decline, 149 recorded sites aggregate a total of approximately 2,000 hectares of built up area.

Late Sassanian (?)–Early Islamic (based on Adams, p. 72)

	Maximum S occupation	*Ab. or partly ab.*	*Approx. % abandoned*
Sites:	437	288	65%
Cities:	9	7	78%
Small urban centers:	4	1	25%
Large towns:	35	24	70%
Others:	367	256	67%

Newly-founded Islamic sites

Cities (incl. cap.):	3	(14,000 ha.)
Small urban centers:	3	(146 ha.)
Large towns:	8	(126 ha.)
Towns:	37	(213 ha.)
Villages:	160	(264 ha.)

The combined Islamic total: 331 recorded sites aggregating approximately 16,000 hectares of built up area including:

Sites

Imperial centers:	2	(14,000 ha.)
Cities:	4	(730 ha.)
Small urban centers:	6	(265 ha.)
Large towns:	57	(337 ha.)
Villages:	234	(367 ha.)

A comparative picture of the relationship of the imperial center with its surrounding areas is depicted in the tables below, and comprises the Parthian, Sassanian, and early Islamic periods. The cities are distinguished from the capitals which are listed as imperial centers.

Sites and average area of occupation

	Parthian		Sassanian		Islamic	
Imperial centers:	0		1	(540 ha.)	2	(7,000 ha.)
Cities:	4	(110 ha.)	8	(162 ha.)	4	(182 ha.)
Small urban centers:	5	(51 ha.)	4	(47 ha.)	6	(44 ha.)
Large towns:	24	(14 ha.)	35	(17 ha.)	28	(14 ha.)
Towns:	50	(6 ha.)	59	(6 ha.)	57	(6 ha.)
Villages:	116	(1.5 ha.)	308	(1.5 ha.)	234	(1.5 ha.)

Conclusion: The total buildup of the Islamic period exclusive of the imperial centers was greater than that of the Parthian period, but also markedly less than that of Sassanian times. However, with the inclusion of Baghdad the Islamic buildup was more than 2.5 times that of the previous period, and with the addition of Sāmarrā four times the combined settlement. The extensive development of the ʿAbbāsid capitals was obviously unprecedented in the historical growth of the region, and must have been stimulated by the injection of human and physical resources from beyond the Diyala Plains.

The extent to which the Islamic conquest and in particular the ʿAbbāsid victory changed the occupational pattern of the Diyala Plains is most revealing. Though the chronological indicators are not sufficiently refined to distinguish between pre- and post-ʿAbbāsid sites for the first two centuries, one would have to assume on the basis of general historical evidence that the intensive Islamic occupation did not begin until the building of Baghdad in 145/762. The urban development of Iraq in the earlier periods was controlled by the needs of the Arab conquests consequently giving rise to the garrison cities (*amṣār*) of al-Kūfah and al-Baṣrah. As the administrative centers of an empire whose focal point was in the Ḥijāz, and later under the Umayyads in Syria, the strategic situation of the *amṣār* on the periphery of the desert and along the Euphrates was ideal. However, when the orientation of the Umayyads later shifted eastward, Wāsiṭ was founded along the Tigris—its strategic importance apparently conceived in terms of the position between the rebellious cities of the *amṣār*. Wāsiṭ thus became the center from which strong regional governors exerted Umayyad influence in southern Iraq.

There is no indication from literary evidence that Ctesiphon and the surrounding settlement of the Diyala Plains achieved any such significant commercial and political importance in pre-ʿAbbāsid times. This impression is partially conveyed by the Chicago survey; and the general conditions described continued until the founding of al-Manṣūr's capital. Thus, for the first time since the fourth century B.C., there was not a city of major significance in this area. The urban and indeed general decline of the Diyala Plains was presumably caused in part by the breakdown in centralized authority resulting from the impending and then actual collapse of Sassanian rule. However, the restoration of authority in Islamic times did not immediately result in the full economic and political recovery of the region because the dominance of Ctesiphon was conditioned by its position as the administrative center of an empire. It was only with the emergence of the ʿAbbāsids and the construction of Baghdad that the Diyala Plains were restored as the hinterland of an imperial center. Unlike their predecessors who looked south and west, first to al-Madīnah and then to

Damascus for political orientation, the ʿAbbāsids sweeping to power from the wealthy eastern provinces founded their rule on the integration of those disparate elements which composed the great empires of Persia and Byzantium before them. Baghdad at the center of this geographical configuration was understandably the logical place to promote such imperial ambitions.

With the enormous and rapid growth of the city, the resultant physiognomy of the Diyala Plains took on the characteristics of a highly caricatured dwarf—a massive urban head surmounting a truncated rural body in a ratio of approximately 7:2. What circumstances could have allowed such a creature to prosper, and with the emergence of Sāmarrā half a century later, even to grow a second head? It is perhaps misleading in this context to speak of a head and a body, for the Islamic imperial center was not conceived to be nourished by its immediate surroundings. The unique development of Baghdad and later Sāmarrā was not the only result of increased trade, commerce, and regional growth. They were like the great Sassanid capitals before them, but even more so instruments for the consolidation of imperial power, and were in this sense artificial cities whose growth was not determined entirely by regional considerations but by the fortunes of the great empire which sustained them. The vitality of the city was a reflex of the general condition of that empire. The progressive dissolution of the ʿAbbāsid Caliphate is thus reflected in the decline of its capital city—not only relative to the physical monuments but to the commercial and artisanal institutions as well. For the decline of the city, like that of the empire, was not merely concomitant with a loss of physical space; it was characterized by a marked disruption of a delicately balanced pattern of existence from which neither could recover. It was only when the power emanating from Baghdad became limited to the Diyala Plains that the characteristics of the city took on the features of the dwarf mentioned above, bringing about first a state of paralysis and then an eventual reduction in the size of the head. When Massignon came to visit Baghdad he did not see the commercial and political hub of a dynasty, "the navel of the universe"; he saw what would have been in earlier times, and what was then, only a provincial city.

Assumption II (Centralized Institutions or Sectional Development?)

It becomes apparent that the images conveyed by the conventional terms for suburb (*rabaḍ*) and city (*madīnah*) have little relevance to the situation of medieval Baghdad where, for example, Madīnat al-Manṣūr the Round City was a palace-complex and where Rabaḍ al-Karkh the southern suburb was essentially a sprawling series of markets. What historical circumstances could have given rise to this undefined urban agglomeration which served as the center of ʿAbbāsid rule; and why does the pattern of its development resist classification within the prevailing conceptual framework advanced by Massignon and others? Or, to restate the question—what is it that distinguishes the city from almost all others of the Islamic realm; for the tremendous growth of Baghdad cannot be explained simply as characteristic of the increasing mercantile urban orientation of Islam. Quite obviously, it is the role played by this city as the administrative capital of the ʿAbbāsid caliphs.

The Historical Growth of an Administrative Capital

The original Round City of al-Manṣūr was not a city in the conventional sense. It was rather an enormous palace-complex combining the residence of the Caliph with the administrative agencies of government. From the moment that one crossed the moat and entered the first of a series of intricate gateways one was made to feel as if this was the personal domain of the sovereign. The architectural features of the walled area, and in particular the green dome of al-Manṣūr's palace, reflected the imperial style of the Caliph and served as a visual symbol of the unity and authority of the state.[33] As the Round City was the heart of a vast empire, it alone was equal in land surface to a full grown city (453 hectares) though not in character of occupation. That is to say, it was originally a city without markets; for the relationship of such a city to its general surroundings is delicately balanced by factors of security and supply. An administrative center must function at some distance from the general populace—a potential source of subversion—but always close enough to be provided with basic services. It therefore comes as no surprise that al-Manṣūr's city was built adjacent to but distinct from the market areas of al-Karkh. However, the Karkh markets of pre-ʿAbbāsid times, important as they may have been, were conceived to supply the surrounding villages and domains. The very construction of the Round City brought thousands of laborers and troops into the general vicinity from the outlying regions of the empire.[34] This conglomeration and the subsequent movement of people to the city soon became part of the fixed population of the area, creating a strain on the established market facilities. So that almost within a decade of its construction it became necessary for the government to invest its own resources in the construction of new markets and wider thoroughfares.

In addition to these basic services, a city such as Baghdad requires the presence of large military forces. Unlike the smaller capitals in the outlying districts where the garrison in times of relative peace is entrusted largely with regional security, the military resources of the administrative center are instruments for the expansion as well as the consolidation of imperial power. These include the reserves which may be sent to any corner of the empire as the exigency of the time requires. Such serves to explain the complex differentiation of military personnel that is found at Baghdad and presumably the larger regional centers of the realm. In addition to the regular army, there was the personal army of the caliph, the various divisions of the security forces, the police, and the paramilitary troops of the city garrison.[35]

As the regular army required installations, the area north of the Round City comprising the suburb of al-Ḥarbīyah was populated originally by various military colonies organized according to regional and tribal groups: each under the command of a general (*qāʾid*) and a functionary (*raʾīs*) who was presumably in charge of affairs which were not of a strict military nature.[36] In time, the new areas of occupation also would have need of basic services; and since they were situated some distance from the markets south of the Round City, it became necessary to establish a second set of markets, perhaps not as large or as comprehensive as that of al-Karkh where the intricate network of canals made for excellent commercial logistics but impressive by most standards as was previously observed.[37] It is clear that the construction of these new markets would have brought numerous merchants and artisans into areas hitherto reserved for military occupation thus disrupting once again the traditional balance of the administrative center. Squeezed by an emerging city on both sides of his palace, al-Manṣūr for reasons of security abandoned the walled city which continued to house various administrative agencies, and built himself a new residence (al-Khuld) along the shore of the Tigris. The new Caliphal residence did not signal an end to the notion of the palace-complex, but was rather an attempt to modify the concept of an administrative center within the difficulties that the Caliph faced. Political as well as strategic considerations had already compelled him to undertake the construction of a second palace-complex and military camp (ʿAskar al-Mahdī or ar-Ruṣāfah as it came to be called) on the unoccupied left bank. The new Caliphal residence bisected the entire northern section of the city. Although al-Manṣūr no longer enjoyed the security of an elaborate protective wall, he was still situated near the pulse of the government, at some distance from the general populace with large and accessible security forces nearby, in al-Ḥarbīyah, and across the river. Following his death, al-Mahdī, the heir apparent, formally moved the government to ar-Ruṣāfah thus attempting to restore the equilibrium of the administrative center.

Aside from the development of the new palace area, the transfer of the government was marked by significant changes in the topography of the city. At the head of the newly constructed bridge which linked East and West Baghdad, was the palace of Khuzaymah b. Khāzim, the prefect of police. From this place which protected the approaches to the East Side, the sources describe various fiefs, some of which al-Manṣūr had granted at the outset of construction. The list includes not only important general and government officials but various members of the royal household, all no doubt anxious to derive the necessary if obvious political advantage of residing close to the Caliph and the government.[38] As a result of building regulations which restricted the type of construction in the new areas,[39] the development of the left bank was by no means limited to the circumscribed vicinity of ar-Ruṣāfah but extended over a much wider surface, as various palaces were also built south and east of the Main Bridge in the vast quarter which came to be known as al-Mukharrim. The Caliphs al-Ma'mūn and al-Mu'taṣim were to reside there in later times, and the sections extending south from the Main Bridge to the Tuesday Market (Sūq ath-Thalāthā') and the Lower Bridge became noted for the fashionable riverside palaces of important government officials, many of which had marinas giving access to the river.[40]

The sections of the lower part of al-Mukharrim were, in turn, supplied by the ancient Tuesday Market which connected to the West Side and al-Karkh via the Lower Bridge. This market derived its name from the monthly fair that was held there in pre-Islamic times on Tuesdays for the people of Kalwādhā and East Baghdad, just as the market of a similar name in al-Karkh serviced the west bank of the river.

Unlike the site of the Round City which was chosen for its advantageous location near the market of al-Karkh, and the tenth-century Caliphal complex, the Dār al-Khilafāh which came to lie adjacent to Sūq ath-Thalāthā', the situation of ar-Ruṣāfah was determined primarily by its strategic position opposite the upper West Side, thereby creating two major problems: the lack of water and the need of services in the absence of a major market area nearby. As the absence of either would have seriously compromised the function of the administrative center, al-Mahdī extended feeder channels from the outskirts of the city via the Khāliṣ Canal, the last of which emptied into a spring on the grounds of his palace.[41] In order to supply the growing population of the upper East Side—the section which came to be called Bāb aṭ-Ṭāq after the principle monument of that name—he also ordered Sa'īd al-Ḥarrashī to construct a market, subsequently known as the Sūq al-'Aṭash, somewhat inland in the general vicinity of the Main Bridge. Every conceivable industrial and commercial enterprise was then transferred there so that it was likened to al-Karkh the great market area of the west bank. This comparison serves to indicate that the Sūq al-'Aṭash was nothing less than a major commercial center for the populace of Bāb aṭ-Ṭāq, thereby duplicating the commercial and industrial services across the river.[42]

When the center of ʿAbbāsid rule was reestablished at Baghdad following the Sāmarrā interlude, the Caliphs chose a spot directly south of the Tuesday Market to build yet another palace-complex, the vast Dār al-Khilāfah. Once again, the administration of the empire was situated adjacent to established market facilities. It remained there until the fall of the dynasty, and this general area was all that was left of the Eastern city in modern times. In addition, various markets of a more limited nature, presumably distributive outlets and often expressed by the diminutive (*suwayqah*), were interspersed at various places. Yaʿqūbī could therefore claim that every location had its own mercantile settlement.[43]

The Tuesday Market and Bāb aṭ-Ṭāq

It is clear that the position of Bāb aṭ-Ṭāq and its markets is crucial to the general problem of the commercial organization of Baghdad; for there can be no provision for a second distinct market area within Massignon's conception of the city. It may be argued (though not convincingly, I think) that the markets of al-Ḥarbīyah were simply large distributive outlets; but Bāb aṭ-Ṭāq was clearly a major market area containing every conceivable commercial and industrial enterprise. In addition to the general comments of Yaʿqūbī on the Sūq al-ʿAṭash, there is a full description of that quarter by one of its residents, Abū-l-Wafā' b. ʿAqīl, a young contemporary of the Khaṭīb.[44] He indicates, with considerable pride, the various locations of his native quarter and lists among them many distinct commercial and artisanal establishments, including the moneylenders and goldsmiths, markets normally found in the center of a major business section. For Massignon, this section must be in the SE quarter of Baghdad someplace near Sūq ath-Thalāthā' and opposite the markets of al-Karkh across the river, thereby preserving the centrality of the commercial institutions. He must, therefore, argue against the view of LeStrange (which is founded on numerous literary references) that Bāb aṭ-Ṭāq is situated near the Main Bridge opposite the Round City and is, in effect, the market area of the upper East Side.[45]

To make his contention more convincing, Massignon cites several accounts from the Khaṭīb on the disposition of the city bridges.[46] Accordingly, there were three bridges spanning the Tigris: one opposite Sūq ath-Thalāthā', another at Bāb aṭ-Ṭāq, and a third in the northernmost part of the city near the Dār al-Mu'izzīyah (= ash-Shammāsīyah). Later, the northernmost bridge was dismantled and moved to Bāb aṭ-Ṭāq forming a double structure. In 383/993, a new bridge was erected at the Wharf of the Cotton Merchants (connecting al-Karkh with the lower East Side); however, this structure fell into disrepair so that the only remaining link between the two cities was the bridge at Bāb aṭ-Ṭāq, which was moved in 448/1056 and erected between the Wharf of the Water Jars (*Mashra'at ar-Rawāyā*) on the West Side and the Wood Cutters Wharf (*Ḥaṭṭabīn*) on the East Side. As the Wharf of the Water Jars was in Modern Times fixed in the SW section of the city, its corresponding dock across the river must have been situated to the SE somewhat *below* Sūq ath-Thalāthā'. Bāb aṭ-Ṭāq according to Massignon was therefore situated in the SE section of the city.

Implicit in this argument is the assumption that the moorings connecting Bāb aṭ-Ṭāq to the West Side were in the same general vicinity following the transfer of the bridge in 1056. However, this impression is not conveyed by the Arabic text. To the contrary, once the bridge was moved it was no longer at Bāb aṭ-Ṭāq but much further downstream. The new position of the single major artery connecting both cities in the eleventh century was not required because the markets were all situated to the south, or because the quarters of the upper East Side had fallen into total ruin. Even if these quarters had lost some of their splendor, it is clear from the continuous reference to various locations situated there that the upper East Side was still very much in evidence.[47] It is also the probable decline of the upper (and later to some extent the lower) West Side which made the Bāb aṭ-Ṭāq bridge obsolescent, as the palaces lining the left bank of the Tigris were demolished to provide building materials for the new construction across the river, i.e.,

Ṭughril's city, and later the expansion of the Dār al-Khilāfah by the Caliph al-Qā'im.[48]

That Bāb aṭ-Ṭāq was north of Sūq ath-Thalāthā' is clear; for the order of the three bridges listed by the Khaṭīb is presumably an indication of their geographic position. Accordingly, Abū ʿAlī b. Shādhān[49] (his authority) saw a bridge at Sūq ath-Thalāthā', another at Bāb aṭ-Ṭāq (further north), and a third in the uppermost part of the city. When the nothernmost bridge was dismantled and moved to Bāb aṭ-Ṭāq, it moved to the next mooring downstream. If the Bāb aṭ-Ṭāq bridge was south of Sūq ath-Thalāthā', it would have been necessary to dismantle the latter as well in order to place the obsolescent Shammāsīyah bridge in its position—a situation that is not impossible but seemingly odd.

However, the centrality of the markets would also have been preserved if Bāb aṭ-Ṭāq was situated slightly to the north of Sūq ath-Thalāthā'. It is necessary to show that they were, in fact, distinct areas of activity, geographically removed from one another. The account of Ibn ʿAqīl, which was unknown to Massignon when he first studied the topography of Baghdad, clearly places Bāb aṭ-Ṭāq in the vicinity of ar-Ruṣāfah. While there is some discussion as to whether that palace precinct was situated across the river from al-Ḥarbīyah or opposite the Round City as Duri maintains,[50] there is no doubt that it was located some distance upstream from the SE markets. This topographical picture is confirmed by an account reported in Ibn al-Jawzī:[51] Some forty years after the death of the Caliph al-Qādir (423/1032) it was decided to rebury his remains in the Royal Cemetery at ar-Ruṣāfah. His coffin was subsequently removed from the Caliphal palace area (near Sūq ath-Thalāthā'), placed on a skiff, and transported upstream to Bāb aṭ-Ṭāq, where it was unloaded at the wharf and carried by bearers to the waiting mausoleum. As the text does not specifically state that the mausoleum was nearby (as seems certain), it is possible to argue that the coffin was carried north for a considerable distance, from Bāb aṭ-Ṭāq which was situated just above Sūq ath-Thalāthā' along the major thoroughfare leading to ar-Ruṣāfah—a road frequently used for state processions. However, if such was the case, why was it necessary to initially transport the coffin by skiff? Why didn't the procession start from the Caliphal palaces, the area in which such spectacles normally began or were ended?[52] Is it because Bāb aṭ-Ṭāq was situated far upstream in the general vicinity of ar-Ruṣāfah where, in fact, the procession on foot actually began? This impression is supported by a second account describing a similar event of earlier times.[53] The order of the procession was: Sūq ath-Thalāthā' to al-Mukharrim, to Bāb aṭ-Ṭāq (presumably the specific location and not the general quarter) and then to Sūq Yaḥyā (near the Main Bridge in the general quarter), from where it crossed the Tigris to al-Ḥarbīyah, i.e., the upper West Side. Bāb aṭ-Ṭāq and Sūq ath-Thalāthā' were distinct areas, each containing its own commercial institutions.

Conclusions

The decline of the Caliphate resulted in a major readjustment of the topography of the city. This was not, as LeStrange apparently assumed, the quick disappearance of entire suburbs but rather the truncation of those areas surrounding the markets and mosques; for the decay of a city does not begin with the essential institutions, but with the spacious aristocratic neighborhoods. The palace construction of Sultans and Caliphs in the late eleventh century was more than offset by the complete destruction of exclusive residential areas on both sides of the city. It is, therefore, not the total land surface of Baghdad that was initially altered, but the character of occupation.[54]

By the end of the eleventh century, frequent mention is made of various quarters which were appropriately described as *kharabāt* "ruins." Thus Yāqūt observed that al-Ḥarbīyah was in his time some distance from the city with its own markets, principal mosque and even an enclosure wall giving it the appearance of a separate city.[55] In the course of time, these too would disappear, with the city contracting around the old Caliphal quarter, and a truncated section of al-Karkh across the river. For Cahen,[56] the emergence of the *kharabāt* marked an end to a unified city which was progressively replaced, after the beginning of the eleventh century, by groups of semi-autonomous quarters, separated by fields of ruins or empty lands or gardens. This explains for him, the duplication, indeed the multiplication of certain markets and principal mosques. This picture is only partially true; for the growth of separate institutions in the *kharabāt* was not entirely the result of a declining city as Cahen assumed, but also the result of suburban development in an emerging city. The widespread markets of Baghdad go back to the earliest period, as the commercial institutions of al-Ḥarbīyah where created in the lifetime of al-Manṣūr, the founder of the city to meet the pressing needs of a rapidly growing population. Similarly, the markets of the upper East Side were developed by his successor al-Mahdī. The pattern of growth was determined by the character of the city as the administrative center of the realm.

Appendix A

Municipal Entities and Mosques

It is clear to us that Baghdad was not so much a city but a city of cities. However, did this notion also find expression among Baghdadis in the Middle Ages?

The preserved fragment of Ibn Ṭayfūr's *History of Baghdad*[1] contains a story concerning the ʿAbbāsid notable Abū Dulaf, who resided in the city during the reign of al-Ma'mūn. He is reported to have taken a slave girl from there, but was unable to find complete contentment as he yearned to live in al-Karkh, the area generally regarded as the southern suburb of the city. The prospective change of residence, however, proved unpopular with the distaff side (no small wonder—Hishām al-Kalbī noted that al-Karkh was infested with the lowest rabble).[2] Baghdad, she said, is my native place (*waṭanī*), and then proceeded to give eloquent expression to her inner feelings by describing her detest for al-Karkh in no uncertain terms, and in verse no less. There is no indication in the text as to what followed; but although our sympathies are with Abū Dulaf, we are given the uneasy feeling that the matter was resolved in favor of his slave girl and for Baghdad vis-à-vis al-Karkh.

Since it is difficult, if not improper, to discuss (let alone understand) the motivation of women, we are left to worry about a second possible problem which is raised by this seemingly innocuous text. What is meant in this context by the expression: Baghdad is my native place (*Baghdād waṭanī*), and how does one distinguish between al-Karkh and Baghdad. If the term *waṭan* refers simply to a particular section of the city, then the expression would be somewhat more clear; for in the following century altercations were known to have taken place between the people of al-Karkh and those of the Baṣrah Gate—a reflection not only of the social and religious conflict between Shīʿites (al-Karkh) and Sunnites (Baṣrah Gate), but of particular pride in one's native quarter as well.[3] However, the words of Abū Dulaf's slave girl seem to imply a good deal more; it is not one quarter of the city vis-à-vis another, but Baghdad itself as opposed to al-Karkh, as if to indicate that al-Karkh is not simply a suburb among many in the city, but a distinct municipal entity which is to be equated with Baghdad itself. And if a suburban area presumed to be part of the city can be a municipal entity, then what in fact is meant by Baghdad?

Municipal Entities

No less distinguished an authority than the jurist Aḥmad b. Ḥanbal is credited with a statement which has a direct bearing on this very problem. As reported by the Khaṭīb:[4] Baghdad (according to Ibn Ḥanbal) comprises everything from the Ṣarāt Canal to Bāb at-Tibn. By way of clarification the Khaṭīb adds: Aḥmad in that statement meant Madīnat al-Manṣūr (the Round City) and what is adjacent to it, since the upper part of the city is the Fief of Umm Jaʿfar (=az-Zubaydīyah) below which is the trench canal (Khandaq Ṭāhir) that divides this fief from the construction that is part of the city (*proper*). Similarly, the lower part of the city, consisting of al-Karkh and what is adjacent to it, is separated from the city (*proper*) by the Ṣarāt Canal.[5]

If I understand this passage correctly, and if the Khaṭīb accurately reflects the meaning of Ibn Ḥanbal's statement, it would seem that a distinction is to be drawn between a city proper and various suburbs. The city proper would then consist of the old Round City (the superstructure was still intact in the lifetime of Ibn Ḥanbal),[6] the suburbs to the north (principally al-Ḥarbīyah) and those directly to the south until the Ṣarāt Canal. The suburbs not covered by Ibn Ḥanbal's statement are the Fief of Umm Jaʿfar (which must have been relatively small) and the southern suburb of al-Karkh which comprised the land between the Ṣarāt, its northern boundary and Nahr ʿĪsā, the southern boundary. The suburbs west of al-Karkh and south of the Ṣarāt are also not part of Ibn Ḥanbal's city. They were, in fact, areas which more accurately convey the impression of real suburbs, i.e. gardens, parks, estates, etc., and not commercial establishments. There is no mention of the East Side which presumably was a separate city for administrative purposes. The impression is thus conveyed that the great capital of the ʿAbbāsid Caliphs was not a unified city, but a complex municipal structure. There was above all the greater urban center, which came to be known as Baghdad, but within that enormous sprawling complex of some 7,000 square hectares—the largest by far in the medieval Near East—there were other municipal components, each retaining a specific identity of its own.[7] It is therefore pertinent to ask what are the characteristic features of these smaller areas in relation to the larger urban organization.

A philological excursus of the various terms which in this text describe specific geographic locations fails to shed light on this question. The terms *rabaḍ* "suburb" and *qaṭī'ah* "fief" are not sufficiently defined as to allow for a precise meaning in this context. The Rabaḍ of al-Karkh was apparently a city unto itself; the term used elsewhere may signify nothing more than an estate. The fief of Umm Ja'far was a suburb of Baghdad, but a qaṭī'ah could imply state grants of all kinds. Similar difficulties can be encountered for a wide range of other topographical terms including the words for town (*balad*) and city (*madīnah*); for how can one speak of Madīnat al-Manṣūr or Madīnat b. Hubayrah for that matter in relation to the madīnah of a remote site like Qaṣr al-Ḥayr ash-Sharqī, where the term found on an inscription perhaps signifies a technical meaning which has become lost in time.[8]

Yet although the words for town and city are rather vague as topographical expressions, the character of an urban center is more or less defined by legal usage, and it is this ideal picture which will help explain the structure of Baghdad and its suburban environment. A Muslim may pray any place, but on Friday he should seek the association of other Muslims and listen to the khuṭbah at mosque designated *masjid al-jāmi'* or principal-mosque. Such mosques are permitted only at larger centers of human occupation, i.e., cities and towns. In fact the existence of a principal-mosque and judicial authority (*qāḍī*) go as a rule together and belong to the criteria which distinquish a city or town from a village (*qaryah*). In the tenth century some smaller localities sought to acquire the status of town or city by establishing these very institutions. The number of principal mosques in any given location was generally limited by law and more particularly in practice to a single structure. However, according to the Ḥanafī school there may be more than one mosque for no particular reason, but Caliphal permission is required. The Shāfi'īs require a valid reason for a second mosque as well as Caliphal permission, thereby indicating that the presence of a second masjid was not overly common.[9] The city of Wāsiṭ, for example, was considered exceptional as it had two such major buildings, one for each side of the Tigris; but this was necessary as the river bisected the city thereby creating two distinct areas.

The Mosques of Baghdad

Note that the Khaṭīb who describes the mosques of Baghdad in detail witnessed Friday prayers at no less than six locations:[10] the Round City, ar-Ruṣāfah, the Caliphal complex, Barāthā, the Fief of Umm Ja'far, and al-Ḥarbīyah. Of these, only the mosque at Barāthā falls technically outside the limits of the city indicated by Aḥmad b. Ḥanbal as it was situated beyond the Ṭāhirid Trench, the western boundary of Baghdad. Although the Khaṭīb considers it one of the mosques of Baghdad, he does not refer to it as a mosque of the city (*masjid al-madīnah*) but rather as a mosque of the vicinity—perhaps in recognition of this fact. In any event, there were no less than six mosques in the general area of the city, of which five were in use concurrently in the tenth century. Considering that there were also three concurrent judicial authorities:[11] one for the upper East Side (ar-Ruṣāfah), a second for the Dār al-Khilāfah, and a third for al-Karkh, one is led to believe that we may see here further indications of separate municipal entities within the larger urban complex. That such separate quarters could have existed in Saljūq times when vast areas of the city fell into disuse is not too difficult to explain; but the creation of additional mosques and judicial authorities was an earlier development, thereby suggesting that the complex municipal structure described in the statement of the Khaṭīb was characteristic of the city two centuries before. The decentralization of the city's economic structure, which I have described in detail elsewhere, was therefore paralleled by a similar trend in other institutions.

This multiplicity of markets, mosques, and cemeteries was necessary because of the extremely large surface area of the city, and the pattern of its growth which was governed in each case by the presence of a palace-precinct consisting of the Caliphal residence and the administrative agencies of the government. A principal-mosque and adjacent market facilities were essential features of this type of urban setting. As the city and its markets encroached upon the palace-precinct, the Caliphs—their security increasingly compromised—felt constrained to move elsewhere in the general vicinity thus duplicating the entire urban setting first at ar-Ruṣāfah (776) and then a century later in the SE section of the city. The general areas abandoned by the Caliph nevertheless continued to prosper. In addition there was the principle-mosque of al-Karkh which al-Manṣūr, the founder of the city, built for the people of that market suburb who were hitherto forced to recite their prayers at his palace. It was erected at a place known as ash-Sharqīyah which was originally chosen to be the palace-precinct of his son and heir-apparent, al-Mahdī. The qāḍī appointed to administer the area was subsequently called the Qāḍī of ash-Sharqīyah, and later the Qāḍī of al-Karkh. In any event, although the Caliph never resided there, the southern suburb (by far largest in the city) had both a principal-mosque and a judicial authority and may thus be considered a municipal entity unto itself. Sometime in the ninth century the Sharqīyah mosque lost its status as *masjid al-jāmiʿ*; however, in light of the Khaṭīb's comment and the continued presence of a qāḍī, it is not unlikely that al-Karkh in some way retained its municipal identity.

When Iṣṭakhrī described conditions of the first half of the tenth century, he reported the existence of three principal-mosques: at Madīnat al-Manṣūr, ar-Ruṣāfah, and the Dār al-Khilāfah.[12] The Khaṭīb confirms this picture but adds that matters changed beginning with the reign of al-Muttaqī.[13] Over a period of the next fifty years new mosques were added at Barāthā,[14] the Fief of Umm Jaʿfar, and even al-Ḥarbīyah which was according to Ibn Ḥanbal and the Khaṭīb part of the city *proper.* What circumstances could have allowed for the creation of these new mosques, and how do they fit into the total picture of the urban setting? 1) Barāthā as it was technically outside the limits of the city, was entitled to a *masjid al-jāmiʿ*, and in fact did have such a building until the reign of al-Muqtadir when it was destroyed as the Shīʿites who frequented the place carried out seditious activities there. However, the structure was rebuilt in the reign of ar-Rāḍī, and al-Muttaqī restored it to the status of principal-mosque by erecting an unused *minbar* from Madināt al-Manṣūr, and appointing (later on a permanent basis) the imām of the Ruṣāfah mosque to conduct prayers there. The Friday services were begun in 329/941 amidst great activity. 2) At the Fief of Umm Jaʿfar there had been a mosque which was not used for Friday prayers. In Dhū-l-Ḥijjah 379/990 a woman of the East Side dreamt that she saw the Prophet at this mosque. He told her that she would die the following day at the time of the *ʿaṣr* prayer, and then placed his palm against the qiblah wall. Upon awakening, she went to the mosque and discovered the imprint of a palm. As the woman died fortuitously at the designated time, the mosque was repaired and enlarged, and petitions were sent to the Caliph aṭ-Ṭāʾiʿ to establish it as a *masjid al jāmiʿ*. It should be noted, however, that it was not the convenient miracle which was the legal basis; the request was rather based on the assertion that the mosque was situated beyond the (Ṭāhirid) Trench which divides it from the town (*balad*), thus making the area in which the mosque was situated a town in its own right. The Caliph granted his permission. The historicity of the woman's dream and her timely demise is not really an issue; it is significant, however, that this account is a confirmation of the Khaṭīb's statement that the Fief of Umm Jaʿfar was a separate municipal entity because below it was the Ṭāhirid Trench which divides the fief from the buildings of the city proper. 3) But what of the mosque at al-Ḥarbīyah which was, following Ibn Ḥanbal and the Khaṭīb, part of the city itself. Was this too an indication of a municipal entity, and if so—how? During the reign of al-Muṭīʿ, a structure was built in that quarter to serve as mosque for Friday prayers, but the Caliph prohibited this. The matter stood this way until al-Qādir asked the jurists for an opinion. Since they agreed that it was necessary to conduct prayers there, the Caliph ordered that the mosque be repaired and furnished, and appointed an imām. This took place in 993.

Yāqūt,[15] writing some two centuries later, notes that in his time al-Ḥarbīyah was confined to the area of Bāb Ḥarb some two *mīl* distant from the city, giving the appearance of a separate town with markets of all kinds, a Friday mosque, and an enclosure wall. He was thus describing one of these truncated sections of the city which were characterized as *kharabāt*, i.e., populated quarters which were originally connected to other sections of the city by a continuous line of occupation, but which had in the course of time become separate from one another as a result of the general decline. It may be noted that the first request for a Friday mosque was viewed unfavorably by the Caliph; indeed al-Ḥarbīyah had been part of the city proper. Can it be that the decision which later permitted the construction of the mosque was based on the increasing isolation of that place resulting from a presumed decline in the area between Bāb Ḥarb and the remaining structures of the Round City? Al-Ḥarbīyah would therefore have become de facto a municipal entity unto itself.

Considering the growth of the Caliphal palaces, the administrative agencies, and the city's economic institutions, all of which have been described elsewhere in detail, the existence of distinct municipal entities within the larger urban setting is still further indication that the topographical development of the ʿAbbāsid capital was different from almost all other cities. It causes one to wonder whether such statements that describe the Islamic city in general terms should also pay particular attention to the significant differences between the larger urban centers of the realm. Studies should perhaps be directed not only in terms of "the Islamic city" but more correctly "Islamic cities."

Appendix B

The Development of the Suburbs and the Economic Policies of the Early ʿAbbāsids

Aside from the very important topographical changes resulting from the development of the suburbs, the manner in which the building program was carried out by the early ʿAbbāsid Caliphs seems to suggest highly sophisticated if not new ideas on the use of state capital. This led ultimately to the direct involvement of the government in such commercial and industrial enterprises, as is reflected in the account of the Khaṭīb concerning the Caliph al-Mahdī and a visiting Byzantine ambassador.[1]

In response to some flattering words, the Caliph promised the ambassador his heart's desire. The Byzantine later indicated to the Wazīr, al-Faḍl b. ar-Rabīʿ, that he would like to develop a commercial establishment at the junction of the Lesser and Greater Ṣarāt, and asked for a loan of 500,000 dirhams, a sum equal to the expected yearly income. The matter was brought to the attention of the Caliph who instructed that he be given twice that sum for development, and that he retain the yearly income subsequent to the completion of the project, a series of great mills which became known as the Mills of the Patrikios. Upon the death of the ambassador, the mills were annexed to the property of the Caliph. This particular account is not only an exemplar of the Caliph's generosity, presumably the intention of the author in presenting the account, but also indicates his ability to determine a good investment; for in time the mills which were situated at the confluence of the Lesser and Greater Ṣarāt, yielded an income of one million dirhams.

The sources speak less favorably of his predecessor al-Manṣūr, whose reputation for parsimony earned him the patronymic "Father of the

Dāniqs" (the *dāniq* being a weight equal to only 1/16 of a dirham). However, there is yet another dimension to the picture of the Caliph's frugality, one which reveals his more sophisticated methods of raising revenues. The great development of the suburbs in 157/774 was financed by the Caliph's personal funds according to a plan which he had himself conceived.[2] Accordingly, the various types (*aṣnāf*) of establishments were assigned specific places of the Caliph's choosing, presumably in the general area already occupied by the major commercial and industrial enterprises. There was, no doubt, some dislocation stemming in part from the demolition of those buildings which projected onto the major roadways that were intended for widening, thereby facilitating the traffic of men and commodities in and out of the rapidly growing city.

This picture of the Caliph's personal generosity in this building activity seems, at first glance, incongruous with other accounts portraying him as doleing out salaries in small coins and cutting down on expenditures for various government projects. However, it becomes somewhat less difficult to understand al-Manṣūr's actions if one assumes that the Caliph's primary interest here is not in expenditures but in revenues. His decision to develop these areas beyond the walls of the original city can hardly be regarded as a spontaneous act of largesse, for previous to this apparently no special taxes were levied on the market properties; however, subsequent to the development of al-Karkh, a special tax (*ghallah* and *ujrah*) was fixed, reportedly according to the size of the establishment. Given the boom conditions in this rapidly growing imperial center, the demand to participate in this program was very great. Consequently, the government's program was unable to provide sufficient facilities for all the expanding commercial interests. In such cases, various entrepreneurs financed the development of their own establishments; but significantly, since no capital outlay was provided for them by the state, they were given preferential treatment in the tax structure.[3] The government was thus providing direct incentives to increase commerce and industrial production in an effort to supply the needs of a growing city and at the same time raise an additional and continuous source of revenue for the state. For the original investment would presumably be returned many times over from the tax receipts. Other reports indicate that it was not until the reign of al-Mahdī that taxes were levied on the market areas. However, this may refer specifically to certain markets of the East Side which were not fully developed until the transfer of the government to ar-Ruṣāfah, the palace area built expressly for him, and/or conceivably a change in the tax structure.

Perhaps favoring this second interpretation is the report that al-Mahdī's tax program was undertaken on the advice of his wazīr, Muʿāwiyah b. ʿUbaydallāh b. Yāsar, an expert in such matters who had previously reformed the fiscal structure of the Sawād by basing the tax formula on a percentage of the yield (*muqāsamah*) rather than a fixed sum (*misāḥah*), although the latter system was not entirely abandoned. In theory the net effect was to make the tax structure more flexible, allowing for a maximum of revenue while minimizing the distress of the agriculturists. For excessive taxation accompanied by agricultural decline will, in the long run, result in a decline in revenues as well as serious social dislocation. Could Ibn Yāsar have instituted similar reforms to protect the entrepreneurs, while at the same time providing the state with a steady source of revenue? Such general measures would not have been an innovation, for a liberal tax program was already in existence during the reign of al-Manṣūr, who gave preferential treatment to industrious merchants and artisans whose building ventures were not covered by government funds. It is indicated that taxes were collected according to the size of the establishment (*taqdīr adh-dhirā*ʿ). However, in another source, he is reported to have assessed them *ʿalā qadri-ṣ-ṣināʿah*[4]—apparently relative to the wealth of the craft. If this last expression does not confuse the two methods, it would seem to indicate that the fixed levy (size of establishment) was supplemented (or replaced?) by a second assessment geared to the income of the more lucrative enterprises. In such fashion the burden of taxation would theoretically have fallen on those more able to sustain it. A silk merchant dealing in expensive wares operating from a relatively small establishment was quite clearly a better source of revenue than, say, a large producer of household pottery. In principle this seems to have a rationale similar to reforms in agricultural taxation, causing one to speculate that the new tax attributed to al-Manṣūr in an incidental statement of a very late source was in fact an innovation of al-Mahdī, thereby reconciling the two accounts. The method of collecting this tax is not stated, but one suspects the levy was placed on merchandise and collected in currency. With the limited means of mass production in the Middle Ages, the great fortunes were still to be made in long distance trade and real estate.

Supervision of the program was entrusted to one Saʿīd al-Ḥarrashī; and according to Yaʿqūbī (ca. 891) the income from the property tax on the markets amounted to 12,000,000 dirhams annually, of which 1,000,000 were realized from the operation of the great Mills of the Patrikios.[5] Unfortunately there is no further breakdown on taxes paid out by individual enterprises. Given the possibility of such revenues, it is not surprising that the state would have had an interest in promoting artisanal and commercial enterprises—a policy which explains perhaps the inevitable rise of the bourgeoisie within the administration of the ʿAbbāsid government,[6] as merchants at a later time entered the highest government circles, and officials of the state actively indulged in various commercial ventures. As for the second half of the eighth century, the personal position of the early ʿAbbāsid Caliphs in developing the market areas most likely gave impetus to the individual initiative of lesser government officials, all presumably anxious to establish for themselves a continuous source of revenue. It is also perhaps no accident that the Ḥanifite law was prevalent at Baghdad and that the Ḥanifīs were the most flexible in their approach to commercial matters.[7]

Short of direct participation in commerce and crafts, and in addition to the fixed salary of government service, what possibilities were opened to them shortly after the expansion of the markets? Given the limited space for construction in the market areas of the highly congested West Side, the rapid commercial and industrial development of the city and the resulting dislocation is likely to have created heavy speculation in real estate based on rising land values. This was apparently the case during the construction of Sāmarrā, an imperial city whose growth in many respects was comparable to Baghdad's. That is to say, there was a feverish building program of enormous magnitude, and a rapidly growing population thus creating critical needs for services, supplies, and living space. Moreover, the propensity of the Caliphs to periodically shift their residences and the administrative agencies of the government caused the beaurocracy to move along with them. It is therefore interesting to note what happens to the properties of the Wazīr, ar-Rabīʿ b. Yūnus when he abandoned his estates on the right bank to take up residence across the river when al-Mahdī moved the Caliphal palace to ar-Ruṣāfah. Upon moving to ar-Ruṣāfah, his fiefs in the general area of al-Karkh were converted into markets from which he presumably realized a healthy source of income.[8] It is a reasonable assumption that this procedure was followed by the other government functionaries moving across the Tigris. They would, therefore, have been able to establish residences in the fashionable new sections of the East Side, while at the same time retaining financially attractive holdings in the older quarters—particularly in al-Karkh.

Moreover, it is curious that many of the suburban fiefs are designated by the term *sūq*, and often the diminutive *suwayqah*. The term *sūq*, "market," is self-explanatory; the *suwayqah* is a small market dealing in foodstuffs and other basic services, which was required in those districts that were situated at some distance from the main commercial centers, i.e., residential areas. Since these terms are clearly defined,[9] the particular suburban places designated by them cannot have been large residential estates. It is possible that these markets were granted outright as fiefs, but one wonders whether the frequent mention of *sūq* and *suwayqah* is evidence that various assignees who received large residential estates before the tremendous expansion of the city converted parts of the residential area into commercial property in order to obtain an added source of revenue when land became very dear.

An example of land utilization of this sort is preserved by Yāqūt in his entry on al-ʿAbbāsīyah, the island between the Lesser and Greater Ṣarāt.[10] After some devious dealing, al-ʿAbbās b. Muḥammad, the ʿAbbāsid notable, managed to have al-Manṣūr grant him this open space, previously used to manufacture bricks for the construction of the Round City. Al-ʿAbbās obtained the right to collect taxes on the property. He had the land cultivated (no doubt to raise the value of the taxes) and sent the rental income to Egypt, presumably in connection with another business scheme.

Were these actions innovations that may be described by that elusive phrase "the ʿAbbāsid revolution," or were they merely a continuation of policies already established in Ummayad times? Were these actions limited to the great capital, or were they also repeated in the smaller provincial towns and cities?

Appendix C

The Architectural Development of al-Manṣūr's Mosque

At the direct center of the Capital, which al-Manṣūr built at Baghdād, were the Caliphal residence and the principal-mosque. Constructed on the analogy of the Umayyad government palaces of al-Kūfah and Wāsiṭ, the palace-mosque complex originally consisted of a residential area 400 cubits square connecting to an adjoining mosque of similar shape one quarter its size.[1] The subsequent history of the mosque is discussed by the Khaṭīb in his topographical introduction to the *Tarīkh Baghdād*, where he indicates that the structure underwent four stages of development:

1. The original building of al-Manṣūr (c. 149/766).[2]
2. The mosque rebuilt and enlarged by ar-Rashīd (192/808–193/808–809).[3]
3. The area of prayer increased by use of the Dār al-Qaṭṭān (c. 260/873–874 or 261/874–875).[4]
4. The construction of a second court by al-Muʿtaḍid (280/893–894) with the addition of the *msqṭt* known as al-Badrīyah.[5]

Since no excavations were undertaken on the presumed site of the Round City, both Herzfeld[6] and Creswell[7] attempted to retrace the architectural development of the mosque according to the respective stages outlined by the Khaṭīb. The literary evidence, however, admits of theoretical possibilities other than those of Herzfeld and Creswell which seem to be more consistent with the intended meaning of the Arabic text. The present remarks are therefore an attempt to offer some divergent views on the changing mosque of the Round City.

Although situated in the center of the Caliph's personal domain, the principal mosque of al-Manṣūr was built to service the entire population of the area surrounding the Round City.[8] The palace-mosque continued to function after al-Manṣūr abandoned his residence for a new edifice (al-Khuld) situated along the Tigris shore somewhat east of the Khurāsān Gate.[9] However, the increasing growth of the city's suburbs made it necessary to establish principal mosques at other locations, i.e., the SW section of al-Karkh and at al-Mahdī's camp in ar-Ruṣāfah on the East Side.[10] By the reign of ar-Rashīd, the Caliph was apparently again confronted with the problem of limited space in the court of the central mosque. In order to relieve the congestion, he demolished (*hdm* and *ndq*) the existing structure, and rebuilt it more solidly over an enlarged area from burnt brick cemented with gypsum.[11] This construction, later referred to as the old court (*ṣaḥn al-ʿatīq*), was begun in 192/808 and was completed the following year, 193/808–809.

No dimensions are given for the old court, but since it is clearly indicated that the mosque was rebuilt over an enlarged area, it is obvious that the structure exceeded the original 200 cubits square. The plans of Herzfeld and Creswell (200 × 200 cubits)[12] must therefore be emended accordingly, as they are apparently based on the description of the original mosque built by al-Manṣūr, and not the ninth-century reconstruction of his grandson, for which several conjectural plans may be suggested:

Enlargement of Length

The simplest method to enlarge the mosque would have been to retain the original structure while piercing the end wall facing the Khurāsān Gate,[13] thereby extending the area for prayer in the length. The text is, however, explicit in stating that the building was demolished, indicating that the walls were razed and rebuilt from the foundations up. It is, of course, possible that the new walls were, for the sake of economy, built directly on the old foundations, in which case the enlargement would have followed the lines suggested above. However, there was no compelling economic reason to retain the original foundations which were laid fifty years earlier. It is difficult to believe that a free-spending reign which is generally regarded as the zenith of ʿAbbāsid splendor should have necessarily compromised in the construction of so major an edifice; for if the construction of a principal mosque was an important event in the history of a city, then the erection of a Caliphal mosque was no less than a momentous occasion, commemorated in this case by an inscription on the wall facing the Khurāsān Gate bearing the date, the name of the Caliph, the architect, the carpenter, and the order of construction. It is more likely that ar-Rashīd intended to create an entirely new structure which could be identified by posterity with the authority and greatness of his reign. The substitution of burnt brick and gypsum for the previous building materials which were more porous and less durable tends to support this view. Since it is then possible that there were new foundations (even if the older foundations were used, it still would have been necessary to extend new foundations to allow for an increase in the area), there is also the possibility that the basic symmetry of the palace-mosque, i.e., a square, was altered as well, so as to give the structure a new and distinctive appearance.

Any increase in the area of ar-Rashīd's mosque is theoretically limited by the later construction of the Caliph al-Mu'tadid, who in 280/893–894 pierced the front wall, which was also the end wall of the palace, and again enlarged the area by adding a second court of approximately the same dimensions (as the first mosque) from the palace structure. If one can assume that al-Muʿtaḍid's court extended as far as the front wall of the palace (approximately 400 cubits wall to wall), it is possible to conclude that ar-Rashīd doubled the size of al-Manṣūr's mosque by extending a second section of similar dimensions along the original axis.[14] However, the ultimate result is then a very long (800 cubits) and narrow (200 cubits) mosque with a symmetry that compromises the careful sense of proportion. Conversely, any attempt to balance the symmetry necessarily limits the area of enlargement since the structures of al-Muʿtaḍid and ar-Rashīd must be of nearly equal dimensions. It therefore seems clear that any increase in length alone is theoretically less than an ideal solution to the problem of enlarging the area of prayer.

Enlargement of Width

The Khaṭīb indicates al-Manṣūr's mosque was enlarged according to its side, giving the impression that the reconstruction may have provided for an extension in the width of the original area.[15] By adding sections 100 × 200 cubits to flank the original area, the Caliph could have doubled the existing dimensions by creating a rectangular structure 200 × 400 cubits.[16] The resulting ratio of length to width is then 1 : 2 for the mosque, and 3 : 2 for the entire structure. Following the addition of al-Muʿtaḍid's court, the basic shape of the mosque would then be altered to a square (400 × 400 cubits), so that the area of prayer was now doubled on two occasions without seeming to compromise the traditional symmetry of the Islamic architecture from this period, while at the same time creating a structure with a new and distinctive appearance.

Although theoretically possible, there are also certain objections to a reconstruction which provides for a rectangular building 200 × 400 cubits. While the great mosques of the early ʿAbbāsid period were built in the shape of rectangles or squares, there is no indication of a structure that was originally conceived as a principal mosque, whose width exceeded its length (2:1). It may be suggested that since the mosque was only a reconstruction of an earlier edifice, ar-Rashīd's architect could have taken certain liberties with the layout of the structure, thereby explaining the peculiar shape. This argument is not convincing, for as previously indicated it was completely rebuilt and redesigned out of functional considerations and presumably the Caliph's desire to perpetuate the glory of his reign. Since the construction of so great a building was most assuredly the product of consummate planning and execution, a mosque of these dimensions (200 × 400) does not seem acceptable. It therefore becomes difficult to argue for an enlargement in the width alone, since given the original square (200 × 200 cubits), such a reconstruction must always result in a rectangle whose width exceeds its length in direct proportion to the area of enlargement.

This contention is supported by additional evidence from the text of the Khaṭīb.[17] In order to connect his court with ar-Rashīd's mosque, the Caliph al-Muʿtaḍid is reported to have pierced the adjoining wall of the palace-mosque creating seventeen aisles, of which four were for the side *riwāq*s, with the remaining thirteen opening directly unto the court (*ṣaḥn*). There is no indication as to the number of horizontal aisles in the sanctuary, but Creswell[18] (following Herzfeld) suggests five based on the analogy of the mosque of Ibn Ṭūlūn and the great mosque at al-Kūfah. To these examples one can add the mosque of Abū Dulaf,[19] the mosque at ar-Rāfiqah,[20] and the palace-mosque constructed by al-Ḥajjāj b. Yūsuf at Wāsiṭ which was analogous to the original structure at Baghdad.[21] From this general observation, one may conclude that the ratio 5:17 was apparently popular in both the square and rectangular mosques of this region.[22]

Since the aisles within each of these mosques were generally of equal width, the side *riwāq*s cut into the vertical area of the court (*ṣaḥn*) by approximately 23 per cent (4:17). If one also includes the end *rīwāq* facing the *miḥrāb* wall, the covered sanctuary of a square mosque cuts into the horizontal area of the court by approximately 41 per cent (7:17). The rectangular mosque can provide a greater court area, but only if the sanctuary is situated along a *miḥrāb* wall whose length is exceeded by the side walls of the structure, thereby ruling out a mosque 200 × 400 cubits. Furthermore, consider applying the ratio 5:17 to a mosque of those dimensions.[23] Sixteen columns are required to provide for seventeen aisles; each side *riwāq* therefore comprised eight columns since the length of the suggested mosque was half its width (200 × 400). Similarly five columns are necessary for the five aisles of the sanctuary, plus two additional columns for the *riwāq* of the far wall, on the analogy of the side *riwāqs*. The horizontal area of the court is then reduced to only $12\frac{1}{2}$ per cent, a figure which is obviously very difficult.

Enlargement by Width and Length

It therefore becomes abundantly clear that ar-Rashīd's best course for enlarging the mosque was to allow for an increase in *both* width and length, which would provide for either a square, or a rectangle of an acceptable ratio—presumably 2:1 or 3:2. Since the theoretical possibilities are limited by the size of the adjoining palace, (400 × 400) the most acceptable rectangle would be 375 × 250 cubits, that is to say, an enlargement of 25 cubits for each side, and 175 cubits in the length, resulting in a ratio of 3:2.[24] The number of acceptable squares is, of course, considerably greater. To arrive at a reasonable choice, one must keep in mind two factors: 1) Since the Round City was still a self-contained unit, ar-Rashīd may have desired to preserve the basic symmetry of the palace-mosque (square adjoining smaller square) while providing for the greatest increase in the area of prayer. 2) The seventeen openings connecting the old court to al-Muʿtaḍid's construction had to cut through an adjoining wall that was possibly five cubits thick. Maximum width would have to be provided for entry, but with enough space between each opening so as to supply sufficient strength for the vaulting.

The rectangular structure (375 × 250), though it provides the greatest area for the court, alters the basic symmetry of the palace-mosque; and after the addition of al-Muʿtaḍid's court, the ratio of length to width would have to be extended 3:1 (750 × 250). Moreover, each vault with supporting sides is only fourteen cubits wide (250–10 for the end walls ÷17 for the arches). Allowing eight cubits for the span of the vault and six for support, it would seem that there is not much passage, once the supporting sides are taken into account. However, a square structure of, let us say, 300 × 300 cubits not only preserves the basic symmetery of the entire edifice, but perhaps allows for more plausible width (10 cubits) and flanking support (7 cubits). While the rectangular mosque is still a possibility, the square building would then seem to offer a more acceptable alternative, although such an argument can hardly be called convincing.

The Dār al-Qaṭṭān and al-Badrīyah

But what of the Dār al-Qaṭṭān and the *msqṭt* known as al-Badrīyah?[25] The Khaṭīb indicates that the Dār al-Qaṭṭān originally housed a government agency (*dīwān*) in the time of al-Manṣūr; but that it was connected to the old court in 260/873–874 or 261/874–875, and thus became a place of prayer (*muṣallā*).

Herzfeld attempts to identify the Dār al-Qaṭṭān with al-Badrīyah but does not elaborate. According to him, the Dār al-Qaṭṭān was a section extending from the south wall of the mosque which he connected to the south wall of the palace. He therefore assumed that the wall between the Dār al-Qaṭṭān and the original mosque was pierced, and that the *minbar*, *miḥrāb*, and *maqṣūrah* were transferred there in keeping with the orientation of the building. This is, however, contrary to the text of the K̲h̲aṭīb which seems to indicate that they were moved to the new mosque. Furthermore, it is reported that ar-Ras̲h̲īd's inscription commemorating the construction of the old court was visible on the outer wall of the mosque on the side of the K̲h̲urāsān Gate, i.e., the north wall. For these reasons, I am inclined to agree with Creswell's reasoning[26] that the mosque was situated along the north wall of the palace, with the Caliph entering directly from his residential precincts into the place of the *maqṣūrah* as was the custom at this time. When the court of al-Mu'taḍid was added to the existing mosque, the *minbar*, *miḥrāb*, and *maqṣūrah* were subsequently moved to the newer section. The Dār al-Qaṭṭān therefore connected to the mosque on the north side of the palace, but there is no indication of how the two buildings were joined.[27] When the K̲h̲aṭīb reports that al-Mu'taḍid added the second mosque because lack of room compelled the populace to pray (*on Fridays*)[28] in places where it is not permissible, he means, according to Creswell, the Dār al-Qaṭṭān. If one follows Creswell, it is clear that the building did not become part of the mosque itself, since it was technically designated as a *muṣallā*, i.e., a place where one may generally pray, but where it is not permissible or at best not recommended to say the Friday prayers. I am inclined to think that the two structures were perhaps connected by some sort of gallery which permitted the overflow crowd to pass from the principal mosque to the secondary place of worship. It is not inconceivable that at a certain point the crowds became so large the great central court itself housed worshipers, as is the case in Jerusalem.

The dimensions of the Dār al-Qaṭṭān are also not reported, but it is safe to assume that the building was smaller than the mosque to which it connected. It is probable that the Dār al-Qaṭṭān was situated quite near the mosque in the central court. Ya'qūbī's description of the Round City, which dates from the reign of al-Manṣūr, reports that there were only two buildings in this central court other than the palace and mosque:[29] One adjacent to the Damascus Gate housed the chief of the guard (*ḥaras*); the other, the location of which is not indicated, was a large portico (*saqīfah*) raised on columns of burnt brick cemented with gypsum. The portico contained the apartment of the chief of police (*s̲h̲urṭah*), and presumably rooms for his men. The building was probably intended for those men who were actually on duty. The remainder of the contingent was, no doubt, quartered in those streets designated for the police and the guards, which were situated in the residential area flanking the arcades of the Baṣrah Gate. The portico of the police, like the Dār al-Qaṭṭān, was, therefore, a government building. What is more, Ya'qūbī, who wrote in the latter part of the ninth century, indicates that in his time this portico was used as a place of prayer (*muṣallā*),[30] thereby suggesting that it may be identified with the Dār al-Qaṭṭān mentioned by the Khaṭīb. The structure of a portico (surrounding a court) would have been ideally suited for conversion into a place of prayer.

As for al-Badrīyah, the *msqṭt* added by Badr, the page of al-Mu'taḍid, I can find no meaning for the term *msqṭt*. However, whatever they may have been, it is clear they were sufficiently impressive to be named after the page of the Caliph. I am left with the impression that they were some kind of ornament rather than a series of chambers.

Appendix D

LeStrange's Maps

These six maps are from G. LeStrange, *Baghdad During the Abbasid Caliphate*, London, 1900. His Map II is not included, and Map VII faces Map III. LeStrange used a different system of transliteration from mine.

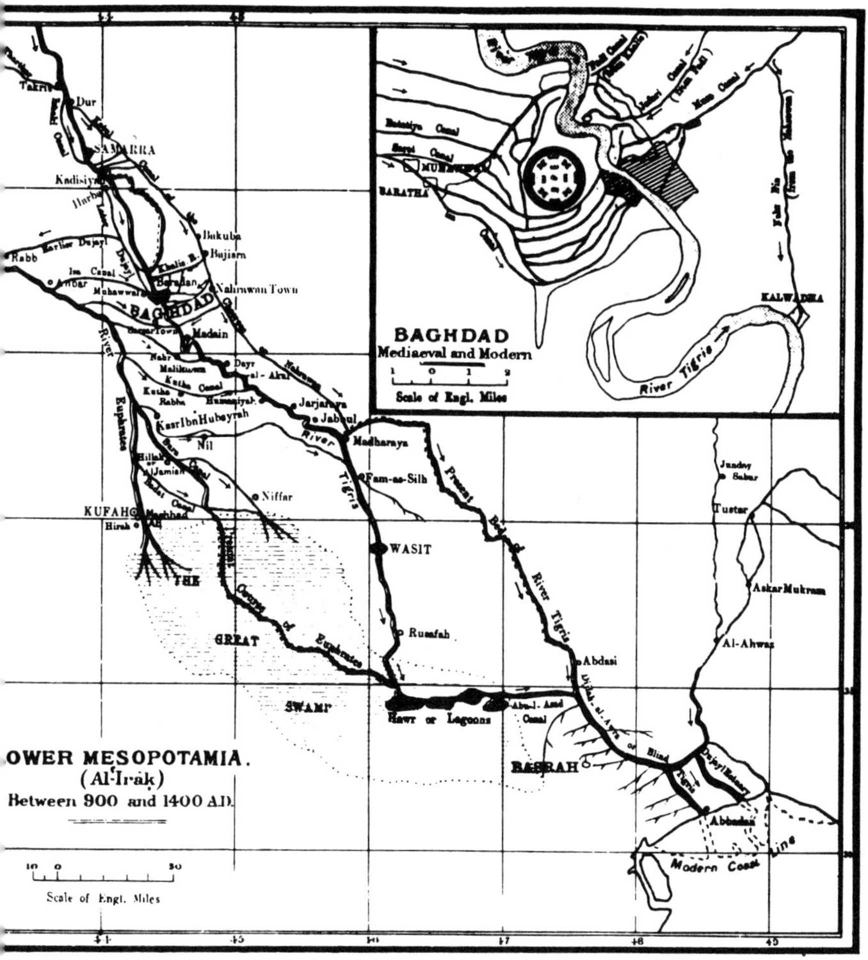

I.

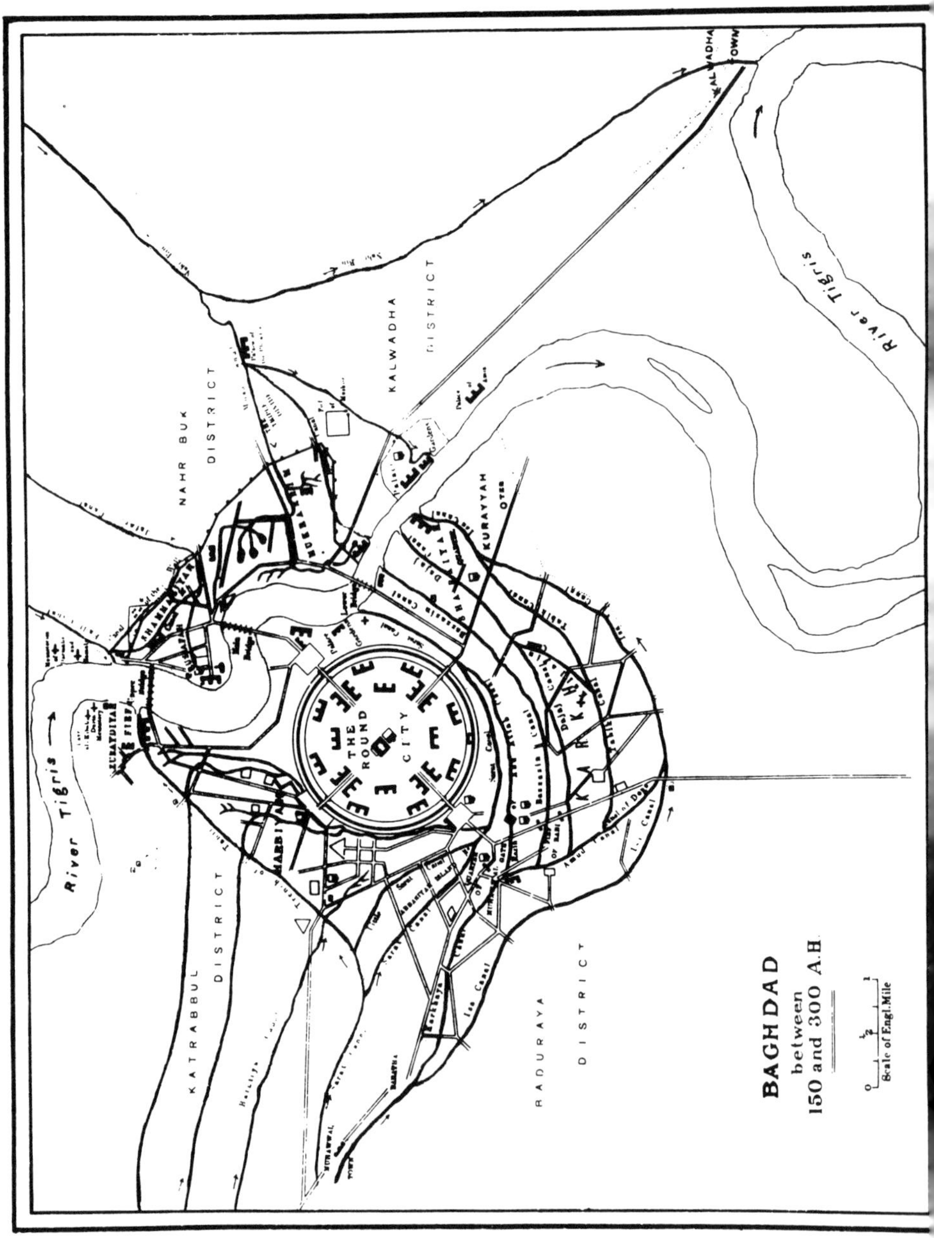
BAGHDAD
between
150 and 300 A.H.
Scale of Engl. Mile
THE ROUND CITY
River Tigris
River Tigris
NAHR BUK DISTRICT
KALWADHA DISTRICT
KATRABBUL DISTRICT
BADURAYA DISTRICT
KALWADHA TOWN
KURAYYAH

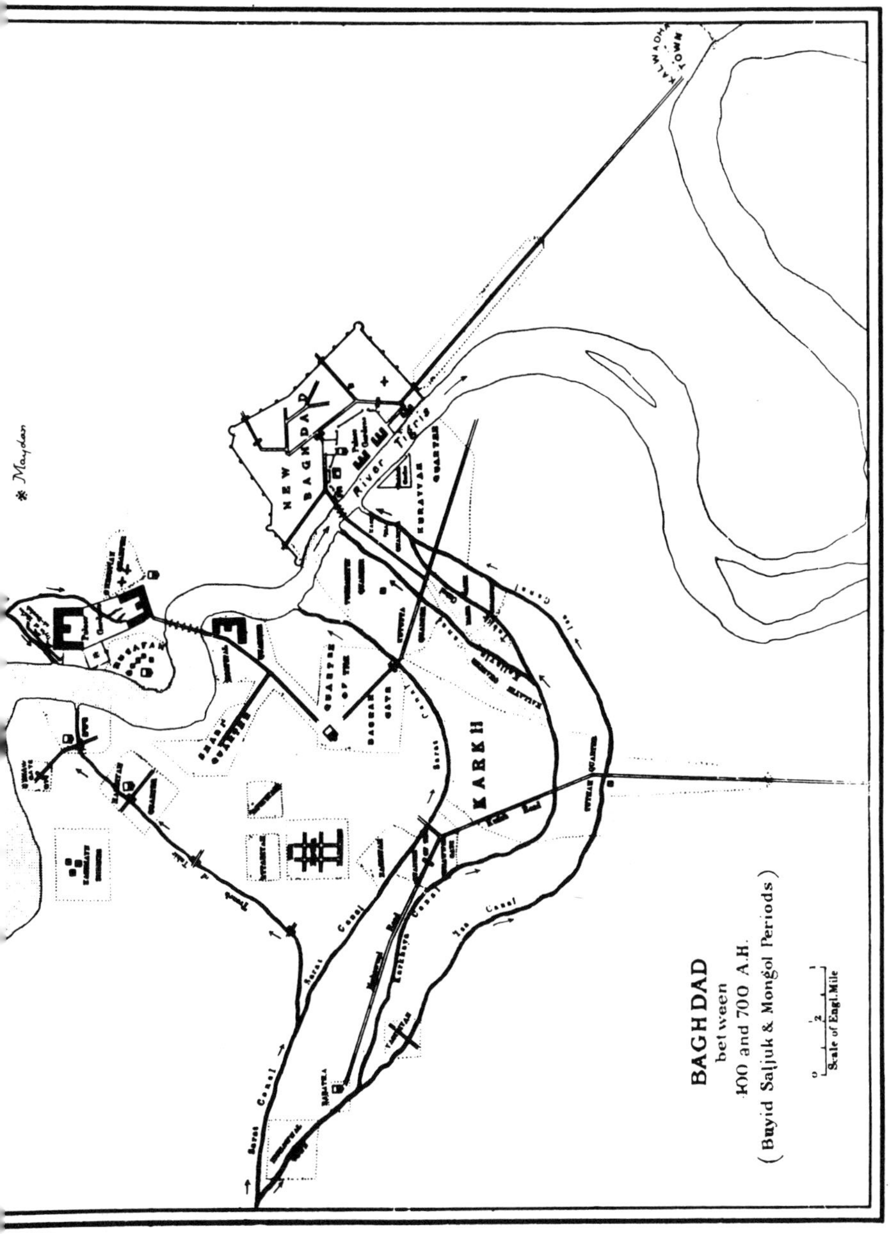
Maydan
NEW BAGHDAD
River Tigris
KARKH
KALWADHA TOWN
Sarat Canal
Isa Canal
BAGHDAD
between
400 and 700 A.H.
(Buyid Saljuk & Mongol Periods)
Scale of Engl. Mile

Map VII.

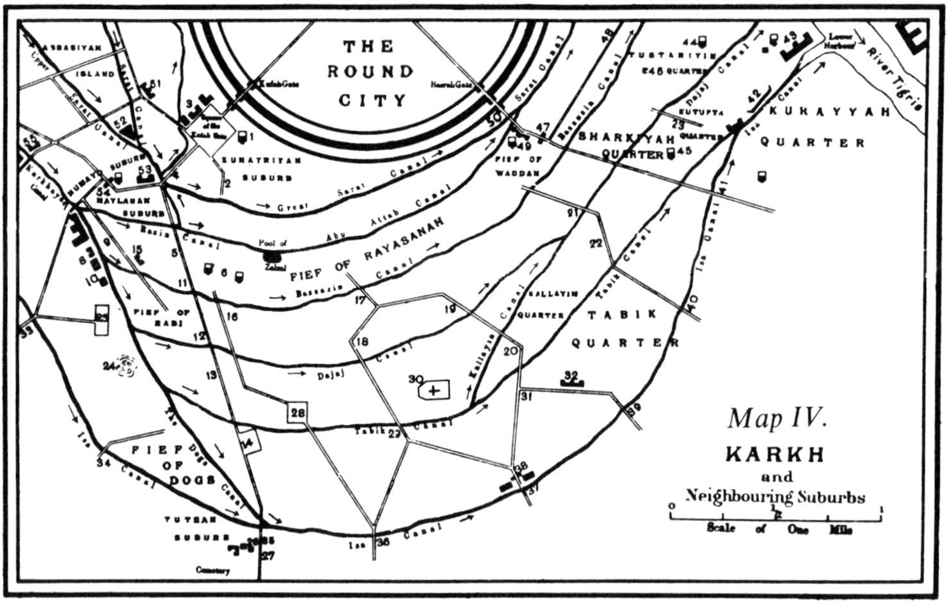

REFERENCES TO MAP NO. IV

1. Mosque of Musayyib with the Tall Minaret.
2. Market of 'Abd-al-Wāhid.
3. Fief of the Gate-keepers, Dīwān of the Ṣadakah (Poor Tax Office). The Stables and Dromedary House.
4. The Old Bridge.
5. Market of Abu-l-Ward.
6. Mosque of Ibn Raghbān and Mosque of the Anbārites.
7. The Hospital Bridge and the Old Hospital (Bīmāristān).
8. The Darrabāt and Mill of Abu-l-Ḳāsim.
9. Quarter of men of Wāsiṭ.
10. Al-Khafḳah (the Clappers).
11. Gate of Karkh.
12. Gate of the Coppersmiths.
13. Market of Ghālib.
14. Square of Suwayd.
15. Road of the Painter and House of Ka'b.
16. The Clothes-merchants' Market (Sūḳ-al-Bazzāzīn).
17. The Butchers' Quarter.
18. Market of the Poulterers.
19. Soap-boilers' Quarter.
20. Canal-diggers' Quarter.
21. Reed-weavers' Quarter.
22. Road of the Pitch-workers.
23. The Cookmen's Quarter.
24. Mound of the Ass.
25. Quadrangle of the Oil-merchant.
26. Shrine of Junayd and of Sarī-as-Sakatī: the Sūfī Convent.
27. The Tuesday Market.
28. Quadrangle of Ṣāliḥ.
29. The Sawwāḳīn.
30. Fief of the Christians and Monastery of the Virgins.
31. The Road of Bricks.
32. The Cotton House.
33. Bridge of the Oil-merchants.
34. The Alkali Bridge.
35. The Thorn Bridge.
36. The Pomegranate Bridge.
37. Maghīd Bridge and Mills.
38. Gate of the Mills.
39. The Garden Bridge.
40. The Ma'badī Bridge.
41. The Banī Zurayḳ Bridge.
42. The Myrtle Wharf and the Melon House (Fruit-market).
43. Palace of 'Īsā, Mosque of Ibn-al-Muṭṭalib, and Tomb of the Caliph Mustaḍī.
44. Shrine of 'Alī called Mashhad-al-Minṭaḳah.
45. Great Mosque of the Sharḳīyah Quarter.
46. The Shrine of Ma'rūf Karkhī and the Cemetery of the Convent Gate.
47. The Ḥarrānī Archway.

47–41. The Baṣrah Gate Road.

47–48. Road to the Lower Bridge, called the Barley Street.

49. Palace and Mosque of Waḍḍāḥ.
50. The New Bridge and the Booksellers' Market.
51. Palace and Market of 'Abd-al-Wahhāb.
52. The Patrician's Mill.
53. Palace in Fief of 'Īsā.
54. The Muḥawwal Gate and Mosque.
55. Bridge of the Greeks and House of the Farrāshes.

REFERENCES TO MAP NO. V

1. The Palace of Ḥumayd ibn 'Abd-al-Ḥamīd.
2. The Barley Gate (Bāb-ash-Sha'īr).
3. The Old Convent at the Ṣarāt Point.
4. Palace of Zubaydah, called the Karār.
5. The Khuld Palace (site afterwards occupied by the 'Aḍudī Hospital).
6. The Royal Stables.
7. Office of the Bridge Works and Hall of the Chief of Police.
8. Palaces of the Princes Sulaymān and Sāliḥ, sons of Manṣūr, on the Street called Darb Sulaymān.
9. The Iron Gate and Bridge, leading to the Dujayl Road.
10. The Water-conduit called 'Abbārat-al-Kūkh.
11. The Ḥarb Gate and Bridge, leading to the Ḥarb Gate Road.
12. Tomb of Ibn Ḥanbal the Imām.
13. Ḳaṭrabbul Gate and Bridge of the Mill of Umm Ja'far.
14. Palace and Mosque of Zubaydah (Umm Ja'far).

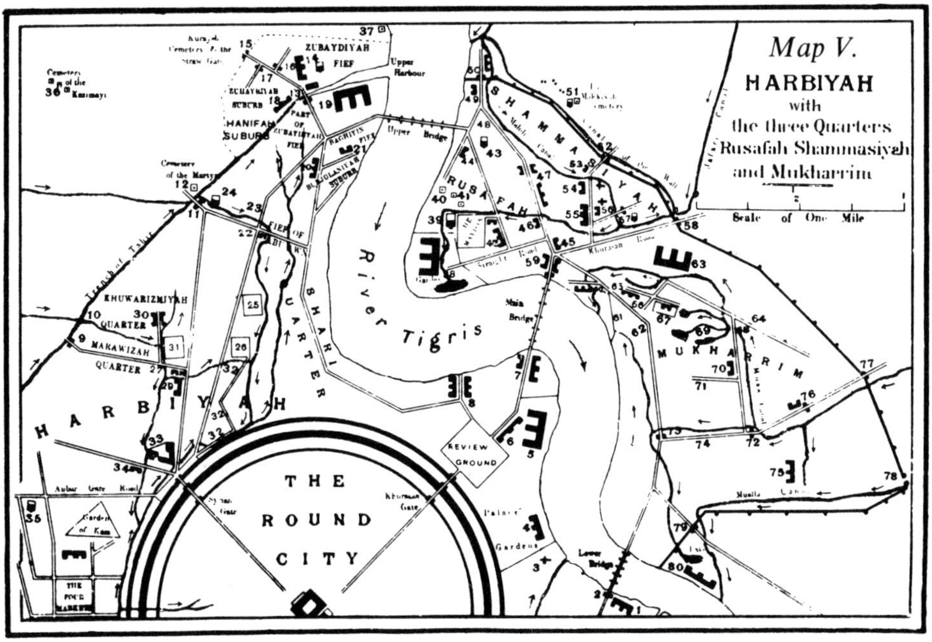

15. The Straw Gate (Bāb-at-Tibn).
16. Gate of the Fief.
17. Bāb-aṣ-Ṣaghīr (the Little Gate).
18. Palace of 'Umārah.
19. Palace of the Ṭāhirid Ḥarīm.
20. The Slaves' House (Dār-ar-Raḳīḳ) and Fief of the Ghulāms (Pages).
21. Palace of Ḥafṣ ibn 'Othmān in Darb Siwār (Street of the Bracelet).
22. Palace of Ibn Abi-'Awn.
23. The Bridge of the Straw-merchants (Ḳanṭarah-at-Tabbānīn).
24. The Ḥarbīyah Mosque.
25. Quadrangle of Abu-l-'Abbās.
26. Quadrangle of Shabīb.
27. The Abu-l-Jawn Bridge.
28. The Palace of Sa'īd-al-Khaṭīb.
29. The Orphan School.
30. Dukkān-al-Abna (the Persian Shops).
31. Quadrangle of the Persians, with Suburbs of Rushayd, of Zuhayr, and of 'Othmān ibn Nuhayk.
32. The Three Arcades of 'Akkī, Ghiṭrīf, and Abu Suwayd.
33. The Prison of the Syrian Gate.
34. Road and Palace of Hānī.
35. The Bukhariot Mosque.
36. The Kāẓimayn Shrines; Tombs of Zubaydah, the Caliph Amīn, and the Buyid Princes.
37. Tomb of 'Abd-Allah, son of Ibn Ḥanbal.
38. Palace of Mahdī in Ruṣāfah.
39. The Ruṣāfah Mosque.
40. Shrine of Abu Ḥanīfah in the Khayzurān Cemetery.
41. The Tombs of the Caliphs.
42. Palaces of Umm Ḥabīb and of Faḍl on the Road of the Maydān.
43. The Khuḍayrīyah Quarter and Mosque; the Khuḍayr Market.
44. Palace of Waḍḍāḥ on Road of Skiffs.
45. Market of Yaḥyā and Road of the Bridge.
46. Palace of Faraj.
47. Palaces of Dūr; Palace of Ja'far the Barmecide.
48. Market of Ja'far and Road of the Mahdī Canal.
49. Market of Khālid and Ḳaṣr-aṭ-Ṭīn (the Clay Castle).
50. The Shammāsīyah Gate and the Palace of Mūnis.
51. Three Gates Suburb, the Place of Vows, and the Chapel of the Festival.
52. The Baradān Gate.
53. The Baradān Bridge and the Palace of Abu-Naṣr.
54. The Ḥuṭam Palace.
55. The Barmecide Fief and Palaces.
56. Dār-ar-Rūm (House of the Greeks), the Nestorian and Jacobite Churches of the Christian Quarter, with the House of the Patriarch.
57. Market of Naṣr, the Mosque and the Iron Gates.
58. The Khurāsān Gate of East Baghdad.
59. The Bāb-aṭ-Ṭāk (Gate of the Archway), Palaces of Khuzaymah, of Prince 'Ubayd-Allah, and of Princess Asmā.
60. The Street of 'Amr the Greek.
61. The Garden of Zāhir at the mouth of the Mūsā Canal, and Palace of Ibn Muḳlah.
62. The Great Road.
63. The Palace of Mu'taṣim.
64. The Long Street.
65. The Palace of Ibn-al-Furāt and the Street of the Vine Tendril.
66. The Thirst Market (Sūk-al-'Aṭsh).
67. Palace, Quadrangle, and Market of Ḥarashī.
68. The Ansār Bridge.
69. The Three Tanks of the Anṣār, of Haylānah, and of Dāūd.
70. Palace of Ibn-al-Khaṣīb in the Road of Sa'd Waṣīf.
71. Market of Ḥajjāj.
72. The Great Pitched Gate.
73. The Mukharrim Gate and the Bridge of 'Abbās.
74. The Hay Market and the Booths.
75. The Palace of Banūjah.
76. The 'Ammār Gate and the Palace of 'Umārah.
77. The Gate of the Horse Market.
78. The Abraz Gate.
79. The Gate of the Tuesday Market.
80. The Firdūs Palace and Lake.

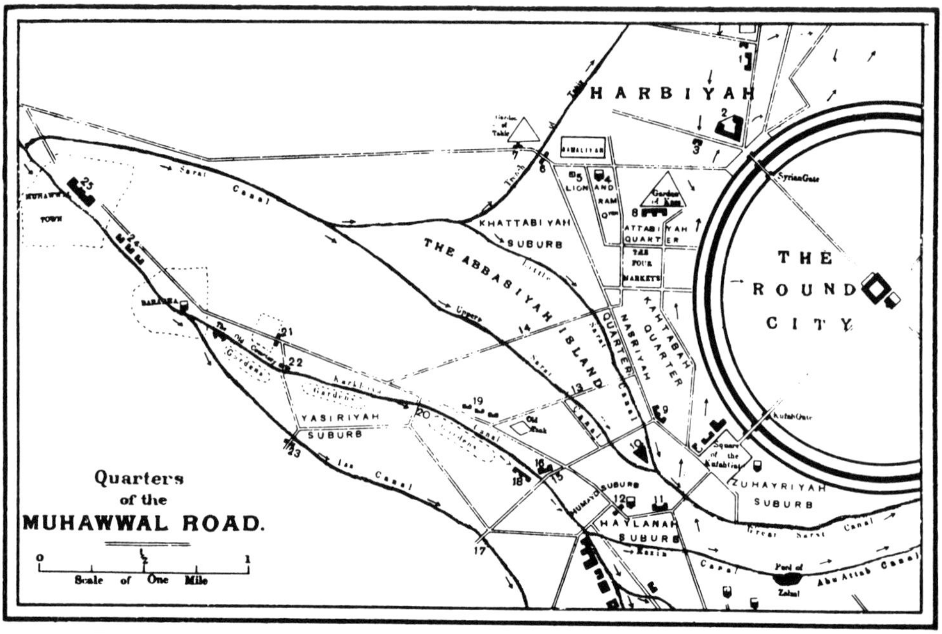

Map VI.

REFERENCES TO MAP No. VI

1. Palace of Sa'īd-al-Khaṭīb and the Orphan School.
2. The Prison of the Syrian Gate.
3. Road and Palace of Hānī.
4. The Bukhariot Mosque.
5. The Shrine of Ibrāhīm-al-Ḥarbī.
6. The Anbār Gate and Bridge.
7. The Garden Gate.
8. Dār-al-Ḳazz (the Silk House) and the Street of Ghāmish.
9. Palace and Market of 'Abd-al-Wahhāb.
10. The Patrician's Mill and Bridge of the Mills.
11. Palace in Fief of 'Īsā.
12. The Muḥawwal Gate and Mosque.
13. The China Bridge.
14. Bridge of 'Abbās.
15. Bridge of the Greeks.
16. House of the Farrāshes.
17. Bridge of the Greek Woman
18. Palace of Ka'yūbah.
19. Houses of the Persians.
20. Bridge and Street of Rocks.
21. The Kunāṣah Gate and Place of the Sweepings, the Tying-place for beasts of burden.
22. Gate of Abu Kabīsah and the Jews' Bridge (Ḳanṭarah-al-Yahūd).
23. The Yāsirīyah Gate, Bridge, and Quarter.
24. Place of the Tanners.
25. Palace of Mu'taṣim at Muhawwal Town.

Appendix E

Illustrations

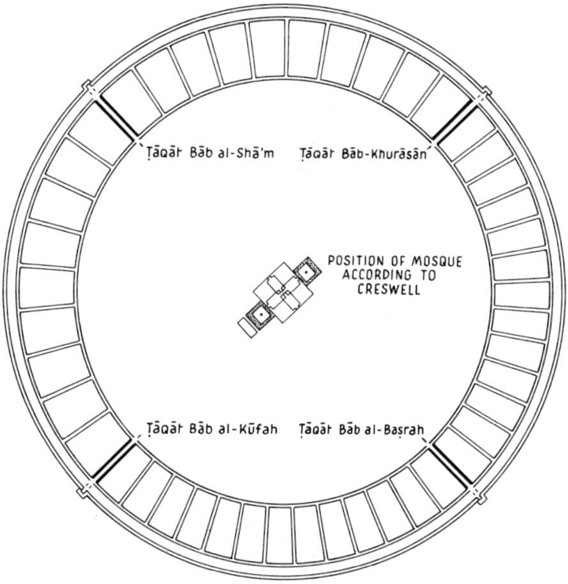

Figure 1. The Round City.
(After Herzfeld and Creswell)

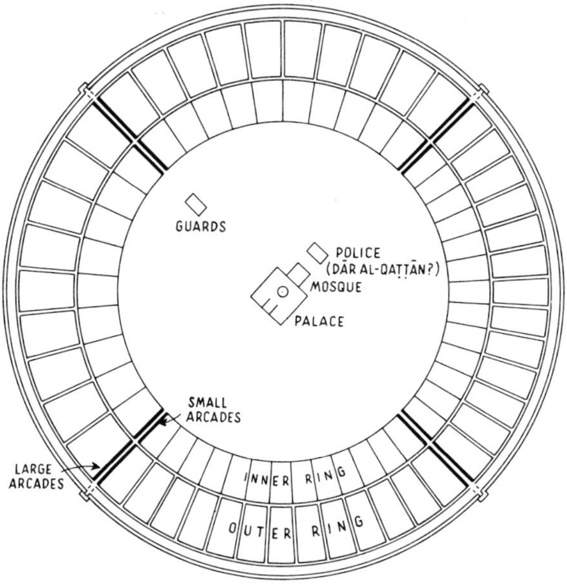

Figure 2. The Round City.

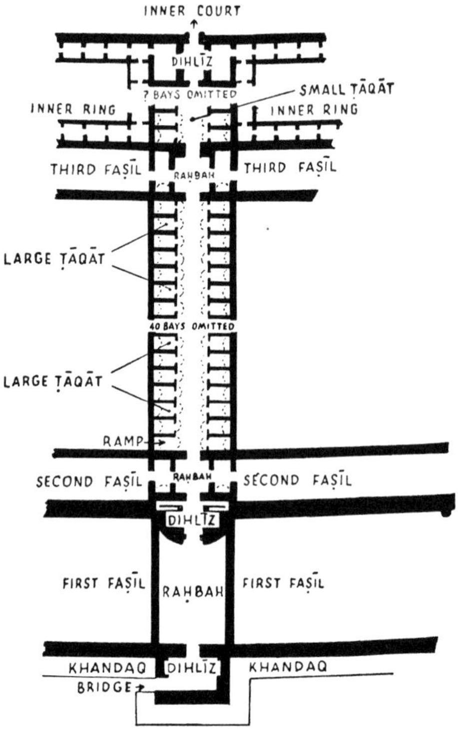

Figure 3. The Large Ṭāqāt.

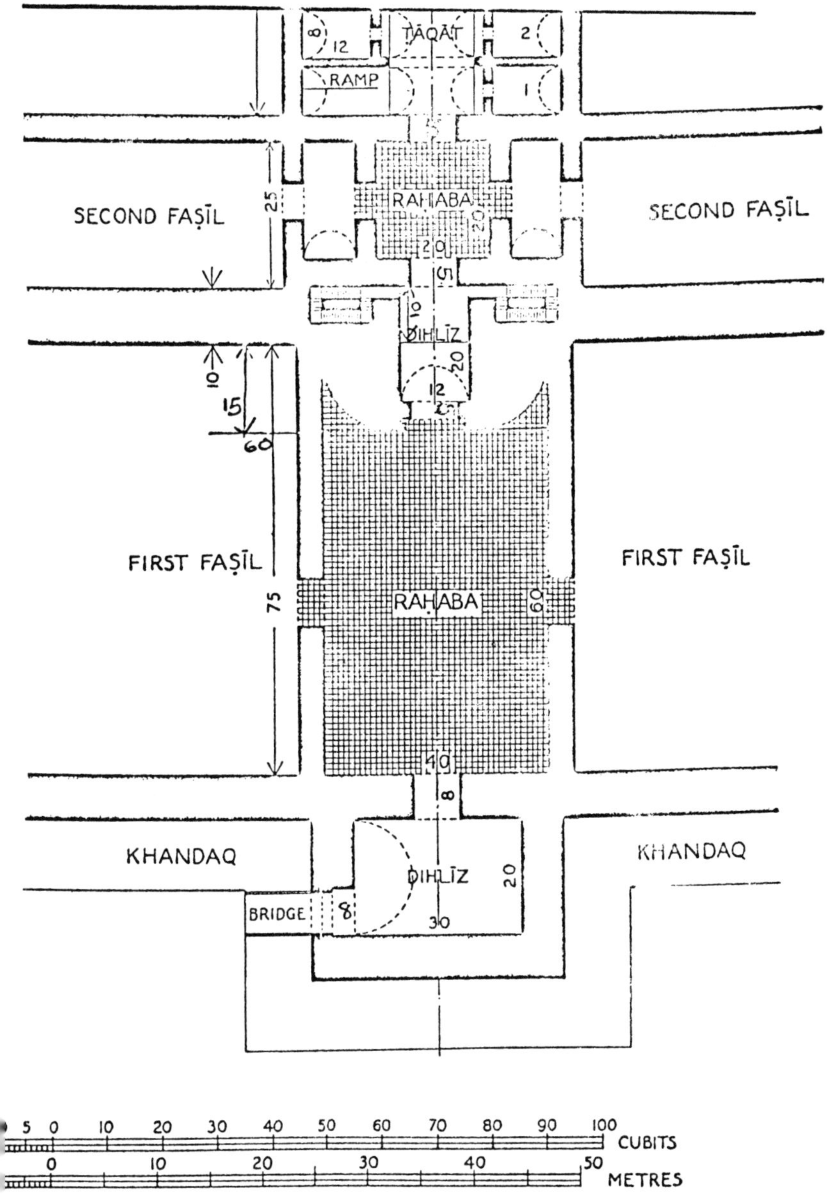

Figure 4. The Gates (Creswell, p. 13).

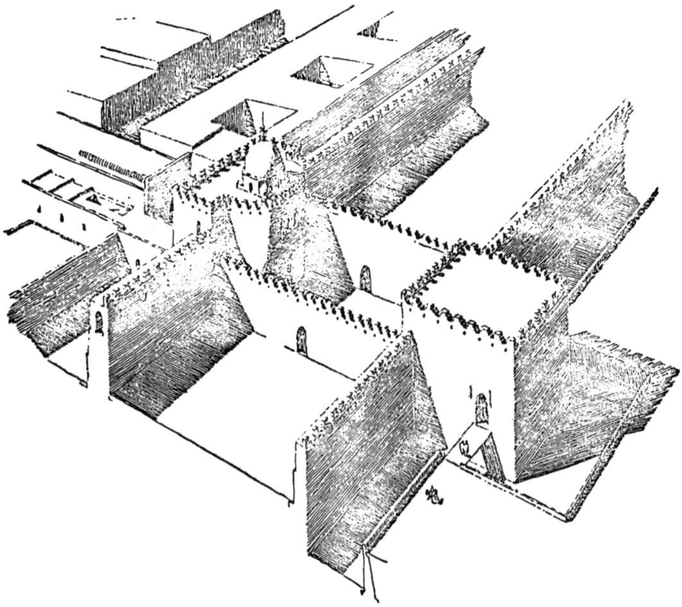

Figure 5. The Gates Reconstructed (*Herzfeld, p. 127*).

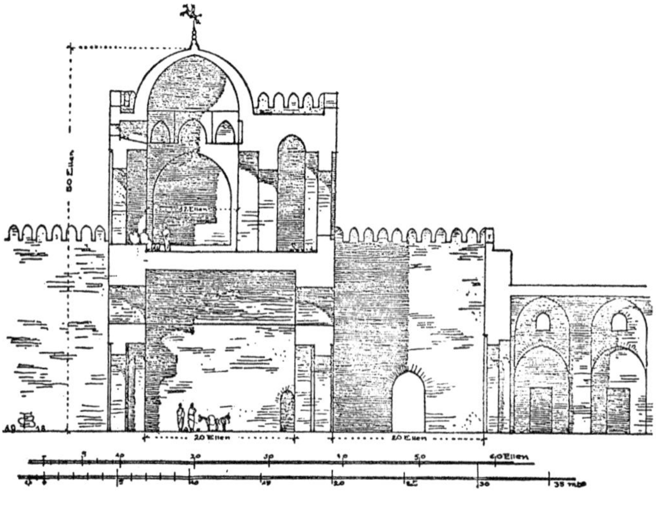

Figure 6. Inner Gate Reconstructed (*Herzfeld, p. 126*).

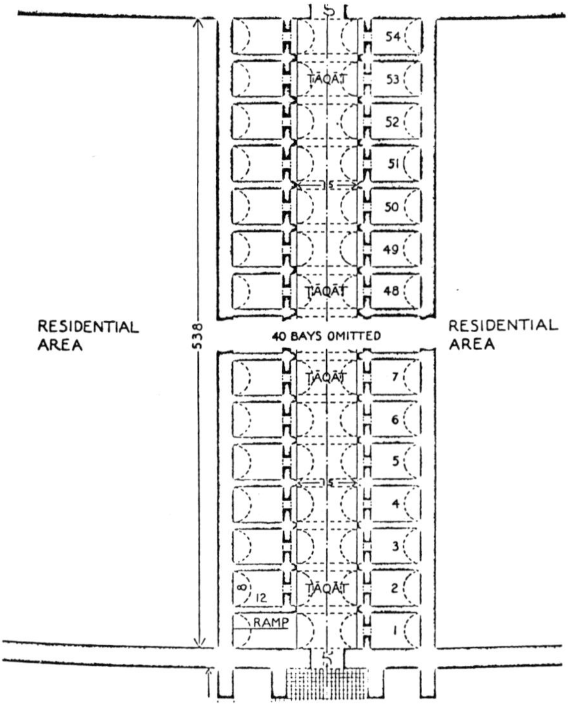

Figure 7. The Large Arcades (Creswell, p. 13).

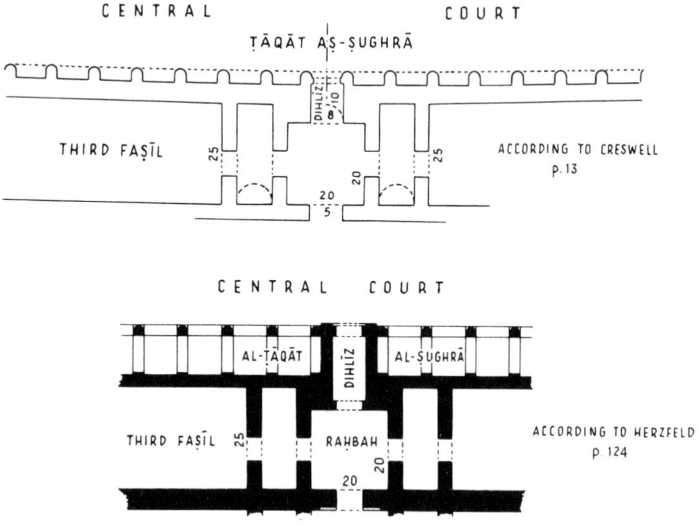

Figure 8. The Small Arcades.

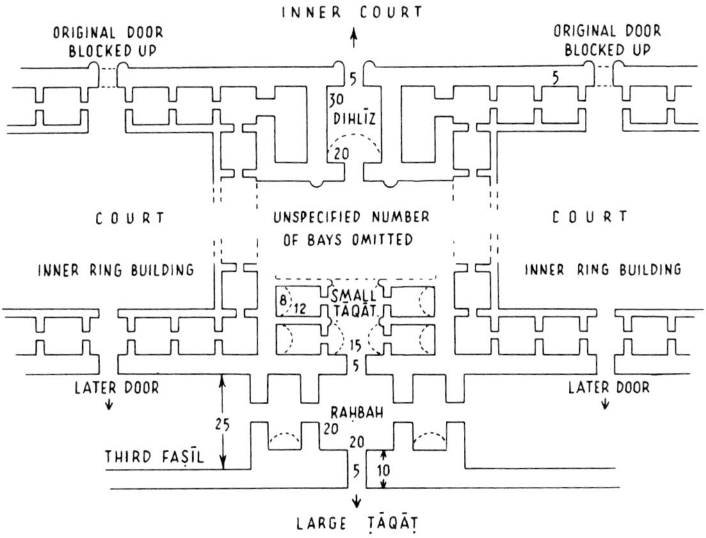

Figure 9. The Small Ṭāqāt (aṣ-Ṣughrā) and the Inner Ring.

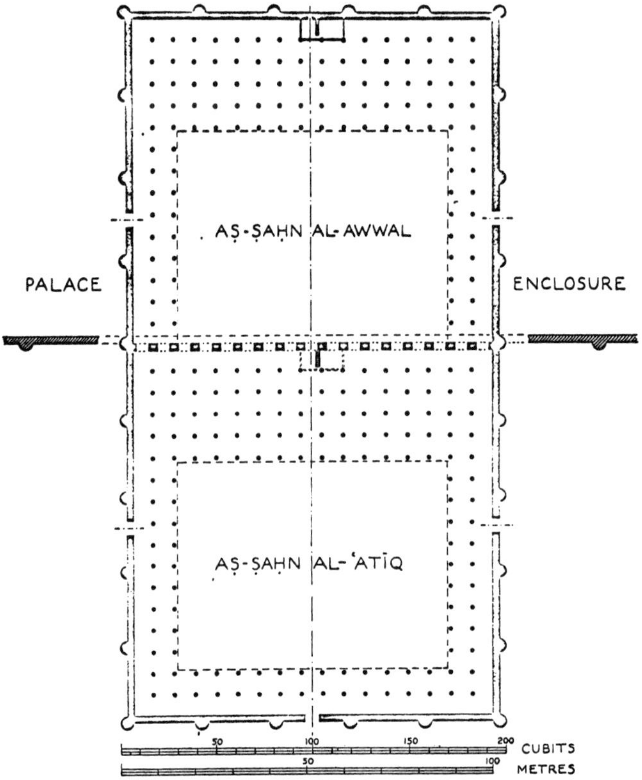

Figure 10. The Mosque of al-Manṣūr (Creswell, p. 34).

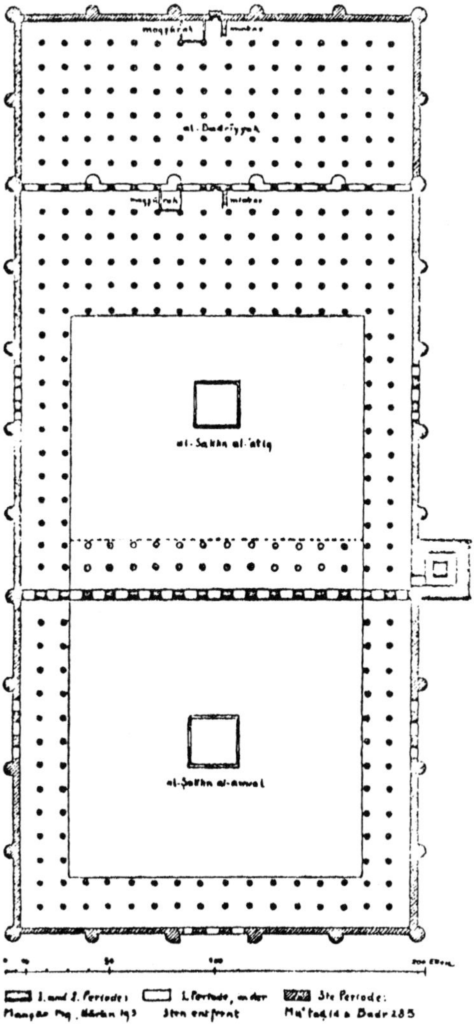

Figure 11. The Mosque of al-Manṣūr (Herzfeld, p. 137).

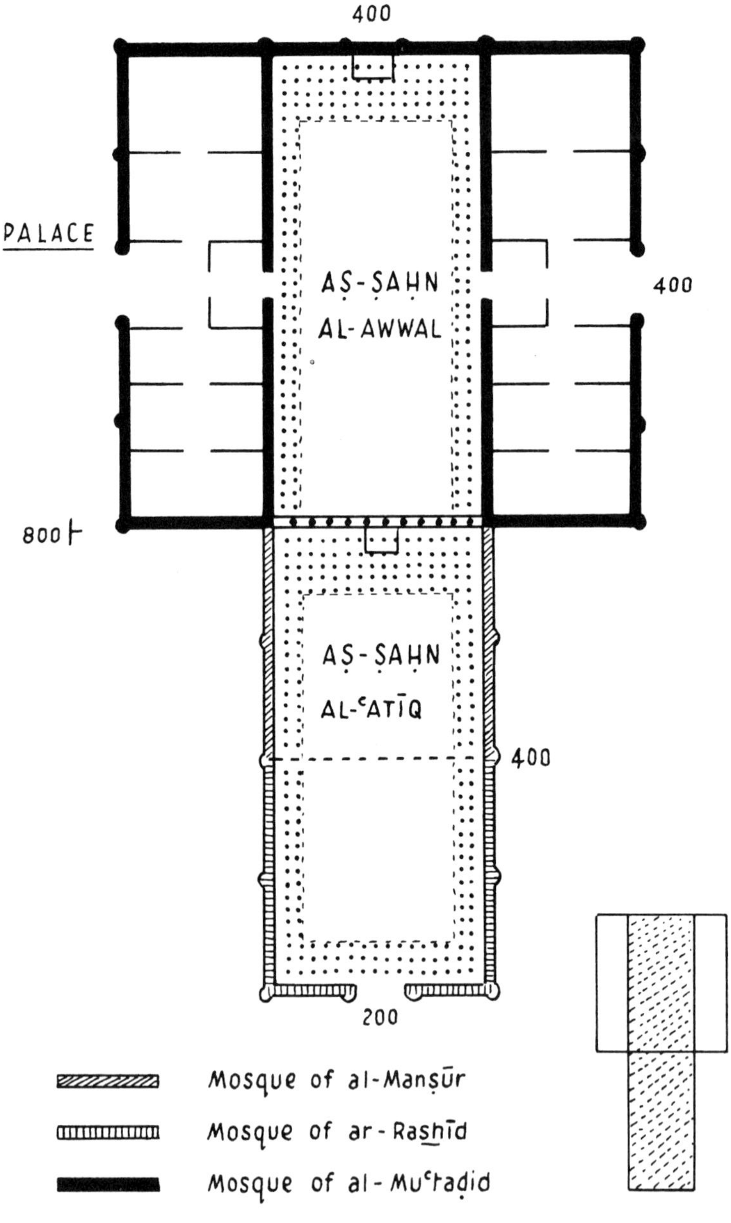

Figure 12. The Enlargement of al-Manṣūr's Mosque according to Length.

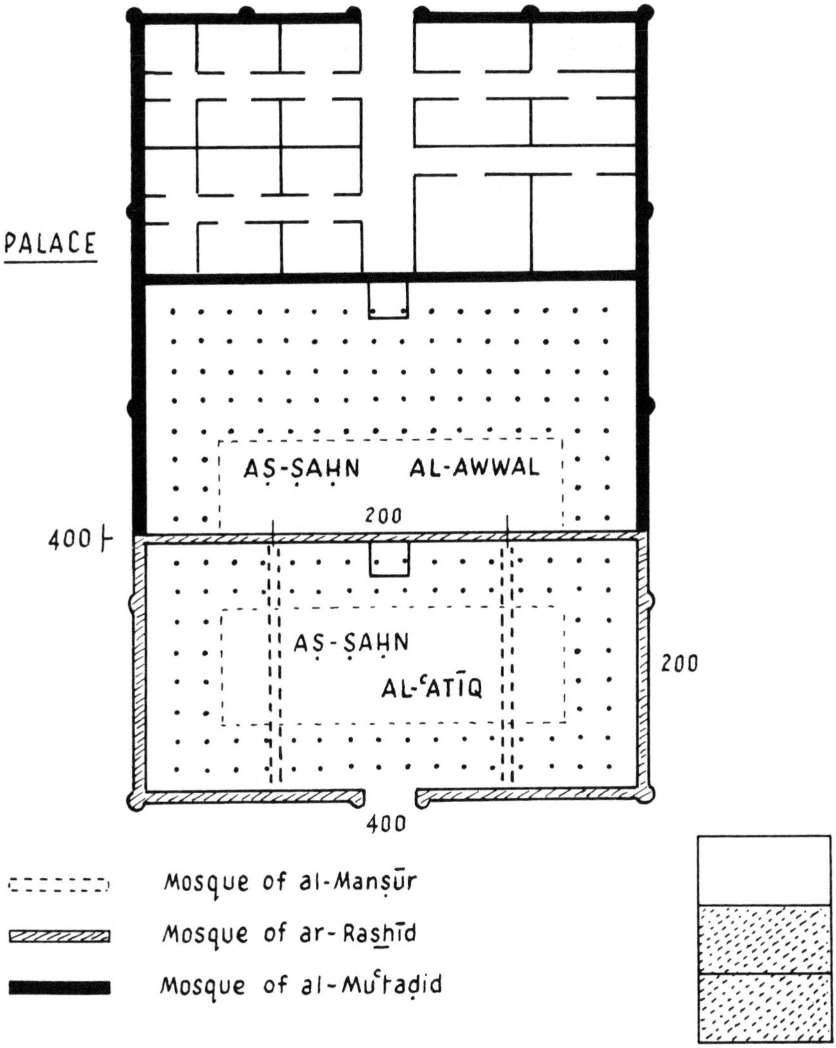

Figure 13. The Enlargement of al-Manṣūr's Mosque according to Width.

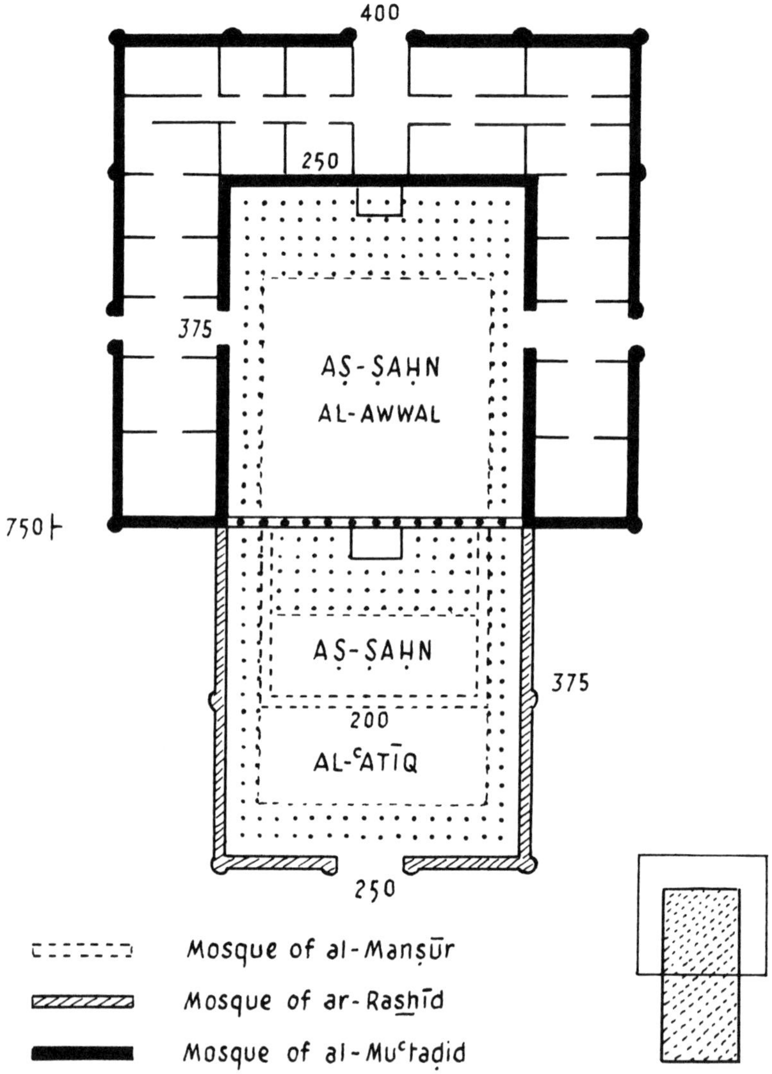

Figure 14. The Reconstruction of al-Manṣūr's Mosque according to Width and Length (Rectangular).

Appendix F

Glossary of Arabic Terms Related to Topography

ājurr	burnt brick
arwiqah	peristyle, galleries
bāb	gate
bayt	house dwelling
dār	residence, palace, building
darb	street
ḍayʿah	domain
dayr	monastery
dihlīz	corridor
dīwān	government bureau
farsakh	league, farasang
faṣīl	intervallum
furḍah	harbor
jaṣṣ	gypsum
jisr	pontoon bridge
khān	cararvanserai
kils	lime
kūrah	district
libn	mud brick
majlis	audience room
manārah	tower, minaret
mashhad	shrine
mashraʿah	wharf
maqbarah	cemetery, burial place
murabbaʿah	square
nahr	canal, river
nūrah	tar
qabr	grave, burial place
qanṭarah	masonry bridge
qaṣr	palace
qaṭīʿah	fief
qubbah	cupola
rabaḍ	estate, suburb
raḥbah	court
rahṣ	burnt brick
riwāq	gallery (of mosque)
rustāq	district
ṣaḥn	court of mosque
ṣārūj	quicklime
shāriʿ	street, quarter
sikkah	side street
sūq	market
suwayqah	dimunitive of above
ṭāq	arch, archway
ṭāqāt	archway, arcades
ṭarīq	road, highway
ṭassūj	district
wilāyah	district

Appendix G

Lists of Caliphs and Amirs

Table 1. The ʿAbbāsid Caliphs from the Beginning of the Dynasty to the Death of the Khaṭīb*

A.H.		*A.D.*	*A.H.*		*A.D.*
132	as-Saffāḥ	750	255	al-Muhtadī	869
136	al-Manṣūr	754	256	al-Muʿtamid	870
158	al-Mahdī	775	279	al-Muʿtaḍid	892
169	al-Hādī	785	289	al-Muktafī	902
170	ar-Rashīd	786	295	al-Muqtadir	908
193	al-Amīn	809	320	al-Qāhir	932
198	al-Ma'mūn	813	322	ar-Rāḍī	934
218	al-Muʿtaṣim	833	329	al-Muttaqī	940
227	al-Wāthiq	842	333	al-Mustakfī	944
232	al-Mutawakkil	847	334	al-Muṭīʿ	946
247	al-Muntaṣir	861	363	aṭ-Ṭā'iʿ	974
248	al-Mustaʿin	862	381	al-Qādir	991
252	al-Muʿtazz	866	422	al-Qā'im	1031

* Based on *Encyclopedia of Islam*, 2nd ed., p. 21.

Table 2. The Būyid Amīrs of Baghdad

A.H.		*A.D.*	*A.H.*		*A.D.*
334	Muʿizz ad-Dawlah	945	379	Bahā' ad-Dawlah	989
356	ʿIzz ad-Dawlah (Bakhtiyār)	967	403	Sulṭān ad-Dawlah	1012
			412	Musharrif ad-Dawlah	1021
367	ʿAḍud ad-Dawlah	977	416	Jalāl ad-Dawlah	1025
372	Ṣamṣām ad-Dawlah	983	435	Abū Khālījār	1044
376	Sharaf ad-Dawlah	987	440	al-Malik ar-Raḥīm	1048

Appendix H

Addendum to Introduction

The Ta'rīkh Baghdād (TB)

Manuscripts: A list describing all the known manuscripts of the *Ta'rīkh Baghdād* may be derived from: J. Horovitz, "Aus den Bibliotheken von Kairo, Damaskus und Konstantinopel," *MSOS* 10 (1907): 61 ff., and H. Ritter, *Orientalia I* (Istanbuler Mitteilungen I) (Istanbul, 1933), pp. 67 ff. Cf. also G. Salmon, *Histoire de Baghdadh*, pp. 13 ff. The following list is limited to those manuscripts which preserve parts of the topographical introduction:

A: London 1281 (ca. 500/1106).
BN: Paris 2128 (633/1235–1236).
B: London Suppl. 665 (ca. 7th/13th century).
AL: Alger 1606 (943/1536–1537).
K: Köprülü 1022–1023 (1084/1673–1674).
AR: Aşir Reisülküttap 604 (ca. 1000/1591–1592).
DI: Damat Ibrahim 889 (1091/1680–1681).
NO: Nuru Osmaniye 3093–3094 (1091/1680–1681).
H: Hekimoğlu 693–394 (ca. 1100/1688–1689).
C[s]: London Suppl. 656 (1243/1825–1826).
D: London 1284 (1254/1838–1839).
T: Cairo, Ta'rīkh 635 (cat. V, 26), no date.

Of these manuscripts, only A, B, and microfilms of NO and DI were available to me. I therefore relied heavily on the printed editions which seem to provide a reliable text.

Editions: Paris (Ṣ): G. Salmon, *L'Introduction topographique à l'histoire de Baghdadh d'Aboū Bakr Aḥmad Ibn Thābit al-Khaṭīb al-Baghdādhī* (Bibliothèque de l'École des Hautes Études, Fasc. 148) (Paris, 1904). Introduction (pp. 1–73), French translation and annotation (pp. 74–181), followed by indexes of names and places, Arabic text (93 pages). The text begins with the chapter on the building of Madīnat as-Salām, and concludes with the chapter on al-Madā'in. It is edited from A, BN, B, C[s], and Cairo Bibl. Khed. 520 (not listed by Horovitz or Ritter, but presumably identical with T).

Cairo (C): Ed. of text not indicated. Complete in fourteen volumes; entire introduction in volume one. The editor based his edition on K (cf. vol. 14, p. 447) and consulted S for the topographical sections.

Table of the Khaṭīb's Sources for Systematic Topography of Baghdad

This table is limited to those chapters containing systematic descriptions of the city. The references are to accounts which presumably originated in works dealing with the topography of Baghdad, rather than incidental topographical information. Other chapters which do not contain lengthy systematic descriptions of the city occasionally preserve accounts which may be part of a topographical work. These accounts are listed separately at the conclusion of this table. "On the authority of" listings are one-line entries; subsequent listings revert to the numbered source until the next "on the authority of" citation.

Madīnat al-Manṣūr

Source	*Page and Lines (according to C)*
1) Muḥammad b. Khalaf[86]	
on the authority of Yaḥyā b. al-Ḥasan b. ʿAbd al-Khāliq	70.19
	70.20–70.21
	70.21–71.1
	72.9 –72.18
	72.19–73.14
	73.21–75.6
on the authority of Aḥmad b. al-Ḥārith———al-ʿAttābī	75.9 –75.15
	76.3 –76.15
	76.16–76.18

East and West Baghdad

1) Muḥammad b. Khalaf Wakīʿ	———	83.17–84.1[87]
on the authority of Aḥmad b. Abī Ṭāhir Ṭayfūr	———	84.8 –84.12
		84.12–84.15
		84.17–85.4
on the authority of Aḥmad b. al-Haytham	———	85.4 –85.7
		85.12–85.16
on the authority of Abū Zayd al-Khaṭīb	———	85.17–85.19
		85.19–86.1
		86.7 –86.12
		87.7 –87.22
		88.3 –88.4
on the authority of Aḥmad b. Abī Ṭāhir Ṭayfūr	———	88.9 –88.11
		88.12–88.15
		90.4 –90.5
		91.1 –91.16
		91.18–92.11[88]
		93.13–94.2
on the authority of Aḥmad b. al-Ḥārith	———	94.5 –94.10[89]
		94.12–94.13
		95.1 –95.17
		95.20–96.3
		96.5 –96.7
		96.7 –96.10
		97.1 –97.5
		97.9 –97.10

East and West Baghdad (continued)

Source		Page and Lines (according to C)
2) Ibrāhīm b. Muḥammad b. ʿArafah al-Azdī Nifṭawayh		85.9 –85.10[90]
		88.17–89.1
		89.1 –90.3
		92.13–92.21
		93.7 –93.9
		94.14–94.22
		95.8 –95.12
		96.11–96.20
		97.9
		98.15–98.21

Chapters other than Those Containing Systematic Descriptions

1) Muḥammad b. Khalaf		
on the authority of Muḥammad b. Mūsā al-Qaysī———al-Khuwārizmī	———	67.9 – 67.12
on the authority of al-Khuwārizmī	———	67.13– 67.14
		107.16–107.20
on the authority of Ibn al-Aʿrābī[91]	———	107.20–108.4
on the authority of Aḥmad b. Khalīl[92]——— his father	———	116.2 –116.6
		120.15–121.2
		125.17–125.20
2) Nifṭawayh	———	67.20– 68.14

The Hydrography of Baghdad

1) Anonymous[93]	———	111.12–112.5
2) ʿAbdallāh b. Muḥammad b. ʿAlī al-Baghdādī	———	112.6 –115.14

Local Histories of Baghdad

The following books are classified as local histories in the lists of Safadī,[94] Sakhāwī (p. 123 in Rosenthal, *Historiography*, pp. 387 ff.), and Ḥajjī Khalīfah (pp. 119–21) which are based, for the most part, on the biographical works subsequent to the Khaṭīb. The list is not all-inclusive but is essentially limited, it seems, to those major works which were still referred to in later times (fifteenth century). Because he was a contemporary of the Khaṭīb, the eventual publication of Ibn ʿAqīl's *K. al-funūn*[95] may disclose new titles of various works from the earlier periods; and hopefully some indications as to their structure and contents.

Author	*Saf.*	*Sakh*	*Ḥ.Kh*
Ibn Abī Ṭāhir Ṭayfūr	×	×	×
al-Kisrawī	—	—	×
al-Khaṭīb	×	×	×
Masʿūd b. al-Bukhārī[96]	—	—	×
as-Samʿānī[97]	×	×	×
M. b. Ḥamīd al-Kātib[98]	—	—	×
Ibn ad-Dubaythī[99]	×	×	×
al-Qaṭīʿī[100]	×	×	×
Ibn an-Najjār[101]	×	×	×
Abū Bakr al-Māristānī	×	—	×
Ibn as-Sāʿī[102]	×	×	×
M. b. A. adh-Dhahabī[103]	—	—	×
Ibn Rāfiʿ[104]	—	×	×
A. b. M. al-Barqī[105]	—	—	×
Rawḍat al-Arīb (anon.)[106]	—	—	×

Appendix I

Abbreviations in Notes and Bibliography

AIEO	*Annales de l'Institut d'Éudes Orientales*, Algiers.
BAHG	*Bibliothek Arabischer Historiker und Geographen*, Leipzig.
BGA	*Bibliotheca Geographorum Arabicorum*, Leiden.
BIFAO	*Bulletin d'Études Orientales de l'Institut Français d'Archéologie Orientale*, Cairo.
BSOAS	*Bulletin of the School of Oriental and African Studies*, London.
C	Al-Khaṭīb, *Ta'rīkh Baghdād* (Cairo ed., vol. 1). See also *TB*.
EI	*Encyclopedia of Islam.*
EMA	K. A. C. Creswell, *Early Muslim Architecture.*
GAL	C. Brockelmann, *Geshichte der Arabischen Literatur.*
GMS	*Gibb Memorial Series.*
JA	*Journal Asiatique*, Paris.
JAOS	*Journal of the American Oriental Society*, New Haven.
JRAS	*Journal of the Royal Asiatic Society*, London.
MIDEO	*Mélanges de l'Institut Dominicain d'Études Orientales*, Cairo.
MIFAO	*Mémoires de l'Institut Français d'Archéologie Orientale du Caire*, Cairo.
MSOS	*Mitteilungen des Seminars für Orientalische Sprachen*, Berlin.
PIEO	*Publication de l'Institut d'Études Orientales*, Algiers.
PIFAO	*Publication de l'Institut Français d'Archéologie Orientale du Caire*, Cairo.
PIFD	*Publications de l'Institut Français de Damas*, Damascus.
RAAD	*Revue de l'Académie Arabe* (*Majallat al-majma' al-ilmī al-ʿarabī*), Damascus.
RSO	*Revista degli Studi Orientali*, Rome.
S	G. Salmon, *L'Introduction topographique à l'histoire de Baghdadh.*
TB	Al-Khaṭīb, *Taʿrīkh Baghdād* (Cairo ed., 14 vols.). See *C* and Appendix H.
WZKM	*Wiener Zeitschrift für die Kunde des Morgenländes*, Vienna.
ZDMG	*Zeitschrift der Deutschen Morgenländischen Gesellschaft*, Wiesbaden.

Notes

Introduction

1. *TB*, 1 : 22–23.
2. Ibid., p. 119.
3. Cf. J. Lassner, "Notes on the Topography of Baghdad—The Khaṭīb al-Baghdādī and the Systematic Descriptions of the City," *JAOS*, 83 (1963): 459–60. Mention should also be made of Yāqūt's great geographical dictionary (*Muʿjam*) and its epitome (*Marāṣid*). Although they are invaluable for any study of the city, they are not discussed here because the information which they contain is generally arranged according to alphabetical entries, and not systematic descriptions. The Introduction is based largely on my notes in *JAOS*. On Arabic geographers in general, see A. Miquel, *La Géographie humaine du monde Musulman jusqu'au milieu du 11e siècle* (Paris, 1967); also I. J. Kratchkovsky, *Arabskäia geografitcheskäia literatura* (Moscow-Leningrad, 1959), part tr. S. A. D. ʿUthmān Hāshim (Cairo, 1963).
4. Ed. M. J. de Goeje (*BGA*, VII) (Leiden, 1892), pp. 238–54; cf. *GAL*, *Supplement*, 1 : 405. See also Miquel, *Index*, p. 405.
5. *Buldān*, p. 254.
6. Ed. H. von Mžik (*BAHG*, V) (Leipzig, 1930); cf. *GAL*, *Supplement*, 1 : 406. Fragment on hydrography edited and translated with notes by LeStrange as Ibn Serapion, *Description of Mesopotamia and Baghdad* (London, 1895); originally published in *JRAS* of that year. See also Miquel, *Index*, p. 409.
7. Cf. *GAL*, 1 :260; *Supplement*, 1 : 405–6. See also Miquel, *Index*, p. 408.
8. Von Mžik's introduction to the text of Suhrāb, vi ff. The *K. ṣūrat al-arḍ* was edited by von Mžik (*BAHG*, III) (Leipzig, 1926). See also Miquel, *Index*, p. 408.
9. Cf. text below.
10. Ed. M. J. de Goeje (*BGA*, V) (Leiden, 1885).
11. De Goeje's introduction to the text of Ibn al-Faqīh, VIII.

12. Mashhad MS., Cat. XVII, 1, 2: photo Berlin MS. sim. or 48.
13. *JA*, 204 (1924): 149 ff.: *Geographische Zeitschrift*, 40 (1934): 368; *ZDMG*, 88 (1934): 43–45; *BSOAS*, 13 (1949–50): 89, n.5. I obtained a photo of this very important MS after the present work was in an advanced state of production; elements of the section on Baghdad are being readied for separate publication.
14. Cf. *GAL*, 1 : 144; *Supplement*, 1 : 210.
15. Cf. *TB*, 5: 236–37; *GAL*, *Supplement*, 1 : 225.
16. Cf. *GAL*, *Supplement*, 1 : 184.
17. This work is presumably the same as the *Akhbār al-khulafā'* (cf. Rosenthal, *A History of Muslim Historiography* [Leiden, 1952], p. 335, n. 6—citing Sakhāwī, *I'lān*, p. 123). This work was later continued by his son 'Ubayadallāh (Rosenthal, op. cit., pp. 72, 386, n. 5). Cf. also Maqqarī, *Annalectes* (Dozy and others), 2: 113.
18. Rosenthal, op. cit., p. 133—citing al-Ḥumaydī, *Jadhwat al-Muqtabis*, Bodleian MS. Or. Hunt. 464 (Uri 783), fol. 45a (= Cairo ed., p. 98).
19. Cf. *TB*, 1 : 88, 94.
20. Ibid, 5: 236.
21. *Fihrist*, p. 114.
22. Cf. *GAL*, *Supplement*, 1 : 381, 404. See also Miquel, *Index*, p. 408, and esp. xix, who identifies him with Muḥammad b. Mūsā Shākir (d. 259/873).
23. Cf. *GAL*, *Supplement*, 1 : 258.
24. Unidentified.
25. Unidentified.
26. Cf. addendum to the Introduction.
27. *TB*, 6: 159.
28. The most complete study of his life and work is that of Yūsuf al-'Ishsh, *Al-Khaṭīb al-Baghdādī mu'arrikh Baghdād wa-muḥaddithuhā* (Damascus, 1364/1945). Cf. also Ibn al-Jawzī, *Muntaẓam*, 8 : 265–70 (apparently = Sibṭ Ibn al-Jawzī, *Mir'āt az-zamān*, Paris, MS. 1506, fol. 131–32, cited in Salmon, *Histoire*, pp. 3–10: Ibn Khallikān, *Wafayāt*, 1 : 27; Dhahabī, *Tadhkirat al-ḥuffāẓ*, 14°, 14 and *GAL*, 1 : 400–1; *Supplement*, 1 : 562–63. See also Miquel, *Index*, p. 408.
29. *TB*, 1 : 69–79; also E. Herzfeld, *Archaölogische Reise Im Euphrat und Tigris Gebiet* (Berlin, 1921), 2: 7–30.
30. *TB* 1 : 69, ll. 9–16.
31. Ibid., ll. 16–18.
32. Ibid., p. 71, ll. 17–20.
33. Ibid., p. 70, l. 19. Yaḥyā was the uncle of the wazīr al-Faḍl b. ar-Rabī'; cf. Ṭabarī, *Index*, p. 633.
34. Ibid., pp. 73–74.
35. Subsequent links in this *isnād* are:
    Al-Ḥasan b. Muḥammad as-Sakūnī, unidentified.
    Muḥammad b. Ja'far an-Naḥwī, d. 402/1011 (*TB*, 2: 158–59).
    Aḥmad b. 'Alī al-Muḥtasib, d. 442/1050 (*TB*, 4 : 324).
    Muḥammad b. 'Alī al-Warrāq, d. 422/1030 (*TB*, 3 : 94–95).
36. *TB*, 1 : 69, ll. 7–8.
37. Ibid., pp. 83–98.
38. The Khaṭīb does devote an entire chapter to the building of the Dār al-Mamlakah, but does not work this information into his systematic description of the city; cf. *TB*, 1 : 105–7.

39. Cf. G. Makdisi, "The Topography of Eleventh Century Baghdad: Materials and Notes," *Arabica*, 6 (1959): 282, 285.
40. *TB*, 1: 111–15.
41. Suhrāb, *'Ajā'ib al-aqālīm as-sab'ah*, pp. 123–24, 131–34 = Ibn Serapion, pp. 24–26.
42. Cf. Miskawayh, *Tajārib*, 2: 406; Ibn al-Jawzī, *Muntaẓam*, p. 168; Ibn al-Athīr, *Kāmil*, 8: 518.
43. *TB*, 1: 79.
44. According to Ibn al-Jawzī, *Muntaẓam*, 8: 266, he wrote fifty-six works; Ibn Khallikān, *Wafayāt*, 1: 76, indicates more than sixty.
45. *Muntaẓam*, 8: 266 (= *Mir'āt az-zamān*, fol. 131 [?], cited in Salmon, *Histoire*, pp. 8–10).
46. Ibn Khallikān, *Wafayāt*, 1: 27.
47. *TB*, 1: 117, 120.
48. For other sources where Ibn Ṭayfūr's work is quoted, see Rosenthal, *Historiography*, p. 386, n. 5.
49. European edited and trans. by H. Kellert (Leipzig, 1908); cf. Rosenthal, op. cit., p. 72, citing Qifṭī, *Ta'rīkh al-ḥukamā'*, pp. 110 ff.
50. Abū Zakarīyā' Yazīd b. Muḥammad b. Iyās al-Azdī, d. 334/945–946; cf. *GAL, Supplement*, 1: 210.
51. Cf. Rosenthal, op. cit., pp. 133, 405 (= Sakhāwī, *I'lān*, p. 133), n. 1, citing *TB*, 5: 417; 6: 132; Sam'ānī, *Ansāb*, fol. 405b–406a; Yāqūt, *Mu'jam*, 3: 114; 1: 223, 685; Ibn Ḥajar, *Lisān*, 3: 257, 261 ff.; *Tahdhīb*, 1: 9.
52. Rosenthal, op. cit., p. 133, citing Cairo Ta'rīkh 2475 (also Ṭaymūr Ta'rīkh 2303); the manuscript was written by Ibrāhīm b. Jamā'ah b. 'Alī in 654/1256. It is possible that a similar type of work was written on the city of Herat by Ibn Yasīn in the ninth century (op. cit., pp. 145, 405–406 = Sakhāwī, *I'lan*, p. 133).
53. Ibid., p. 405, n. 1, citing Mas'ūdī, *Murūj*, 1:6.
54. Rosenthal, op. cit., pp. 82–84.
55. D. 288/901 or 292/904–905 (cf. *GAL, Supplement*, 1: 210; Yāqūt, *Irshād*, 2: 256. Also see Rosenthal, op. cit., pp. 83–84, 144–45, citing MS. Cairo Ṭaymūr Ta'rīkh 1483, written in 629/Dec. 1231; p. 406 (= Sakhāwī, *I'lān*, p. 134). Baḥshāl arranged the biographical entries according to "generation"; however, he used the older *qarn* arrangement, and not the *ṭabaqāt*. For the type of topographical information contained in this work, see F. Safar, *Wāsiṭ, The Sixth Seasons Excavations* (Cairo, 1945), pp. 1 ff.
56. Rosenthal, op. cit., pp. 145 ff.
57. *TB*, 1: 131–214.
58. Rosenthal, op. cit., p. 147.
59. Ibid., pp. 386–87 (= Sakhāwī, *I'lān*, pp. 123–24).
60. Cf. Qifṭī, *Ta'rīkh al-ḥukamā'*, p. 110.
61. Rosenthal, *Historiography*, pp. 149 ff.; cf. also the remarks of Ṣ. al-Munajjid in preface to the *Faḍā'il ash-Shām wa-Dimashq* of 'Alī b. Muḥammad ar-Ruba'ī al-Mālikī (Damascus, 1951), pp. 5–6. I have not been able to obtain a copy of the *Faḍā'il*.
62. *Mu'jam*, 1: 445 *s.v.* Bābil; 4: 445 *s.v.* al-Madā'in.
63. There are various forms of this name; cf. T. Nöldeke, *Geschichte der Perser und Araber zur Zeit der Sasaniden* (Leiden, 1879), pp. 14, 348, 480; F. Justi, *Iran. Namenbuch*, pp. 148 ff.
64. *Nishwār*, 1: 165; this account is translated in F. Rosenthal, *Aḥmad b. aṭ-Ṭayyib as-Sarakhsī*, A.O.S. mon. ser. 26 (1943), p. 80. A similar story is found in *TB*, 1: 118—on

the authority of Hilāl aṣ-Ṣābi' = Yāqūt, *Mu'jam*, II, p. 255—citing a *K. Baghdād* of Hilāl aṣ-Ṣābi'. Cf. also F. Heer, *Die historischen und geographischen Quellen in Jāqūt's geographischen Wörterbuch* (Strassburg, 1898), p. 34. Hilāl aṣ-Ṣābi' was a major source of historical information for the Khaṭīb. Cf. also n. 66 below.

65. *TB*, 1 : 117 ff.
66. Ed. M. 'Awād (Baghdad, 1383/1964), esp. pp. 18 ff. Cf. also n. 64 above.
67. *TB*, 1 : 44 ff.
68. Ibid., pp. 120 ff.
69. Cf. J. Sourdel-Thomine, "Les anciens lieux de pèlerinage damascains d'après les sources arabes," *Bulletin d'Études Orientales*, 16 (1952–54): 65 ff.
70. *Kashf aẓ-ẓunūn*, 2: 120–21. He gives the author as Abū Sahl Yazdjard b. Mahmandār al-Kisrawī.

70a. The preserved fragment of this work in the Mashhad MS of Ibn al-Faqīh gives no indication of a systematic account; however, this does not preclude the existence of such an account.

71. D. 285/899. Cf. Rosenthal, *Sarakhsī*, pp. 13 ff.
72. Ibn an-Nadīm, *Fihrist*, p. 262; Qifti, *Ta'rīkh al-ḥukamā'*, p. 78 omits *wa-akhbāruha*; Ibn Abī Uṣaybi'ah, *'Uyūn al-aṭibbā'*, 1 : 215; Ḥajjī Khalīfah, op. cit. 4 : 447. The Mashhad MS of Ibn al-Faqīh preserves a large fragment if not the entire *Faḍā'il* of Sarakhsī. There is no indication of a systematic description, but this does not preclude the existence of an additional section of the *Faḍā'il* on topography.
73. Cf. Rosenthal, *Sarakhsī*, pp. 50 ff.
74. Ed. M. B. al-Atharī (Baghdad, 1342/1923); partial tr., and annotation by G. Makdisi, "The Topography of Eleventh Century Baghdad: Materials and Notes," *Arabica*, 6 (1958): 185–97.
75. On the disputed authorship of this work, see Makdisi, op. cit., p. 183, n. 4.
76. *Manāqib*, pp. 25–28 = Makdisi, *Topography*, pp. 185–97.
77. Op. cit., p. 184, n. 1.
78. E. Reitemeyer, *Die Städegründungen der Araber im Islam*, (Munich, 1912), pp. 50–59.
79. M. Streck, *Die alte Landschaft Babylonien* (Leiden, 1900), pp. 47–101.
80. G. LeStrange, *Baghdad During the Abbasid Caliphate* (London, 1900).
81. L. Massignon, *Mission en Mésopotamie 1907–1908* (Cairo, 1912), *MIFAO*, XXXI, 2: 66 ff.
82. Cf. text above.
83. *Topography*, p. 183.
84. Cf. for example *TB*, 1 : 118.
85. Such a study was begun by Makdisi for the period of the Saljūqs; cf. his *Topography*, pp. 281 ff.

Chapter 1

1. General information about the building of Madīnat as-Salām can be found in G. Salmon, *L'Introduction topographique à l'histoire de Baghdadh* (Paris, 1904), pp. 42–46; G. LeStrange, *Baghdad during the Abbasid Caliphate* (London, 1900), pp. 1–46; M. Streck, *Die alte Landschaft Babylonien* (Leiden, 1900), pp. 53–63; E. Reitemeyer, *Die Städtegründungen der Araber im Islam* (Munich, 1912), pp. 50–59; *EI*, 2nd edition, *s.v.*, Baghdad. For detailed descriptions of the city plan and its architecture, see F. Sarre and E.

Herzfeld, *Archäologische Reise im Euphrat und Tigris Gebiet* (Berlin, 1921), 2: 106–33; K. A. C. Creswell, *Early Muslim Architecture* (Oxford, 1940), pp. 4–30.

2. ʿAlī b. Abī ʿAlī al-Muʿaddil at-Tanūkhī, d. 447/1055 (*TB*, 12: 115).
   Talhah b. Muhammad b. Jaʿfar Abū-l-Qāsim ash-Shāhid, d. 380/990 (*TB*, 9: 351).
   Abū Jaʿfar Muḥammad b. Jarīr aṭ-Ṭabarī, d. 311/923 (*GAL*, 1: 142, 184, 189; *Supplement*, 1: 217).
3. According to the Khaṭīb (*TB*, 1: 60), this name was chosen because the site of Baghdad was adjacent to the Tigris which was known as Qaṣr as-Salām. The same account is reported by Ibn al-Jawzī (*Manāqib*, p. 2) who depends on the Khaṭīb as his source. The editor of the *Manāqib* corrects the text to read Wadī-s-Salām (*Manāqib*, p. 2, n. 2), presumably because the form Wadī-s-Salām is mentioned in this context as another name for the Tigris (*TB*, 1: 58; Yāqūt, *Muʿjam*, 1: 678; Samʿānī, *Ansāb*, fol. 86a, Ibn al-Athīr, *Lubāb*, 1: 133). The same is true of the form Nahr as-Salām (Yāqūt, op. cit., 3: 112). The reading of *wādī* (river bed of *peace*) or *nahr* (river of *peace*) seems more plausible here than that of *qaṣr* (palace?) but does not suggest that it is a correct etymology. However, Qaṣr as-Salām is also mentioned as a place adjacent to the Tigris in the general vicinity of Baghdad. We are informed that al-Manṣūr crossed the Tigris there in his quest to find a suitable location for his new city, and that this site, near al-Jisr, was then occupied by a monastery (Ṭabarī, *Annales*, 3.1: 273; Yāqūt, op. cit., 1: 680). In another report Ṭabarī indicates that al-Manṣūr camped at the monastery which was located at the place now known as al-Khuld (op. cit., p. 280). Situated near al-Jisr, al-Khuld was on the west bank of the Tigris directly contiguous to the original city of al-Manṣūr. If the two accounts in Ṭabarī can be correlated, it is possible that Qaṣr-as-Salām was the name ascribed to a specific area directly adjacent to the spot later occupied by al-Manṣūr's city. This, however, does not necessarily suggest an explanation for the name Madīnat as-Salām. Yāqūt presents two additional explanations. One account (op. cit., p. 677) indicates that the name was adopted by al-Manṣūr from an earlier Persian form "*hilid*" which is said to mean in Arabic "leave in peace" (*khallū bi-s-salām*). The second account explains that as-Salām denotes God, and what was desired was a name which contained the nuance of "The City of God" (op. cit., p. 678).
4. Little is known about the administration of public works in early ʿAbbāsid times (cf. E. Herzfeld, "Die Genesis der Islamischen Kunst und das Mshatta Problem," *Der Islam*, 1 (1910): 60–63; *Archäologische Reise*, 4: 117, n. 8; also F. Rosenthal, *The Muslim Concept of Freedom* (Leiden, 1960), pp. 77 ff.). The essential feature of such a program with regard to the building of Baghdad was the importing of skilled and unskilled labor from the provinces (Yaʿqūbi, *Buldān*, p. 238; Ṭabarī, *Annales*, 3.1: 276–77; Muqaddasī, p. 121; Yāqūt, *Muʿjam*, 1: 681–82). In recruiting his labor force, al-Manṣūr tapped the regions of Syria, al-Mawṣil, al-Jabal, al-Kūfah, Wāsiṭ, and al-Baṣrah (Ṭabarī, ibid.; Muqaddasī, ibid.; Yāqūt, op. cit., p. 681). No mention is made of Egypt or of Khurāsān. According to Yaʿqūbī (ibid.), actual construction did not begin until 100,000 workers of various kinds had arrived. The number is no doubt exaggerated but it nevertheless reflects a large scale undertaking (cf. Part II B). Salaries were fixed according to the division of labor, and were apparently paid out at given intervals. The price index, cited in connection with this account, indicates that the purchasing power of the skilled laborer was more than adequate to his needs, thus giving the general impression of an emerging boom town (cf. Khaṭīb, p. 70). The overall supervision of construction was given to four generals, one for each quarter of the city (Ṭabarī, op. cit., pp. 272, 278, 322); technical supervision was entrusted to groups of trained experts.

This was the system generally followed during large-scale government operations of this kind.

5. Dīnawarī, *Akhbār*, p. 379; Ya'qūbī, *Buldān*, p. 238; Ṭabarī *Annales*, 3.1: 272, 274, 277, 278; Muqaddasī, p. 121; Yāqūt, *Mu'jam*, 1: 680, 682. The overall plan of the Round City seems to have been al-Manṣūr's personal creation, although the actual task of tracing the city plan was entrusted to al-Ḥajjāj b. Arṭāt and a group of men from al-Kūfah (cf. Khaṭīb, p. 70). In order to see the form of the city plan, the Caliph ordered that the lines be traced with ashes (Ṭabarī, op. cit., p. 277; Yāqūt, op. cit., p. 682). When this was accomplished, the Caliph gave the site his personal inspection, walking about and looking at the outline of the *faṣīls*, gates, arcades, courtyards, and the city moat. He then ordered for cotton seeds which were subsequently placed along the ash marks. The seeds were doused with naphtha and set on fire. After viewing the flaming outline, he commanded that the foundations be laid on exactly these lines (Ṭabarī, op. cit., p. 277—however, Ṭabarī, op. cit., p. 278 indicating that Khālid b. Barmak traced the plan of the city). The picture obtained from the sources raises a problem demanding serious attention—that is to say, the art-historical problem which is posed by the existence of a variegated labor force of skilled artisans (see note 4 above). It would seem that such a method allows for wide diversity within very rigid limits; i.e., the execution of decorative motif and style within certain fixed architectural patterns which are pre-determined by the general taste of the grand patron. To what extent did al-Manṣūr look at his city beyond the first general impression that he was obviously concerned with; and to what extent was this initial impression pre-determined by considerations of aesthetics, architectural function and conscious political symbolism?
6. Such a statement is also found in Ya'qūbī, *Buldān*, p. 238. There are, however, numerous references in Islamic literature to other round cities. The circular plan was employed in Eastern Asia Minor and Western Persia since Assyrian times. This is particularly true with regard to military architecture (Creswell, pp. 18–21, Herzfeld, 2: 132–33). To date, the closest parallels to Madīnat as-Salām appear to be Hatra, Dārābjird, Gūr, and Ctesiphon (al-Madā'in), all sites dating from Parthian–Sassanian times. According to Creswell, "it was probably the plan of Dārābjird which directly inspired the Round City of al-Manṣūr." In support of this assumption, he cites a text from Ḥamzah al-Iṣfahānī that the circular walls of Dārābjird were first constructed when al-Ḥajjāj b. Yūsuf (d. 96/714) was governor of Iraq—that is to say, roughly within fifty years of the construction of Baghdad (Creswell, p. 21, citing Ḥamzah al-Iṣfahānī, *Ta'rīkh*, p. 37). Modern exploration does indeed indicate the presence of a round city in earlier times, but there is no evidence to link the present remains of Dārābjird with the supposed reconstruction of the city walls in Umayyad times. Literary evidence to the contrary, the circular city of Dārābjird seems to date from Parthian or Sassanian times (cf. Sir A. Stein, "An Archaeological Tour of Ancient Persis," *Iraq*, 3: 191–93). Furthermore, it is difficult to believe, on historical grounds alone, that this inconspicuous provincial town should have served as a direct prototype to the great 'Abbāsid capital. For the relationship of these cities to Baghdad, see Part II A.
7. The Caliph is reported to have laid the first brick himself (Ṭabarī, *Annales*, 3.1: 274; Yāqūt, *Mu'jam*, 1: 680), while reciting an appropriate verse from the Qur'ān (7.125, cf. Ibn aṭ-Ṭiqṭaqā, *Fakhri*, p. 219). Nawbakht, the Astrologer: one of al-Manṣūr's court astrologers (Mas'ūdī, *Murūj*, 8: 290), and the first of a line of distinguished figures bearing his name (*EI*, *s.v.* Nawbakht). According to Ya'qūbī (*Buldān*, p. 238), he was assisted in this task by Māshā'llāh, d. 200/815 (*EI*, *s.v.* Māshā'llāh b. Sāriyat).

8. Muḥammad b. 'Ali al-Warrāq, d. 422/1030 (*TB*, 3 : 94–95).
   Aḥmad b. 'Alī al-Muḥtasib, d. 442/1050 (*TB*, 4 : 324).
   Muḥammad b. Ja'far an-Naḥwī, d. 402/1011 (*TB*, 2 : 158–59).
   Al-Ḥasan b. Muḥammad as-Sakūnī, unidentifiable.
   Muḥammad b. Khalaf, d. 306/918 (*TB*, 5 : 236–37 ; *GAL*, *Supplement*, 1 : 225).
   Muḥammad b. Mūsā al-Qaysī, unidentified.
   Muḥammad b. Mūsā al-Khuwārizmī, the Mathematician, d. 232/846. (*GAL*, 1 : 215–16, 225; *Supplement*, 1 : 381, 404).
9. For the Caliph's expedition in search of a capital, and the reasons motivating his move from al-Hāshimīyah to Baghdad, see Part II A. Ya'qūbī (*Buldān*, pp. 237–38) indicates that the Caliph remained at al-Hāshimīyah until al-Mahdī left on his campaign against the Ṣaqālibah in 140/757. Al-Manṣūr then left for Baghdad and traced the city plan on Rabī I, 141/758. This is supported by a second statement (*Historiae*, 2 : 449) that the city plan had already been traced when the Caliph left Baghdad (144/761) in order to meet al-Mahdī who was returning from Khurāsān. After greeting him at Nihāwand, al-Manṣūr pushed on to al-Kūfah and then encamped at al-Hāshimīyah. He returned to Baghdad the following year (op. cit., p. 450). Ya'qūbī thus gives the impression that as many as four years may have elapsed between the conception of the city and the actual construction. For it is likely that actual construction began in 145/762. The earlier authorities generally agree upon this date (Balādhurī, *Futūḥ*, p. 295; Ibn Qutaybah, *K. al-ma'ārif*, p. 192; Ṭabarī, *Annales*, 3.1 : 277; Mas'ūdī, *Tanbih*, p. 360; Muqaddasī, p. 121; also Yāqūt, *Mu'jam*, 1 : 680, 682). Ṭabarī indicates the site had been chosen by an advance party in 144/761. On the other hand, 142/759 is a date found in the *Muntaẓam* (Creswell, 2 : 19, n. 7—citing Aya Sofya MS., No. 3095, fol. 68a—based on Ṭabarī?), however, the author of the *Manāqib* (p. 8) prefers the more accepted date citing the Khaṭīb as his source. According to Dīnawarī (*Akhbār*, p. 379), construction was underway in Baghdad as early as 139/756. Later Arabic historians follow the opinion generally accepted by the earlier authorities in preferring the date 145/762 (Ibn al-Athīr, *Kāmil*, 5 : 425, 427; Abū-l-Faraj, *Chronographia*, p. 123; *Historia*, p. 218; Ibn aṭ-Ṭiqṭaqā, *Fakhrī*, p. 219; Abū-l-Fidā', *Ta'rikh*, 2: 14; Abū-l-Maḥāsin, *Annales*, 1 : 376).
10. Muḥammad b. al-Ḥusayn b. al-Faḍl al-Qaṭṭān, unidentified.
    'Abdallāh b. Ja'far b. Durustawayh an-Naḥwī, d. 347/958 (*GAL*, 1: 112, *Supplement*, 1: 174).
    Ya'qūb b. Sufyān, d. 277/891 (*GAL*, *Supplement*, 3 : 1195, new edition, 2 : 662 : F. Rosenthal, *A History of Muslim Historiography* [Leiden, 1952], p. 320, *n.* 4).
11. Construction was interrupted by an 'Alid revolt in al-Madīnah (Ṭabarī, *Annales*, 3.1 : 278). Al-Manṣūr thus was forced to leave Baghdad with his troops and pull back to al-Kūfah (Mas'ūdī, *Tanbih*, p. 360), and did not return to Baghdad for the duration of the conflict (Ṭabarī, op. cit., p. 281). Only when the rebels had been successfully disposed of did al-Manṣūr transfer the state offices and treasuries from al-Hāshimīyah, thus establishing Baghdad as his capital in the year 146/763 (Balādhurī, *Futūḥ*, p. 295: Ibn Qutaybah, *K. al-ma'ārif*, p. 192: Ṭabarī, op. cit., pp. 281, 319: Mas'ūdī, *Tanbih*, p. 360). The statements in Yāqūt (*Mu'jam*, 1 : 580) and Muqaddasī (p. 121) which indicate that the city was completed in 149/766 probably denote the competition of the enclosure-wall adjacent to the moat as is reported by the Khaṭīb and Ṭabarī (*Annales*, 3.1 : 278; Balādhurī, *Futūḥ*, p. 295, however, indicates the date to be 147/764–65). This may refer to the inner wall.

12. Abū-l-Qāsim al-Azharī. He is frequently mentioned in *TB*, but I have not been able to find any biographical entry for him.
    Aḥmad b. Ibrāhim b. al-Ḥasan d. 383/993 (*TB*, 4 : 18–20).
    Abū ʿAbdallāh Ibrāhīm b. Muḥammad b. ʿArafah al-Azdī d. 323/935 (*GAL*, Supplement, 1 : 184).
    The astrologer who is the source of this account is identified in Yāqūt (*Muʿjam*, 1 : 684) as Abū Sahl Tirmādh b. Nawbakht, d. 170/786 (*EI*, *s.v.* Nawbakht; cf. n. 7). Yāqūt's account is a close variant of the Khaṭīb's report, and this is true as well for the poem which follows (Yāqūt, op. cit., p. 685).
13. Qur'ān 57.21, 62.4.
14. ʿUmārah b. ʿAqīl, fl. 9th century (*GAL*, *Supplement*, 1 : 122). A close variant of the poem is found in Yāqūt, *Muʿjam*, 1 : 685.
15. Manṣūr an-Namarī, fl. 8th century (Iṣfahānī, *Aghāni*, 12 : 16–25).
16. Abū ʿAbdallāh Aḥmad b. Muḥammad b. ʿAbdallāh al-Kātib d. 425/1033 (*TB*, 5 : 44–50).
    Abū Jaʿfar Muḥammad b. Aḥmad b. Muḥammad, client of the Banū Hāshim, known as Ibn Mutayyam d. 370/980 (*TB*, 1 : 344).
    Aḥmad b. ʿUbaydallāh b. ʿAmmār d. 314/926 (*TB*, 4 : 252–253).
    Abū ʿAbdallāh Muḥammad b. Dāwūd b. al-Jarrāḥ d. 296/908 (*GAL*, *Supplement*, 1 : 224–225).
17. A literal reading of the text indicates that al-Amīn boarded the boat in order to divert himself (*tanazzaha*). Descriptions of this Caliph's frivolity, even in times of crises, are not uncommon. Nevertheless, I have not, as yet, found any indication that the Caliph did, or for that matter was able to, seek the pleasures of the river during the last stages of the siege of Baghdad when his position was precarious (cf. F. Gabrieli, "La Successione di Hārūn ar-Rashīd e la Guerra fra al-Amīn e al-Ma'mūn", *RSO*, 11 : 341–97). However, the historians do mention that the Caliph boarded a boat in order to surrender to the rival general Harthamah, and thus throw himself upon the mercy of his brother (Dīnawarī, *Akhbār*, p. 395; Ṭabarī, *Annales*, 3.2 : 913–14; Masʿūdī, *Murūj*, 6 : 472–74). When the Caliph reached Harthamah's boat, it was attacked by the vessels of Ṭāhir b. al-Ḥusayn, a fellow general in the army of al-Ma'mūn. The boat was overturned in the skirmish and al-Amīn swam to safety. He was recognized and captured by one of Ṭāhir's security officers (Yaʿqūbī, *Historiae*, 2 : 536; *Dīnawarī*, ibid.; Masʿūdī, op. cit., p. 477; Ṭabarī, op. cit., pp. 920–21). There are contradictory accounts which describe the final hours of al-Amīn. An eyewitness to these events, relates that he was captured, and imprisoned with the Caliph at the house of Abū Ṣāliḥ, the scribe. At midnight a group of Persians entered the chamber and slew the Caliph after a brief scuffle. Al-Amīn's head was severed and sent to Ṭāhir. His body was left behind and was removed the following day (Ṭabarī, op. cit., pp. 919–24; Masʿūdī, op. cit., pp. 478–82). I have not been able to find any source which indicates that Muḥammad al-Amīn was killed in mid-river. For accounts which indicate that the Caliph was killed at Ṭāhir's camp, cf. n. 19.
18. Abū Bakr Muḥammad b. Yaḥyā aṣ-Ṣūlī, d. 335/946 or 336/947 (*GAL*, *Supplement*, 1 : 218–19).
    Aḥmad b. Abī Yaʿqūb al-Kātib, d. 284–897 (cf. *GAL*, *Supplement*, 1 : 405).
19. This account is apparently based on Yaʿqūbī, *Buldān*, p. 238 and indicates that the Caliph was killed at Ṭāhir's camp which was situated in a garden near the Bāb al-Anbār (Masʿūdī, *Murūj*, 6 : 471; Salmon, *Histoire*, pp. 49–50). Other historical accounts which indicate that al-Amīn was actually killed in Ṭāhir's camp are cited in Dīnawarī, *Akhbār*, p. 395; and Masʿūdī, op. cit., p. 477. However, Yaʿqūbī (*Historiae*, 2 : 536) indicates that

al-Amīn was killed at another location, and that his death came at the hands of an executioner sent by Ṭāhir from his camp. According to Ṭabarī, he was taken to the house of one Ibrāhīm b. Ja'far al-Balkhī which was situated at the Kūfah Gate and killed there (Ṭabarī, *Annales*, 3.2: 917).

Chapter 2

1. Abū 'Umar al-Ḥasan b. 'Uthmān b. Aḥmad al-Falw al-Wā'iẓ, d. 426/1035 (*TB*, 7 : 362). Ja'far b. Muḥammad b. Aḥmad b. al-Ḥakam al-Wāsiṭī, d. 353/964 (*TB*, 7: 231–232). Abū-l-Faḍl al-'Abbās b. Aḥmad al-Ḥaddād, unidentified. Aḥmad b. al-Barbarī, unidentified.
2. The data of the Khaṭīb on the area of the city is to be compared with that of Ya'qūbī, *Buldān*, p. 238, who indicates that the distance from gate to gate (4) was 5,000 black cubits. This gives a total area in round numbers of 32,000,000 sq. cubits. It is difficult to make comparative estimates owing to the chaotic state of Arabic metrology. Unless otherwise stated, the calculations are figured according to the "black cubit," for which Hinz gives a value of 54.04 cm. (Cf. W. Hinz, *Arabische Masse und Gewichte*; [Leiden, 1955], pp. 54 ff.; *EI*, 2nd edition, *s.v.* Dhirā'). According to this report, the area of the inner circle in round numbers is, therefore, 468,000 cubits, and its diameter 772 cubits. The outer circle is 576,000 cubits and its diameter 856 cubits. (Cf. Creswell, *EMA*, 2: 7—calculating 1 *jarīb* = 3,600 sq. cubits according to M. Sauvaire, "Matériaux pour servir à l'histoire de la numismatique et de la métrologie musulmanes," *JA*, 8 (1886): 485 ff.).
   However, the Khaṭīb also cites five additional reports with conflicting figures:
   1) On the authority of Badr, the page of al-Mu'taḍid (Khaṭīb, p. 69, ll. 16–18) indicating that the city was 2 *mīl* by 2 *mīl* (*mīlayn mukassir fī mīlayn*). As one *mīl* = 4,000 black cubits (Hinz, p. 63), this gives a total area of 64,000,000 sq. cubits (following Creswell, p. 7). Note, however, Herzfeld who reads 2 *mīl* sq., thus obtaining an area of approximately 16,000,000 sq. cubits, which agrees with the account of Ya'qūbī mentioned above (*Archäologische Reise*, 2: 107, n. 3).
   2) On the authority of Rabāḥ, the architect (Khaṭīb, p. 71, ll. 17–20) indicating the distance between each gate is one *mīl*, thus giving a total area of 16,000,000 sq. cubits (Herzfeld, p. 107; Creswell, p. 8).
   3) On the authority of Yaḥyā b. al-Ḥasan b. 'Abd al-Khāliq (Khaṭīb, p. 70, l. 19) agreeing with the figure mentioned above.
   4. On the authority of Wakī' (Khaṭīb, pp. 73–74) indicating that the diameter measured from the Khurāsān Gate to the Kūfah Gate was 1,200 cubits; and from the Baṣrah Gate to the Damascus Gate it was 1,200 cubits, thus giving an area of approximately 1,000,000 sq. cubits.
   5) On the authority of Wakī' (Khaṭīb, p. 72) where it is indicated that the distance between the Khurāsān Gate to the Kūfah Gate is 800 cubits, and from the Damascus Gate to the Baṣrah Gate it is 600 cubits. The account is obviously in error as this would indicate the city was not round.
   As for the expenditures, according to Yāqūt, he spent 18,000,000 dinars (*Mu'jam*, 1: 683). However, the figure seems much too high. Although the legal ratio of dinars to dirhams was 1:10, the actual rate of exchange varied. During this period it was 1:14 (cf. Salmon, *Histoire*, p. 82, n. 1).

3. S: *Abū-ṭ-Ṭayyib al-Bazzāz.*
4. S: *Al-Khaṭīb al-Ḥāfiẓ.* This variant is common in S.
5. S and C: 4,883 dirhams (corrected to 4,833,000) and 123,000 *fals.* Correct to 4,000,833 dirhams, and 100,023,000 *fals*, as in Ṭabarī, *Annales*, 3.1: 326. Cf. also Muqaddasī, p. 121; Ibn aṭ-Ṭiqṭaqā, *Fakhri*, p. 220. The ratio of copper coins (*fals*) to silver (dirhams) varied according to locality. There is no information on the exchange rate in Baghdad. (Cf. A. Udovitch, "The Bronze Coinage of the ʿAbbāsids", unpublished paper, American Numismatic Society, Summer Seminar 1961, pp. 20 ff.; also, *EI*, 2nd edition, *s.v.*, fals. One *qīrāṭ* = $\frac{1}{12}$ of a dirham, 1 *ḥabbah* = $\frac{1}{24}$ of a dirham. These denominations, as well as the *dāniq* which is mentioned below, were actually weights, and not coins (cf. Sauvaire, "Materiaux," *JA*, VII, 15 (1880): 251, 256). According to Udovitch (citing the Khaṭīb), "It is inconceivable that these minute pieces of silver were weighed out every evening in order to pay the thousands of laborers.... The small sums were obviously paid in copper or bronze coins, the denomination created expressly for this purpose. The weight divisions of the dinar and dirham were monies of account pegged to the fluctuating and diversified value of the *fals.* The *dāniq*, *qīrāṭ* and *ḥabbah* were both for official and private purposes, the only standard way to express small sums of money" (op. cit., pp. 22–23).
6. S: *Abū-l-Faḍl*; read *al-Faḍl* as in C.
   Abū-l-Ḥasan Muḥammad b. Aḥmad b. Rizq al-Bazzār (*TB*, 1: 302–3).
   Jaʿfar b. Muḥammad al-Khuldī, d. 348/959 (*TB*, 7:226–31).
   Al-Faḍl b. Makhlad ad-Daqqāq (*TB*, 12: 371).
   Dāwūd b. Saghīr b. Rustam al-Bukhārī (*TB*, 8: 367).
   This account is quoted in part in the biographical entry of Dāwūd b. Ṣaghīr.
7. For given periods historical sources may preserve some information on the changing prices of various commodities. This passage is, however, of particular importance since it also cites salaries according to the occupational structure, thus giving a picture of the purchasing power of artisans and workers under specific conditions, i.e., under the public works program. The picture obtained from these sources would seem to indicate that the labor force at Baghdad was able to obtain their basic needs without difficulty, perhaps giving the impression of an emerging boom town. For a recent collection of data on this type of problem see E. Ashtor, "Essai sur les prix et les salaires dans l'Empire Califen," *RSO*, 36 (1961): 19–69. As for the weights and measures: One *dāniq* = $\frac{1}{16}$ of a dirham (cf. Sauvaire, "Materiaux," *JA*, VII, 15 (1880): 247), and one *raṭl* = approximately 406.25 gm. (cf. Hinz, p. 31).
8. ʿUthmān b. Aḥmad ad-Daqqāq, d. 344/955 (*TB*, 11: 302–3).
   Al-Ḥasan b. Salām as-Sawwāq, d. 277/890 (*TB*, 7: 326).
   Abū Nuʿaym al-Faḍl b. Dukayn, d. 219/834 (*EI*, 2nd ed., *s.v.* Abū-Nuʿaym).
9. Abū Nuʿaym, the source of this account, died in 219/834. There is, however, no way of fixing a precise date for the comparative prices at Jabbānat Kindah. Such a place was known to have been situated in al-Kūfah (Yāqūt, *Muʿjam*, 2: 16). The reference here is therefore not necessarily to "un quartier de Baghdadh que nous ne pouvons situer, faute de renseignement précis," as Salmon assumes (*Histoire*, p. 82, n. 5). It should be noted that at different periods prices appear to have varied considerably from one location to another, although these places were situated in the same general area. This great fluctuation of price in part can be traced to the diverse metrological system which was operative at that time. See A. Ehrenkreuz, "The Kurr System in Medieval Iraq," *JESHO*, 5 (1962): 309–14; "The Taṣrīf and Tas'īr Calculations in Medieval Mesopotamian Fiscal Operations," *JESHO*, 7 (1964): 46–56. There are, of course, many other

factors which control prices. Unfortunately, it is not always possible to determine what they are in specific situations.

10. *Qiṭ'ah*: A cut-up piece of a dirham (cf. A. Grohmann, *Einführung und Chrestomathie zur arabischen Papyruskunde* [Prague, 1955], 1: 211–12). Although disapproved of, the clipping of coinage was a common practice. One *makkūk* = 5.625 kg. (Hinz, p. 44).
11. Aḥmad b. Maḥmūd ash-Sharawī, d. 274/887 (*TB*, 5: 155 ff.). Al-Ḥajjāj b. Arṭāt, who was one of the four chief engineers, was also partly responsible for the development of the suburbs (cf. Ya'qūbī, *Buldān*, p. 241—where he is incorrectly listed as al-Ḥajjāj b. Yūsuf; see also Ṭabarī, *Annales*, 3.1: 276, 321; Muqaddasī, p. 121). The other engineers were 'Abdallāh b. Muḥriz, 'Imrān b. al-Waḍḍāḥ and Shihāb b. Kathīr. They were assisted by the astrologers Nawbakht, Ibrāhīm b. Muḥammad al-Fazarī and aṭ-Ṭabarī. According to the historian, aṭ-Ṭabarī, al-Ḥajjāj was also entrusted with the task of tracing the plan of al-Manṣūr's mosque (*Annales*, 3.1: 321).
12. Abū-n-Naṣr al-Marwazī, unidentified.
    Aḥmad b. Ḥanbal, the famous jurist d. 241/855 (cf. *EI*, 2nd edition, *s.v.* Aḥmad b. Ḥanbal).
13. The Fief of Umm Ja'far was also known as az-Zubaydīyah. It was situated on the west side, north of the city, bounded by Bāb at-Tibn to the west, the Tigris to the east and the Ṭāhirid Trench (Khandaq) to the south. This last canal formed the boundary between the fief and the city proper, although at some period it may have extended south of the trench. This place is not to be confused with a location of the same name which was situated south of the Round City at Nahr al-Qallā'īn (Ya'qūbī, *Buldān*, p. 250; Suhrāb, *'Ajā'ib*, pp. 132, 133 = Ibn Serapion, pp. 24, 25; Khaṭīb, pp. 89, ll. 10–11; 110, 112, ll. 11–17; Yāqūt, *Mu'jam*, 2:517; 4: 141). Cf. also LeStrange, *Index*, p. 381; Map V. The statement by Aḥmad b. Ḥanbal is apparently confirmed by reports concerning the mosque of Umm Ja'far (Khaṭīb, p. 110 *sub anno* 379. However, he confuses the fief with az-Zubaydīyah situated at Nahr al-Qallā'īn; Ibn al-Athīr, *Kāmil*, 9: 48). It is indicated that the Caliph (aṭ-Ṭā'i') was asked to establish the mosque of the fief as a mosque for the Friday prayers. This request was based on the assertion that the mosque was situated beyond a trench which divided it from the town, and thus the fief was a town in its own right. The Caliph granted his permission. Note that according to the statement of Ibn Ḥanbal, the southern boundary of the city was the Ṣarāt Canal. This same body of water also formed the northern boundary of al-Karkh. If the statement attributed to this famous legal scholar was a juridical opinion, it would seem that for legal and/or administrative purposes, the southern suburb of al-Karkh was by the middle of the ninth century a distinct entity, thus lending support to the view that greater Baghdad was not an integrated city, but a series of interdependent areas, each giving rise in time to its own markets, mosques, cemeteries, and autonomous institutions (cf. Appendix A).
14. The Kabsh (Ram) and Asad (Lion) consisted of two large quarters (*shāri'*) near an-Naṣrīyah approaching the Ṭāhirid Trench (Khandaq), the northwest boundary of the city (Yāqūt, *Mu'jam*, 4 : 233). Cf. also LeStrange, pp. 111, 133, Map VI. According to Makdisi—citing the *Muntaẓam*, 8: 181; and *Mir'āt az-zamān*, fol. 26b—the Kabsh was still a populated quarter in 449/1057 for it is listed among the various places that were damaged in the great conflagration that occurred in that year ("The Topography of Eleventh Century Baghdad: Materials and Notes," *Arabica*, 6 (1959): 283, n. 5). He does note a variant reading in the Paris MS. of the *Mir'āt* which substitutes *al-Kutubiyīn* for al-Kabsh, and also the *Bidāyah*, 12: 71 which has *al-Kanīs*, but he believed these to be copyists' errors. However, of all the identifiable places mentioned in this fire, none, with the possible exception of Bāb ash-Sha'īr (cf. n. 36), are in the general vicinity of

an-Naṣrīyah, or the Ṭāhirid Trench (west of the Round City), but all are in or near al-Karkh (south of the Round City). Al-Kutubiyīn was situated in the eastern part of al-Karkh (Ya'qūbī, *Buldān*, p. 245—aṣḥāb al-kutub). The reading of the Paris MS. may, therefore, be more correct. However, by the time of Yāqūt it had disappeared. For the grave of Ibrāhīm al-Ḥarbī, see LeStrange, p. 133, Map. VI, ref. no. 5.

15. Abū-l-Ḥusayn Hilāl b. al-Muḥassin al-Kātib, d. 447/1056 (cf. *GAL*, 1 : 323 ff.).
Abū-l-Ḥasan Bishr b. 'Ali an-Naṣrānī al-Kātib, unidentified.

16. According to Ṭabari, the Caliph wanted to appoint Abū Ḥanīfah as the qāḍī of the city, but he refused to accept this appointment. However, al-Manṣūr did get him to accept the task of supervising the construction of bricks and the recruiting of laborers. He continued to do so until the completion of the enclosure wall which surrounded the moat of the Round City (*Annales*, 3.1 : 278).

17. Muḥammad b. Isḥāq al-Baghawī (*TB*, 1 : 242).
These figures are accepted by Herzfeld and Creswell, (Herzfeld, pp. 108–9, 121 ; Creswell, pp. 8, 10). Since 1 *mil* = 4,000 black cubits, the circumference was 16,000 cubits. Herzfeld assumes that the walls were 10 cubits thick at the base, giving a total of 160,000 bricks, plus 2,000 left over for the towers (for the towers, see text, below). The 150,000 bricks of the middle course provide for a wall $9\frac{1}{4}$ cubits thick, plus 2,000 left over for the towers. The upper part of the wall was $8\frac{1}{2}$ cubits thick with 4,000 left over for the towers and battlements. Although these figures for the thickness of the walls do not agree with those mentioned in the Arabic sources, they are regarded as more plausible (cf. n. 25 below). The bricks were generally cemented with clay (Ya'qūbī, *Buldān*, p. 238), however, where burnt brick was used, a lime mortar was employed (cf. for example Khaṭīb, p. 79). Although burnt bricks were more porous than today, when combined with quicklime (*ṣārūj*) their comprehensive strength improved considerably. They were, therefore, frequently used in foundations, at the base of retaining walls, wherever good insulation was necessary, and in tunnel-vaults and domes (cf. R. J. Forbes, *Ancient Technology*, 1: 72–74). Reeds (*qaṣab*) were set in as a bond between the courses (Yāqūt, *Mu'jam*, 1 : 681). This, as Creswell indicates, was an ancient Babylonian practice which continued into Sassanian times (Creswell, pp. 22–23).

18. Cf. Ṭabarī, *Annales*, 3.1 : 322. According to Ya'qūbī, two types of bricks were used in building the city: the large bricks which were 1 cubit square and weighed 200 *raṭl*, and the half brick which was 1 × $\frac{1}{2}$ cubits and which weighed 100 *raṭl* (*Buldān*, p. 238). The bricks were cemented with wet clay. In order to produce these bricks, wells were dug and conduits were constructed to bring the waters of the Karkhāyā Canal into the city; these conduits also supplied the city with drinking water (ibid.). On the water supply of the city, see Khaṭīb, pp. 78–79.

19. Cf. Ṭabarī, *Annales*, 3.1 : 321 ; Ibn aṭ-Ṭiqṭaqā, *Fakhri*, p. 220—on the advantages of the Round City. Note also Creswell's argument that this shape leads to an economy of construction (p.21). More difficult to evaluate are the cosmic implications of circular planning developed in H. P. L'Orange, *Studies in the Iconography of Cosmic Kingship in the Ancient World* (Cambridge, 1953). However, the most plausible explanation is that the Caliph simply followed an ancient precedent of building military camps according to a circular shape (cf. ch. 1, n. 6).

20. See Figs. 3, 4. There is no indication as to the width of the moat in any of the published texts. However, Duri, in his article on Baghdad, mentions that it was 40 cubits wide, without indicating his source (cf. *EI*, 1, 2nd edition, p. 895, —based on the Mashhad MS. of Ibn al-Faqīh [?]). There is no way of determining if this figure is correct; but if

the moat was 40 cubits wide, it would have been necessary to extend a dock from the opposite shore to meet the entrance-bridge which was set 12 (or 22) cubits from the city wall in the side of the projecting gateway. The projection of the gateway, including its front wall (10 cubits), was 30 cubits (40 according to Herzfeld). Herzfeld and Creswell, who were unaware of Duri's figure, calculated the width of the moat by subtracting the width of the entrance (presumably the same as the bridge: 8 cubits) plus that of the gateway wall (10 cubits) from the total length of the gateway. The moat was therefore 12 (or 22) cubits wide (p. 119; pp. 10–11). I am inclined to agree with Duri's figure. Note that the moat at ar-Raqqah, whose fortifications were modeled after Baghdad, was approximately 40 cubits wide (Creswell, p. 41). Ya'qūbī reports (*Buldān*, p. 239) that the base of the city wall was lined with a quay (*musannāh*) of burnt brick cemented with quicklime (*ṣārūj*) and, according to Ibn Rustah, the same was true for the shoreline of the opposite wall (p. 108). He indicates that the bricks were cemented with gypsum (*jaṣṣ*); but this is unlikely, since quicklime made the bricks less porous, and was, therefore, generally used at the base of a retaining wall, or in the construction of conduits (see n. 17 above; also K͟haṭīb, p. 79). There is no indication as to the width of this quay.

21. Meaning the Gold Palace (*al-Qaṣr adh-D͟hahab*) and the adjoining mosque, which were situated in the center of the inner courtyard (cf. Ya'qūbī, *Buldān*, p. 240; Ibn Rustah, pp. 108–9; Muqaddasī, p. 121; text, Figs. 1 and 2). According to the K͟haṭīb, the palace was 400 cubits by 400 cubits, and the mosque 200 cubits by 200 cubits. This is identical with the figures given by Yāqūt for the palace and mosque of al-Hajjāj b. Yūsuf in Wāsiṭ (*Mu'jam*, 4: 885). These figures and the position of the palace to the mosque are confirmed by an Iraqi expedition to that site (F. Safar, *Wāsiṭ, the Sixth Seasons Excavations* [Cairo, 1945]). A structure of the same dimensions was found at al-Kūfah (M. 'Alī Mustafā, "Taqrīr al-awwal," *Sumer*, 10 [1954]: 73–85). For other possible connections between these structures see n. 22 below and Part II A. Herzfeld and Creswell have reconstructed the palace on a central plan with a dome in the middle and four courts leading to *iwāns* on each side of the domed chamber. This was based on the analogy of Abū Muslim's palace at Merv (Herzfeld, pp. 134–35; Creswell, p. 4, fig. 2; cf. also Fig. 1). However, note the objections of O. Grabar who believes it was on a longitudinal axis ("Al-Mushatta, Baghdad and Wāsiṭ," in *Studies in Honor of Phillip K. Hitti* [London, 1959], pp. 99–108).

22. Cf. Yāqūt, *Mu'jam*, 1: 683, who regards the story as nonsensical. Yāqūt (d. 1229), of course, never had an opportunity to view the green dome, for as the K͟haṭīb indicates below, the structure collapsed during a storm in the year 329/941 (cf. also Ibn al-Jawzī, *Muntaẓam*, 6: 317; and Ṣūlī, *Ak͟hbār*, p. 229 *sub anno* 330). It apparently inspired the creation of a mechanical device described and illustrated in Jazarī's, *K. fī ma'rifat al-ḥiyal al-handasiyah* (cf. F. J. Martin, *The Muslim Painting of Persia, India and Turkey* [London, 1912], 2, pl. 2—where the source of the horseman on the miniature is described as St. Michael). There can be no doubt that the green dome and its horseman—whatever his function—was a guidepost for the region. It is remarkable that the palace-mosque of al-Ḥajjāj at Wāsiṭ, which was built according to similar dimensions, was also surmounted by a green dome which could be seen at some distance from the city (Balād͟hurī, *Futūḥ*, p. 290; Ya'qūbī, *Buldān*, p. 322; Ibn Rustah, p. 187). It is reported that such green domes serving as audience halls were also found at ar-Ruṣāfah, the functioning capital of the Umayyads in the reign of His͟hām (724–743), and at the palace of Mu'āwiyah in Damascus (Grabar, p. 106). The palace of al-Manṣūr's original capital

in al-Hāshimīyah, also may have featured such a structure (Ṭabarī, *Annales*, 3.1: 418 ff.). The question therefore arises: Was al-Manṣūr consciously imitating an established Umayyad tradition? For a full discussion see Part II A.

23. Ibrāhīm b. Makhlad al-Qāḍī, d. 410/1020 (*TB*, 6: 189–91).
Ismā'īl b. 'Alī al-Khuṭabī, d. 350/951 (*TB*, 6: 304 ff.).

24. Following Herzfeld (with some modifications), the size of the towers can be deduced in the following fashion: Since the main gateways were 40 cubits wide (see Fig. 4), the distance along the curtain wall between each gate was 3,960 cubits. Since there were 28 towers along the curtain wall, the pitch of each tower was 141 cubits. Along the wall extending from the Baṣrah to the Kūfah Gate, there was an additional tower, giving a pitch of 136½ cubits. So great a pitch indicates that the towers were not merely buttresses, but hollow projecting towers with chambers that enabled archers to give flanking fire. Although there is no mention of the shape, it can be assumed that they were round, according to the current usage. The towers at ar-Raqqah were semi-circular, and were reportedly modeled after the fortifications at Baghdad. We have already noted (above n. 17) that approximately 2,000 bricks were left over from each course for the towers. In addition, there is a gain of 12 × 20 = 240 bricks from the corridor inside each of the gates, giving a total gain of 960 plus 2,000 bricks. Assuming that the gates were double towers, a figure of approximately 24 cubits (2,960 ÷ 121) is obtained (pp. 121–22). If the towers were semi-circular, they would project approximately 40 cubits. Creswell modifies this view somewhat. He claims that the bricks that can be gained by cuts in the main wall can be calculated only according to the width of the wall. The number of bricks gained from the corridor is, therefore, 12 × 10 = 120 for each gate. In addition, there are those bricks (313 in number) gained because each of the rings of the wall going inward contains less bricks than the former. The total number of bricks gained is, therefore, 2,000 plus 480 plus 313 = 2,793. When divided by the number of towers (121), the total number of bricks left over for each course of the tower is approximately 23, or nearly equal to Herzfeld's figures (pp. 11–12). Herzfeld also argues for an internal gallery in the curtain wall, such as at Ukhayḍir. However, if such a gallery existed, it would have made for a saving in the number of bricks used for the construction of the walls, forcing a readjustment of his estimate for the size of the towers, or the first two courses (p. 126; also see n. 25 below).

25. Ya'qūbī indicates that the height of the wall to the top of the battlements was 60 black cubits (*Buldān*, p. 239); Ṭabarī and Muqaddasī indicate that the wall was 20 cubits thick at the top (*Annales*, 3.1 : 278; p. 121). According to Ya'qūbī, the width was 90 black cubits at the base of the retaining wall, and 25 at the top (*Buldān*, p. 239). In his *Historie*, 2: 449, the width is given as 70 cubits, but the course is not indicated. Ṭabarī and Muqaddasī report that it was 50 at the base, but give no figures for the middle courses (*Annales*, 3.1: 278; p. 121). These figures do not seem possible, because they indicate that the width of the wall was too great for the height. Even if some figures are reversed, it is not at all likely that the thickness of the wall could have been so great in relation to its height. One can object to the figures of the Khaṭīb on similar grounds. For other possible dimensions (10, 9¼, 8½ cubits) see n. 18. Note that Herzfeld assumes that, similar to Ukhayḍir, there was an internal gallery in the curtain wall which was situated at the level of the last offset, and which connected the upper chamber of the main gateway (2: 126; also Creswell, p. 12). There are, to be sure, certain similarities between both structures, and according to W. Caskel, they are of contemporary construction (W. Caskel, "Uhaidir," *Der Islam*, 39 (1964): 28–37). Therefore, it is perhaps

useful to compare the two with regard to dimensions, though one must keep in mind that different building materials were used. At Ukhayḍir, a most insignificant fortress (175 × 169 m.) when compared to Baghdad, the relationship of width to height of the enclosure wall was approximately 1:7, or 2.6 m.:19 m. (Creswell, pp. 54–55). A similar ratio at Baghdad would result in an enclosure wall 70 cubits high if Herzfeld is correct in assuming a width of 10 cubits. At ar-Raqqah, which is of course much smaller (1,500 m. east-west, and the same north-south), and where the walls were supposedly built after the pattern of Baghdad, the main wall was approximately 11½ cubits thick or 5.85 m. (Creswell, p. 39). I am, therefore, inclined to agree with Herzfeld on the thickness of the wall, although it may be somewhat wider than he assumed. Unfortunately, the walls of ar-Raqqah are not sufficiently preserved to give us an indication as to their height.

However, according to Yaʿqūbī, the *faṣīl* was 100 cubits wide (*Buldān*, p. 239). No information is given for the dimensions of the outer wall. Herzfeld assumes a proportion of 4:5, in relation to the main wall (35 cubits high, and according to him 10 cubits thick), which gives it a height of 28 cubits and a thickness of 8 cubits. There is no indication that the outer wall was protected by towers, but Herzfeld is of the opinion that there may have been small, round buttresses like those at Sāmarrā, which served a structural rather than any military function. (Herzfeld, p. 119; also Creswell, p. 11). The ratio of 4:5 is more or less upheld by the findings at ar-Raqqah where the outer wall was 4.50 m. thick and the inner protective wall 5.85 m. thick (Creswell, pp. 39–42). However, it is clear that Herzfeld's estimated height of both walls must be raised considerably. It is inconceivable that walls of Baghdad were not higher than those at Ukhayḍir (approximately 38 cubits—see n. 25 above).

According to Yaʿqūbī (*Buldān*, p. 239), the length of the corridor was 80 cubits. Herzfeld indicates that the corridor of the outer gateway was situated along the axis of the main gate (p. 123). The projection of the outer gateway was, therefore, 40 cubits, including 10 for the wall of the gateway.

However, I am inclined to agree with Creswell that the entrance leading to the main gateway was situated in the long wall. The projection of the outer gateway was, therefore, only 30 cubits (p. 12).

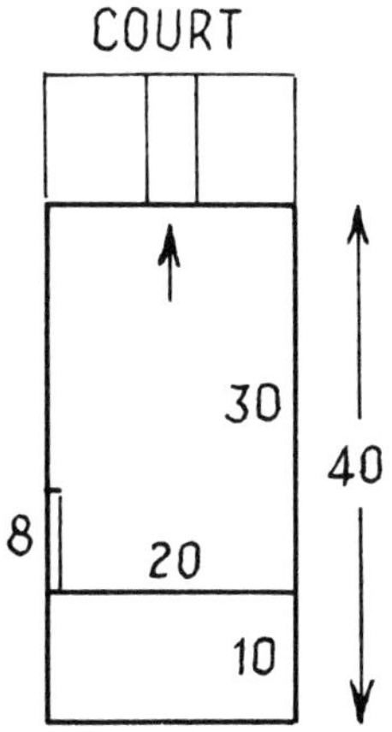

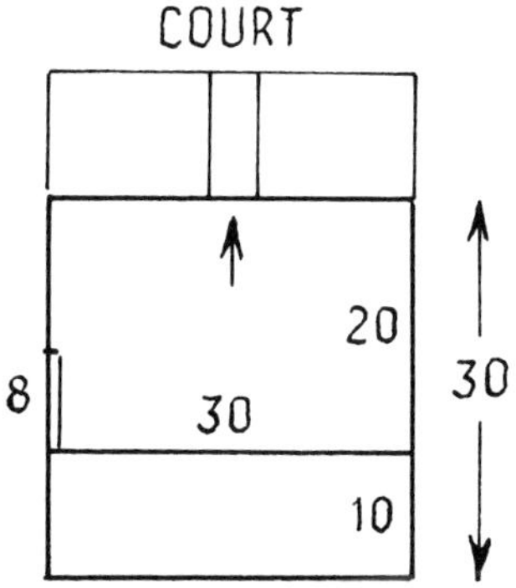

Herzfeld points out that the ratio of width to length (2:3) is also found for the halls of Sāmarrā (p. 123). For other examples of the bent entrance, see Creswell, p. 23 ff.

28. Ya'qūbī indicates that this court was paved with stones (*Buldān*, p. 239). The figure given for the length of this court seems to contradict the earlier statement in which the Khaṭīb indicates that the width of the entire *faṣil* was 60 cubits. From this statement, we can deduce that the width of the *faṣil* was 60 cubits until the line of the projecting gateway (see Figs. 3 and 4). To this figure we must add the projection of the gateway in order to obtain the total width of the *faṣil*. The projection of the gateway consisted of the corridor (10 cubits) plus the outer wall of the gateway. If we allow 5 cubits for the outer wall of the gateway, we obtain a total of 15 cubits for the gateway and 75 for the *faṣil* (cf. also Herzfeld, pp. 120–21; Creswell, p. 11).
29. Cf. text below; Figs. 6 and 7.
30. An account in Ya'qūbī indicates that it was also possible to reach the upper chamber by means of a ramp, but it is not stated how this structure connected to the gateway. The ramp inclined on the haunches of a vault constructed partly of burnt brick cemented with gypsum, and partly of large mud bricks. The inside of the vault served as a room for the guard. At various stages of the ramp, there were gates that could be locked (*Buldān*, pp. 239–240; also Creswell, pp. 15–16).
31. Ibn Rustah indicates that these domes were green (p. 108). If he does not confuse them with the green dome of the palace, he would seem to indicate that these royal audience halls built into the walls of the city were symbolically, as well as architecturally, an extension of the palace area, i.e., the personal residence of the Caliph which was situated in the great central court. This very important point is developed in detail in Part II B. The entire gateway was 30 cubits long and 40 cubits wide. These figures are obtained (based on Herzfeld) in the following fashion: The thickness of the end walls is not stated, but was assumed to be at least 5 cubits thick at each end, in order to be able to withstand assault and support the upper story. To this figure we add the length of the corridor (20 cubits), thus obtaining a total of 30 cubits. The width of the gate was equal to that of the court that led to it, i.e., 40 cubits (Herzfeld, p. 125; Creswell, p. 12). The chambers, upper and lower, may be analogous to the domed structure of Manṣūr's palace, which consisted of two superposed domed chambers of equal height (cf. Khaṭīb p. 73). Let us assume (following Creswell), that the domed chambers and the vaulted hall below were of equal height. If we allow 1 cubit for the apex of the dome, and one for the apex of the vault (according to Creswell 2 cubits), we obtain chambers with an equal height of 24 cubits, plus 2 cubits = 50 cubits, or the height given by the Khaṭīb. The palace chambers referred to above had a width equal to half their heights. The width of the corridor, as reported in the Khaṭīb was 12 cubits. We should expect, therefore, that the height of the chambers was 24 cubits, which confirms the figure previously obtained. In the palace chambers, the vertical walls were half the total height, the zone of transition making up the other half. The same was probably true of the upper chamber in the gateway (Creswell, pp. 13–14; cf. also Fig. 6).
32. No figures are available on the size of these doors; however, Ya'qūbī indicates that the entranceway was high enough to allow for the passage of a horseman with his lance or standard raised upright (*Buldān*, pp. 238–39). Herzfeld states that the long lance of the modern Bedouin is 10 cubits. He, therefore, assumes that the doorway was 10 cubits high (apparently he does not consider the horse, the point at which the lance is held, or the possibility that this expression is an idiom). The doorways at Sāmarrā had a ratio of width to length of 2:3. The width of the doorway at Baghdad would, therefore

be 6⅔ cubits. At Ukhayḍir, the doorways were 6 cubits wide and 9 cubits high (Herzfeld, pp. 124–25). It required a group of men to open and shut these doors (Yaʿqūbī, op. cit.).

33. Aḥmad b. al-Ḥārith, d. 258/872 or 259/873 (*TB*, 4: 112–23). Al-ʿAttābī, perhaps the poet Kulthūm b. ʿAmr, d. beg. fifth century (cf. *EI*, 2nd edition, *s.v.* al-ʿAttābī).
34. Ṭabarī indicates that the five gates from Wāsiṭ were set into the four main gateways, and the entrance (?) to the palace of al-Manṣūr (*Annales*, 3.1 : 321). Herzfeld, however, assumes that it was placed in the outer gateway of the Baṣrah Gate, since this is the only gateway unaccounted for in the report of the Khaṭīb (Herzfeld, p. 128). In the medieval Near East, the transfer of gates from one city to another is believed to be a symbolic act indicating an expression of authority. When Saʿd b. Abī Waqqāṣ conquered Ctesiphon and settled at al-Kūfah, he modeled his palace after the Īwān Kisrā and removed the iron gates from that building for his own use. Similarly, the gates of al-Ḥajjāj at Wāsiṭ were brought from az-Zandaward. Presumably, it was necessary for Baghdad to assume the symbolic trappings of authority which had previously accrued to Wāsiṭ and the capitals of the Umayyad realm. For a full discussion see Part II A.
35. Cf. Ṭabarī, *Annales*, 3.1 : 379, *sub anno* 157. The construction of al-Khuld marked an end to the Round City as the residence of the Caliph. However, the structure continued to be used as an administrative center. The new palace was ideally located, for it bisected the entire northern section of the city, and was stratigically situated between the major areas of military settlement—ar-Ruṣāfah on the East Side, and al-Ḥarbīyah on the West Side. Access to the east bank was gained by four bridges, three of which were reserved for the Caliph's private use and that of his retinue (cf. Khaṭīb, p. 116). Although al-Manṣūr no longer enjoyed the security of an elaborate protective wall, he was still situated near the pulse of the government, at some distance from the general populace, with large and accessible security forces nearby. For the relationship of al-Khuld to ar-Ruṣāfah see Chapter 4 and Part II B. Cf. also LeStrange, *Index*, p. 369; Map V, ref. no. 5. For ar-Rabīʿ b. Yūnus (d. 169/785), see D. Sourdel, *Le Vizirat ʿAbbāside*, Damascus (1959–1960), 2, *Index*: 779.
36. Apparently Bāb ash-Shaʿīr was originally situated near the Round City, adjacent to the Tigris; however, Yāqūt notices that in his time it was located some distance from the river (*Muʿjam*, 1 : 445). LeStrange therefore concludes, though somewhat puzzled, that there had been two places of that name (p. 139). I cannot see Makdisi's contention that the Round City was situated further to the east, and therefore obviates the necessity for two such places (*Topography*, p. 284, n. 7; also L. Massignon, *Mission en Mésopotamie* [*1907–1908*] [Cairo, 1912], *MIFAO* XXI, 2: 18–19). The location mentioned here is obviously the Bāb ash-Shaʿīr which was situated at the harbor along the Tigris. Cf. Ṭabarī, *Annales*, 3.1 : 380.
37. The allusion is to the verse in the Qur'ān (25:16) which mentions the Palace of Eternity (Khuld) that is promised to the God-fearing.
38. The reference here is presumably to the fortress-like Maṭbaq Prison which was situated on the street of that name between the Kūfah and Baṣrah Gates (Yaʿqūbī, *Buldān*, p. 240). It is clear from this statement, as well as a subsequent report of the Khaṭīb (p. 76), that the superstructure of the Round City's gate complex and residences was not only standing as late as the tenth century, but it was very much in use. Note that riots broke out that year on the West Side because of rising prices and shortages. The minbars of several mosques were smashed and Friday prayers were suspended. The bridges spanning the Tigris were set on fire, perhaps in an attempt to keep government

troops from reaching al-Karkh. The rioters also sacked the residence of the Ṣāḥib ash-Shurṭah, and liberated the prisons. Order was finally restored when the Caliph sent troops, and the shortage of foodstuffs was made up from the government warehouses. The report of the Khaṭīb is no doubt connected with these events (cf. Hamadhānī, *Takmilat*, pp. 156–57; Ibn al-Athīr, *Kāmil*, 8: 85–86).

39. In Herzfeld's view, the length of the arcade as reported by the Khaṭīb is obviously too small since the adjoining rooms had to house 1,000 men. Creswell assumes that each room was 8 cubits wide and 12 cubits deep, with 2 cubits allowed for the partition walls, and 5 for each of the end walls. Since the arcades stood free of the *faṣīl* wall, there were 54 rooms in all, and not 53 as Herzfeld believed. The total length of the arcade area was, therefore, 54 × 8 plus 53 × 2 plus 5 × 2 = 548 cubits. The arches must have corresponded with the partition walls for the sake of abutment. The springing must have been high, for Ya'qūbī indicates that the vault was pierced with Byzantine windows (*kīwā' rūmīyah*) which admitted light but no rain (*Buldān*, p. 239). A tunnel vault would have presented abutment difficulties. Wooden roofing is not possible since both Ya'qūbī (op. cit.) and Ibn Rustah (p. 108) indicate that the arcades were constructed of burnt brick and gypsum. Creswell suggests a series of transverse arches such as those at Ukhayḍir and elsewhere (Herzfeld, p. 129; Creswell, p. 16; also Figs. 3 and 7).

40. The dimensions of the corridor are not given. Herzfeld makes it 10 cubits wide and 15 long. The total length of the gateway past the arcade is therefore 35 cubits; 20 for the court and 15 for the corridor. Let us assume that the length of the second *faṣīl* is equal to the first (25 cubits), and that the end wall which is adjacent to the great inner court is 5 or less cubits wide. The gateway would therefore project 5 cubits beyond the end wall. Herzfeld (p. 129) allows for a series of free standing arches which connect to this wall, thereby forming the little arcades. Cf. also Fig. 8. Creswell, however, makes the corridor 8 cubits wide and 10 cubits long. The total length of the gateway is, therefore, even with the end wall. He assumes that the little arcades were a series of blind arches set on half piers on the analogy of the Court of Honor at Ukhayḍir, and the *ziyādahs* of the great mosque at Sāmarrā (Creswell, p. 17). Both attempts at reconstructing the small arcades leaves much to be desired. Herzfeld's structure, aside from obvious abutment difficulties, results in a very long and very narrow passageway leading nowhere along a very wide circumference. Creswell's pseudo-archway is theoretically possible, but it does not seem likely that such a structure would have been called the small arcade in contrast to the large arcade previously described. For a more plausible explanation of the small arcade see n. 41 below, and particularly Part II B.

41. The Khaṭīb does not mention any other buildings which may have been situated in the great central court. Ya'qūbī, however, mentions two additional buildings. One was adjacent to the Damascus Gate, housing the Chief of the Guard and his men. The other, the location of which is not indicated, was a large portico (*saqīfah*) raised on columns of burnt brick cemented with gypsum. This portico contained the apartment of the Chief of Police, and, presumably, rooms for his men (*Buldān*, p. 240). Surrounding the court were the residences of al-Mansur's younger children, his servants in attendance, and the slaves. In addition, there was also the treasury (*bayt al-māl*), the arsenal (*khizānat as-silāḥ*), the *dīwān* of the palace personnel (*al-aḥshām*), the public kitchen, and various other government offices (ibid.). Despite these explicit statements, and although it can be assumed that these buildings were an important element in the original city plan, there is no provision for these structures in the plan of the Round City as reconstructed by Herzfeld and Creswell (Fig. 1). LeStrange (pp. 30–31; Map II)

is somewhat more faithful to the Arabic text, but lacking any clear picture of their arrangement, he arbitrarily placed the buildings around the palace-mosque. However, evidence from Ṭabarī (*Annales*, 3.1 : 322–23) would seem to indicate the existence of a second ringed structure which housed the above-mentioned offices and residences. Such a structure must have been similar to the ringed area formed by the streets of the Round City, and flanked by the large arcades. The existence of a second ringed area thus, also, provides a suitable explanation for the small arcades. Flanking the inner ring, they were identical in function with the large arcades but simply had fewer arches thus explaining the name. For a full discussion see Part II B, also Figs. 2, 3, and 9. This statement concludes the Khaṭīb's description of the Round City. It should be noted that the site of this city has never been excavated. The reconstructions of the city are based on literary sources and are highly conjectural. The absence of excavated sites in the area from this period renders difficult any discussion of architectural origins.

42. Abū Bakr b. Abī Mūsā al-Hāshimī, d. 330/999 (*TB*, 5: 64).
43. I have been unable to find any other specific reference to this flood, but it is known that Baghdad was hard hit by inundations during this period (cf. Miskawayh, *Tajārib*, 2: 8; Ibn al-Jawzī, *Muntaẓam*, 6: 300, 315–16). In particular, the floods reported for the years 328/940 and 329/941 could very well have caused the damage described by the Khaṭīb. The circumstances of these two floods were almost identical. The waters of both the Tigris and the Euphrates swelled until the dams gave way in the vicinity of al-Anbār. The Ṣarāt, one of the major tributaries of the Euphrates leading to Baghdad, then overflowed inundating the thoroughfares of the west side, leveling houses and other structures. Qubbīn, from where the flood in our text emanated, was a district (*wilāyah*) in Iraq (cf. Yāqūt, *Mu'jam*, 4: 35). The Ṭāqāt al-'Akkī (correct C: *Ṭāq*) was a place in al-Ḥarbīyah, the northwest suburb of the city (cf. Khaṭīb, p. 83, l. 17).
44. 'Amr b. Baḥr al-Jāḥiẓ, d. 255/869 (*EI*, 2nd edition, *s.v.* al-Djāḥiẓ).
45. Az-Zawrā', meaning "the crooked." This was a name which supposedly applied to the West Side (Mas'ūdī, *Tanbīh*, p. 360; Yāqūt, *Mu'jam*, 1: 678). According to Mas'ūdī, it was so named because the *qiblah* was not precisely fixed, and the people had to turn from the orientation (of the mosque) in order to face Mecca (op. cit., p. 360). LeStrange records two other explanations: The first indicated that Baghdad took the name az-Zawrā' from the Tigris, which was bent as it passed by the city. He also notes, citing Mustawfī (ca. 14th cent.), "that while the Arabs spoke of Baghdad as Madīnat as-Salām, it was in preference named az-Zawrā' by the Persians, which almost looks as though this Arabic word az-Zawrā', "crooked," "may have stood for some more ancient Iranian name now long forgotten." (LeStrange, p. 11—citing Mustawfī, *Nuzhat al-qulūb*, p. 146). Salm al-Khāsir, d. 186/802 (cf. *GAL*, *Supplement*, 1 : 113).
46. Al-Ḥusayn b. Muḥammad al-Mu'addib, d. 213/828–29 or 214/829–30 (*TB*, 8 : 88). Ibrāhīm b. 'Abdallāh ash-Shaṭṭī, d. 391/1000–1001 (as-Sahmī, *Ta'rīkh Jurjān*, p. 99 ff.). Abū Isḥaq al-Ḥujaymī, unidentified. Muḥammad b. al-Qāsim, d. 182/798–99 or 183/799–800 (*TB*, 3 : 170 ff.).
47. Al-'Abbās b. al-'Abbās b. Muḥammad b. 'Abdallāh b. al-Mughayrah al-Jawharī, d. 328/940 (*TB*, 12: 157–58). 'Abdallāh b. Abī Sa'd al-Warrāq (*TB*, 9 : 473).
48. 'Abdallāh b. Muḥammad b. 'Ayyāsh at Tamīmī, unidentified. 'Ayyāsh b. al-Qāsim; his grandfather is mentioned in *TB*, 12: 279–80. I can find no biographical entry for him.
49. From the text of the Khaṭīb, there would appear to be two distinct accounts—one

concerning Dāwūd b. ʿAlī, the other ʿAbd aṣ-Ṣamad. However, Dāwūd b. ʿAlī is reported to have died in 133/750, before the building of Baghdad (Ṭabarī, *Annales*, 3.1 : 73). The Khaṭīb, perhaps, confuses Dāwūd b. ʿAlī and Abd aṣ-Ṣamad with ʿĪsā b. ʿAlī. A parallel account, which is preserved in Ṭabarī, (*Annales*, 3.1 : 322–23) indicates the following sequence of events: ʿĪsā b. ʿAlī complained to the Caliph that the walk from the court gate (unspecified) to the palace tired him out, and the Caliph suggested that he could be carried in a litter. ʿĪsā remarked that he would be ashamed to do that, but that he would be willing to ride one of the pack mules. There is no indication that this request was carried out. Following this discovery, the Caliph gave orders for the people (residing in the inner ringed area facing his residence; see Figs. 2, 3, and 9) to shift the gates (which opened onto the central court) so that they faced the *faṣīls* of the arcades (*ṭāqāt*). No one was permitted to enter the courtyard except on foot. Markets were then transferred to each of the four arcades (previously occupied by guards) and remained there until the Caliph, fearful of the security problem which they posed, removed them from the Round City when the matter was brought to his attention by a visiting Byzantine Ambassador (cf. Khaṭīb below; also Ṭabarī, *Annales*, 3.1 : 323–24). Also see Part II B for the importance of this account in reconstructing the architectural and historical development of the city.

50. S: *Shams*. However, Yaʿqūbī indicates that the waters of the Karkhāyā entered the city via conduits even before the walls were constructed, since water was necessary for the manufacture of the bricks and the clay cement. The Karkhāyā also supplied water for the laborers (*Buldān*, p. 238). Such was, of course, possible with regard to engineering. The account of Yaʿqūbī is, therefore, presumably correct, while in its present form that of the Khaṭīb is a later invention concocted to neatly explain certain changes in the architectural arrangement of the Round City and the subsequent development of the suburbs. It is perhaps suggested by the previous account concerning the Caliph's uncle, Dāwūd b. ʿAlī (cf. n. 49 above); for the account of the ambassador, with considerable modification, follows the account of Dāwūd b. ʿAlī in Ṭabarī as well as the Khaṭīb (*Annales*, 3.1 : 323). This, however, is not to deny that such an embassy could have existed, or for that matter that the Byzantine's advice on security was not solicited. It does, however, lead me to believe that in its present embellished form the Khaṭīb's account was suggested by later events (the redevelopment of the suburbs). For the suburb of alʿAbbāsīyah see Khaṭīb, p. 91, ll. 12–14.

51. The breakdown at the canal system was a fact of major topographical and political importance. The Khaṭīb's observation that these canals had fallen into disuse by his own time is therefore revealing. For in his chapter on the hydrography of the city (Khaṭīb, pp. 111–15), he describes the canal system as it existed ca. 925 without reworking the topographical information at his disposal. His failure to do so is what one might expect from a scholar whose particular competence was not geography, but rather the religious sciences. This becomes more clear upon examining the work of the Khaṭīb in relation to other histories of Baghdad. It also indicates that major sections of his work are based on earlier sources and thus reflect a period not contemporary with his own (cf. Introduction, p. 41). The harbor mentioned here is the lower harbor (cf. LeStrange, p. 85; Map IV).

Chapter 3

1. Al-Karkh: a loan word from Aramaic *Karka* meaning "fortified city," "city" (Fraenkel, *Fremdwörter*, 20; Pauly-Wissowa, *Real-Encyclopädie*, 4: 2122, 2124; *Supplement*,

1 : 275, 283). In Islamic times, the word is associated with various towns. Found in areas of Aramaic culture before the Islamic Conquest, such towns are distinguished from one another by adding the name of their geographic location, e.g. Karkh Baghdād, Karkh Sāmarrā (cf. Yāqūt, *Mushtarik*, pp. 368–370; *Mu'jam*, 4: 252–57). In Baghdad, al-Karkh refers to a specific area (Bāb al-Karkh) and more generally to the whole of the West Side below the Round City (cf. Iṣṭakhrī, p. 84; also Ibn Ḥawqal, p. 164). According to Ya'qūbī, whose account reflects conditions of the 8th century, the limits of al-Karkh in length were Qaṣr Waḍḍāh (north) and the Tuesday Market (south). The limits in width were the Fief of ar-Rabī' (west) and the Tigris (*Buldān*, p. 246). See LeStrange, Maps III, IV, and VII.

2. It is understandable that al-Manṣūr should have chosen this general area when he decided to relocate the markets of the Round City. Before the building of Madīnat al-Manṣūr, the old market of the West Side (Sūq Baghdād) was situated in al-Karkh, and there is reason to believe that the Karkh markets continued to service the large population of that area when the Round City was built (Ṭabarī, *Annales*, 2.2: 910, 914). The position of the old market is fixed by Balādhurī as somewhere near Qarn aṣ-Ṣarāt, the point at which the Ṣarāt Canal empties into the Tigris (*Futūḥ*, p. 246). According to Ṭabarī, the markets were also relocated at the Damascus Gate and Bāb Ṭāq al-Ḥarrānī. The former markets were then reoccupied by the guards and police of the Round City (*Annales*, 3.1 : 324). A full discussion of this move is found in Part II B. As for the specific locations mentioned in the transfer: the Karkh Gate opened unto the suburb from the west. It was found along Nahr al-Bazzāzin between the residence of Ka'b and the Clothes Merchants' Quarter (*al-Bazzāzin*). (Suhrāb, *'Ajā'ib*, p. 133 = Ibn Serapion, p. 26; also see LeStrange, *Baghdad*, p. 63; Map IV, ref. no. 11). Bāb ash-Sha'īr was situated close to the Round City near the Tigris (cf. Khaṭīb, p. 75, l. 15). The Bāb al-Muḥawwal was a vaulted gateway situated somewhere below the junction of the two Ṣarāt Canals (Ya'qūbī, *Buldān*, p. 244; Yāqūt, *Mu'jam*, 1 : 451). It gave its name to the surrounding quarter which was at first connected with al-Karkh. By the thirteenth century, it had become a separate location which was distinguished by its own mosque, and a prosperous market place (Yāqūt, op. cit., 1 : 451; 4 : 432). The people of this quarter were Ḥanbalite Sunnite, and as such were frequently in conflict with the Shī'ites of al-Karkh. Also see LeStrange, pp. 46, 146; Map IV, ref. no. 54. Cf. also *TB* 1 : 25–27; and Ch. 5, n. 56.

3. According to Ya'qūbī, the task of building the suburb, which lay between the Kūfah and Baṣrah Gates including Bāb al-Muḥawwal, Bāb al-Karkh and their environs, was entrusted to al-Musayyab b. Zuhayr, ar-Rabī', and 'Imrān b. al-Waḍḍāh, the engineer (*Buldān*, pp. 241, 246). That is to say, supervision was entrusted to a general, a public official, and a technical expert. This is consistent with programs of public works where security is provided by the army, financial administration by the state, and technical services by trained professionals. The area indicated here refers to the whole of the West Side below the Round City. See LeStrange, Map III. The development of the suburbs also included the areas to the west and to the north of the Round City (Ya'qūbī, *Buldān*, pp. 241–42).

4. A similar account of this seditious Muḥtasib is found in Ṭabarī (*Annales*, 3.1 : 324). According to his report, Abū Zakarīyā' made cause with the Shī'ites by inducing the rabble to revolt. Al-Manṣūr then dispatched Abū-l-'Abbās aṭ-Ṭūsī who quieted matters. Abū Zakarīyā' was seized, and then executed by Mūsā, a chamberlain of Abū-l-'Abbās in the courtyard (*raḥbah*) of the Bāb adh-Dhahab. The Caliph then gave orders to widen the city roads and facilitate the transfer of the markets to al-Karkh, which in later times

were heavily populated by S̲h̲ī'ites (K̲h̲aṭīb, p. 81). This security measure was followed by the construction of a second principal mosque for the population of al-Kar k̲h̲, who had previously recited their prayers at the mosque of the Round City (see text below). Thus, the market people had no recourse to the Round City with the exception of a few distributive outlets for foodstuffs; for at the suggestion of Abān b. Ṣadaqah, al-Manṣūr left a grocer (*baqqāl*) in each of the city's four quadrants. He was permitted to sell only greens and vinegar (Ṭabarī, *Annales*, 3.1: 324–25). C: *Zakariyā'*, read *'Abdallāh*.

5. Al-Ḥārit̲h̲ b. Abī Usāmah, d. 282/896 (*GAL, Supplement.* 1: 258).

6. A similar account of the ambassador's visit is found in Ṭabarī (*Annales*, 3.1: 323; also see Yāqūt, *Mu'jam*, 4: 254). Cf. also the report mentioned in Ṭabarī, op. cit., p. 324. The account, like that of the seditious muḥtasib, would seem to indicate that the Caliph's primary concern was security. A less convincing explanation for the transfer of the markets is reported by Yāqūt. He indicates that the Caliph ordered the merchants from the city because the smoke from their shops blackened the city walls (Yāqūt, *Mu'jam*, 4: 255).

7. S: *Ḥunays*; B: *Ḥubayn*. According to Ṭabarī, he was assisted in this task by Jawwās b. al-Musayyab (*Annales*, 3.1: 323; K̲h̲arrās̲h̲ as reported in Yāqūt, *Mu'jam*, 4: 254).

8. Situated along the Baṣrah Gate Road before Bāb Ṭāq al-Ḥarrānī (Balād̲h̲urī, *Futūḥ*, p. 295; Ya'qūbī, *Buldān*, p. 245; Yāqūt, *Mu'jam*, 4: 123—citing the K̲h̲aṭīb). It gave its name to the surrounding suburb (*rabaḍ*) which in the time of Ya'qūbī contained numerous markets, including the shops of over one hundred booksellers (Ya'qūbī, op. cit., p. 245). According to Balād̲h̲urī, this palace, which was situated on the other side (east) of Bāb al-Kar k̲h̲, was built as a residence for al-Mahdī before he erected his palace at ar-Ruṣāfah, and was variously known as Qaṣr al-Waḍḍāḥ, Qaṣr al-Mahdī, and as̲h̲-S̲h̲arqīyah (op. cit., p. 295; also see Ya'qūbī, ibid. He indicates that the suburb as̲h̲-S̲h̲arqīyah, which stood in the vicinity of this palace, was prepared as a fief for al-Mahdī before it was decided to move him to ar-Ruṣāfah on the East Side). LeStrange (p. 198) in addition lists a Qaṣr al-Waḍḍāḥ for the East Side. His source is probably Yāqūt, who also reports that a palace of this name was built for al-Mahdī near ar-Ruṣāfah (op. cit., p. 123). However, this last report may stem from a misunderstanding of the account mentioned by Balād̲h̲urī (cf. also LeStrange, pp. 58, 92, 198; Map IV, ref. no. 49). For as̲h̲-S̲h̲arqīyah, see Yāqūt, *Mu'jam*, 3: 279, who indicates that it was situated east of the Baṣrah Gate. See also LeStrange, pp. 90, 94, Map IV, ref. no. 49.

9. Cf. Ya'qūbī, *Historiae*, 2: 481; Yāqūt, *Mu'jam*, 4: 254—citing the K̲h̲aṭīb. Nevertheless, other accounts indicate that rents were being charged during the reign of al-Manṣūr (Balād̲h̲urī, *Futūḥ*, p. 295; Ṭabarī, *Annales*, 3.1: 323–24; also Yāqūt, op. cit., p. 254). The tax was levied according to the size of the establishment (Ṭabarī, op. cit., p. 323; however, note Yāqūt, op. cit., p. 254, where he reports that they were levied *'alā qadri-ṣ-ṣinā'ah*—meaning wealth of the craft?). Those merchants occupying the government-built markets were subject to a higher rate of taxation, as no capital outlay was required of them (Ṭabarī, op. cit., pp. 323–24). The yearly rent (*ujrah*) on the markets of both East and West Baghdad was cited by Ya'qūbī as 12,000,000 dirhams. This sum included the rent-income from the mills of the Patrikios, which is said to have been 1,000,000 dirhams (Ya'qūbī, *Buldān*, p. 254). On the mills, see K̲h̲aṭīb, pp. 91 ff. Abū 'Ubaydallāh, Mu'āwiyah b. 'Ubaydallāh b. Yāsar, d. 169/784–785 or 170/785–786 was a scribe and later wazīr for al-Mahdī. It should be noted that he was considered an expert on taxation, having directed the taxation reforms in the Sawād of Iraq (cf. D. Sourdel, *Vizirat*, 1: 96 ff.). As for the rent collector S and C read *al-K̲h̲ursi*; perhaps

to be read *al-Ḥarrashī* (cf. *'Arīb*, p. 43d; Ṭabarī, *Index*, p. 230). Cf. also Appendix B.

0. Dār al-Baṭṭīkh (The Melon House) was a fruit market situated at the juncture of Nahr 'Īsā and Nahr Ṭābaq. (Suhrāb, *'Ajā'ib*, p. 133 = Ibn Serapion, p. 26; Yāqūt, *Mu'jam*, 2: 517; also see LeStrange, pp. 84–85; Map IV, ref. no. 42). As for the Darb al-Asākifah (Road of the Shoemakers), Yāqūt also indicates that the Dār al-Baṭṭīkh was situated there before it was moved to al-Karkh (*Mu'jam*, 2; 517). The exact location is, however, not specified. A street (*shāri'*) bearing the same name was known to have existed at a later time (eleventh century) on the upper East Side somewhere near Bāb aṭ-Ṭāq (Ibn al-Jawzī, *Manāqib*, p. 26; *Muntaẓam*, 8: 56; G. Makdisi, "The Topography of Eleventh Century Baghdad: Materials and Notes," *Arabica*, 6 [1959]: 188). However, this no doubt refers to a second market servicing the populace on the left bank of the Tigris. The street referred to in our text was presumably somewhere on the lower West Side. A more precise fix may be determined on the basis of a report describing the great Karkh fire of 332/944 (Ṣūlī, *Akhbār*, pp. 261–62). In Dhū-l-Qa'dah, a violent fire broke out in the general area of the lower West Side with the flames extending to the Cobbler's Market (Asḥāb an-Ni'al)... and the quarter of the Clothes Merchants (al-Bazzāzīn). Another report for the year 309/921 indicates that fire ravaged the Sandal-Maker's Market (al-Ḥadhdhā'īn) on the lower West Side (*Muntaẓam*, 6: 159). The existence of more than one market for the manufacture of footwear indicates that shoemaking was a diversified industry. It may be assumed that all the manufacturers were located in the same general vicinity, i.e., on the street of the shoemakers (al-asākifah). The position of the Clothes Merchants can be definitely fixed in the western part of al-Karkh (cf. LeStrange, Map III). As the cobblers were situated nearby, the position of the Darb al-Asākifah can now also be fixed. This would seem to indicate that the fruit market was originally situated in the western part of al-Karkh, but was later moved closer to the river. I can find no information on the other two streets.

1. 'Uqbah b. Ja'far b. Muḥammad b. al-Ash'ath, d. 204/819 (Ibn Abī Ṭāhir Ṭayfūr, *Ta'rīkh Baghdād*, p. 350).
   Uhbān b. Ṣayfī Mukallam adh-Dhi'b (Tha'ālibī, *Thimār*, pp. 309 ff.)
   'Īsā b. Ja'far, a grandson of al-Manṣūr, d. 172/788 (cf. Ṭabarī, *Index*, p. 433). His own palace and that of his brother Ja'far were also in this vicinity (cf. Khaṭīb, p. 92).

2. Al-Ḥasan b. Abī Ṭālib al-Khallāl, d. 439/1047 (*TB*, 7: 425).
   Abū 'Umar Muḥammad b. al-'Abbās al-Khazzāz, d. 382/992-93 (*TB*, 3: 121–22).
   Abū 'Ubayd an-Nāqid; unidentified.
   Muḥammad b. Ghālib at-Timtām, d. 283/896 (*TB*, 3: 143–47).
   Abū Muslim 'Abd ar-Raḥmān b. Yūnus, d. 234/848 (*TB*, 10: 258–59).
   Muḥammad b. 'Umar al-Wāqidī, d. 207/822 (*GAL, Supplement*, 1: 207–8).

3. Originally those sectarians who rejected (*rafaḍa*) the Caliphs, Abū Bakr and 'Umar. The term is generally used synonymously with Shī'ite. During the period of the Būyids (945–1055), there was frequent strife between the Shī'ites of al-Karkh and the Sunnites of the surrounding areas (cf. for example, Ibn al-Jawzī, *Muntaẓam*, 8: 140–42, 149–50; Ibn al-Athīr, *Kāmil*, 9: 373–74, 395–96). These frequent altercations resulted in great losses of property and goods, and even led to the erection of protective walls around the large quarters inhabited by these groups. The previously-mentioned account of Abū Zakarīyā', the seditious muḥtasib (cf. text above) seems to indicate that the large Shī'ite population of the market areas goes back to the earliest period of the city's history. This settlement of the suburban areas according to religious, and also regional, and occupational grouping (cf. Part II B), led in time to the development of autonomous

institutions within the larger city organization (cf. C. Cahen, "Mouvements populaires et autonomisme urbain dans l'Asie musulmane du moyen age," *Arabica*, 5 [1958]: 225–50; 6 [1959]: 25–56, 233–65. For specific references to the market areas, see A. A. Duri, "Nushū' al-aṣnāf wa-l-ḥiraf fi-l-Islām," *Majallat kulliyat al-ādāb*, Baghdad University, 1 [1959]: 133 ff.).

14. C: *Bakr*
    Al-Ḥasan b. Abī Bakr b. Shādhān d. 426/1034 (*TB*, 7: 279).
    Ibrāhīm b. Shādhān; the father al-Ḥasan. I can find no further information about him.

Chapter 4

1. Referring here to the new area of the upper East Side directly opposite the northwest suburb of al-Ḥarbīyah. On the relationship of these two areas, see Part II B. According to Iṣṭakhrī, p. 83, the name, among others, also came to signify more generally the entire East Side. The location referred to here was originally called 'Askar al-Mahdī (see text below). According to LeStrange, ar-Ruṣāfah (meaning the causeway) became its more general name. Perhaps in reference to a causeway which went across the swampy ground (levels were taken in the reign of al-Mu'taṣim and this area was found to be $2\frac{2}{3}$ cubits lower than the Round City—see text below). Note however, Iṣṭakhrī, p. 83, who indicates that it was called ar-Ruṣāfah after a palace of a similar name which was built by Hārūn ar-Rashīd near the principal-mosque that was situated there. In the time of Yāqūt, the area was almost entirely in ruin, as the East Side had contracted around certain areas further downstream (*Mu'jam*, 2: 783; also see LeStrange, *Index*, p. 376, esp. pp. 41–42, 187–89, Map V).
2. The date given here and in Ṭabarī (*Annales*, 3.1: 364–65) for the beginning of construction conflicts with a statement of Ya'qūbī (143/760–761). The date, as reported in Ya'qūbī, is not possible since according to virtually all the authorities, the building of the Round City itself was not begun until 145/762 (cf. *Buldān*, p. 251; for dates on the construction of the Round City see Khaṭīb, pp. 66, 67). Moreover, there is evidence that the construction of the palace area on the East Side must have been concurrent with al-Mahdī's triumphal return from the eastern provinces, an event which assuredly took place in the year 151 (cf. Part II B). There is, however, some disagreement as to the state of construction. For according to another report in Ṭabarī (op. cit., p. 460), the moat was not dug and the wall (*ḥā'iṭ*) not built until 159/775–776. See also the text of the Khaṭīb below. At this time, the main source of water for the East Side was the Nahr al-Mahdī (cf. Khaṭīb, p. 115, ll. 4–6).
3. Aḥmad b. Kāmil al-Qāḍī, d. 350/961 (*GAL*, *Supplement*, 1: 226).
   Muḥammad b. Mūsā (al-Barbarī?); see Ch. 13, n. 20.
   Muḥammad b. Abī-s-Sarī, unidentified.
   Al-Haytham b. 'Adī, d. 206/821–822 or 207/822–823 (*GAL*, *Supplement*, 1: 213).
4. Abū-l-Bakhtarī Wahb b. Wahb, d. 200/815–816, was the Qāḍī of 'Askar al-Mahdī under ar-Rashīd (*TB*, 13: 481–87).
   Ja'far b. Muḥammad is presumably the Imām Ja'far aṣ-Ṣādiq, d. 148/765 (cf. D. Donaldson, *The Shi'ite Religion* [London, 1933], pp. 129–42).
5. 'Alī b. Muḥammad b. 'Abdallāh al-Mu'addil, d. 415/1024 (*TB*, 12: 98–99).
   Muḥammad b. Aḥmad b. al-Barrā', d. 291/904 (*TB*, 1: 281–82).
   'Alī b. Yaqtīn was an official in the service of al-Mahdī, and also Keeper of the Privy Seal for al-Hādī (cf. Ṭabarī, *Index*, p. 403). A variant of the following account found in

Ṭabarī indicates that the event took place in Māsabadhān during the last days of al-Mahdī (*Annales*, 3.1 : 525).

6. Al-Ḥusayn b. ʿAlī aṣ-Ṣaymarī, d. 436/1045 (*GAL, Supplement*, 1 : 636).
   Muḥammad b. ʿImrān al-Marzubānī, d. 384/994 (*GAL, Supplement*, 1 : 43, 157).
   Muḥammad b. Yaḥyā (aṣ-Ṣūlī?).
   Muḥammad b. Mūsā al-Munajjim, i.e., al-Khuwārizmī.
   Aḥmad Ibn Abī Du'ād, d. 240/854–855, Wazīr of al-Muʿtaṣim (cf. D. Sourdel, *Vizirat*, 2, *Index*: 753).
7. Cf. Balādhurī, *Futūḥ*, p. 295; Masʿūdī, *Tanbīh*, p. 360; Yāqūt, *Muʿjam*, 3 : 677. An account which explains al-Manṣūr's decision to develop the upper East Side for his son is preserved in Ṭabarī (*Annales*, 3.1 : 365–67). The Caliph, fearing a revolt in his army, decided to divide his troops at the suggestion of Qutham b. al-ʿAbbās. One detachment was camped on the East Side, the other remained at the Round City, so that the Caliph could play one faction against the other. Al-Mahdī then took charge of this area, settling in the palace built for him. On the strategic importance of this area and its relationship to the caliphal residence (al-Khuld), as well as the northwest suburb of al-Ḥarbīyah, see Part II B.

Chapter 5

1. The Ṭāqāt al-ʿAkkī was the first of three arcades to be erected in al-Ḥarbīyah, the northwest suburb. It was situated on the road which led to the Square (*Murabbaʿah*) of Shabīb b. Rūḥ (Yāqūt, *Muʿjam*, 3: 489). The arcade is not to be confused with a fief (*qaṭīʿah*) of the same name that was situated between the Baṣrah and Kūfah Gates. (Yāqūt, op. cit., 3 : 489; 4 : 142–43). Next to be erected was the Ṭāqāt al-Ghiṭrīf; and the last, and most southernly of the three arcades was the Ṭāqāt of Abū Suwayd. It was constructed as a vaulted archway, with adjoining arcades. The Fief and Estate (*Rabaḍ*) of Suwayd, his son, were situated nearby (Yāqūt, op. cit., 3: 488). Cf. also LeStrange, p. 130; Map V, ref. no. 32. For the Cemetery of the Damascus Gate, see Khaṭīb, pp. 120–21.
2. Yaʿqūbī mentions a street (*sikkah*) of that name as having been situated in the Round City between the Kūfah and Damascus Gates (*Buldān*, p. 241). The estate was probably in al-Ḥarbīyah like the other places mentioned here, but a more precise location cannot be fixed.
3. C and S: *yuqālu Shīrawayh*; emended to *darb yuqālu lahu Shīrawayh*.
4. C and S: *ad-darb an-nāfidh* for(?) *fī-d-darb an-nāfidh*. The Estate of Abū ʿAwn was located in the Shāriʿ Quarter which extended along the Tigris shore from the Khurāsān Gate to the Upper Bridge (Yaʿqūbi, *Buldān*, p. 249). It was more precisely situated in Shāriʿ Dār ar-Raqīq (cf. n. 53 below) on the road leading to the Palace of ʿAbdallāh b. Ṭāhir (Yāqūt, *Muʿjam*, 2: 750). Cf. also LeStrange, pp. 124–25; Map V, ref. no. 22. The map identification is based on the assumption that the palace of his son Ibn Abī ʿAwn is also located on this estate (cf. Suhrāb, *ʿAjā'ib*, p. 134 = Ibn Serapion, pp. 27–28). The Palace of ʿAbdallāh b. Ṭāhir is more generally called the Ḥarīm aṭ-Ṭāhirī (cf. Yāqūt, *Muʿjam*, 2: 255). It was situated along the Tigris adjacent to Shāriʿ Dār ar-Raqīq in upper Baghdad (*aʿlā Baghdād*). In the reign of al-Muʿtaḍid it became a secondary residence of the Caliphs, who were then dwelling on the East Side (*ʿArīb*, p. 22). In the tenth century it was turned into a state prison, where the deposed Caliphs resided. Although, by the time of Yāqūt, the adjacent areas had fallen into ruin, this particular

section remained populated. Appearing like a separate town amidst the ruins, it contained, in addition to dwellings, various markets which serviced the populace. A surrounding wall provided for protection (Ibn al-Jawzī, *Manāqib*, p. 27, Yāqūt, op. cit., pp. 255–56; 3: 494). Cf. also LeStrange, pp. 120, 121, 145, 327; Map V, ref. no. 19. Makdisi, *Topography*, p. 191, n. 7.

5. The Estate of Abū Ayyūb was situated along the Anbār Gate Road (Ya'qūbī, *Buldān*, p. 248). The suburb of Ḥarb is also referred to as al-Ḥarbīyah (cf. Yāqūt, *Mu'jam*, 2: 750). For al-Ḥarbīyah, see n. 26 below.

6. Situated along the unnamed canal which begins near the Ḥarb Bridge and continues on to the Damascus Gate. It was located between the Plot of Abū-l-'Abbās to the north and the three arcades to the south (Suhrāb, *'Ajā'ib*, p. 134 = Ibn Serapion, p. 28; Yāqūt, *Mu'jam*, 3: 489; Balādhurī, *Futūḥ*, p. 296—reported as a place of interest without mention of location.) Cf. also LeStrange, pp. 126, 129, 130; Map V, ref. no. 26. The reading S̲h̲abīb b. Wa'j is found in Balādhurī, *Futūḥ*, p. 296. According to Yāqūt it is read S̲h̲abīb b. Rāḥ (*Mu'jam*, 3: 489). Muḥammad b. 'Umar al-Ji'ābī, d. 355/870 (*TB*, 3: 26–31).

7. Not to be confused with the fief of the same name which was located near the Prison and Markets of the Damascus Gate (cf. Ya'qūbī, *Buldān*, p. 248). It was situated between the Fief of Ibn Abī 'Awn and the Square of S̲h̲abīb (Suhrāb, *'Ajā'ib*, p. 134 = Ibn Serapion, pp. 27–28). Yāqūt fixes the location of this place along the Damascus Gate Road between al-Ḥarbīyah and the Baṣrah Gate (Quarter). He also indicates that the plot was situated adjacent to the Square of the Persians (*Mu'jam*, 4: 485; for the Square of the Persians, see n. 21 below). Cf. also LeStrange, p. 126; Map V, ref. no. 25.

8. Abū Ja'far Muḥammad b. Mūsā b. al-Furāt, presumably the father of the famous family of public officials known as the Banū-l-Furāt (cf. D. Sourdel, *Vizirat 'Abbāside*, 2, *Index*: 762–63; table IV, p. 747).

9. S: *Banū Zadāri*. According to Ṭabarī, al-Manṣūr consulted a certain *dihqān* when he decided to build his city. The village of that *dihqān* stood where the Square of Abū-l-'Abbās is presently located (*Annales*, 3.1: 274–75). The *dihqāns* were the head men of villages in ancient Iran. They formed a class lower than that of the nobility, and were in turn subdivided into five classes, each distinguishable by its dress. The main function of the *dihqān* was to levy taxes, and they continued to exercise this function in Islamic times (cf. C. Huart, *Iran and Iranian Civilization* [London, 1927], p. 143; A. Christensen, *L'Iran Sous Les Sassanides* [Copenhagen, 1936], pp. 106–7; R. Frye, *The History of Bukhara* [Cambridge, 1954], p. 106, n. 21).

10. According to Yāqūt, it was named after a man called Wardān (*Mu'jam*, 4: 920). Cf. also LeStrange, p. 126. The Square of Abū Qurrah is not to be confused with the street (*sikkah*) of that name, which is located by Ya'qūbī in the Round City between the Kūfah and Damascus Gates (*Buldān*, p. 241).

11. Ibrāhīm b. 'Īsā b. Abū Ja'far al-Manṣūr (*TB*, 6: 134). For this account, see Ṭabarī, *Annales*, 3.1: 279.

12. C and S: *Sharqaniyah*; read *S̲h̲arafaniyah* as in Ṭabarī, *Annales*, 3.1: 279; Yāqūt, *Mu'jam*, 3: 277. Cf. also LeStrange, p. 129.

13. C and S:*Abī-l-Jawz*; read *Abī-l-Jawn* as in Suhrāb, *'Ajā'ib*, p. 134 = Ibn Serapion, p. 27; Ṭabarī, *Annales*, 3.1: 279; Yāqūt, *Mu'jam*, 3: 277. Cf. also LeStrange, p. 129; Map V, ref. no. 27.

14. S: *Mukhālid*. Located by Ya'qūbī between the Damascus and Kūfah Gates near the Fiefs of the Qaḥāṭibah (*Buldān*, p. 246; also Yāqūt, *Mu'jam*, 2; 751—no location

indicated). Sulaymān was in charge of developing the suburbs in that area during the reign of al-Manṣūr (Ya'qūbī, op. cit., pp. 242, 246, 248).

15. Identified as a place on the West Side, but the exact location is not indicated. By the time of Yāqūt, it had fallen into ruin (*Mu'jam*, 2: 750).
16. C: *Rawwād*; S: *Raddād*. Perhaps the same as the Fief of Raddād b. Zādān which, according to Ya'qūbi, was situated near the Estate of Abū Ayyūb al-Khūzī (*Buldān*, p. 248).
17. S following BN: *Būsan*; A: *Būsā*, read *Būs* (cf. Yāqūt, *Mu'jam*, 1: p. 758). The Estate of Ḥumayd was a section (*shāri'*) situated along the Upper Ṣarāt near Bāb al-Muḥawwal and the Fief of the Rug-Makers (*Farrāshīn*). Also inhabiting this section were the relatives of Qaḥṭabah b. Shabīb (Ya'qūbī, *Buldān*, p. 244, Suhrāb, *'Ajā'ib*, p. 132 = Ibn Serapion, p. 25). Yāqūt describes it as lying in ruin adjacent to an-Naṣrīyah (cf. n. 18 below), and the Estate of al-Haytham b. Sa'īd (Yāqūt, *Mu'jam*, 2: 750). Cf. also LeStrange, pp. 140–41; Map VI.
18. S: *Nuṣayr*. It extended originally to the Dujayl Road (*Shāri'*). Yāqūt, however, observes, that the area between the road and the estate is presently occupied by Shahār Sūj, al-'Attābiyīn, and Dār al-Qazz. It was still thriving in the time of Yāqūt (*Mu'jam*, 2: 167, 522, 751–752; 4: 786). Cf. also LeStrange, pp. 137, 148; Map VI.
19. According to Yāqūt, it was situated near Rabaḍ al-Khuwārizmīyah (*Mu'jam*, 2: 751). Cf. also LeStrange, p. 128; Map V, ref. no. 30. For the Quraysh Cemetery, see Khaṭīb, p. 120 who places this cemetery in the vicinity of Bāb at-Tibn further to the north. This account appears to disagree with Yāqūt's report that this estate was situated near Rabaḍ al-Khuwārizmīyah which was located much further south. If Yāqūt is correct, perhaps one should read Maqābir ash-Shuhadā' for Maqābir Quraysh. For the Cemetery of the Martyrs (*Shuhadā'*), see Khaṭīb, pp. 126–27. Yāqūt, op. cit., 4: 586—placing it in the vicinity of Qanṭarat Bāb Ḥarb, i.e., near al-Khuwārizmīyah.
20. Not to be confused with the Fief of Zuhayr b. Muḥammad which was situated near Bāb at-Tibn (cf. n. 27 below). Located on the Fiefs of al-Mussayab b. Zuhayr (cf. n. 22 below), perhaps suggesting that the text read here: The Estate of al-Musayyab b. Zuhayr. This Suburb was near the Suwayqah of 'Abd al-Wāḥid b. Ibrāhīm. In Yāqūt's time, this entire area lay in ruins (*Mu'jam*, 2: 964; see, however, 2: 751, where it is located in the vicinity of al-Khuwārizmīyah). Cf. also LeStrange, Maps IV, VI.
21. Al-Ḥarbīyah was heavily populated with Persian clients of the 'Abbāsids. This particular suburb was situated along the Dujayl Road adjacent to the Plot of Abū-l-'Abbās (Suhrāb, *'Ajā'ib*, p. 134 = Ibn Serapion, p. 27; Yāqūt, Mu'jam, 4: 485). Cf. also LeStrange, pp. 127–28; Map V, ref. no. 31.
22. According to Ya'qūbī, these fiefs extended from the Kūfah Gate to the city entrance adjacent to the Baṣrah Gate (*Buldān*, p. 243). His palace and the mosque with the tall minaret (*al-manārah aṭ-ṭawīlah*) were also situated there. The palaces of his father and brother were found nearby (ibid., also see n. 20 above). Al-Mussayab is reported to have built the quarter between the Baṣrah and Kūfah Gates, together with ar-Rabī', and 'Imrān b. al-Waḍḍāḥ (Ya'qūbī, op. cit., p. 241). He was later appointed Ṣāḥib ash-Shurṭah (op. cit., p. 243). The Suwayqah of 'Abd al-Wahhāb was situated opposite the Kūfah Gate along the lower Ṣarāt. The Palace (*Qaṣr*) of 'Abd al-Wahhāb was also situated here. Both the Suwayqah and palace had fallen into ruin by the ninth century (Ya'qūbī, *Buldān*, p. 242; Yāqūt, *Mu'jam*, 3: 201). LeStrange, by reading "Little Ṣarāt" for "Lower Ṣarāt" (*Ṣarāt as-Suflā*), mistakenly places the Suwayqah to the right of the Kūfah Gate, pp. 59, 141; Map VI, ref. no. 9. As for the cemetery entrance, the Khaṭīb seems to refer to the Bāb ad-Dayr Cemetery (cf. Khaṭīb, p. 121, 1. 21). Streck's

identification of this location with the Cemetery of the Quraysh is not possible since that cemetery was located at Bāb at-Tibn, far north of the Round City. (*Babylonien*, p. 106). The Bāb ad-Dayr Cemetery was apparently the burial ground for the eastern part of al-Karkh.

23. Situated between the Kūfah and Damascus Gates along the road named after al-Ḥasan b. Qaḥṭabah. His fief was also located there (Ya'qūbī, *Buldān*, p. 246; Suhrāb, *'Ajā'ib*, pp. 132, 134 = Ibn Serapion, pp. 25, 27). Cf. also LeStrange, pp. 140–41, Map VI.
24. Situated along the shore road, running from the Khurāsān Gate to the Upper Bridge (Ya'qūbī, *Buldān*, pp. 242, 249). According to Ya'qūbī, it was occupied originally by Ḥafṣ b. 'Uthmān and his companions; the palace of Ḥafṣ was later taken over by Isḥāq b. Ibrāhīm (op. cit., p. 249, Khaṭīb, p. 93, l. 6). Cf. also LeStrange, p. 108; Map V, ref. no. 21. An estate (*rabaḍ*) named after Ḥamzah b. Malik is located by Yāqūt on the West Side. He reports that it was in ruin during his time. The exact location is not indicated (*Mu'jam*, 2: 750). For al-Burjulānīyah, see Yāqūt, 1: 550.
25. According to Yāqūt, it was situated adjacent to the Fief of the Persians, i.e., in al-Ḥarbīyah (*Mu'jam*, 2: 750). Ya'qūbī locates a place of this name, between the Kūfah and Damascus Gates (*Buldān*, p. 246). Apparently it was so named because it was inhabited by the companions of al-Ḥārith b. Ruqād al-Khuwārizmī.
26. Originally it referred to the entire northern suburb of the West Side (cf. Iṣṭakhrī, p. 83; also Ibn Ḥawqal, p. 164). Ya'qūbī indicates that in his time there was not a larger or more important suburb in Baghdad, and that it contained roads and markets equal to any in the city. It was populated largely by inhabitants of Persian origin who settled in neighborhoods according to regional grouping. Each group had a military and civilian head (*Buldān*, p. 248). In the time of Yāqūt, it was confined to the area of Bāb Ḥarb two *mīl* distant from the city. The surrounding environs had fallen into ruin, so that it gave the appearance of a separate town with markets of all kinds, a principal-mosque and an enclosure wall which was built for protection (*Mu'jam*, 2: 234). Cf. also LeStrange, *Index*, p. 365; Map V.
27. Not to be confused with the Fiefs of Zuhayr b. al-Mussayab which were situated between the Kūfah and Baṣrah Gates (cf. n. 20 above). This estate was situated near Bāb at-Tibn. In the time of Yāqūt, this estate lay in ruin (Balādhurī, *Futūḥ*, p. 296; *Mu'jam*, 2: 964; 4: 132). Cf. also LeStrange, p. 117; Map V.
28. Also called Shār Sūq (Ya'qūbī, *Buldān*, p. 247). It was situated between the Kūfah and Damascus Gates adjacent to an-Naṣrīyah, Dār al-Qazz, and al-'Attābīyin (op. cit., p. 247, Yāqūt, *Mu'jam*, 2: 522 reads Shahār Sūq). It consisted of a large market, various residences, and side streets (*sikkah*). Cf. also LeStrange, pp. 136–37; Map VI. According to Salmon, Shahār Sūj is Persian for "square," lit. "four sides" (Modern Persian *chahār sū*) and this is the probable origin of the Arabic *murabba'ah* which I have translated as "square" (*Histoire*, p. 108, n. 1).
29. It was situated between the Damascus and Kūfah Gates, below Shāri' Qaṣr Hāni' and adjacent to Shahār Sūj (Balādhurī, *Futūḥ*, p. 297; Ya'qūbī, *Buldān*, pp. 247, 248—cited as Rabaḍ al-Quss; Suhrāb, *'Ajā'ib*, p. 134 = Ibn Serapion, p. 27). According to Ya'qūbī, Bustān al-Quss was named after a client of al-Manṣūr (op. cit., p. 247).
30. 'Abd al-Wahhāb was the first member of the royal family to be granted a fief outside the city. His estate (*rabaḍ*) was situated on the Lower Ṣarāt opposite the Kūfah Gate and was called Suwayqat 'Abd al-Wahhāb. Ya'qūbī reports that his palace was in ruins, and that other information seems to indicate that was true for the rest of the fief as well. This would seem to indicate that the buildings of the Suwayqah were no longer standing

at the end of the ninth century (cf. Ya'qūbī, *Buldān*, p. 242).

31. Situated along the Lower Ṣarāt near the New Bridge (al-Qanṭarah al-Jadīdah) in front of the Baṣrah Gate (Ya'qūbī, *Buldān*, p. 243; Yāqūt, *Mu'jam*, 4: 189; also see Suhrāb, *'Ajā'ib*, p. 132 = Ibn Serapion, p. 25). They were inhabited by descendants of the Anṣār, and the tribes of Quraysh, Rabī'ah, Muḍar, and al-Yaman (Ya'qūbī, op. cit., p. 243). The early settlers who did not live to see the foundation of Baghdad are mentioned by the Khaṭīb in a long biographical section which precedes all the biographical entries in his work (*TB*, 1: 131–214).
32. Cf. Ya'qūbī, *Buldān*, p. 243, who lists a Dār 'Ayyāsh in this general vicinity.
33. S: *Ibn Abī Sa'īd.*
    Muḥammad b. al-Ḥasan b. Aḥmad al-Ahwāzī, d. 428/1036–1037 (*TB*, 2: 218).
    Abū Aḥmad al-Ḥasan b. 'Abdallāh b. Sa'īd al-'Askarī, d. 382/993 (*GAL, Supplement*, 1: 193).
    Abū-l-'Abbās b. 'Ammār, d. 314/926 (*TB*, 4: 252–53).
    Ibn Abī Sa'd, d. 274/887–888 (*TB*, 10: 25 ff.).
    Aḥmad b. Kulthūm; unidentified.
    Abū 'Uthmān al-Māzinī, d. 248/863 (*GAL, Supplement*, 1: 168).
    Al-Jammāz, unidentified.
    Muḥammad b. Abī Rajā', unidentified.
    Abū Dulāmah, d. 160/776–777 or 170/786–787 (cf. *EI*, 2nd edition *s.v.* Abū Dulāmah).
34. For a similar poem attributed to Abū Dulāmah, see Ibn Khallikān, *Wafayāt*, 1: 192; also M. Ben Cheneb, *Abū Dolāma*, Algiers (1922), p. 134—a close variant.
35. This prison was demolished by Mu'izz ad-Dawlah and its rubble was used as building material in the construction of his palace at ash-Shammāsīyah in 350/961–962 (Ibn al-Jawzī, *Muntaẓam*, 7: 33). Cf. also F. Rosenthal, *The Muslim Concept of Freedom* (Leiden, 1960), p. 59, n. 171. Al-Qarār was situated near Qaṣr al-Khuld above Qarn as-Ṣarāt, the point at which the great canal entered into the Tigris (cf. text below).
36. Situated along the shore road next to (south of) the Fief of Ṣāliḥ, his brother (cf. text below) in the Shāri' Quarter (Ya'qūbī, *Buldān*, p. 249). The Fief of Ṣāliḥ which was further north was bounded by the dwelling of Najīḥ, the client of al-Manṣūr, and the Fief of Abū 'Awn. Cf. also LeStrange, p. 108; Map V, ref. no. 8. I am inclined to believe that the map identification of LeStrange places this fief much too far to the south. It seems more likely that the adjacent fiefs of these two royal princes originally occupied more of the coast line between al-Jisr and the upper bridge since the Fief of Abū 'Awn was situated further north in Shāri' Dār ar-Raqīq. The dwelling of Najīḥ, according to Ya'qūbī (op. cit., p. 249), later became the possession of 'Abdallāh b. Ṭāhir, whose holdings were situated in the vicinity of the upper bridge.
37. S: *Ṭuhayr.* Streck (*Babylonien*, p. 110) believes that this suwayqah may be that of al-Haytham b. Sa'īd b. Ẓuhayr which was situated, according to Yāqūt, on the West Side near the city of al-Manṣūr (*Mu'jam*, 3: 201). Ibn Sa'īd's estate was farther west (n. 17, above). Ṭabarī (*Annales*, 3.1: 378, *sub anno* 156) reports the death of al-Haytham b. Mu'āwiyah, the deposed governor of al-Baṣrah. He died in Baghdad while lying with a slave girl and was buried in the Hāshimite Cemetery.
38. Not to be confused with the fief of that name on the East Side (cf. Ya'qūbī, *Buldān*, p. 252; Yāqūt, *Mu'jam*, 2: 521). According to Yāqūt, it was situated adjacent to Rabaḍ Abī Ḥanīfah and near the Estate of 'Uthmān b. Nuhayk on a spot that was a garden for the Persian Kings before the building of Baghdad (ibid.). 'Umārah, along with Hishām b. 'Amr at-Taghlibī and Shihāb b. Kathīr, was in charge of developing the area

extending along the Tigris shore from the K̲h̲urāsān Gate to the Qaṭrabbul Gate (Ya'qūbī, op. cit., p. 242). Cf. also LeStrange, pp. 117–18; Map V, ref. no. 18.

39. Not to be confused with the street (*sikkah*) of that name which was originally situated in the Round City between the Baṣrah and K̲h̲urāsān Gates (cf. Ya'qūbī, *Buldān*, p. 241). Another location which was a street in the Round City, between the Baṣrah and K̲h̲urāsān Gates, is mentioned below, i.e., the Sikkah of Muhalhil (Ya'qūbī, op. cit., 240). The Field of Abū-s-Sarī, a fief located in al-Ḥarbīyah which is mentioned here, calls to mind the street of that name which was also situated in the Round City between the Baṣrah and K̲h̲urāsān Gates (op. cit., pp. 240, 248). The locations listed in this section of the K̲h̲aṭīb's chapter are all outside the walls of the Round City. It seems that the three above-mentioned locations were originally streets in the Round City, whose occupants were concurrently or later granted estates in the suburbs.

40. Probably on the estate (*rabaḍ*) of that name which is situated between the Kūfah and Damascus Gates (cf. Ya'qūbī, *Buldān*, pp. 247–48).

41. Balād̲h̲urī mentions a Sulaymān b. Qīrāṭ, who was master of Saḥrā' Qīrāṭ in Madīnat as-Salām. No location is indicated (*Futūḥ*, p. 310; also see Yāqūt, *Mu'jam*, 3: 216— refers to a Salmān b. Qīrāṭ, whose father was master of Saḥrā' Qīrāṭ).

42. The island was situated in the Tigris below the point where the Ṭāhirid Trench (*K̲h̲andaq Ṭāhir*) empties into the river (Suhrāb, '*Ajā'ib*, p. 132 = Ibn Serapion, p. 24). He also had a residence at al-Baghayīn, which had previously belonged to Ḥafṣ b. 'Ut̲h̲mān (Ya'qūbī, *Buldān*, p. 249). Cf. also LeStrange, p. 119; Map V.

43. Situated east of al-Qanṭarah al-Jadīdah between Nahr Abī 'Attāb and the Ṣarāt. Adjacent to the right is the Fief of Isḥāq as̲h̲-S̲h̲arawī, and to the left is Birkat Zalzal (cf. Ya'qūbī, *Buldān*, p. 244; Suhrāb, '*Ajā'ib*, p. 132 = Ibn Serapion, p. 24; Yāqūt, *Mu'jam*, 3: 201). Cf. also LeStrange, pp. 60–61; Map IV, ref. no. 5. The identity of Abū-l-Ward is uncertain (cf. below). Ya'qūbī indicates that he was Kawt̲h̲ar b. al-Yamān, Keeper of the Treasury (*bayt al-māl*; op. cit., p. 244). Cf. also G. Wiet, *LesPays*, p. 23, n. 1.

44. Watered by a tributary (Nahr Abī 'Attāb) of the Karkhāyā, it was situated between the Ṣarāt and al-Karkh, and between the Muḥawwal Gate and the Suwayqah of Abū-l-Ward (Suhrāb, '*Ajā'ib*, p. 132 = Ibn Serapion, p. 25; Yāqūt, *Mu'jam*, 1: 592–93; 3: 201; 4: 252). Before the building of Madīnat al-Manṣūr, a village called Sāl is said to have been situated on the ground between this pond and Qaṣr al-Waḍḍāḥ (op. cit., 1: 593). Cf. also LeStrange, pp. 52, 61–62; Map IV. According to Yāqūt, Zalzal provided for the endowment of the pond in the event of his death (op. cit., p. 593; cf. also Salmon, *Histoire*, p. 112, n. 2).

45. Yāqūt reads Umm Jundub (*Mu'jam*, 1: 593). The identification of the names and places listed in this poem are discussed by Salmon: Salmā and Umm Sālim were celebrated women in the poems of the pre-Islamic poets, Zuhayr and Imrū'-l-Qays. Ad-Dak̲h̲ūl and Ḥawmal are identified by Yāqūt as places in al-Yamāmah (op. cit., 2: 370, 559) and are mentioned in Imrū'-l-Qays' *Mu'allaqāt* (cf. *Histoire*, p. 112, n. 3).

46. B: *Bayāwari*; cf. also Yāqūt, *Mu'jam*, 4: 142—citing this account. However, no entry is listed for either name. For al-Farawsyaj, see Yāqūt, op. cit., p. 252; 3: 886. Bādūraya is a district (*ṭassūj*) west of Baghdad. It is said to comprise mostly land east of Nahr 'Īsā (Suhrāb, '*Ajā'ib*, p. 123 = Ibn Serapion, p. 15; Yāqūt, op. cit., 1: pp. 460–61—it comprises all the land east of the Ṣarāt). The Fief of Rabi' consisted of an inner and an outer fief. One was situated to the right of Bāb al-Karkh, the other near the Nahr al-Qallā'īn Quarter (cf. Ya'qūbī, *Buldān*, p. 245; Ṭabarī, *Annales*, 3.1: 279, 280; Yāqūt, *Mu'jam*, 4: 142, 843). However, no mention is made in the sources as to which fief was

situated in which section. Ya'qūbī indicates that it was inhabited by clothes merchants (*bazzāzin*) from K̲h̲urāsān who dealt exclusively in their native goods (op. cit., pp. 245–46). It was one of the most populous quarters of the city (Muqaddasī, p. 121). Cf. also LeStrange, pp. 58, 67–68, 322; Map IV.

47. Salmon (*Histoire*, pp. 113, 114, n. 1) seems to suggest that the inner fief was located in the Round City *entre les deux murailles*. Bayn as-Sūrayn, however, does not refer to the walls of the city, but to a large section of al-Kark̲h̲, which Yāqūt describes as one of the nicest and most densely populated areas of that quarter. It was eventually destroyed by Ṭug̲h̲ril Bak (*Mu'jam*, 1: 799). Cf. also G. Wiet, *LesPays*, p. 23, n. 7. The street of Jamil was situated in the Anbārite Mosque Quarter (cf. text below; also Yāqūt, op. cit., 2: 119). When al-Mahdī became Caliph and moved the government to ar-Ruṣāfah, the leading figures of the regime also relocated to the East Side, ar-Rabī' b. Yūnus among them. As conditions were crowded on the West Side, the situation appears to have been ripe for speculation in real estate, particularly in the development of market areas. Ar-Rabī', after moving to the East Side, converted his western holdings into market areas in order to secure the rental income. He and his son al-Faḍl, who followed him, were therefore absentee landlords (cf. Ya'qūbī, *Buldān*, p. 252). For a full discussion, see Appendix B. The Suwayqah of G̲h̲ālib is mentioned by Yāqūt as a place in Baghdad, but the exact location is not indicated (op. cit., 3: 201; also 4: 919—in connection with this account). Cf. also LeStrange, p. 67: Map IV, ref. no. 13. For Wart̲h̲āl, see Yāqūt, op. cit., 4: 919; also p. 843—it was situated on land occupied by the Nahr al-Qallā'īn Quarter. Cf. also LeStrange, pp. 67, 83, 91.

48. The reference here is to their residences near the K̲h̲urāsān Gate (cf. K̲h̲aṭīb, p. 87). The Barmakids also had extensive holdings on the East Side (cf. Salmon, *Histoire*, p. 113, n. 3; LeStrange, pp. 200, 202, 206; Map V, ref. no. 55).

49. Situated in al-Kark̲h̲ along the banks of Nahr al-Kilāb (Suhrāb, *'Ajā'ib*, p. 133 = Ibn Serapion, p. 26). Cf. also LeStrange, p. 78; Map IV.

50. The streets (*sikkah*) within the Round City are listed in Ya'qūbī (*Buldān*, pp. 240–241). The street of S̲h̲ayk̲h̲ b. Amīrah was situated between the K̲h̲urāsān and Baṣrah Gates in the Round City (Ya'qūbī, op. cit., p. 240).

51. Yāqūt refers to Sulaymān b. Ja'far b. Abī Ja'far, the grandson of al-Manṣūr, who died in 199/814–815 (*Mu'jam*, 2: 563). It was situated opposite al-Jisr (Ibn al-Jawzī, *Manāqib*, p. 27; Yāqūt, op. cit., p. 563), and is not to be confused with the street (*sikkah*) of the same name that lay between the K̲h̲urāsān and Baṣrah Gates (Ya'qūbī, *Buldān*, p. 240). A Darb Sulaymān also existed on the East Side in ar-Ruṣāfah (Ibn al-Jawzī, op. cit., p. 28). Cf. also LeStrange, p. 108; Map V, ref. no. 8.

52. Situated in the Round City between the Baṣrah and Kūfah Gates (Ya'qūbī, *Buldān*, p. 240). Ya'qūbī also mentions a structure which contained the quarters of the commander of the guard (and presumably rooms for his men) as having been situated within the great central court in the vicinity of the Damascus Gate (ibid.). This building was presumably for the men who were actually on duty in the palace area; the rest of the contingent were no doubt housed in the above-mentioned street. The same procedure seems to have been true for the police (*s̲h̲urṭah*). That is to say, when on duty they stayed at a building in the great general court, but their general quarters were situated on a street between the Baṣrah and Kūfah Gates.

53. Not to be confused with the quarter of the same name that was situated in al-Kark̲h̲ (cf. below). Az-Zubaydīyah was the northernmost fief of the West Side. It was bounded by Bāb at-Tibn to the west and the Tigris to the east. The southern boundary was

formed where the Khandaq Ṭāhir emptied into the river at the upper harbor, although sometime it may have extended further south into the Fief of the Baghayīn (cf. Ya'qūbī, *Buldān*, p. 250; Suhrāb, *'Ajā'ib*, pp. 132, 133 = Ibn Serapion, pp. 24, 25; Yāqūt, *Mu'jam*, 2: 517; 4: 141). The location given by these authorities agrees with other statements by the Khaṭīb which indicate that the Khandaq Ṭāhir forms the boundary between the "city" and az-Zubaydīyah (cf. Khatib, p. 71). It is, therefore, puzzling that the Khaṭīb should refer to it here as being situated between the Khurāsān Gate and Sharī' Dār ar-Raqīq (cf. below). Cf. LeStrange, *Index*, p. 381; Map V. It first belonged to Ja'far b. al-Manṣūr but later it passed into the possession of Zubaydah and was occupied by her servants (Ya'qūbī, op. cit., p. 250; Yāqūt, op. cit., p. 141). The Caliph al-Muqtadir also took up residence there (*'Arīb*, p. 81). By the fourteenth century, this quarter lay in ruins having suffered considerable damage from floods (*Marāṣid*, 2: 432). Sharī' Dār ar-Raqīq was adjacent to the Ṭāhirid Ḥarīm. In the course of time, it gave its name to the surrounding area. An eleventh century account preserved by Ibn al-Jawzī indicates that it is a vast quarter with many magnificent dwellings (*Manāqib*, p. 27). Yāqūt, writing two centuries later, however, describes this quarter as mostly in ruin. (Ya'qūbī, op. cit., p. 248; Yāqūt, op. cit., 2: 519, 804; 3: 231; 4: 141). Cf. also LeStrange, pp. 123–24; Map V, ref. no. 20. The southern fief called az-Zubaydīyah was situated in the Nahr al-Qallā'īn Quarter of al-Karkh (cf. Khaṭīb, p. 110, ll. 14–15; Suhrāb, *'Ajā'ib*, pp. 132, 133 = Ibn Serapion, pp. 24, 25; Yāqūt, op. cit., 2: 917). Cf. also Appendix A.

54. A town between al-Baṣrah and Wāsiṭ (cf. Yāqūt, *Mu'jam*, 3: 132–33). S reads *Sāmarrā* but cites BN *Simmar*.
55. Situated behind the Suwayqah of Abū-l-Ward on the Fief of Ibn Raghbān (cf. n. 58 below). The Anbārites referred to here were scribes in the Dīwān al-Kharāj (Ya'qūbī, *Buldān*, p. 245). Cf. also LeStrange, p. 61; Map IV, ref. no. 6. For the public officials mentioned below who resided there, see Sourdel, *Vizirat 'Abbāside*, 2, *Index*: 751, 761, 769.
56. Ṭāq al-Ḥarrānī was situated between ash-Sharqīyah and Qaṣr al-Waḍḍāḥ (Ya'qūbī, *Buldān*, p. 245; see also Yāqūt, *Mu'jam*, 3: 489–90). Cf. also LeStrange, pp. 90, 91, 92, 96; Map IV, ref. no. 47. According to Ya'qūbī, he was 'Amr b. Sim'ān (op. cit., p. 245). It later gave its name to the surrounding area which extended from al-Qanṭarah al-Jadīdah to the Bāb al-Karkh road (*shāri'*). Before the building of Madīnat al-Manṣūr, the Old Market was called Sūq Baghdād (Balādhurī, *Futūḥ*, p. 246; *TB*, 1: 25–27). It comprised the area from Ṭāq al-Ḥarrānī to Bāb ash-Sha'īr and the places adjacent to the Tigris shore (Balādhurī, ibid; Yāqūt, *Mu'jam*, 3: 613). For Bāb ash-Sha'īr, see Khaṭīb, p. 79, l. 14. Cf. also Ṭabarī, *Annales*, 2.2: 910, 914; and Ch. 3, n. 2.
57. 'Īsā b. Aḥmad b. 'Uthmān al-Hamadhānī: he is mentioned often, but I can not find a biographical entry for him (cf. *Muntaẓam*, *Index*, 6–9). Abū-l-Ḥasan b. Rizqawayh, i.e., Muḥammad b. Aḥmad b. Muḥammad b. Aḥmad b. Rizq, who was also a direct authority of the Khaṭīb.
58. Situated on his fief behind the Suwayqah of Abū-l-Ward near the Fiefs of Raysānah and Kawthar b. al-Yamān. The Anbārite Mosque seems to have been located on this fief also (Balādhurī, *Futūḥ*, p. 296; Ya'qūbī, *Buldān*, pp. 244–245; Yāqūt, *Mu'jam*, 4: 142). Before the building of Baghdad, this area was reported to have been a dungheap (Yāqūt, op. cit., p. 524). According to Ya'qūbī, it was named after Ḥabīb b. Raghbān (op. cit., p. 245). Cf. also LeStrange, pp. 61, 95; Map IV, ref. no. 6.
59. Cf. Ṭabarī, *Annales*, 3.1: 280; Yāqūt, *Mu'jam*, 3: 486, 4: 841. According to Ya'qūbī, it was named after one Ṭābaq b. aṣ-Ṣamīh (*Buldān*, p. 250). Cf. see also G. Wiet, *LesPays*,

p. 34, n. 4. The Palace of ʿĪsā is not to be confused with his fief which was on the east bank of the Ṣarāt near Bāb al-Muḥawwal. (Yaʿqūbī, *Buldān*, p. 244.) It is situated on the bank of the Rufayl, where it empties into the Tigris. By Yāqūt's time, it had been destroyed without a trace, although the name continued, as the market servicing this heavily populated area was called Sūq Qaṣr ʿĪsā (Yāqūt, *Muʿjam*, 4: 117, 841). Cf. also LeStrange, p. 146; Map IV, ref. no. 43.

60. The course of the ʿĪsā Canal is described in the Khaṭīb's chapter on the hydrography of Baghdad (cf. pp. 111 ff.). The dwellings of the Maʿbadites were situated on the fief of that name near the Bridge (*Qanṭarah*) of ʿAbdallāh b. al-Maʿbadī (Yāqūt, *Muʿjam*, 4: 191, 842). This land later passed into the possession of Muḥammad az-Zayyāt, the Wazīr of al-Wāthiq, who converted it into a garden (ibid.). Cf. also LeStrange, p. 75; Map IV, ref. no. 40. For the Dār al-Baṭṭīkh, see Khaṭīb, p. 81, l. 6; and for the Dār al-Quṭn, see Yāqūt, op. cit., 2: 523; also LeStrange, p. 84, Map IV, ref. no. 32. The Fief of the Christians is not to be confused with the large Christian Quarter (Dār ar-Rūm) on the East Side. The monastery of the Virgins (ʿAdhārā) was located here (Yāqūt, op. cit., 2: 680; 4: 143). Cf. also LeStrange, pp. 82–83; Map IV, ref. no. 30.

61. The section of the Wāsiṭ Mosque was situated along the Karkhāyā near the Mill of Abū-l-Qāsim (Suhrāb, *ʿAjāʾib*, p. 133 = Ibn Serapion, p. 25). Cf. also LeStrange, p. 63; Map IV, ref. no. 9. I have as yet been unable to identify the Ṣīnīyāt Trench. A bridge of that name (the reading is subject to question) is known to have spanned the Ṣarāt near the Mills of the Patrikios (cf. Khaṭīb, p. 112; for the Mills, see text below).

62. The text reads: extends until the Ṣīnīyāt Trench, until al-Yāsirīyah. Perhaps a passage is missing. The text seems to be describing locations along the Karkhāyā Canal (in the direction of the ʿĪsā[?] to the south). Al-Yāsirīyah was situated along Nahr ʿĪsā (and bounded by the Karkhāyā?) two *mīl* (4 km.) from Baghdad and one *mīl* from al-Muḥawwal. It was noted for its gardens, and a bridge which spanned the canal (Suhrāb, *ʿAjāʾib*, p. 123 = Ibn Serapion, p. 14; Yāqūt, *Muʿjam*, 4: 842, 1002). Cf. also LeStrange, pp. 74, 151, 152; Map VI, ref. no. 23. Barāthā was situated along Nahr ʿĪsā where the Karkhāyā branches off at the outskirts of Baghdad near al-Muḥawwal (Yaʿqūbī, *Buldān*, p. 244; Iṣṭakhrī, p. 84; also Ibn Ḥawqal, p. 165; Yāqūt, *Muʿjam*, 1: 532–34; 4: 252). In Yāqūt's time this section was in ruin. For the etymology of Barāthā, see S. Fraenkel, *Fremdwörter*, 20. Cf. also LeStrange, pp. 153–56; Map VI. I prefer to read "quarter" for shāriʿ. That is to say, Barāthā is situated to the west of Shāriʿ al-Yāsirīyah, and al-Farawsyaj is situated to the east.

63. The Darb al-Ḥijārah was situated along the Karkhāyā somewhat above Bāb al-Muḥawwal (Suhrāb, *ʿAjāʾib*, p. 132 = Ibn Serapion. p. 26; also Yāqūt, *Muʿjam*, 4: 252—based on the Khaṭīb). Cf. also LeStrange, p. 151; Map VI, ref. no. 20. I am inclined to believe that it was located somewhat west of LeStrange's map identification and nearer Barāthā. The text of the Khaṭīb is difficult. It seems to indicate the existence of a section called Nahr Karkhāyā, which was situated between the Ṣarāt east of Qanṭarat al-ʿAbbās, and the Karkhāyā east of Darb al-Ḥijārah. Lying to the west of these sites between the two waterways was part of Barāthā.

64. Yāqūt, citing the Khaṭīb, mistakenly refers to the Mills of Umm Jaʿfar, which were situated on Khandaq Ṭāhir in al-Ḥarbīyah (cf. Yāqūt, 4: p. 252; for the Mills of Umm Jaʿfar, see Suhrāb, *ʿAjāʾib*, p. 132 = Ibn Serapion, p. 24). A statement in Ṭabarī is the only reference to the Abū Jaʿfar Mill that I have been able to find (*Annales*, 3.2: 887). The exact location is, however, not indicated. The attempt by LeStrange to identify this location with the Mills of the Patrikios does not seem possible as the latter were situated

at the junction of the two Ṣarāt canals, and thus could not have bisected the Karkhāyā as the Khaṭīb indicates (cf. LeStrange, p. 142). Moreover, the Mills of the Patrikios were built in the time of al-Mahdī. It is interesting that although Nahr Rufayl was known from early Islamic times (seventh century), it is not mentioned by Suhrāb (cf. Yāqūt, *Mu'jam*, 4: 839). Judging from the account in Yāqūt, it would seem that this waterway may have become part of Nahr 'Īsā where the great canal enters the Tigris, since Yāqūt indicates that it emptied into the Tigris near Qaṣr 'Īsā; that is where the 'Īsā Canal empties into the river (op. cit., pp. 117, 190). Cf. also LeStrange, pp. 71–72.

65. It is the island formed between the Greater and Lesser Ṣarāt. It was cultivated by the Caliph's brother al-'Abbās b. Muḥammad. Its crops are reported to have grown the year round (Ya'qūbī, *Buldān*, pp. 242–43; Yāqūt, *Mu'jam*, 6: 300–1). Three bridges spanning the lower Ṣarāt gave access to the island (cf. Khaṭīb, p. 112). Al-'Abbās later received a fief on the East Side (Ya'qūbī, op. cit., p. 252). Cf. also LeStrange, pp. 142, 149; Map VI; Appendix B.

66. The mills were situated at the junction of the Lesser and Greater Ṣarāt on the eastern tip of al-'Abbāsīyah (Ya'qūbī, *Buldān*, p. 243; Suhrāb, *'Ajā'ib*, p. 132 = Ibn Serapion, p. 24; Yāqūt, *Mu'jam*, 2: 760). One hundred millstones (*ḥujar*) were used there, and the annual income amounted to one million dirhams (Ya'qūbī, op. cit., p. 243; also see n. 68 below). By the fourteenth century nothing remained of this great establishment (*Marāṣid*, 1: 463). Cf. also LeStrange, *Baghdad*, pp. 142–44, 306; Map VI, ref. no. 10. Salmon identifies this Patrikios as Tarasius, the Armenian who defected the Muslims at the battle of Maleh in 781 (*Histoire*, p. 120, n. 2, citing Ibn al-Athīr, *Kāmil*, 6: 42). However, according to Yāqūt, the Byzantine died in 163/779–780 (op. cit., p. 760).

67. Abū 'Abdallāh al-Ḥusayn b. Muḥammad b. Ja'far al-Khāli', d. 422/1031 (*TB*, 8: 105–6). Ya'qūb b. al-Mahdī, i.e., son of the Caliph. For al-Faḍl b. ar-Rabī', d. 208/823–824, see Sourdel, *Vizirat 'Abbāside*, 2, Index: 761. A similar account which is not based on the Khaṭīb is found in Yāqūt (*Mu'jam*, 2: 759–60).

68. The account in Yāqūt (*Mu'jam*, 2: 760), confirms that "and 500,000 better" is not "*sans doute une répétition superflue du passage précédent*" (S: p. 38, n. 2). The story is not only an indication of the Caliph's generosity, but also of his ability to determine a good business investment. For a full discussion of the new economic policies of the early 'Abbāsids, see Appendix B.

69. I do not know of any fief by that name on the West Side. The Khaṭīb and Ya'qūbī both list a Fief of Khuzaymah on the East Side (cf. Khaṭīb, p. 93, ll. 13–14, Ya'qūbī, *Buldān*, pp. 251, 253). Cf. also LeStrange, p. 218, Map V, ref. no. 59.

70. Qarn aṣ-Ṣarāt was situated at the confluence of the Tigris and the Ṣarāt Canal (Ya'qūbī, *Buldān*, p. 235). Cf. also LeStrange, p. 101; Map V. The Fief of 'Īsā b. 'Alī b. 'Abdallāh b. 'Abbās was not situated along the shore but further inland near Bāb al-Muḥawwal (cf. Ya'qūbī, *Buldān*, p. 244; also Yāqūt, *Mu'jam*, 4: 143, location not indicated). The Khaṭib apparently refers to the Fief of 'Īsā b. Ja'far, which Ya'qūbī locates along the bank of the Tigris (op. cit., p. 245). Cf. LeStrange, p. 146, and also n. 71 below. According to LeStrange, Ibn Serapion indicates that the 'Īsā Canal was built by 'Īsā b. Mūsā, a nephew of the Caliph al-Manṣūr. I have not been able to find such a statement in Ibn Serapion (cf. LeStrange, *Baghdad*, p. 72; Ibn Serapion, p. 73—commentary to the text).

71. S and C: *'Īsā b. Ja'far wa Ja'far b. Abī Ja'far*: suggested emendation *li'Īsā wa liJa'far* (cf. S, p. 39, n. 1). I preserve the original reading in my translation. It seems more likely that the text is corrupt, and I suspect the correct reading is: The section of the Tigris Shore (*Shāṭi' Dijlah*) which runs from the Palace of 'Īsā to the dwelling at Qarn aṣ-Ṣarāt

presently occupied by Ibrāhīm b. Aḥmad was granted as a fief to ʿĪsā b. Jaʿfar. Qaṣr ʿĪsā is named after ʿĪsā b. ʿAlī, that is to say, b. ʿAbdallāh b. ʿAbbās after whom Nahr ʿĪsā is also named. The Harbor (*Furḍah*) and Fief of Jaʿfar are named after Jaʿfar b. Abī Jaʿfar. This reading also resolves the difficult identification mentioned in n. 70 above.

72. Not to be confused with the Palace of Ḥumayd b. Qaḥṭabah, which was named after Ḥumayd b. ʿAbd al-Ḥamīd, a general in the army of al-Maʾmūn. It stood on the bank of the Tigris near the Lower Bridge. (Cf. LeStrange, pp. 45–96; Map V, ref. no. 1—citing *Aghānī*, 18: 106.)

73. ʿAlī b. Muḥammad b. ʿAbdallāh al-Muʿaddil, d. 415/1024 (*TB*, 12: 98–99).
Al-Ḥusayn b. Ṣafwān al-Bardhaʿī, d. 340/952 (*TB*, 8: 54).
Abū Bakr ʿAbdallāh b. Muḥammad b. Abī-d-Dunyā, d. 201/816 (*GAL*, *Supplement*, 1: 247).
Al-Ḥasan b. Jahwar, unidentified.
Alī b. Abī Hāshim al-Kūfī, unidentified.
I have been informed by F. Rosenthal that these verses are quoted in a Princeton MS of Ibn Abī-d-Dunyā's *K. al-Iʿtibār*.

74. Situated in the Fief of the Baghayīn below the harbor market and az-Zubaydīyah. This palace originally belonged to Ḥafṣ b. ʿUthmān whose companions were residing in the general vicinity (cf. Yaʿqūbī, *Buldān*, pp. 249–50; also n. 24 above).

Chapter 6

1. In tracing the topographic history of Baghdad, LeStrange speaks of a shift on the East Side during the eleventh century. This change of position southward created, in effect, a new city enclosed by the wall of al-Mustazhir (pp. 217–18, 316–17, 323). Massignon, supported by Herzfeld, argues for the fixity of the city based on *un fait constant et général, la fixité de la réparition topographique des corps de métiers dans une cité islamique détérminé, à partir du moment de sa fondation* (*Mission*, 2: 90–92; *Archäologische Reise*, 2: 147–48). Canard agrees with Massignon on the fixity of the markets, but argues for the southward shift of the East Side (*Hamdanides*, pp. 158–63). Cf. also G. Makdisi, *Topography*, p. 179, and Part IIC.

2. Cf. Khaṭīb, p. 92, l. 13 for a fief of Khuzaymah b. Khāzim on the West Side. This fief was the first location off the Main Bridge as one entered the Bāb aṭ-Ṭāq area. Khuzaymah b. Khāzim was the chief of police under al-Mahdī. It is likely this location was chosen for him so as to protect the approaches to ar-Ruṣāfah and the upper part of al-Mukharrim, i.e., the Caliphal residence and administrative center of the government.

3. The Ṭāq Asmāʾ was a great archway which formed part of her palace. It was situated between ar-Ruṣāfah and Nahr al-Muʿallā (meaning in al-Mukharrim) and gave its name to the entire quarter, which became known as Bāb aṭ-Ṭāq. It is reported to have been a meeting place for poets during the reign of ar-Rashīd (Yāqūt, *Muʿjam*, 1: 445; 3: 489). Cf. also LeStrange, pp. 218, 320; Map V, ref. no. 59; Makdisi, *Topography*, p. 185, n. 4. According to Yāqūt, it was granted to Ibn Jahshiyār by al-Muwaffaq (op. cit., 3: 489). Bayn al-Qaṣrayn is cited by Yāqūt as a large place in Bāb aṭ-Ṭāq between the palaces of Asmāʾ and ʿUbaydallāh (op. cit., 1: 799). Cf. also LeStrange, p. 218. For Bāb aṭ-Ṭāq see Part II C.

4. Situated on the road which led to the Fief of al-Faḍl b. ar-Rabīʿ (Yaʿqūbī, *Buldān*, p. 253). According to Yaʿqūbī, the merchants there specialized in selling curios (*ṭarāʾif*) from China (ibid.; also see G. Wiet, *LesPays*, p. 41, n. 3). Yāqūt indicates a market for water

jugs was located there (*sūq al-jirar*). By the thirteenth century it had given its name to the entire quarter which was known as al-Khuḍayrīyah (*Mu'jam*, 2:453; *Marāṣid*, 1:357). Cf. also LeStrange, pp. 173, 197–98; Map V, ref. no. 43.

5. Situated in the vicinity of al-Jisr between the palaces of the amīrs and wazīrs (Ya'qūbī, *Buldān*, p. 253; Ibn 'Aqīl's description in *Manāqib*, pp. 17, 26; Ibn al-Jawzī, *Muntaẓam*, 5: 146; 9: 82; Yāqūt, *Mu'jam*, 3: 195). It was the large market servicing the area of Bāb aṭ-Ṭāq. According to Salmon and LeStrange, it was destroyed when the Saljūqs entered Baghdad in 447/1055 (*Histoire*, p. 65; *Baghdad*, pp. 199–201, 206; Map V, ref. no. 45). It is, however, mentioned in the *Manāqib* (cf. above); and Ibn al-Jawzī (*Muntaẓam*, 9: 85) reports that its inhabitants participated in the building of al-Mustazhir's wall in 488/1095. It must have been destroyed sometime afterward, for Yāqūt (thirteenth century) reports that no trace of it existed in his time. He follows the Khaṭīb in indicating that it was named after Yaḥyā b. Khālid, the Barmakid, and later passed into the possession of Umm Ja'far. After the civil war between al-Ma'mūn and al-Amīn, al-Ma'mūn granted Sūq Yaḥyā as a fief to Ṭāhir b. al-Ḥusayn (op. cit., p. 195; cf. however, Ya'qūbī, op. cit., p. 253, who reports that it was named after a Yaḥyā b. al-Walīd). Cf. also M. Canard, *Hamdanides*, 1: 161, 164; Makdisi, *Topography*, p. 186, n. 6.
6. C and S: *Addāt*; read *Yāsar*. The Suwayqah was situated between ar-Ruṣāfah and Nahr al-Mu'allā; this expression is usually the way Yāqūt indicates the Mukharrim quarter (Yāqūt, *Mu'jam*, 3: 201—he incorrectly reads Mu'āwiyah b. 'Amr.) The Khaṭīb also lists a square (*murabba'ah*) of that name on the East Side (*TB* 13: 136).
7. C: *'Umārah b. Abī-l-Khaṣīb, the client of Rūḥ b. Ḥātim. Some say he was the client of al-Manṣūr.* It was situated along Shāri' al-Maydān. It later passed into the possession of ar-Rabī' b. Yūnus, and then on to Umm Ḥabīb during the reign of al-Ma'mūn. In later times it served as an abode for 'Abbāsid princesses before they took up residence at al-Mahdī's palace in ar-Ruṣāfah (Yāqūt, *Mu'jam*, 4: 108—reads 'Abbād b. al-Khaṣīb). I can find no evidence of LeStrange's statement that its grounds were annexed to those of al-Mahdī's palace (p. 197; Map V).
8. Situated along the Nahr al-Mahdī (Suhrāb, *'Ajā'ib*, p. 131 = Ibn Serapion, p. 23; also see Yāqūt, *Mu'jam*, 3; 201—exact location not indicated). Cf. also LeStrange, pp. 207, 214, 215; Map V, ref. no. 57.
9. *S: al-Jurshī*; C: *al-Khursī*; perhaps read *al-Ḥarrashī*. According to Ya'qūbī it was situated near the Fief of Badr, the location of which is not indicated (*Buldān*, p. 252). Suhrāb fixes its location somewhere in al-Mukharrim (*'Ajā'ib*, p. 130 = Ibn Serapion, p. 22). By the time of Yāqūt it was completely destroyed, and its previous location unknown. However, he mentions it as being in the general area between Nahr al-Mu'allā and ar-Ruṣāfah, i.e., al-Mukharrim. Another account cited by him places it between ar-Ruṣāfah and Bāb ash-Shammāsīyah near the Dyke of Mu'izz ad-Dawlah (*Mu'jam*, v. 3, p. 194). Ya'qūbī (*ibid.*) indicates that every conceivable type of market came to be located there and he likened it to al-Karkh. Sūq al-'Aṭash was, therefore, the major market area servicing the upper East Side; just as al-Karkh serviced the lower West Side, and Sūq ath-Thalāthā' the lower East Side. Cf. also LeStrange, pp. 221–24; Map V, ref. no. 66, and M. Canard, *Hamdanides*, p. 161—who attempts to identify this market with Sūq ath-Thalāthā' (cf. n. 25, below). As Canard follows Massignon on the fixity of the city markets (cf. Part II C), it is necessary for him to place all the great markets of the East Side in the same general vicinity, i.e., the lower part of al-Mukharrim. It is clear, however, that this market was located much further upstream near the Main Bridge in the upper part of al-Mukharrim (cf. *'Arib*, pp. 28–29; Ṣūlī, *Akhbār*, p. 90).

10. S; *Abū-n-Naṣr.*
11. Cf. Khaṭīb, p. 115, l. 10. According to Yāqūt, Ibn al-Ḥuṭam built the Baradān Bridge and owned the surrounding land (*Mu'jam*, 4: 187).
12. Alī b. Muḥammad b. al-Mughīrah al-Jawharī, ca. 1000 (*TB*, 8: 105).
13. Salmon assumes that the three gates are Bāb al-Baradān, Bāb al-Ḥadīd, and the Bāb Khurāsān of East Baghdad (*Histoire*, p. 123, n. 1). It seems more likely that the Khaṭīb refers here to the three gates situated along the wall of East Baghdad, that is to say, Bāb ash-Shammāsīyah, Bāb al-Baradān, and Bāb Khurāsān. The area mentioned therefore covers most of the East Side (cf. Canard, *Ṣūlī*, 1, p. 203, n. 4—citing Ṭabarī, *Annales*, 3: 1576; Mas'ūdī, *Murūj*, 6: 443). LeStrange mentions a place just outside the city wall (Thalāthat Abwāb) which Ya'qūbī reports to be the outer limits of the Eastern City (*Buldān*, p. 269). However, according to LeStrange, there is no record of this place being written with the definite article (Thalathāt al-Abwāb); cf. LeStrange, p. 203, n. 2; Map V. The Shāri' al-Maydān was a long thoroughfare extending from ash-Shammāsīyah to Sūq ath-Thalāthā' (*Mu'jam*, 3: 231–32; for Sūq ath-Thalāthā', see n. 25, below). Cf. also LeStrange, *Baghdad*, Map. V.
14. Located on his fief (Ya'qūbī, *Buldān*, p. 253; Yāqūt, *Mu'jam*, 4: 485—exact location not indicated). Cf. LeStrange, pp. 221–22; Map V, ref. no. 67.
15. Situated above Sūq Yaḥyā (cf. n. 5 above). According to Yāqūt, it was a fief granted to him by ar-Rashīd. It was destroyed along with the residences of his son 'Umar when the latter was punished by al-Mutawwakil (*Mu'jam*, 2: 522; also see text below). Faraj and his son were public officials in the service of the 'Abbāsid rulers (cf. Sourdel, *Vizirat 'Abbāside*, 2, *Index*: 762, 785). *Umm al-walad* designates a concubine who bears her master a son. If the son is recognized by the master, the concubine will be set free upon her master's death (cf. *EI*, *s.v.*, Umm al-walad).
16. Yazīd died in 64/683. 'Abd aṣ-Ṣamad died accordingly 121 years later in 185/801–802 (cf. Ibn Khallikān, *Wafayāt*, 1: 296). According to Ibn Khallikān, Muḥammad b. 'Alī died in 126/743–744 (ibid.). Dāwūd b. 'Alī died in 133/750. Since 'Abd aṣ-Ṣamad is reported to have died fifty-two years later, this account is consistent with the date 185/801–802 mentioned above.
17. Cf. Yāqūt, *Mu'jam*, 2: 564—exact location not indicated. A hospital was established there in 311/924 by the Wazīr Abū-l-Ḥasan b. al-Furāt (cf. Ibn al-Jawzī, *Muntaẓam*, 6; 174; Ibn Abī Uṣaybi'ah, *'Uyūn al-anbā'* 1: 224). For other hospitals at Baghdad, see Chapter 10, n. 9.
18. Situated in the vicinity of Bāb al-Muqayyar (Ya'qūbī, *Buldān*, p. 253; also Yāqūt, *Mu'jam*, 2: 767—exact location not indicated).
19. Situated in al-Mukharrim. The Mūsā Canal is reported to have ended on the palace grounds (Suhrāb, *'Ajā'ib*, p. 129 = Ibn Serapion, p. 21). Cf. also LeStrange, pp. 226–27: Map V, ref. no. 75. S reads *al-Bānūjah.*
20. S: *al-'Abbāsīyah.* The Suwayqah is mentioned by Yāqūt (*Mu'jam*, 3: 200—no location indicated). The palace was presumably situated there. Al-'Abbās received his fief after having developed al-'Abbāsīyah on the West Side (Ya'qūbī, *Buldān*, p. 252). The move to the East Side was, no doubt, prompted by the shift of the Caliphate to ar-Ruṣāfah. For al-'Abbāsīyah on the West Side, see text above.
21. C: *'Ubaydallāh b. Aḥmad aṣ-Ṣayrafī.*
    Ibn Durayd, d. 321/934 (*GAL*, *Supplement*, 1: 172–74).
22. Abū 'Alī al-Kharaqī, unidentified.
    'Abdallāh b. Aḥmad b. Ḥanbal, d. 290/903 (*TB*, 9: 375–76).

23. Muḥammad b. Abī ʿAlī, unidentified.
Muḥammad b. ʿAbd al-Munʿim b. Idrīs; his father is mentioned in *TB*, 11: 131–34, but I can find no biographical information on him.
Hishām b. Muḥammad, d. 206/821 (*GAL, Supplement*, 1: 211).

24. Cf. Balādhurī, *Futūḥ*, p. 249. Al-Mukharrim refers to the general area between ar-Ruṣāfah and Nahr al-Muʿallā (Yāqūt, *Muʿjam*, 4: 441).

25. Situated near the Lower Bridge, this section was watered by the Nahr al-Muʿallā (Suhrāb, *ʿAjaʾib*, p. 130 = Ibn Serapion, p. 22). Before the building of Madīnat al-Manṣūr, a market was held there once a month on a Tuesday for the people of Kalwādhā and Baghdad, thus giving the market its name. (Yāqūt, *Muʿjam*, 3: 193–94.) This market is not to be confused with one of a similar name, which according to Yaʿqūbī, was situated on the West Side (*Buldān*, p. 246). Cf. also LeStrange, *Index*, p. 378; Map V, ref. no. 79; Massignon, *Mission*, 2: 92–93—in modern times: Canard, *Hamdanides*, 1: 159–62: esp. p. 161, where it is identified with Sūq al-ʿAṭash (cf. n. 9 above). For the name Sūq ath-Thalāthāʾ, see E. Herzfeld, *Archäologische Reise*, 2: 105–6. Kalwādhā is a district (*ṭassūj*) adjacent to East Baghdad. It was in ruin by the time of Yāqūt (cf. *Muʿjam*, 4: 301). Cf. also LeStrange, *Index*, p. 368; Map III.

26. By the time of Yāqūt, it lay in ruin (*Muʿjam*, 3: 200—exact location not indicated). Cf. also LeStrange, p. 226; Map V, ref. no. 71—located near a Dār Ibn al-Khaṣīb. He apparently refers to Ibn Abī Khuṣayb mentioned below.

27. Situated in al-Mukharrim (Yāqūt, *Muʿjam*, 2: 521). Cf. also LeStrange, p. 227; Map V, ref. no. 76—referred to as al-Khaṣīb. The Palace of ʿUmārah b. Abī-l-Khaṣīb was situated further north along Shāriʿ al-Maydān (cf. n. 7 above).

28. The exact location of ʿĪsābādh is not known. According to Yāqūt, al-Mahdī granted it to his son ʿĪsā. Later, he built a palace (*Qaṣr as-Salām*) there at the cost of 50,000,000 dirhams (*Muʿjam*, 3: 752–53; and text below). Cf. also LeStrange, p. 194, n. 1. Although the Royal Palace was situated in ar-Ruṣāfah, there is reason to believe that once Qaṣr as-Salām was built, much of the administrative work was carried out in ʿĪsābādh (Ṭabarī, *Annales*, 3.1: 517). At first, temporary quarters were built of mud-brick; later the permanent residence was erected in burnt-brick. According to Ṭabarī, the foundations were laid in Dhū-l-Qaʿdah, 164/781, and the Caliph took up residence there in 166/782–783 (op. cit., pp. 501, 517).

29. This seems to be a contradiction of the previous statement, but the text admits of no other translation.

30. On the advice of Harthamah, ar-Rashīd made Ibrāhīm b. al-Aghlab the master of al-Ifriqīyah on payment of 40,000 dinars. This took place in 184/800. For the Aghlabid dynasty, see *EI*, 2nd edition, *s.v.*, Aghlabids.

31. Cf. Yāqūt, *Muʿjam*, 3: 363—no location indicated. He also had holdings on the West Side along the shore of the Tigris (cf. Khaṭīb, p. 87, ll. 10–11). This new residence (?) was prompted, perhaps, by the shift of the Caliphate to ar-Ruṣāfah.

32. Situated outside Baghdad on the Khurāsān Road (Yāqūt, *Muʿjam*, 4: 25—who gives al-Ḥusayn b. Sukayn).

33. It was situated near Ḥawd Haylānah and Ḥawd al-Anṣār. All three were supplied by branch canals of the Nahr Mūsā (Suhrāb, *ʿAjāʾib*, p. 130 = Ibn Serapion, p. 22). According to Yāqūt, it was named after one Dāwūd b. al-Mahdī b. al-Manṣūr who is reported to have a fief near Sūq al-ʿAṭash (*Muʿjam*, 2: 362). As al-Manṣūr's uncle, Dāwūd b. ʿAlī, died before the building of Madīnat as-Salām (cf. Khaṭīb, p. 78, n. 49), this account

of the K̲h̲aṭīb seems to be in error. For other identifications of Dāwūd, see text below. Cf. also LeStrange, p. 223 ; Map V, ref. no. 69.

34. Situated near Ḥawd al-Anṣār and Ḥawd Dāwūd (cf. n. 33 above). According to Yāqūt, she was a stewardess (*qahramānah*) in the service of al-Manṣūr, and was called Haylānah because when hurried, she frequently commanded, "Let's go now" (Hayya-l-ānah?; cf. n. 36 below). She also had an estate on the West Side near Bāb al-Muḥawwal (*Mu'jam*, 2: 362–63; p. 752 refers to Haylānah the concubine of ar-Ras̲h̲īd; see text below). For Rabaḍ Haylānah, see LeStrange, p. 146.

35. S: *al-Jawhari al-Ḥasan b. 'Ali b. Muḥammad*; see Ch. 12, n. 22.
    Aḥmad b. Muḥammad b. 'Īsā al-Makkī, d. 322/934 (*TB*, 5 : 64).
    Muḥammad b. al-Qāsim b. K̲h̲allād ; see Ch. 2, n. 46.
    Al-Asma'ī, d. 213/828 (*GAL, Supplement*, 1 : 164–65).

36. Apparently some colloquial expression. Salmon's translation, "*Elle et maintenant lui*," does not seem likely (cf., *Histoire*, p. 128, n. 1). It may be noted that Yāqūt mentions this account in relation to Haylānah, the stewardess of al-Manṣūr (cf. n. 34 above). The name is probably Greek "Helene" (Salmon, ibid.).

37. The above-mentioned *isnād* occurs in Ṣūlī, *Awrāq*, but I have not been able to obtain biographical information about al-Iṣbahānī, al-G̲h̲allābī, and Muḥammad b. 'Abd ar-Raḥmān.
    Al-'Abbās b. al-Aḥnaf, d. 193/808 (*EI*, 2nd edition, *s.v.*).

38. Situated along the bank of the Tigris below Sūq at̲h̲-T̲h̲alāt̲h̲ā'. The palace was originally built by Ja'far the Barmakid. He presented it to al-Ma'mūn who in turn allowed al-Ḥasan b. Sahl to reside there. Upon the death of al-Ḥasan, the palace passed into the hands of his daughter Būrān. She later turned it over to al-Mu'taḍid (cf. K̲h̲aṭīb, p. 99).

39. Probably Dār Dīnār aṣ-Ṣug̲h̲rā which, according to Yāqūt, was situated on the East Side (between Sūq at̲h̲-T̲h̲alāt̲h̲ā' and the Tigris). He also mentions a Dār Dīnār al-Kubrā, but gives no indication of its location (*Mu'jam*, 2 : 518–19). One of these buildings was first converted into a prison in the time of al-Mu'tazz (Ṭabarī, *Annales*, 3 : 1693; Ṣūlī, *Akhbār*, p. 139, who indicates that the lower prison was moved to Dār Dīnār in 329/940 during the reign of al-Muttaqī. Dār Rajā' is mentioned by Yāqūt, but the exact location is not indicated (op. cit., p. 519). Judging from this account, the Palace of al-Mu'taṣim must have been located closer to the shore than is indicated by LeStrange (Map V). It is more likely that the Palace stood on the left side of the great shore road (cf. Suhrāb, '*Ajā'ib*, p. 130 = Ibn Serapion, p. 22). It is also possible to identify the Palace of al-Ma'mūn that is mentioned here. Al-Ma'mūn was known to have had three palaces on the East Side; the Qaṣr al-Ḥasanī which was located downstream below Sūq at̲h̲-T̲h̲alāt̲h̲ā', and two others, one near Qaṣr al-Ma'mūnī (al-Ḥasani), and the other near Bustān Mūsā (Ibn Abī Ṭāhir Ṭayfūr, *Ta'rikh* [Cairo], pp. 9–10). The palace mentioned here is one of these two palaces, presumably the one at Bustān Mūsā. For the famous family of public official called Wahb, see Sourdel, *Vizirat 'Abbāside, Index*, p. 786.

40. These figures are found in Ya'qūbī (*Buldān*, pp. 250, 254).

Chapter 7

1. Although his official residence was at ar-Ruṣāfah, al-Mahdī often stayed at his pleasure palace at 'Īsābād̲h̲ which also served as an administrative center of the Caliphate (cf. K̲h̲aṭīb, p. 96, l. 12). After al-Hādī was murdered there, his successor Hārūn ar-Ras̲h̲īd moved back to the West Side, residing at al-K̲h̲uld, as did his son al-Amīn. Following the

civil war and the death of his brother al-Amīn, al-Ma'mūn did not return to Baghdad but chose instead to remain in Khurāsān among his Persian allies. His palace in Baghdad (in which he never resided as Caliph) became the residence of al-Ḥasan b. Sahl. Upon returning from Khurāsān in 204/819, he at first stayed in ar-Ruṣāfah, and then built for himself two residences along the left bank of the Tigris in al-Mukharrim (cf. n. 2 below). Al-Mu'taṣim before moving to Sāmarrā, lived in a palace nearby. The next seven Caliphs lived at Sāmarra allowing for the ill-fated attempt of al-Musta'īn to re-establish his rule at the capital of al-Manṣūr. When al-Mu'tamid returned from Sāmarrā (279/892), the 'Abbāsid Caliphs once again made their capital at Baghdad. Unlike the previous Caliphs who resided at Baghdad, al-Mu'tamid and his successors established their residence on the East Side below Sūq ath-Thalāthā'. The Caliphal residence (Dār al-Khalīfah, also al-Khilāfah, and, referring to the general area: The Ḥarīm) consisted of three large palaces (Qaṣr al-Firdaws, Qaṣr al-Ḥasanī, Qaṣr at-Tāj) that were surrounded by a complex of minor buildings, and enclosed by a semi-circular wall. Access to Dār al-Khalīfah was obtained by disembarking along the Tigris shore, or by one of the eight gateways which were situated along the enclosure wall. The exact relationship of these components to one another is not clear. A fourth palace (ath-Thurayyā), built at a distance of two *mīl* (4 km.) from the Dār al-Khalīfah, connected to the major complex by means of underground passageways. Hilāl aṣ-Ṣābi' (*Rusūm*, p. 8) reports that in his time (d.1056) the area of the Dār al-Khilāfah had been reduced to half of what it was as a result of the civil disorders which began in the reign of al-Muqtadir; that is to say, the areas connecting the major complex and the zoological garden and Thurayyā palace had fallen into ruin. Cf. Suhrāb, *'Ajā'ib*, p. 129 = Ibn Serapion, pp. 21–22: Yāqūt, *Mu'jam*, 2: 254–55: LeStrange, *Baghdad*, pp. 242–78: Map VIII; Canard, *Hamdanides*, 1: 169–74; Map IV.

2. The palace was originally built at great expense by al-Ma'mūn's tutor Ja'far al-Barmakī for his own pleasure. Fearing that the Caliph (ar-Rashīd) might not look with favor on so magnificent an edifice, he turned the palace over to al-Ma'mūn, the Caliph's son. The name was subsequently changed from Qaṣr al-Ja'farī to Qaṣr al-Ma'mūnī. Al-Ma'mūn added a hippodrome and zoological garden, and dug a canal leading from the Nahr al-Mu'allā (cf. Khaṭīb, p. 115, ll. 5–6) which provided for drinking water. An eastern gate was constructed to give access to the unoccupied land beyond, and nearby residences were built for his special personnel and his companions. The place of these residences were called al-Ma'mūnīyah. Following the civil war, when al-Ma'mūn was still in Khurāsān, al-Ḥasan b. Sahl was allowed to reside in the palace. When al-Ma'mūn returned from Khurāsān (204/819) he set up quarters for himself in ar-Ruṣāfah, and then built two more residences along the right bank of the Tigris near the Qaṣr al-Ma'mūnī, and Bustān Mūsā (Ibn Abī Ṭāhir Ṭayfūr, *Ta'rīkh* [Cairo], pp. 9–10). One of these two palaces is apparently referred to by the Khaṭīb in his description of the Tigris' shore (Khaṭīb, p. 98, l. 17). Al-Ḥasan had arranged the marriage of his daughter Būrān to al-Ma'mūn in 202/817, but the wedding did not take place until 210/825–826. Since Būrān was residing at the Qaṣr al-Ma'mūnī, it was decided that the palace should be granted to al-Ḥasan, and it subsequently became known as Qaṣr al-Ḥasanī (cf. Yāqūt, *Mu'jam*, 1: 806–8: *EI*, *s.v.* al-Ḥasan b. Sahl; 2nd edition, *s.v.*, Būrān). Cf. also LeStrange, pp. 243–46; Map VIII, ref. no. 1. On al-Mu'taḍid's claim, see n. 3 below.
3. Yāqūt reports that it was al-Mu'taḍid who first undertook the construction of at-Tāj. He mentions that workers had been assembled from various regions to dig the foundations of this new palace. The Caliph was, however, obliged to leave on a campaign.

Upon his return, he observed smoke entering the would-be palace precinct (cf. Ibn al-Jawzī, *Muntaẓam*, 5.2: 144). He then abandoned his plans for this site and decided to build a palace for himself two *mīl* (4 km.) from there. This palace became known as Qaṣr ath-Thurayyā. It was al-Muktafi who completed at-Tāj, by taking building materials from the ruins of the Sassanid palaces at nearby al-Madā'in. The battlements of these palaces were thrown down, and the burnt-brick was used at at-Tāj. New precincts were added to the palace area. The palace was damaged by fire in 549/1154, and later partially rebuilt. Makdisi, arguing against LeStrange, finds no evidence that the palace was completely destroyed at this time (*Topography*, p. 134, n. 2—citing Ibn al-Jawzī, *Muntaẓam*, 10: 157, 169, 173; Ibn al-Athīr, *Kāmil*, 9: 51). It was finally demolished to make way for a new building during the reign of al-Mustaḍī' (574/1178). Cf. Yāqūt, *Mu'jam*, 1: 808–9; LeStrange, *Index*, p. 368; Map VIII, ref. no. 2.

4. Ath-Thurayyā was built by al-Mu'taḍid at a cost of 400,000 dinars, when he abandoned his plans for the construction of at-Tāj. Covering an area of 3 farsakh (?), it was situated at a distance of two *mīl* (4 km.) from the Dār al-Khalīfah, and was connected to Qaṣr al-Ḥasanī by underground passageways. According to Yāqūt, it was destroyed during the first great flood in Baghdad, which probably indicates the series of floods that struck the East Side during the middle of the eleventh century. LeStrange indicates that it was destroyed in 466/1073–1074 although it is possible that the palace was destroyed during the first flood (461/1069) since it is mentioned in connection with that flood and not the later innundation (cf. Mas'ūdī, *Murūj*, 8: 116; Ibn al-Jawzī, *Muntaẓam*, 8: 254, 285; Yāqūt, *Mu'jam*, 1: 808, 924; also see LeStrange, *Index*, p. 379; Map III; Makdisi, *Topography*, pp. 286–90).
5. Yāqūt, in reporting the transfer of Būrān's residence, indicates that the Caliph involved was al-Mu'tamid (*Mu'jam*, 1: 808). However, al-Mu'tamid did not come to settle at Baghdad until the year of his death (273/892). LeStrange suggests that the transfer may have been effected during a temporary visit in 270/883 (pp. 248–49). Ibn al-Jawzī in reporting the events of the year 280/893–894, indicates that al-Mu'taḍid was the first Caliph to reside in the Qaṣr al-Ḥasanī (*Muntaẓam*, 5.2: 143). It is, of course, possible that although the palace was ceded to al-Mu'tamid, he did not make it his official residence. The palace was renovated by al-Mu'taḍid, who built the underground chambers which served as a state prison (cf. Khaṭīb, p. 109; Ibn al-Jawzī, op. cit., pp. 143–44). In the reign of al-Muktafī, these chambers were torn down in order to transform the prison area into a mosque (cf. Khaṭīb, p. 109; Ibn al-Jawzī, *Muntaẓam*, 6: 33). In 294/907 an audience room called at-Tāj was added to the palace structure (Ibn al-Jawzī, op. cit., 6: 60).
6. S: *'Alī b. Muḥammad al- Khuwārizmī.*
   Aḥmad b. 'Alī al-Munajjim, tenth century (*TB*, 4: 318–19).
   'Alī b. Hārūn al-Munajjim d. 352/963 (*TB*, 13: 119–20).
   'Alī b. Muḥammad al-Ḥawārī, the Ṣāhib Khizānat al-Farsh. Cf. n. 13.
7. Detailed information on the distribution of palace personnel is also found in Ṣābī', *Rusūm*, pp. 8–9. He indicates that in the time of al-Muktafī (289/902–295/908) there were 20,000 ghilmān ad-dār (cf. below) and 10,000 Negroes and Slavs. In the time of al-Muqtadir, there were 11,000 male servants—7,000 Negro and 4,000 white Slavs. The female servants *hurrah* and *mamlūkah* numbered 4,000; and in addition there was the Ḥujarite guard (*al-ḥujrīyah*) numbering many thousands. These palace servants were also called ghilmān al-ḥujar, and ghilmān ad-dār. According to Canard, they were so called because they resided in quarters designated as al-ḥujar (the chambers), although it seems that the name is derived from their functions as guards

in the palace precincts. However, they also seem to have joined the Caliph in his campaigns. They were first formed by al-Muʿtaḍid and placed under the command of the chief eunuchs or their assistants. (Canard, *Ṣūlī*, 2: 49, n. 3—citing Ṭabarī, *Annales*, 3.4: 2262, 2265; Hilāl, *Wuzarā'*, pp. 12–13). The security patrol (*nawbah*) consisted of 5,000 troops (*rajjālat al-muṣaffiyah*), 400 palace guards (*ḥaras*), and 800 room servants (*farrāsh*). The city garrison (*shiḥnat al-balad*) was under the supervision of the *ṣāḥib al-maʿūnah* and numbered 14,000 infantry and cavalry.

8. C and S: *Abū-l-Qāsim*, read *Abū-l-Ḥasan*.
   Abū Aḥmad Yaḥyā al-Munajjim, d. 300/912 (*GAL, Supplement*, 1: 225).
   Abū-l-Ḥasan ʿAlī b. Yaḥyā, d. 275/888–89 (*TB*, 12: 121).
9. LeStrange (*Baghdad*, p. 259) understood this statement to mean that the house of the Caliph in Baghdad covered ground equalling in extent the whole city of Shīrāz, the chief town of Fārs, and the capital... of the Būyid prince (ʿAḍud ad-Dawlah). The similarity between the two places is more likely in the fact that both Shīrāz and the Dār al-Khilāfah were encompassed by an enclosure wall containing several gateways (cf. LeStrange, *Eastern Caliphate*, p. 249).
10. The purpose of this mission was to arrange for the exchange of captives. Accounts of this visit are found in Miskawayh, *Tajārib*, 1: 53–55; Ibn al-Jawzī, *Muntaẓam*, 6: 143–44; Ibn al-Athīr, *Kāmil*, 8: p. 79; and particularly Ṣābi', *Rusūm*, pp. 11 ff.; and Ibn az-Zubayr, *Dakhā'ir*, pp. 131–39. This entire passage from the Khaṭīb has been translated and discussed by LeStrange, "A Greek Embassy to Baghdad in 917 A.D.," *JRAS* (1897), pp. 35–45. Cf. also M. Hamidullah, "Nouveaux Documents," *Arabica*, 7 (1960): 293–97. B. Dolger, *Corpus*, II: 69. On the question of ʿAbbāsid ceremonial. see D. Sourdel "Questions de Cérémonial ʿAbbāside," *REI*, 38 (1960): 120–48.
11. The Byzantine party consisted of a young man, an old man, and various pages (*ʿArīb*, p. 64; Ibn al-Jawzī, *Muntaẓam*, 6: 143). According to Ibn az-Zubayr, the younger man was forty years of age, the older sixty (*Dakhā'ir*, p. 132). The former was in charge of the embassy; the latter acted as his interpreter, and should death have befallen the younger man, he was empowered to take charge of the negotiations (cf. text below). They were accompanied by Abū ʿUmar (*Dakhā'ir*: ʿUmayr) ʿAdī b. Aḥmad b. ʿAbd al-Bāqi' aṭ-Ṭarsūsī, the commander of the Syrian frontier. The sequence of events leading up to the actual interview with the Caliph seems rather confused in this account and the one which follows. The ambassadors, in this report, apparently first passed from Bāb ash-Shammāsīyah along the great shore road until reaching the Dār al-Khilāfah. There, they stopped at the palace of Naṣr al-Qushūrī, the Chamberlain, which was adjacent to the residence of the Caliph (Ṣābi', *Rusūm*, p. 12; for Naṣr al-Qushūrī, see Sourdel, *Vizirat ʿAbbāside*, 2, *Index*: 776). They did not see the Caliph, but were then escorted to the palace of Ibn al-Furāt, the Wazīr. This palace was not situated near the Dār al-Khilāfah but upstream by the Main Bridge in Sūq al-ʿAṭash near Bayn al-Qaṣrayn (cf. Suhrāb, *ʿAjā'ib*, p. 130 = Ibn Serapion, p. 22: *ʿArib*, pp. 28–29; Ṣūlī, *Akhbār*, p. 90; Hilāl, *Wuzarā'*, pp. 23, 28, 34; LeStrange, Map III). The audience-room of the wazīr is described as having a gilt roof, and as having been furnished at a cost of 30,000 dinars. The wazīr sat on a splendid prayer rug with a lofty throne behind him. The room was crowded with public officials and attendants. When in the presence of the wazīr, the Byzantines asked for a redemption of captives. The wazīr indicated he would speak to the Caliph about an interview, and they returned to the Residence of Ṣāʿid where they were staying (Miskawayh, *Tajārib*, 1: 53–54, Ibn az-Zubayr, op. cit., pp. 132 ff.). This account of the Khaṭīb might lead one to believe that the wazīr's palace was located at the Dār

al-Khilāfah, and that the entire visit took place at one time; but such does not seem to have been the case (cf. n. 12 below).

12. The source of this account ʿAlī b. al-Ḥusayn d. 450/1055 (*Muntaẓam*, 9: 200–1). There is no mention in his report of a visit to the palace of Naṣr al-Qushūrī, or of a visit to the Wazīr Ibn al-Furāt. It would appear that the ambassadors were first detained at Takrīt which was 180 km. from the city on the way to al-Mawṣil, i.e., in the direction of the Syrian frontier (cf. Yāqūt, *Muʿjam*, 1: pp. 861–63). After being detained there for two months, they reached the city and were then settled at the residence of Ṣāʿid b. Makhlad, and where, according to the text, they remained two months prior to the interview. Ibn az-Zubayr, however, indicates that the Byzantines reached the city on the second of Muḥarram and saw the Caliph on the fifth (*Dakhāʾir*, pp. 131, 134). Perhaps the text of the Khāṭib should read two days for two months—the latter confusing the stay in Baghdad with the detaining of the Byzantines in Takrīt. Although the account of Ibn az-Zubayr also omits the visit to Naṣr al-Qushūrī, it suggests, with the help of Miskawayh, what the actual sequence of events may have been. After arriving at Baghdad, the Byzantines were apparently settled at the residence of Ṣāʿid (cf. Sourdel, *Vizirat ʿAbbāside*, 1: 315 ff. for Ṣāʿid b. Makhlad). It was situated on the east bank of the Tigris presumably in ash-Shammāsīyah (Hilāl, *Wuzarāʾ*, pp. 262, 431). Ibn al-Furāt, the Wazīr gave orders to furnish the residence with all the necessary utensils and supplies. The Byzantines requested an interview with the Caliph but were informed that they first had to consult the Wazīr. This meeting was arranged by Abū ʿUmar ʿAdī b. Aḥmad b. Abd al-Bāqi', who had escorted them from the frontier and acted as their interpreter (*Tajārib*, 1: 53). They were then led to Ibn al-Furāt (after a visit to Naṣr al-Qushūrī?) and following this interview returned to the residence of Ṣāʿid. From there they went to see the Caliph.

13. C: *al-Badghāʾiyah*, S: *al-Badinnāʾiyah*; read *al-Baṣinnāʾiyah* from Baṣinnā, a small city in the vicinity of al-Ahwāz famed for its weavers (cf. Yāqūt, *Muʿjam*, 1: 656). Al-Bahnasā was a town in Egypt situated on the west side of the Nile (Yāqūt, op. cit., 1: 771). Dabīq was also situated in Egypt (op. cit., 2: 548). The materials produced there grew so popular they were manufactured in the east as well, although they were still referred to as Dabīq clothwork (cf. R. B. Serjeant, "Islamic Textiles," *Ars Islamica*, 13: pp. 89, 94, 97, 98, 100; v. 15, pp. 15, 76; G. Wiet, "Tissues et Tapisseries," *Syria*, 16: 282–83). Jahram was a city in Fārs famous for the manufacture of rugs (Yāqūt, op. cit., 2: 167). Dawraq was situated in Khuzistān (op. cit., pp. 618–20). The distribution of the curtains is also reported by Ibn az-Zubayr, *Dakhāʾir*, pp. 133–34. He indicates that the curtains from Wāsiṭ, Baṣinnā, and Armenia numbered 25,500; 8,000 were produced for the Caliphs al-Ma'mūn, al-Muʿtaṣm, al-Wāthiq, al-Mutawakkil, and al-Muktafī. The interior decoration was apparently arranged by ʿAlī b. Muḥammad al-Ḥawārī (*ṣāhib khizānat al-farsh*). The Bāb al-ʿĀmmah was the fifth gate situated along the enclosure wall of the palace complex (cf. Yāqūt, *Muʿjam*, 2: 255; LeStrange, pp. 274–76, Canard, *Hamdanides*, Map IV, ref. no. 5).

14. Yāqūt indicates that it was built by al-Muqtadir, and was so named because of a tree which was situated in a circular pond opposite the īwān. The tree was crowned with jewels in the shape of fruits (Yāqūt, *Muʿjam*, 2: 520–21). A similar tree is known to have existed at the court of Tīmūr (ca. 1405). It was as tall as a man and contained rubies, emeralds, turquoises, sapphires, and pearls shaped like fruit. The gilded birds sat on the branches as if to eat the fruit (cf. Ruy Gonzales de Clavijo, *Embassy to the Court of Timur*, Hakluyt Society, Ser. I, 26 [1859]: 161). The artificial tree in the Dār ash-Shajarah

is not to be confused with a second contraption that was actually located in the throne room of the Caliph. This second tree is not mentioned by the Kẖaṭīb but is described by Ibn az-Zubayr (*Dakẖā'ir*, p. 138). Unlike the first tree, whose birds were set into motion by the wind, the device of the throne room was a mechanical contrivance operated hydraulically. When the ambassadors stood before the Caliph, he gave a command and a cupola opened. Emerging from the ground were representations of whistling birds perched upon a tree while scented water emptied into receptacles presumably setting the whole device into motion. Such automata were known in antiquity and continued into the Middle Ages in both Europe and the Near East. Of particular interest is the Byzantine throne of Theophilus (tenth century), the so-called "Throne of Solomon" (cf. G. Brett, "The Automata in the Byzantine Throne of Solomon," *Speculum*, 29 [1954]: 477 ff.). It has been said that Theophilus' Palace of Bryas was built after models in Baghdad, and it has been suggested that all the automata were imported from Baghdad at this time (cf. A. Grabar, "Le Succès des arts orientaux à la cour byzantine sous les Macedoniens," *Münchner Jahrbuch der bildenden Kunst*, Ser. III, 2 [1951]: 56). Could this visit of the Ambassadors have inspired the creation of the Byzantine device?

15. C: *fī nāward kẖababan taqrīban*, S: *kẖayyan taqrīban*. The text appears corrupt. These horsemen are described by Yāqūt and the text here is reconstructed from Yāqūt's description. He indicates that there were twenty-five to the right, and an equal number to the left, dressed in silk brocade, and girded with swords. Holding lances, they turned on a single line so that the horsemen on the right faced those on the left (*Mu'jam*, 2: 521).

16. The *Dakẖā'ir* of Ibn az-Zubayr (p. 136) gives somewhat different figures. He indicates that there were 5,000 breastplates in Qaṣr al-Firdaws (Kẖaṭīb: 10,000); and that the Ambassadors were conducted to the Court of the Ninety after touring thirteen palaces (Kẖaṭīb: twenty-three palaces).

17. The interpreter addressed the wazīr, and he relayed the message to the Caliph who was stationed 100 cubits from the ambassadors (*'Arīb*, p. 64; Ibn al-Jawzī, *Muntaẓam*, 6: 144). For Mū'nis, the alternate interpreter of the Caliph, see Sourdel, *Vizirat 'Abbāside*, 2, *Index*: 774–75. According to protocol, the wazīr had to stand five cubits to the right of the throne. Other officials of lesser rank and in descending order took their respective positions to the right and to the left. The ambassadors, according to this account, did not kiss the ground. Note, however, Miskawayh reports that they kissed the ground where they were told to stand by Naṣr al-Qushūrī. At one time, it was apparently not the custom to kiss the ground or a rug, as Hilāl aṣ-Ṣābi' indicates various personages of importance substituted other forms of salutation. However, by his time (d. 1056) it became an accepted procedure to kiss the hand, the ground, or a rug (*Rusūm*, pp. 31, 78, 79). They (the ambassadors) then read the letter asking for an exchange of prisoners. The Caliph agreed and made arrangements to send Mū'nis to facilitate this matter. After the ambassadors left, Mū'nis and some officers were dispatched with 170,000 dinars to arrange the transfer. The redemption of the captives was carried out that year in Rabi' II. The total number of prisoners redeemed was 1,586 (*Tajārib*, 1: 55; Ibn az-Zubayr *Dakẖā'ir*, p. 139).

18. Other accounts put the number of dirhams at 20,000 (cf. *'Arīb*, p. 64; Ibn az-Zubayr, *Dakẖā'ir*, p. 139). Ibn az-Zubayr (ibid.) also indicates that two purses were placed before them, and fifty more were loaded, each containing 5,000 dirhams. This seems somewhat at variance with the account of the Kẖaṭīb and the figure mentioned above. If the purses contained the ransom money (170,000 dinars seems very high) then the higher estimate

of the K͟haṭīb is more likely to be correct since the official exchange rate of dinar to dirham (although the actual rate varied) was approximately 1:10. If the purses contained gift money, the lower estimates (which also seem high) would seem to be more correct. I am inclined to believe that the 20,000 dirhams was gift money for the ambassadors and was presumably brought in the two purses that were presented to them; the rest was therefore the ransom money. According to the K͟haṭīb, they left the Dār al-K͟hilāfah by boat for Dār Ṣā'id where they were staying. Ibn az-Zubayr, however, indicates that they traveled on land (op. cit., p. 139). Perhaps he refers to their leaving Baghdad.

Chapter 8

1. The term Dār al-Mamlakah (the Government Palace) is used here to indicate the residence of the Būyid Amīrs and, later, the Saljūq Sulṭāns. It is clear that this term refers not to a single palace, but to several palaces situated wherever the Sulṭān may have resided (cf. Makdisi, *Topography*, pp. 302–5). The K͟haṭīb here refers to a palace which was situated in the upper part of al-Muk͟harrim. This is *not* to be confused with the great Dār al-Mamlakah of Mu'izz ad-Dawlah. That palace (Dār al-Mu'izzīyah) was, without doubt, situated in ash̲-S̲h̲ammāsīyah. The first Dār al-Mamlakah was also that of Mu'izz ad-Dawlah (d. 356/967) and originally was located where the Palace of Mū'nis stood. This was not at Bāb ash̲-S̲h̲ammāsīyah, as LeStrange claims (p. 232) but further down stream at Suq ath̲-T̲h̲alāthā' (cf. Miskawayh, *Tajārib*, 1: 396; Ṣābi', *Rusūm*, pp. 136–37; Ibn al-Jawzī, *Muntaẓam*, 7: 2; 8: 31). In the year 350/961, Mu'izz ad-Dawlah made plans to build a new palace which came to be situated near Bāb ash̲-S̲h̲ammāsīyah. He purchased the dwellings adjacent to Bustān aṣ-Ṣaymarī, and no doubt demolished them so he could have room on which to build the palace complex, which included a parade ground and stables. He took the iron gates of ar-Ruṣāfah; and the palace which was situated there, and also those of Madīnat al-Manṣūr. He also demolished the New Prison in order to obtain building materials. Skilled workers are said to have been brought in from various regions including al-Ahwāz, al-Mawṣil, and Iṣfahān. Mu'izz ad-Dawlah also began work on his dyke but it was not completed at the time of his death (Ibn al-Jawzī, op. cit., p. 31). The estimated expenditure for this venture is put by Ibn al-Jawzī at twelve million dirhams = one million dinars; Miskawayh and Yāqūt indicate thirteen million dirhams (Miskawayh, op. cit., pp. 182–83; Ibn al-Jawzī, op. cit., 7: 2; Yāqūt, *Mu'jam*, 3: 318). Cf. also LeStrange, pp. 231–41; Map VII; and K. 'Awād, "Ad-Dār al-Mu'izzīyah," *Sumer*, 10 (1954): 197–217. His successor, 'Izz ad-Dawlah (d. 367/977), chose to establish his residence at the palace formerly occupied by al-Muttaqī on the West Side. 'Izz ad-Dawlah, however, did make use of the Dār al-Mamlakah as a military camp (Ibn al-Jawzī, op. cit., 8: 31). Before and after the building of Dār al-Mu'izzīyah, the area adjacent to Bāb ash̲-S̲h̲ammāsīyah was frequently used for stationing troops. 'Aḍud ad-Dawlah, in turn, built his palace further to the south in al-Muk͟harrim, and it is described in this chapter by the K͟haṭīb. Makdisi indicates that this palace and the Dār al-Mu'izzīyah are identical (*Topography*, pp. 303–4). Such is apparently the opinion of LeStrange as well, although he concedes some of the Būyid palaces must have extended further south into al-Muk͟harrim. However, nowhere does the K͟haṭīb indicate that the Dār al-Mamlakah, reconditioned by 'Aḍud ad-Dawlah, belonged originally to al-Mu'izz. It

was, according to the text, the palace of his page, Subuktakīn. As Ibn al-Jawzī explicitly states that after ʿIzz ad-Dawlah took power, he left the Dār al-Muʿizzīyah for the Palace of al-Muttaqī (on the West Side), LeStrange and Makdisi conclude that the empty Dār al-Muʿizzīyah was then occupied by Subuktakīn. I know, however, of no evidence for this transfer. Furthermore, the *Muntaẓam* adds that (after ʿIzz ad-Dawlah moved to the West Side), the Dār al-Mamlakah of al-Muʿizz remained abandoned although Būyid after Būyid came to power (op. cit., p. 31). The Dār al-Muʿizzīyah and the ʿAḍudī Dār al-Mamlakah were two distinct places; the first was situated in ash-Shammāsīyah, the second in the upper part of al-Mukharrim (cf. also n. 2 below).

2. It would appear that ʿAḍūd ad-Dawlah's successor Ṣamṣām ad-Dawlah (d. 376/987) also resided in al-Mukharrim, and this was apparently true of Sharaf ad-Dawlah as well; although in the last year of his life he was advised, by his doctors, to return to the Dār al-Muʿizzīyah for reasons of health (Ibn al-Jawzī, *Muntaẓam*, 7 : 147 *sub anno* 379/989). Unlike his predecessors, Bahā' ad-Dawlah did not choose to stay at the ʿAḍudī Dār al-Mamlakah, but instead he renovated the original palace of al-Muʿizz further down stream at Sūq ath-Thalāthā'. In doing so, he contributed to the deterioration of the palace area in ash-Shammāsīyah, thereby taking burnt brick from the stables there, to be re-used in his own construction. On another occasion he attempted to strip the gilded roof of the banquet hall in order to re-use the material for a palace in Shīrāz. The undertaking, however, proved too expensive and the Dār al-Muʿizzīyah was left to deteriorate, its building material and fixtures eventually were taken by the army (Ibn al-Jawzī, op. cit., 8 : 31; Ibn al-Athīr, *Kāmil*, 9 : 256). The subsequent Būyids, no doubt, remained at Sūq ath-Thalāthā'. This permitted Jalāl ad-Dawlah to continue the demolition of the Dār al-Muʿizzīyah (for building material?) and to convert the Bayt as-Sittīnī at al-Mukharrim into a stable in which he kept his horses and grooms. When Ṭughril Bak entered Baghdad, he erected a wide wall which extended along a large part of al-Mukharrim. Having decided to build a palace there, he renovated the ʿAdudī Dār al-Mamlakah (cf. Ibn al-Jawzī, op. cit., p. 169; Ibn al-ʿAthīr, op. cit., p. 422; Makdisi, *Topography*, p. 304).
3. S: *mā kāna wahā minhā*, which may be translated: The dilapidated structures restored.
4. That is to say, coins which were not debased. There is, as yet, no complete study of Būyid coinage; but a high percentage of the Būyid gold coins found in the collection of the American Numismatic Society show evidence of debasement. The earlier coins (al-Muʿizz, ʿAḍud ad-Dawlah) still display a standard of fitness over 90 per cent; but by the time of Bahā' ad-Dawlah the dinars displayed a standard of under 50 per cent, thus reflecting the deplorable coinage conditions in the metropolitan areas of the ʿAbbāsid Caliphate (cf. A. Ehrenkreuz, "Studies in the Monetary History of the Near East in the Middle Ages II—The Standard Fitness of Western and Eastern Dinars Before the Crusades," *JESHO*, 6 [1963]: 243–77, esp. 256).
5. Excavations on this canal were begun in 371/981–982 and the work was not completed until the following year (Ibn al-Jawzī, *Muntaẓam*, 7 : 107, 112). Nahr al-Khāliṣ did not enter Baghdad but emptied into the Tigris two leagues below ar-Rāshidīyah. Its waters were carried to Baghdad by the Nahr al-Mahdī, which intercepted one of its branch canals just above Bāb ash-Shammāsīyah. This seems to indicate that the canals which branched off from the Khāliṣ were no longer serviceable at this time (cf. Khaṭīb, p. 115). For the poor state of Baghdad's canals during Būyid times, see Miskawayh, *Tajārib*, 2 : 406. The reference to Darb al-Silsilah is confusing, for it was the street leading to the Niẓāmīyah College near Sūq ath-Thalāthā' further downstream. This

account, if correct, would seem to indicate that this street extended almost the entire length of the city.

Chapter 9

1. The same figures are given for the palace and mosque of al-Ḥajjāj b. Yūsuf at Wāsiṭ (cf. Yāqūt, *Muʿjam*, 4: 885) and have been confirmed by excavations there (cf. F. Safar, *Wāsiṭ, The Sixth Seasons Excavations*, Cairo [1945]). A structure of similar dimensions was found at al-Kūfah (cf. M. ʿAlī Muṣṭafā, "Taqrīr al-awwal," *Sumer*, 10: 73–85). On the similarity of these buildings, see O. Grabar, "Al-Mushatta, Baghdad, and Wāsiṭ," *The World of Islam, Studies in Honor of Phillip K. Hitti* (London, 1959), pp. 98–108; also Part II A. The plan of the mosque was traced by al-Ḥajjāj b. Arṭāt who also laid the foundation (Ṭabarī, *Annales*, 3.1: 321–22). For reconstructions of the mosque at Baghdad, see Figs. 10–14. The passage on the columns is difficult. It is not clear whether the columns indicated in the last sentence refer to the five or six near the minaret, or those of the mosque in general. Herzfeld is of the opinion that the columns near the minaret are distinguished from the others by their monolithic shafts. This is not stated directly in the Arabic text but Herzfeld thinks it is implied. The following sentence indicates a new trend of thought dealing with the columns generally. The word *mulaffaqah* is difficult, but it must be understood as a "composite capital." In the spoken Arabic of the Mawṣil region, the term *dikmah malfūf* indicates "the volute of a capital," therefore suggesting to Herzfeld a possible reading of *mulaffafah*. Cf. *Archäologische Reise*, 2: 135, n. 6; also LeStrange, p. 34—freely translating: All the columns supported round capitals, each made of a block of wood which was set on the shaft like a drum; Salmon. *Histoire*, pp. 145–46—*à l'exception de cinq ou six colonnes près du minaret car dans chacune de celles-ci, il y avait des morceaux ajustés tout autour du bois de la colonne* —indicating, contrary to Herzfeld's view, that the five or six columns would be distinguished from the others because they are composed of more than two pieces.
2. Ibn al-Aʿrābī, ninth century (*TB*, 11: 373). The orientation of the *qiblah* was not correct because the mosque had to be built along the axis of the palace which was symmetrical with the gates and not the *qiblah* direction. The mosque at ar-Ruṣāfah was built before the palace of al-Mahdī so that there was no need to compromise on the orientation (cf. Ṭabarī, *Annales*, 3.1: 322; also Muqaddasī, p. 121).
3. Herzfeld (p. 136, n. 1) is of the opinion that the wooden columns continued in use, or were replaced with similar columns, since an inscription dedicating the mosque expressly mentions the name of the carpenter. Furthermore, Ibn al-Faqīh (ca. 900) indicates that the mosque was built from burnt brick and gypsum, raised on columns of teakwood (p. 109). However, the services of the carpenter would also have been required for the roof, which was constructed of teakwood and inset with laipis lazuli (ibid.). The inscription on the outer wall facing the Khurāsān Gate supports Creswell's contention that the mosque was situated along the north wall of the palace, and not the south wall as Herzfeld had assumed. Creswell, who generally agrees with Herzfeld's reconstruction (see Figs. 10 and 11), points out that if the mosque was situated along the south wall, the *qiblah* wall would not be contiguous with the palace, and the Caliph would then be unable to pass from the latter directly into the *maqṣūrah*, as was the practice in the first centuries of Islam. Moreover, there is the difficulty of the Dār al-Qaṭṭān which will be discussed below in nn. 5 and 7. Cf. Creswell, 2: 33–34; Herzfeld, 2: 135; also LeStrange, p. 34, who places the mosque along the eastern wall of the palace. The suggestion of

M. Jawād and A. Sūsah that the mosque was situated along the right corner of the wall facing the Khurāsān Gate, and that the entire palace-mosque was out of line with the gateway, does not seem plausible (cf. "Madīnat al-Manṣūr wa jāmi'uhā," *Sumer*, 22 [1966]: 4 ff., and fig. 1, 6).

4. No dimensions are given for this structure which subsequently became known as the old court. However, since it is clearly indicated that the mosque was rebuilt over an enlarged area, it is obvious that the building exceeded the original 200 cubits square. The plans of Herzfeld and Creswell (200 × 200 cubits) must therefore be amended accordingly, as they are apparently based on the description of the original mosque built by al-Manṣūr and not the ninth century reconstruction of his grandson (cf. Figs. 12, 13, 14). Several conjectural plans of this reconstruction are suggested in Appendix C.
5. Cf. Ibn al-Jawzī, *Muntaẓam*, 5.2: 21 *sub anno* 260. This is no indication of how this structure was connected with the mosque. According to Herzfeld, it was an extension along the south wall of the mosque which he places along the south wall of the palace (cf. Fig. 11). If this is correct, it is necessary for him to assume that when the new mosque was built by adding part of the palace, the wall between the Dār al-Qaṭṭān and the mosque was pierced, and that the *minbar*, *miḥrāb*, and *maqṣūrah* were transferred there in keeping with the orientation of the building, instead of being taken to the new mosque as the Khaṭīb explicitly indicates. I am inclined to agree with Creswell that the mosque was situated along the north wall of the palace. The *minbar*, *miḥrāb*, and *maqṣūrah* were then moved to that section of the palace which had become part of the mosque. It is not clear what use was made of the Dār al-Qaṭṭān once the new mosque was built (cf. Herzfeld, pp. 137 ff.; Creswell, pp. 32–34; also nn. 6 and 7 below). The number of horizontal aisles in the sanctuary is not indicated. Herzfeld suggests five as in the mosque at al-Kūfah, which was also a square, and because the ratio of 5:17 can be found in the mosque of Ibn Ṭūlūn (op. cit., p. 136). Similarly one can include the mosque of Abū Dulaf (Sāmarrā), the mosque at ar-Rāfiqah, and the palace mosque constructed by al-Ḥajjāj b. Yūsuf at Wāsiṭ, which was analogous to the original structure at Baghdad (cf. Creswell, p. 280, fig. 223; for the mosque at ar-Rāfiqah, p. 46, fig. 33—the plan reveals only three aisles but the space clearly indicates room for five). From this general observation, one can conclude that the ratio 5:17 may have been popular in both the square and rectangular mosques of this region. Note that Ibn Ṭūlūn came from Sāmarrā. The text of the Khaṭīb indicates that arcades opened directly into the courts of the mosque area. These arcades were apparently roofed over; for Muqaddasī, in describing the mosque at Fasā in Fārs, indicates that it consisted of two courts separated by a covered passage, similar to the mosque at Madīnat as-Salām (p. 431). Cf. also Creswell, p. 32.
6. The construction of the new mosque area was entrusted to the Qāḍī Yūsuf b. Ya'qūb. The total expenditures amounted to 20,000 dinars (Ibn al-Jawzī, *Muntaẓam*, 5.2: 143). When the Khaṭīb reports that al-Mu'taḍid added the second mosque because lack of room compelled the populace to pray (on Fridays) in places where it is not permissible, he indicates, according to Creswell, the Dār al-Qaṭṭān. That is to say, the Dār al-Qaṭṭān was technically designated as a *muṣallā*, i.e., a place where one may generally pray, but where it is not permissible, or at best not recommended to say the Friday prayers. It is not indicated how this structure connected to the mosque, but if Creswell is correct it could not have become an integral part of the larger building, since it would then have been unnecessary to enlarge the area of prayer (cf. Appendix C). Note that Ya'qūbī's description of the Round City reports that there were only two buildings in this central court other than the palace mosque (*Buldān*, p. 240). One adjacent to the Damascus

Gate housed the chief of the guard; the other the location of which is not indicated was a large portico containing the apartment of the chief of police, and presumably rooms for his men. The portico of the police, like the Dār al-Qaṭṭān, was, therefore, a government building. What is more Ya'qūbī, who wrote in the latter part of the ninth century, indicates that in his time this portico was used as a place of prayer (*muṣallā*), suggesting, perhaps, that it may be identified with the Dār al-Qaṭṭān mentioned by the Khaṭīb.

7. This passage in the text is not clear as I have been unable to find any meaning for the word (*msqṭt*). Herzfeld thinks that this may be a reference to what was known as the Dār al-Qaṭṭān, but does not elaborate. Note that the Dār al-Qaṭṭān was connected to the mosque in the reign of al-Mu'tamid, the previous Caliph (cf. Herzfeld, p. 137; also Fig. 11). Moreover, the text indicates that *msqṭt* were added from, or perhaps even to the palace of al-Manṣūr, but not to the mosque. The identification of al-Badrīyah with the Dār al-Qaṭṭān is therefore not possible.
8. S: *nazala*, which translates: stayed at.
9. This statement is borne out by the tenth-century geographer Iṣṭakhrī (p. 84) who indicates that there were three principal mosques in Baghdad: at Madīnat as-Salām, ar-Ruṣāfah, and the Dār al-Khilāfah. What then became of the principal-mosque in al-Karkh which was built by al-Manṣūr when he redeveloped that suburb (cf. Khaṭīb, p. 80, ll. 21–22)? This must have been the mosque in ash-Sharqīyah mentioned by Ya'qūbī. He indicates that by this time the *minbar* had been removed, that is to say, it was no longer considered a principal mosque (cf. *Buldān*, p. 245). The reason for the development of the Karkh mosque was to enable the market people to say their Friday prayers without having to enter the Round City. This not only relieved possible congestion in the great mosque, but also maintained the security of the palace precinct (cf. Part II B). In time, the Round City ceased to be the major administrative center that it had been. The Caliph had long since moved from the palace there, and for half a century from Baghdad altogether. When al-Mu'taḍid returned the Caliphate to the city, he set up residence on the East Side, and demolished some chambers in al-Manṣūr's palace in order to widen the area of prayer. Is it possible that the people of the markets had returned to the original mosque nearby in order to say their prayers; for the problem of security had long since passed? Did the surviving sections of the Round City now become an extension of the southern suburbs? This would explain the need for the people of al-Ḥarbīyah, the northern suburb, to petition for a mosque of their own (cf. text below).
10. The raid on the Barāthā Mosque took place in the year 313/925 following some difficulty with agents of the Qarmaṭians, the Shī'ite petty dynasty in southern Iraq. The Caliph al-Muqtadir dispatched Nāzūk (chief of police) to seize all those present, and he found thirty worshippers. In their possession were white clay seals bearing an inscription of allegiance to the Shī'ite Muḥammad b. Ismā'īl which had been distributed by an agent of the Qarmaṭians. The Wazīr Abū-l-Qāsim al-Khāqānī then sought to demolish the mosque (as it was a hotbed of subversion) and accordingly sought a legal decision from the jurists. They decreed that it was a mosque of apostasy that would serve to divide the true believers, and if it were not demolished, it would continue to be a shelter for subversive elements. As a result it was destroyed by Nāzūk and the area was made into a burial ground (cf. Ibn al-Jawzī, *Muntaẓam*, 6: 195–96). When the mosque was rebuilt by Bajkam in 329/941, prayers were conducted by a Sunnite Imām. However, in the following century, it was necessary to halt worship there temporarily as the name of 'Alī and various Shī'ite epithets were added to the Khuṭbah following the mention of the Prophet. Prayers were only resumed after the required apologies were made (cf.

Ibn al-Jawzī, *Muntaẓam*, 6 : 317 ; Yāqūt, *Mu'jam*, 1 : p. 532 ; Ṣūlī, *Akhbār*, p. 136 *sub anno* 327 ; Miskawayh, *Tajārib*, 2 : 8 ; Ibn al-Athīr, *Kāmil*, 9 : 278 *sub anno* 421 in reference to the last event).

11. This was apparently the *minbar* expressly built for Hārūn's mosque in 192/808 (cf. Ṣūlī, *Akhbār*, p. 192). Aḥmad b. al-Faḍl b. 'Abd al-Malik al-Hāshimī, d. 350/961 (*TB*, 4 : 131).
12. The fief referred to here is also known as az-Zubaydīyah. It was situated north of the city beyond Khandaq Ṭāhir which formed the boundary between it and the city. This account of the Khaṭīb confuses this fief with one of a similar name which was located south of the city in Nahr al-Qallā'īn (cf. Khaṭīb, p. 71, ll. 3–4).

Chapter 10

1. The major part of the Khaṭīb's chapter on the canals of the city is derived on the direct authority of 'Abdallāh b. Muḥammad b. 'Alī al-Baghdādī (unidentified). It is virtually identical in content and language with Suhrāb, *'Ajā'ib*, pp. 123–24, 131–34 = Ibn Serapion, pp. 14–15, 24–26. Since the *'Ajā'ib*, the earliest known source of this information was reportedly composed ca. 925, the account of the canals obtained from the Khaṭīb does not stem from his time, but from a much earlier period. With the decline of the city in the tenth century, some of the canals and bridges of Baghdad had fallen into ruin. Although the Khaṭīb made a casual reference to this development elsewhere in his work (cf. Khaṭīb, p. 79), he left the dated description of the canals unchanged, and without comment. His failure to rework the topographical information at his disposal is indicative of his interest and competence in religious scholarship rather than geography, a fact of considerable importance for evaluating his work in relation to other local histories. For full details, see Introduction, p. 33. The account of the Khaṭīb is of particular importance because it describes the various places of the city as situated along its major water routes. Many of these locations are not accounted for in the other preserved descriptions of the city. Those places which are also listed by the Khaṭīb in his lengthy description of East and West Baghdad are treated in detail in the earlier chapters, and can be referred to by consulting the Index.
2. Nahr 'Īsā was one of the four major canals leading to the general vicinity of Baghdad; the others being Nahr al-Malik, Nahr Ṣarṣar, and Nahr aṣ-Ṣarāt (Muqaddasī, p. 124). A tributary of the Euphrates, it was deep enough to allow large boats coming from ar-Raqqah to deliver foodstuffs from Egypt and Syria (Ya'qūbī, *Buldān*, p. 250). Since the canal emptied into the Tigris below Qaṣr 'Īsā, it connected both major waterways (Iṣṭakhrī, pp. 84–85; Ibn Ḥawqal, pp. 164–65). As a result, the city was strategically situated amidst the major inland water routes of the empire, in addition to the great highways leading to the East and the Arabian peninsula. When the construction of dams along the Ṣarāt made it impossible for large boats to reach the Tigris, the 'Īsā alone remained open to heavy traffic. The course of Nahr 'Īsā is reported by Yāqūt, whose account is based on the Khaṭīb (*Mu'jam*, 4 : 842). He reports that in his time only Qanṭarat az-Zayyātīn, and Qanṭarat al-Bustān remain standing. However, the *Marāṣid* indicates that these bridges were surely destroyed before then, and that the only bridges standing in the time of Yāqūt were Qanṭarat al-Yāsirīyah, Qanṭarat ash-Shawk, and Qanṭarat Banī Zurayq (3 : 250). Cf. also Yāqūt (op. cit., pp. 190, 191, 839). Ibn al-Jawzī, writing in the twelfth century, reports that Qanṭarat Banī Zurayq fell into Nahr 'Īsā in 433/1042. There is no indication that the bridge was repaired then (*Muntaẓam*, 8 : 108). A century earlier (323/935) Qanṭarat al-Ushnān and its environs

were ravaged by fire. According to Ṣūlī it was not rebuilt in his time (*Akhbār*, p. 68). Cf. also LeStrange, Maps IV, VI. Qanṭarat Dimimmā was located at the village of the same name which was situated near al-Fallūjah (Yāqūt, *Mu'jam*, 2: 600). The *ṭassūj* of FīrūzSābūr is the administrative district of al-Anbār (cf. Yāqūt, *Mu'jam*, 3: 929; LeStrange, *Eastern Caliphate*, pp. 65–66).

3. According to Yāqūt, a large market was situated at Qanṭarat al-Ushnān (*Mu'jam*, 4: 191, 839). Cf. also LeStrange, p. 75; Map IV, ref. no. 35. The mills near Qanṭarat al-Maghīd are not to be confused with the Mills of the Patrikios which were situated at the junction of the Lesser and Greater Ṣarāt (cf. Khaṭīb, pp. 91 ff.). The Ma'badite Bridge was named after 'Abdallāh b. Muḥammad al-Ma'badī whose fief and mills were also situated here (cf. Khaṭīb, p. 91, l. 5). On the subsequent history of these locations, see n. 2 above.
4. This waterway consisted of two canals, the Greater Ṣarāt (al-Kubrā), which was a tributary of Nahr 'Īsā, and the Lesser Ṣarāt somewhere below at al-Muḥawwal. The two canals formed the island of al-'Abbāsīyah between them, and then merged again into a single canal which emptied into the Tigris (Ya'qūbī, *Buldān*, p. 242; Iṣṭakhrī, p. 84; Ibn Ḥawqal, p. 165). The Ṣarāt, which dates back to Sassanian times (Yāqūt, *Mu'jam*, 3: 377) was apparently a major commercial artery. In time, the building of dams along the canal made it impossible for large boats to continue until the Tigris. The goods, therefore, had to be unloaded and transferred to smaller vessels (Iṣṭakhrī, p. 85; Ibn Ḥawqal, p. 165; Muqadassī, p. 120). The larger boats continued to travel along Nahr 'Īsā. The course of Nahr aṣ-Ṣarāt is reported by Yāqūt whose account is based on the Khaṭīb (*Mu'jam*, 3: 377–78). He reports that in his time only, al-Qanṭarah al-'Atīqah and al-Qanṭarah al-Jadīdah remain standing. Ibn al-Jawzī reports that all the bridges spanning the Ṣarāt collapsed during a flood in 370/981. They were, however, rebuilt more solidly (*Muntaẓam*, 7: 105). For al-Qanṭarah al-'Atīqah and al-Qanṭarah al-Jadīdah, see text below. Cf. also LeStrange, Maps IV, VI.
5. Yāqūt reads aṣ-Ṣabībāt (*Mu'jam*, 3: 378). The etymology of the name is not clear. LeStrange calls it the Porcelain Bridge (*Ṣīn* being the Arabic name for China), but indicates that the word may be of Aramaic origin signifying date palms (cf. Ibn Serapion, p. 290, n. 2). Yāqūt mentions az-Zabad as a place in West Baghdad but no precise location is indicated (*Mu'jam*, 2: 914).
6. Dating back to Sassanian times, the Old Bridge was situated at the junction of the Lesser and Greater Ṣarāt. It was a solid vaulted structure built of burnt brick cemented with gypsum (Ya'qūbī, *Buldān*, pp. 243–44; Ṭabarī, *Annales*, 3.1: 280). It sustained considerable damage during the flood of 329/940 and is reported to have been destroyed when the bridges of the Ṣarāt collapsed during the flood of 370/981 (Ibn al-Jawzī, *Muntaẓam*, 6: 300; 7: 105; Ibn al-Athīr, *Kāmil*, 9: 6–7). The bridge was subsequently repaired, but was destroyed again in 433/1042 (Ibn al-Jawzī, op. cit., 8: 108). Apparently it was rebuilt once again for Yāqūt mentions that it was still standing in his time (*Mu'jam*, 3: 378). Cf. also LeStrange, p. 60: Map IV, ref. no. 4. The New Bridge was located near the Baṣrah Gate; a large market is reported to have been situated there (Ya'qūbī, *Buldān*, p. 245). Built by al-Manṣūr, it was later destroyed in the civil war following the death of ar-Rashīd (Ṭabarī, *Annales*, 3.2: p. 906), and was subsequently repaired several times (*'Arīb*, p. 132; Ibn al-Jawzī, *Muntaẓam*, 7: 105; Ibn al-Athīr, *Kāmil*, 9: 6–7). Its ruins were still visible in Yāqūt's time, although a newer bridge spanning the Ṣarāt had been erected somewhat below it (*Mu'jam*, 4: 188–89). Cf. also LeStrange, pp. 92–93; Map IV, ref. no. 50.

7. The course of Khandaq Ṭāhir is indicated by Yāqūt. However, he is incorrect in reporting that the canal flowed into the Tigris opposite the Baṣrah Gate (*Mu'jam*, 3: 378; *Marāṣid*, 2: 151). This canal which is reported as the northern boundary of Madīnat al-Manṣūr (cf. Khaṭīb, p. 71) also marked the western limits of the Ḥarbīyah Quarter, and thus provided a defensive barrier for the western approaches to the city. It is not surprising, therefore, that when al-Musta'īn was defending the city from his adversaries at Sāmarrā, he decided to build a protective wall along the Trench, and then eastward, encompassing the Round City and parts of al-Karkh, until it reached the Tigris. The subsequent history of this wall is not known. I suspect it was a defensive barrier, rather than a complex enclosure wall with fortifications, and thus was soon destroyed, its materials to be re-used in local construction. Although it is also not clear when the canal was originally dug, it most likely goes back at least to the earliest occupation of al-Ḥarbīyah in the reign of al-Manṣūr. Cf. also LeStrange, Maps V, VI. As for places situated along its course not previously discussed in this text: Yāqūt reports that no trace of the Bāb al-Ḥadīd remained in his time (*Mu'jam*, 2: 650). The Bāb al-Ḥarb was situated in al-Ḥarbīyah near the tomb of Aḥmad b. Ḥanbal (Yāqūt, *Mu'jam*, 2: 234). Cf. also LeStrange, p. 112; Map V, ref. no. 11. Bāb Qaṭrabbul was situated in the vicinity of az-Zuhayrīyah (Yāqūt, *Mu'jam*, 2: 964). Cf. also LeStrange, *Index*, p. 269; Map V, ref. no. 13.
8. The course of the Karkhāyā is reported in Yāqūt whose account is based on the Khaṭīb. He indicated that no trace of this canal could be found in his time (*Mu'jam*, 4: 252). Cf. also LeStrange, Maps IV, VI. The course of Nahr Razīn is also reported in Yāqūt whose account is again based on the Khaṭīb (*Mu'jam*, 4: 252). The lower part of Nahr Razīn which empties into the Greater Ṣarāt is known as Nahr Abī 'Attāb (Suhrāb, p. 132 = Ibn Serapion, p. 25). Cf. also LeStrange, Map IV.
9. This refers to the first hospital of the city established by Hārūn ar-Rashīd on the West Side (cf. Ibn Abī Uṣaybi'ah, *'Uyūn al-anbā'*, 1: 174–75; Qifṭī, *Ta'rīkh al-ḥukamā'*, pp. 383–84). A second institution was established during the reign of al-Mu'taḍid and was situated on the East Side in al-Mukharrim (Ibn Abī Uṣaybi'ah, op. cit., p. 221). In 302/914 'Alī b. 'Īsā, the Wazīr of al-Muqtadir, endowed a hospital in the northwest suburb al-Ḥarbīyah, and Abū 'Uthmān Ṣā'id b. Yāqūt ad-Dimishqī was entrusted with the administration of all these institutions. His duties were later entrusted to Sinān b. Thābit (op. cit., p. 234). This same Sinān b. Thābit founded two hospitals in the year 306/918. (Ibn al-Jawzī, *Muntaẓam*, 6: 142; Ibn Abī Uṣaybi'ah, op. cit., pp. 221–22). The first was situated on the East Side at Sūq Yaḥyā and became known as the Bīmāristān as-Sayyidah; the second, a smaller hospital, was located at the Damascus Gate, and was called the Māristān al-Muqtadirī. In 311/924 still another hospital was built at Darb al-Mufaḍḍal by the Wazīr Abū-l-Ḥasan b. al-Furāt (Ibn al-Jawzī, op. cit., p. 174, Ibn Abī Uṣaybi'ah, op. cit., p. 224). For hospitals in general, see *EI*, 2nd edition, *s.v.* Bīmāristān.
10. Yāqūt mentions Nahr ad-Dajāj as a branch canal of the Karkhāyā but does not describe its course (*Mu'jam*, 4: 838–39). It was apparently first dug by al-Manṣūr to service the populace of al-Karkh and was so named because the poultrymen used to stop there (Ya'qūbī, *Buldān*, p. 250; Khaṭīb, p. 79). It also gave its name to the surrounding area, which was damaged in the great Karkh fire of 449/1057 (Ibn al-Jawzī, *Muntaẓam*, 8: 181). The Food Market, situated along the course of Nahr ad-Dajāj, was also damaged in that fire (ibid.). A similar market (*Sūq al-Ma'kūl*) is also reported for the East Side (*Manāqib*, p. 26). The food in the markets was served ready to eat (cf. also *Makdisi*,

Topography, pp. 188, n. 13, 283, n. 4; and LeStrange, Map VI). For k͟harrāzīn (cobblers) C reads k͟hazzāzīn (silk merchants).

11. The course of Nahr Baṭāṭiyā is described in Yāqūt whose account is based on the K͟haṭīb (*Mu'jam*, 4: 835). Cf. also LeStrange, Map III. For Maskin, see Yāqūt, *Mu'jam*, 4: 529. Similar to the Kark͟hāyā which flowed into al-Kark͟h, the Dujayl was the main carrier of drinking water into the northwest suburb of al-Ḥarbīyah. However, unlike the Kark͟hāyā whose waters originated in the Euphrates, the Dujayl was a tributary of the Tigris. The drinking water was brought into the city via conduits constructed of burnt brick and quicklime (Ya'qūbī, *Buldān*, p. 250). According to the K͟haṭīb, they were all above ground except for the conduits of al-Ḥarbīyah, i.e., the waters branching off from the Dujayl (cf. text below). Similar underground conduits were apparently found in Fusṭāṭ by an archeological team headed by G. Scanlon. Their complete findings are as yet unpublished.

12. C and S: *al-Kark͟h*, read *al-Kūk͟h* as in Suhrāb, p. 133 = Ibn Serapion, p. 27.

13. S: *al-Jadīd*.

14. Suhrāb, 134 = Ibn Serapion, p. 27 reads *nahr yuqālu lahā Dukkān al-Abnā'*. However, see Suhrab 134 c. where the suggested reading is *nahr yuqālu lahā* [...] *yamurru* [*bi*]-*Dukkān al-Abnā'*, which may be translated: A canal called [...] which passes the shops (*Dukkān*) of the Abnā'. In early 'Abbasid times, the term *Abnā' ad-Dawlah* referred to members of the 'Abbāsid house, and by extension, to certain of their clients (cf. *EI*, 2nd edition, *s.v.* al-Abnā'). Note that al-Ḥarbīyah was heavily populated with the Persian clients of the 'Abbāsids.

15. S: *al-Bānūjah*; the reference is to al-Bānūqah the daughter of al-Madhī.

16. The description of the East Side Canals is based on Suhrāb, pp. 129–131 = Ibn Serapion, pp. 21–23. Cf. also LeStrange, Map V. The course of Nahr Mūsā is briefly described by Yāqūt whose account is based on the K͟haṭīb (*Mu'jam*, 4: 842). Nahr Bīn was a branch canal of the Nahrawān. It did not flow in Baghdad, but irrigated Kalwād͟hā before emptying into the Tigris two leagues (*farsak͟h*) below the city (cf. Suhrāb, p. 129 = Ibn Serapion, p. 21; Iṣṭak͟hrī, p. 83; Ibn Ḥawqal, p. 164). Cf. also LeStrange, Maps III, V.

17. C and S: *K͟handaq al-'Abbās*. *Qanṭarat al-'Abbās* (Suhrāb 130 = Ibn Serapion, p. 22) was on the West Side (p. 75, above).

18. C and S: *al-Mu'arrash*, read *al-'Ars͟h* as in Suhrāb, p. 130 = Ibn Serapion, p. 22.

19. A tributary of Nahr Bīn, it flowed underground (probably within the city) until reaching Qaṣr al-Firdaws. This canal, and the great quarter of the same name, which was still thriving in the time of Yāqūt, were named after al-Mu'allā b. Ṭarīf, the client of al-Mahdī (Yāqūt, *Mu'jam*, 4: 845–46).

20. C: *Biyayraz*, S: *Biyabraz*, read *Abraz* as in Suhrāb, p. 130 = Ibn Serapion, p. 22.

21. C and S: *Mūs͟hajir*. Suhrāb reads *Mūs͟hajin* (p. 130 = Ibn Serapion, p. 22). The reading is doubtful.

22. Upon reaching Bāb as͟h-S͟hammāsīyah, Nahr al-Faḍl emptied into the Tigris (Suhrāb, p. 131 = Ibn Serapion, p. 23). Its parent canal, the K͟hāliṣ, like Nahr Bīn to the south, did not enter Baghdad, but emptied into the Tigris, in this case two leagues (*farsak͟h*) below ar-Rās͟hidīyah. A tributary of Nahr Tamarrā, it was a major waterway permitting the traffic of large boats (Suhrāb, pp. 128, 131 = Ibn Serapion, pp. 20, 23; Iṣṭak͟hrī, p. 84; Ibn Ḥawqal, p. 165). When 'Aḍud ad-Dawlah built his palace in al-Muk͟harrim, he extended feeder-canals from the K͟hāliṣ to Baghdad. (Cf. K͟haṭīb, p. 106). Cf. also Le-Strange, Map I. Bāb as͟h-S͟hammāsīyah was situated in the uppermost quarter of East Baghdad marking the northeast boundary of the city (Yāqūt, *Mu'jam*, 3: 318). When

al-Musta'īn fortified Baghdad, he built a wall extending from this gate to Sūq ath-Thalāthā', and repaired the gates along the fortification (Ṭabarī, *Annales*, 3.4: 1551). For a discussion of the East Side walls erected in the eleventh century, see LeStrange, *Index*, p. 380; Massignon, *Mission*, 2: 96–99; Canard, *Hamdanides*, 1: 162–163; Makdisi, *Topography*, pp. 298–302. Of these canals only the Mahdī entered the city itself. According to Suhrāb, it originates just above Bāb ash-Shammāsīyah. After entering the city at this place, it flows to the Suwayqah of Ja'far and passes the Nahr al-Mahdī Road (p. 131 = Ibn Serapion, p. 23; also Ya'qūbī, *Buldān*, p. 251). When 'Aḍud ad-Dawlah built his palace in al-Mukharrim he was forced to water the area with a newly dug canal from the Khāliṣ (cf. Khaṭīb, p. 106). This would seem to indicate that this waterway and its parent canal Nahr al-Faḍl had ceased to be effective carriers of the Khāliṣ' waters. The Baradān Bridge is mentioned by Yāqūt but no location is indicated (*Mu'jam*, 4: 187). It was reconstructed when al-Musta'īn built his wall from Bāb ash-Shammāsīyah to Sūq ath-Thalāthā' (Ṭabarī, 3.4: 1551). Cf. also LeStrange, *Index*, p. 360; Map V, ref. no. 52; Canard, *Hamdanides*, 1: 163. The Dār ar-Rūmīyīn was, according to Yāqūt, located in the Christian Quarter of upper East Baghdad (*Mu'jam*, 2: 662; 3: 317). Cf. also LeStrange, p. 149, Map V, ref. no. 56.

23. C and S: *al-Faḍl*, read *as-Sūr* as in Suhrāb, p. 131 = Serapion, p. 23.

Chapter 11

1. Pontoon bridges (*jisr*) were used to connect East and West Baghdad since the inundation of the river made masonry bridges (*qanṭarah*) impractical. The pontoon bridge also had the advantage of being mobile and easy to repair. In times of strife the bridges could be dismantled and traffic between the two sides cut. Conversely the bridges were also easy to erect so as to facilitate the transfer of men and materials (cf. for example, Ibn al-Jawzī, *Muntaẓam*, 8: 56–57, 132). The account of the Khaṭīb is also mentioned in Ṭabarī, *Annales*, 3.1: 380. This bridge is identified by LeStrange as Jisr al-Awwal, the bridge which Ya'qūbī indicates connected the West Side with al-Mukharrim and which LeStrange considers to be the Lower Bridge of the City (p. 175; Map IV; also Ya'qūbī, *Buldān*, p. 254). According to Canard, this was the Main Bridge, connecting the markets of al-Karkh with Sūq ath-Thalāthā' (*Hamdanides*, 1: 168). He therefore agrees with LeStrange as to the identification of the bridge, i.e., the bridge connecting the lower West Side with the lower East Side. However, LeStrange is of the opinion that the Main Bridge of the city (*al-Jisr*) was situated further north at Bāb aṭ-Ṭāq (cf. n. 6 below). The identification of the Baghdad bridges is made more difficult by such relative terms as first bridge (*al-Awwal*) and upper bridge (*al-A'alā*). There is, apparently, some confusion as to what these names indicate in different periods. Ya'qūbī's Jisr al-Awwal is not to be confused with the bridge of the same name that spanned the Tigris between al-Ḥarbīyah and the upper East Side in the tenth century (Ṭabarī, op. cit., 3.4: 2242, 2252; *'Arib*, pp. 5, 8).
2. Aḥmad b. al-Khalīl b. Malik, ninth century (*TB*, 4: 131). The reference to Bāb al-Bustān refers either to Bustān az-Zāhir (East Side), or more likely to the gardens (*bustān*) adjoining the Caliphal Palace at al-Khuld (West Side). The three bridges gave the Caliph private access to al-Mahdī's camp on the East Side, thus pointing out the strategic location of al-Khuld between ar-Ruṣāfah, the Round City, and the suburb of al-Ḥarbīyah (cf. Part II B). However, once construction was well underway on the East Side, new

market areas to service this region became necessary, and thus the great markets near Bāb aṭ-Ṭāq came to be constructed. The Caliph (al-Mahdī) then resided at the new palace complex in ar-Ruṣāfah. It was presumably about this time that al-Manṣūr's bridges were replaced or perhaps supplemented by the Main Bridge of the city which spanned the Tigris in the same general area (cf. n. 6 below).

3. A location directly south of Baghdad in the district of Kalwāḏhā (Yāqūt, *Mu'jam*, 2: 665). According to LeStrange, this was a double bridge which served to connect the Caliph's palace at az-Zandaward with the West Side (pp. 175, 295, 297; Map III).
4. According to Ya'qūbī, there were three bridges spanning the Tigris in the time of ar-Rashīd (*Historiae*, 2: 510). The account of the Khaṭīb would seem to indicate that the Caliph either replaced or repaired an older bridge at Bāb ash-Shammāsīyah which connected the East Side with West Baghdad, since such a bridge (Jisr al-A'lā) is reported by Ṭabarī to have existed during the reign of al-Mahdī (*Annales*, 3.1 : 470–71). During the tenth century this bridge was also known as Jisr al-Awwal (op. cit., 3.4 : 2242, 2252; *'Arīb*, pp. 5, 8). This is not to be confused with the Jisr al-Awwal which was situated further downstream (cf. no. 1 above). The bridge apparently fell into disrepair for some undisclosed period of time in the tenth century as Ṣūlī reported for 327/938–939 (*Akhbār*, p. 138; also see Iṣṭakhrī, p. 84; Ibn Ḥawqal, p. 165; Ibn al-Jawzī, *Manāqib*, p. 20. Cf. also LeStrange, p. 179; Map V; Canard, *Hamdanides*, 1 : 168).
5. S: *al-'Izziyah*, perhaps read *al-Mu'izziyah* as in C. The Arabic sources indicate that at various times in the tenth century there were only two bridges spanning the Tigris. (Iṣṭakhrī, p. 84; Ibn Ḥawqal, p. 165; Hilāl, *Wuzarā'*, p. 21; Ṣūlī, *Akhbār*, p. 138). This may have been the result of a temporary state of disrepair, or the intentional dismantling of one of the bridges. By 422/1030 the only bridge remaining was the Main Bridge connecting Bāb aṭ-Ṭāq with the West Side (cf. Ibn al-Jawzī, *Muntaẓam*, 8: 56–57). Cf. also Makdisi, *Topography*, p. 186, n. 2).
6. This bridge, which connected Bāb aṭ-Ṭāq with the West Side, was the main bridge of the city. According to LeStrange, it was traversed by the eastern highroad which led from the Khurāsān Gate of the East Side to the Khurāsān Gate of the Round City. Its western end was therefore near the Khuld Palace, its eastern end near Bāb aṭ-Ṭāq. The account in the Khaṭīb seems to indicate that the upper bridge was dismantled and moved to Bāb aṭ-Ṭāq forming a double bridge (pp. 178, 181; Map V). Disagreeing with LeStrange, Massignon argues that the Main Bridge has, more or less, remained at the same spot, and was closer to where the modern bridge (1907) stands. The bridge therefore could not have been located as far north as LeStrange claims, but was situated between al-Karkh and the markets of the East Side (Sūq ath-Thalāthā'), thus uniting the fixed markets of East and West Baghḏad (*Mission*, 2: 88–91). However, a report mentioned by Ibn al-Jawzī for the year 422/1030 indicates that the only remaining Tigris bridge was the one connecting Bāb aṭ-Ṭāq with the West Side. Presumably this was the Main Bridge. Canard, who follows Massignon on the fixity of the markets, is, therefore, forced to conclude that Bāb aṭ-Ṭāq and Sūq ath-Thalāthā' were situated in the same general area despite all the evidence to the contrary (cf. Canard, *Hamdanides*, 1 : 161, 168; Makdisi, Topography, p. 185, n. 4). On the Massignon theory, see Part IIC.
7. According to Ibn al-Jawzī, the bridge was repaired and erected at Bāb aṭ-Ṭāq, thus giving access to Bustān az-Zāhir which served as a camping ground for the troops of al-Basāsīrī, the Wazīr (*Muntaẓam*, 8: 132 *sub anno* 450). It is probable that the bridge was dismantled after his fall from power and relocated at Mashra'at al-Qaṭṭānīn which was situated further down stream near Sūq ath-Thalāthā'.

Chapter 12

1. Aḥmad b. Muḥammad b. ʿImrān, unidentified.
   Muḥammad b. Yaḥyā an-Nadīm, i.e., aṣ-Ṣūlī.
   This *K. Baghdād* of Aḥmad b. Abī Ṭāhir Ṭayfūr presumably refers to his *Akhbār al-khulafā'* (cf. F. Rosenthal, *Historiography*, p. 335, n. 6—citing Sakhāwī, *I'lān*, p. 123). Like the Khaṭīb this work also featured a topographical introduction dealing with the sections of the city (*khiṭaṭ*) and the residences of its distinguished inhabitants (Ḥumaydī, *Jadhwat al-Muqtabis*, p. 98). Other works dealing with Baghdad, the *Faḍā'il* of Tanūkhī, and the *Risālah* of Mahdundādh al-Kisrawī also contained statistics relating to the city (cf. Tanūkhī, *Nishwār*, 1: 165; Ṣābi', *Rusūm*, p. 18 ff.; M. ʿAwād, "K. faḍā'il Baghdād li Yazdjard b. Mahmandār al-Fārisī," *RAAD*, 19 [1944]: 322 ff. —also published as a separate pamphlet in Baghdad, 1947). Was there a tradition for local histories of Baghdad to contain a chapter dealing with statistical data? For a full discussion of the Khaṭīb's work in relation to other local histories of the city, see Introduction, pp. 34–40.
2. One *jarib* = 1,592 sq. m. (cf. W. Hinz, *Arabische Masse und Gewichte*, p. 65). Duri explains the larger of the two estimates as the result of extended building on the East Side during the reign of al-Muqtadir (*EI*, 2nd edition, p. 898). However, the source of this account, Aḥmad b. Abī Ṭāhir Ṭayfūr, died in 893, some fifteen years before al-Muqtadir became Caliph. Moreover, the smaller estimate agrees with still another account by Aḥmad b. Abī Ṭāhir Ṭayfūr which reports statistics from the time of al-Muwaffaq (c. 884; cf. note 10 below). However, other figures reported by Ibn Ḥawqal (p. 164 = Iṣṭakhrī, p. 83) indicate that the length of Baghdad along the Tigris shore from Bāb ash-Shammāsīyah to the Dār al-Khilāfah is five *mīl*, and the width from Bāb Khurāsān (East Side) to al-Yāsirīyah is also five *mīl*. LeStrange (p. 324 ff.), on the basis of these figures, calculates the area of the city at 25 sq. miles, although the Arabic *mīl* (2,000 m.) and the English mile (1,728 yds.—metric mile 1,500 m.) are not the same. Moreover, without information on Arabic metrology which has been collected since his time, he assumed this figure corresponded, more or less, to the data given by the Khaṭīb. Such, however, is not the case (cf. n. 10 below). The total area given by LeStrange is larger than the figures mentioned by the Khaṭīb, since 25 sq. *mīl* = 100 sq. km., whereas 43,750 *jarīb* is somewhat less than 70 sq. km., and 53,750 *jarib* is somewhat less than 86 sq. km. The difficulty may be resolved if one can assume that the width of Baghdad was measured according to different points of reference. Note that according to another account of the Khaṭīb the length of Baghdad was 250 *ḥabl*, the width only 175 *ḥabl* (cf. n. 10 below). The reference to al-Yāsirīyah is presumably to the boundary of Baghdad at its westernmost limits. The length of Baghdad as measured along the Tigris shore was, no doubt, constant for both the East and West Sides. This is not necessarily true for measuring the breadth of Baghdad; and this distinction may serve to explain the difference between the statistics of the Khaṭīb and those derived by LeStrange from Ibn Ḥawqal. The calculations of LeStrange are, in any case, not acceptable.
3. The figure of 1,500,000 given in the Khaṭīb is claimed for the total population of the city by Duri (cf. *EI*, 2nd edition, p. 899). In addition to the baths (cf. n. 6 below) he cites a report which indicates that the Mosque of al-Manṣūr was measured to determine its capacity, and that the figure reached was 64,000, a figure obviously exaggerated in view of the mosque's size (Ibn al-Faqīh, fol. 62a). Other figures supporting the large

population estimate are given in Ya'qūbī who indicates that Baghdad contained in the time of al-Manṣūr (?) 10,000 streets (*darb*) and side streets (*sikkah*), 35,000 mosques, and 15,000 baths (*Buldān*, pp. 250, 254). Also cited by Duri is the account in which al-Muqtadir ordered Sinān b. Thābit to examine doctors, and license only those who were qualified; they totaled 860 (Ibn Abī Uṣaybi'ah, *'Uyūn al-anbā'*, 1: 221, 224, 310; Ibn al-Athīr, *Kāmil*, 8: 85). According to the Khaṭīb the number of *summayrīyah* and *ma'baranīyah* vessels operative in the Tigris were counted in the time of al-Muwaffaq and totaled 30,000 (cf. text above; also Ibn al-Jawzī, *Manāqib*, p. 24). Other reports try to establish the density of population according to the consumption of foodstuffs (cf. n. 9 below). Attempts to estimate the population of the city by the number of baths seem to have been popular. Such an account attributed to Yazdjard b. Mahmandār al-Fārisī (al-Kisrawī) is mentioned by Hilāl aṣ-Ṣābi' (*Rusūm*, p. 18 ff.). The author's figures, though he considered them modest, are comparable to those of the Khaṭīb. He indicates that certain prevalent estimates as to the number of baths (200,000, 130,000, and 120,000) are exaggerations for the benefit of the listener and are uncritically accepted by the general populace. By halving the lowest estimate he arrives at a more reasonable figure of 60,000 baths. He then gives the number of people servicing each bath which, in addition to the five listed by the Khaṭīb, includes a purser (*ṣāḥib aṣ-ṣundūq*), thus obtaining a figure of 360,000. Analogous to al-Manṣūr's time, he also determines the number of houses in relation to the number of baths. Kisrawī modestly halved the accepted figure of 400 and thus obtained a total of 12,000,000 houses. As some residences housed twenty people and others only two or three, he halved the greater number (20) and doubled the lesser (3), and then halved the combined total (16). This sum (8) when multiplied by the number of houses results in a total population of 96,000,000, a figure which is, of course, impossible. It almost seems inconceivable that no hint of an actual census is to be found in all these discussions. A thorough study of the sources will yield more speculative information of this kind. These statistics, while they are consistently large, are nevertheless suspect. At present there does not seem to be any way of making these figures more tangible, although other data would seem to indicate a population of about 200,000—600,000 is not altogether impossible. See Part II C.

4. *'Īd*: meaning festival. The Muslim year has two canonical festivals, the 'Īd al-Aḍḥā, "the sacrificial festival," and the 'Īd al-Fiṭr, "the festival of breaking the fast of Ramaḍān"; the first occurs on the 10th of Dhū-l-Ḥijjah, the second on the 1st of Shawwāl (cf. *EI*, *s.v.* 'Īd al-Aḍḥā, 'Īd al-Fiṭr). I have corrected the figures given by the Khaṭīb as they do not tally. According to S and C, they are 1,158½ jars and 609,510 *raṭl*.
5. Ibrāhīm b. Hilāl aṣ-Ṣābi', d. 384/994 (*GAL*, *Supplement*, 1: 153; also the introduction to M. 'Awād's edition of the *Rusūm*). For a similar story, see Tanūkhī, *Nishwār*, 1: 65; also Ṣābi', *Rusūm*, pp. 20 ff.—perhaps the source of this account. The Khaṭīb = Yāqūt, *Mu'jam*, 2: 255—citing a *K. Baghdād* of Hilāl aṣ-Ṣābi'; cf. Introduction, p. 38.
6. Ya' qūbī indicates that in the time of al-Manṣūr (?), there were 5,000 bathhouses on the East Side, and 10,000 on the West Side, and that the number had increased since then (*Buldān*, pp. 250, 254). Hilāl aṣ-Ṣābi', on the authority of his grandfather, reports that there were 27,000 baths in the time of al-Muqtadir, but that the number continuously declined in Būyid times: 17,000 under Mu'izz ad-Dawlah (945–967); somewhat in excess of 5,000 under 'Aḍud ad-Dawlah (977–983), over 1,500 under Bahā' ad-Dawlah (count taken in 382/99–99), and in Hilāl's time (d. 1056) only approximately 150 (cf. *Rusūm*, pp. 20 ff.). The figure given for the period of al-Mu'izz is somewhat at variance

with the account of the Khaṭīb. What is particularly interesting is that there should have been more baths in the time of al-Mu'izz, than in that of 'Aḍud ad-Dawlah when the city is reported to have undergone extensive rebuilding and expansion (cf. Miskawayh, *Tajārib*, 2 : 404–9 ; 3 : 69 ; Ibn al-Athīr, *Kāmil*, 8 : 158). Hilāl, amazed at the current number of baths in relation to previous times, sought confirmation of the larger figures. He observed that attached to some thirty residences of the Bāb al-Marātib section there were fifteen baths. According to him, this section, which was a prestige area, contained in the time of al-Mu'taḍid no less than 50,000 inhabitants. At that time, each house had at least one bath, some had more. This estimated population of the Bāb al-Marātib section is, of course, exaggerated. Moreover, one may note that the very wealthy Ḥanbalite merchant Abū 'Abdallāh b. Jaradah had a residence there valued at tens of thousands of dinars. It was composed of no less than thirty buildings and a garden, but contained only a single bath (G. Makdisi, *Topography*, p. 288; *Autograph Diary of an Eleventh Century Historian of Baghdad*, II, in *BSOAS*, 18 [1956]: p. 248 and n. 6). The figures on the baths reflect the general decline of the city in Būyid times (cf. n. 8 below), but are otherwise difficult to evaluate.

7. C: *ṭuruz*; perhaps correct to *ṭarrāzūn* meaning manufacturers of embroidered garments (*ṭirāz*).
8. That is to say, the war between al-Amīn and al-Ma'mūn (cf. F. Gabrieli, "La Successione di Hārūn ar-Rashīd et la Guerra fra al-Amīn e al-Ma'mūn," *RSO*, 11 [1928]: 341–97). The siege of Baghdad (c. 813), resulting from the conflict of the two brothers, is graphically described by the Arab chroniclers who report wide-spread devastation (cf. Ṭabarī, *Annales*, 3.2: 864 ff.; Mas'ūdī, *Murūj*, 4: 441 ff.; summed up in LeStrange, pp. 306 ff.). There are, however, very few references to actual places which were destroyed; and those mentioned, such as the Qanṭarah al-'Atīqah and the Qanṭarah al-Jadīdah, are known to have existed in later times (cf. text of Khaṭīb). Moreover, even the superstructure of the Round City was intact and occupied during the tenth century (cf. ch. 2, n. 38). I am inclined to believe that the damage from this siege on the topography of the city was marginal, that most of the destroyed areas were soon rebuilt, and thus came to be described in the later topographical accounts. It was rather the prestige of the city as the capital of the Islamic world which declined, if ever so slowly, after the civil war, as the Islamic empire became increasingly decentralized and the status of the Caliphate diminished. Al-Ma'mūn's real capital was not at Baghdad, but at Merv with his Persian allies in Khurāsān. His successor, al-Mu'taṣim, officially moved the capital to a new administrative center at Sāmarrā where it remained for over half a century, despite an ill-fated attempt in 865 by the Caliph al-Musta'īn to re-establish himself in Baghdad (Ṭabarī, *Annales*, 3.4: 1553–78). It was this attempt which brought about some changes in the topography of the city, principally in the construction of defensive fortifications for both the East and West Sides (summed up in LeStrange, pp. 310 ff.). But it was only with the return of the Caliphate in 892 that extensive building programs were undertaken in the general vicinity of the new Caliphal complex (cf. text, ch. 7). Nevertheless, it is reported that beginning with al-Muqtadir's tumultuous reign (908–932) even these new royal areas, and what is adjacent to them, became truncated so that by the time of Khaṭīb's exile (1055) this general area was only half of what it had been (Ṣābi', *Rusūm*, pp. 7 ff.). The great physical decline of the city must be attributed, for the most part, to major changes which took place in the administration of Iraq under the Būyids, and the Saljūqs who followed them. A full study of the city in these last periods is, unfortunately, still not available.

9. Abū-l-Ḥasan Muḥammad b. Ṣāliḥ al-Hāshimī, d. 369/979 (*TB*, 5: 363–65). A version of this story is found in Tanūkhī, *Nishwār*, 1 : 66, and similar accounts attempt to gage population according to the consumption of foodstuffs. Tanūkhī thus notes that the amount of lettuce brought in (345/956) from Kalwādhā, Qaṭrabbul, and the surrounding environs was 2,000 *jarīb* worth 50,000 dinars, and concludes, "What then must be the size of a city where in a single season of a year, one type of vegetable was consumed to a value of 50,000 dinars" (ibid.). Hilāl aṣ-Ṣābi' notes that in addition to statistics on bathhouses (cf. n. 3 above), Yazdjard al-Kisrawī attempted to estimate the population of Baghdad on the basis of clothing and foodstuffs. He indicates that on each side of Baghdad, 60,000 dinars were spent on cooked beans (*baqillā*) every day, thereby resulting in a total of 120,000 dinars for the entire city, and supporting the higher population estimate he previously arrived at (cf. *Rusūm*, p. 20). However, information of this sort is almost impossible to evaluate. One *kurr* of peas mentioned below equals 2.437 kg. (Hinz, pp. 42–43).
10. According to LeStrange, this estimate may have been made when al-Muwaffaq returned to Baghdad from his campaign against the Zanj in 884. The figures must be reversed in order to indicate that the West Side was the larger section of the city (cf. n. 2. above; also Ibn Ḥawqal, p. 164 = Iṣṭakhrī, p. 83; LeStrange, pp. 324–25—he incorrectly reports that the East Side was the larger of the two based on this account). The length and width of the city are estimated in terms of *ḥabl*, and the total area is given in *jarīb*. According to the statistics of the Khaṭīb, we can determine that 1 sq. *ḥabl* = 1 *jarīb* (250 × 105 = 26,250). Hinz indicates that the *ḥabl* = 21.616 m., but his information is for Spain rather than the Eastern part of the Islamic World (p. 62). Note that the length of Baghdad, as indicated by Ibn Ḥawqal (p. 164) and Iṣṭakhrī (p. 83), is 5 *mīl*. Since each *mīl* is the equivalent of 2 km. (=2,000 m.; cf. Hinz, op. cit., p. 63; according to Duri 1,848 m.), the total length of Baghdad, as measured along the river, was 10,000 m. One *ḥabl* is then equal to 40 m. (10,000 ÷ 250). The *jarīb*, according to Hinz, is 1,592 sq. m. or 39.9 m. sq. (op. cit., p. 65; 36.9 according to Duri). The figures are therefore consistent, and an exact figure has been determined for the *ḥabl* as measured in Baghdad. The statistics of the Khaṭīb indicate that the length of the city is larger than its breadth by a ratio of 10:7; and that the breadth of the West Side is larger than that of the East Side by a ratio of 3:2. This is at variance with the accounts of Ibn Ḥawqal and Iṣṭakhrī which seem to report the length and breadth of the city to be equal. It may be assumed, however, that the length of the city as measured along the Tigris shore was constant, but the breadth may have varied depending on the points of reference. For Ibn Ḥawqal these are the Khurāsān Gate in East Baghdad and al-Yāsirīyah on the West Side. A careful study of Duri's map indicates that a line drawn from the Khurāsān Gate in East Baghdad to the Kūfah Gate of the Round City is consistent with the ratio of length to breadth; and also the ratio of the breadth of the West Side to that of the East Side. If the reported ratio is correct and if the map is accurate, these locations could possibly have been the points of reference for the measurement of the city as indicated in the Khaṭīb. For a full discussion, see J. Lassner, "The *Ḥabl* of Baghdad and the Dimensions of the City—a Metrological Note," *JESHO*, 6 (1963): 228–29.

Chapter 13

1. The Cemetery of the Quraysh is linked with the Bāb at-Tibn Cemetery. It was situated beyond Khandaq Ṭāhir in the vicinity of Bāb at-Tibn. It is also linked with the Shūnīzī

Cemetery (cf. text below), and the Cemetery of the two Kāẓims (*Kaẓimayn*), in honor of the two Shī'ite Imāms who are buried there—Mūsā al-Kāẓim and his grandson Muḥammad b. 'Alī. It would, therefore, seem that all these cemeteries were part of a single burial complex extending over a wide area just beyond the limits of the city. The name Quraysh was also apparently used to designate the Khayzurān Cemetery on the East Side (cf. Yāqūt, *Mu'jam*, 1 : 443 ; 2 : 522 ; 3 : 339 ; 4 : 79, 587 ; Ibn Ḥawqal, p. 164). Cf. also LeStrange, pp. 158, 160–65, 193, 350–53 ; Map V ; Massignon, *Mission*, 2 : 78, 105–6 ; Donaldson, *The Shi'ite Religion*, pp. 152–60, 188–208. Mūsā b. Ja'far is the Imām Mūsā al-Kāẓim, d. 183/799–800 or 180/802 (cf. Donaldson, op. cit., pp. 152–60). His grave was called the Shrine (*Mashhad*) of Bāb at-Tibn. This shrine and that of his grandson were destroyed in the riot of 443/1051 (Ibn al-Jawzī, *Muntaẓam*, 8 : 149–50 ; Ibn al-Athīr, *Kamil*, 9 : 395–396). However, they were rebuilt some time later (cf. LeStrange, p. 162 ff. ; also Massignon, *Mission*, 2 : 99–100).

2. S : *al-Ḥasan b. Ibrāhīm———'Alī al-Khallāl.*
   Al-Ḥasan b. al-Ḥusayn al-Astarābādhī, d. 412/1021–1022, (*TB*, 7 : 300).
   Aḥmad b. Ja'far al-Qaṭī'ī, d. 368/979 (*TB*, 4 : 73–74).
   Al-Ḥasan b. Ibrāhīm al-Khallāl, c. 940 (*TB*, 7 : 272).
3. Muhammad b. al-Ḥusayn al-Ḥanbalī, d. 458/1066 (*TB*, 2 : 256).
   Abū Ṭāhir b. Abī Bakr, unidentified.
4. Al-Qaṭī'ah, i.e., the Fief, meaning the Fief of Umm Ja'far which was also known as az-Zubaydīyah, and which was situated near the Bāb at-Tibn Cemetery. The Tomb of Aḥmad b. Ḥanbal apparently refers to his burial place in the Cemetery of the Ḥarb Gate as mentioned by the Khaṭīb (cf. also Yāqūt, *Mu'jam*, 4 : 586 ; *Marāṣid*, 3 : 129 ; Ibn al-Athīr, *Kāmil*, 10 : 63 ; 11 : 164 ; 12 : 216). LeStrange, however, observes that two later authorities, Ibn Jubayr and Ibn Battūṭah place the tomb near that of Abū Ḥanīfah on the upper East Side ; but also indicate the existence of a tomb for Ibn Ḥanbal on the West Side as does the contemporary Persian geographer Qazwīnī. He is led to believe that Aḥmad b. Ḥanbal was never buried on the East Side, but after his tomb near al-Ḥarbīyah was destroyed by flood, he was mistakenly venerated at the burial place of his son 'Abdallāh which was situated in the Fief (West Side) opposite the Shrine of Abū Ḥanīfah across the river (LeStrange, pp. 159–60, 165–67, Map V, ref. no. 12). Note, however, Massignon's objections to the above-mentioned theory, and his own contention that Aḥmad b. Ḥanbal's body was exhumed and moved to a new burial place on the East Side (*Mission*, 2 : 101–2). Bishr b. al-Ḥārith mentioned as having also been buried in the Cemetery of the Ḥarb Gate d. 226/840 or 227/841 (cf. *EI*, 2nd. edition, *s.v.* Bishr al-Ḥāfī). For the position of his tomb in modern times (1907), see Massignon, *Mission*, 2 : 79–80.
5. Ismā'īl b. Aḥmad al-Ḥayrī, d. 430/1038–1039 (*TB*, 6 : 313).
   Muḥammad b. al-Ḥusayn as-Sulamī, d. 412/1021 (*GAL*, *Supplement*, 1 : 361 ff.).
   Abū Bakr ar-Rāzī, d. 376/986 (Sulmaī, *Ṭabaqāt*, p. 18 ff.).
   'Abdallāh b. Mūsā aṭ-Ṭalḥī, unidentified.
   Aḥmad b. al-'Abbās, unidentified.
6. Ma'rūf al-Karkhī, d. 200/815–816 (*EI*, *s.v.* Ma'rūf al-Karkhī). This tomb burned down accidentally in 495/1067, when some wood and matting caught fire, burning the walls and the dome. The building was reconstructed by order of the Caliph al-Qā'im. It was rebuilt with burnt brick cemented by gypsum, and the work was completed the following year (cf. Ibn al-Jawzī, *Muntaẓam*, 9 : 246, 248 ; Ibn al-Athīr, *Kāmil*, 10 : 37–38 ; also Makdisi, *Topography*, p. 286). It was situated in the Bāb ad-Dayr Cemetery near the

Baṣrah Gate less than one *mīl* from the Tigris (along the lower course of the Ṣarāt?). This cemetery was apparently the burial ground for the eastern part of al-Karkh (cf. Yāqūt, *Mu'jam*, 2: 650; 4: 137; also LeStrange, *Index*, p. 371; Massignon, *Mission*, 2: 108). Also see M. Jawād "Al-'Imārāt al-Islāmīyah al-'itqīyah al-qā'imah fī Baghdād," *Sumer*, 3 (1947): 55 ff. Manṣūr b. 'Ammār, d. 225/840 (*TB*, 13: 71 ff.).

7. Al-Ḥasan b. Abī Ṭālib (al-Khallāl?).
   Yūsuf b. 'Umar al-Qawwās, d. 385/995 (*TB*, 14: 325–27).
   Muḥammad b. Shujā', unidentified.
   Abū Yūsuf b. Bakhtān (*TB*, 14: 280).
8. S: *Ismā'īl b. Bakr as-Sakūnī*, C: *Abū Bakr.*
   Al-Ḥusayn b. 'Alī at-Tanājirī, d. 439/1048 (*TB*, 8: 79–80).
   Muḥammad b. 'Alī al-Mu'addib, unidentified.
   Uthmān b. Ismā'īl as-Sukkarī, d. 323/934–935 (*TB*, 11: 296).
   Ismā'īl b. Bakr, d. 280.893–894 (*TB*, 6: 293–94).
   Aḥmad b. Ibrāhīm ad-Dawraqī, d. 240/855 (*TB*, 4: 6–7).
9. This cemetery is identified by Streck with the place called al-Kunāsah (*Babylonien*, p. 159). For al-Kunāsah see Ya'qūbī, *Buldān*, p. 244; also LeStrange, pp. 150–51; Map VI, ref. no. 21. For the Shūnīzī Cemetery see n. 1 above, and text below. Yāqūt indicated that a Ṣūfī convent (*khānaqāh*) was situated there (*Mu'jam*, 3: 338). Sarī as-Saqaṭī, d. 256/870 or 257/871 (Ibn Khallikān, *Wafayāt*, 1: 201; also LeStrange, pp. 79–80). According to Yāqūt, the following ascetics were also buried there: al-Junayd, Ja'far al-Khuldī, Ruwaym, and Samnūn al-Muḥibb (*Mu'jam*, 3: 338). At-Tūthah was situated opposite Qanṭarat ash-Shawk. It was still populated in the time of Yāqūt when it was like a separate town (*Mu'jam*, 1: 889; also LeStrange, p. 75; Map VI). The last passage on the Cemetery of the Quraysh is cited by Ibn Khallikān in his biography of Sarī as-Saqaṭī.
10. Abū-l-Ḥasan b. Miqsam, d. 380/990 (*TB*, 4: 429).
    Abū 'Alī aṣ-Ṣaffār, unidentified.
11. Ibrāhīm b. 'Umar al-Barmakī, d. 445/1054 (*TB*, 6: 139).
    'Ubaydallāh b. 'Abd ar-Raḥmān, d. 384/994 (*TB*, 10: 368–70).
    'Abd ar-Raḥmān b. Muḥammad, d. 336/947–948 (*TB*, 10: 289–90).
12. Qur'ān, 112.1.
13. S: *al-Ḥusayn*, C: *Abū-l-Ḥusayn.*
    Muḥammad b. 'Alī aṣ-Ṣūrī, d. 441/1049 (*TB*, 3: 103).
    Muḥammad b. Aḥmad b. Jumay', unidentified.
    Abū 'Abdallāh al-Maḥāmilī, unidentified.
14. This was apparently also identifiable with the Cemetery of the Quraysh (East Side); cf. n. 1 above. The graveyard was situated somewhat north of ar-Ruṣāfah (cf. LeStrange, pp. 191 ff.; Map V). Muḥammad b. Isḥāq b. Yāsar, d. ca. 151/767. He was the author of a biography (*sīrah*) of the Prophet in two parts, the second of which is the *K. al-Maghāzī* mentioned below (cf. *GAL*, *Supplement*, 1: 226). The grave of Abū-Ḥanīfah was situated next to the tombs of the Caliphs at ar-Ruṣāfah (cf. Yāqūt, *Mu'jam*, 2: 783; also LeStrange, pp. 190 ff.; Map V). The earliest mention of a shrine is found in Muqaddasī (p. 130) who indicates that one Abū Ja'far az-Zammām erected a platform (*suffah*), apparently at the side of the tomb, which was presumably for prayer and meditation. In 436/1044–1045, a mosque was built over his grave. In 453/1061–1062 Sharaf al-Malik decided to remake the shrine and demolished the existing structure and some of the surrounding buildings in order to reconstruct it on new foundations over a larger area. The new shrine consisted of a brick building surmounted by a cupola which was built over his grave, and a college

(*madrasah*) which was erected behind it. The extensive construction required the acquisition of further land, and consequently many bodies were exhumed to be buried elsewhere. The structure was completed in 459/1067 (cf. Ibn al-Jawzī, *Muntaẓam*, 8: 245; for the later history of the sanctuary, see LeStrange, pp. 190–92; M. Jawād, "An-Niẓāmīyah fī Baghdād," *Sumer*, 9 (1953): 324; G. Makdisi, "Muslim Institutions of Learning in Eleventh Century Baghdad" *BSOAS*, 24 (1961): 19 ff., 17–19 for other Hānīfite institutions). Although Abū Hanīfah belongs to the first generation of Baghdadi's, it was not until 436 that a mosque was built over his grave, and not until 459 that a shrine complex was erected to venerate his memory. This apparently supports the view that the development of such shrines belongs to a period no earlier than the tenth century.

15. ʿUmar b. Ibrāhīm al-Muqri', d. 393/1002–1003 (*TB*, 11: 269–70).
    Mukram b. Aḥmad, d. 345/956 (*TB*, 13: 221).
    ʿUmar b. Isḥāq b. Ibrāhīm, unidentified.
    ʿAlī b. Maymūn, unidentified.
    Ash-Shāfiʿī, d. 204/820 (*EI*, *s.v.* Ash-Shāfiʿī).
16. Cf. Yāqūt, *Muʿjam*, 4: 397—mentions a village of that name in the immediate vicinity of Baghdad, but does not indicate its exact location. According to LeStrange, this cemetery was situated outside Bāb al-Baradān, and was also known as the Bāb al-Baradān Cemetery (pp. 204, 307; Map V, ref. no. 51). However, the text of the Khaṭīb seems to refer to two separate locations: al-Mālikīyah, and the Bāb al-Baradān Cemetery.
17. S: *qabr an-nudhūr mashhad an-nudhūr*.
    In the time of Yāqūt, it was situated a half *mīl* from the city wall. The *Marāṣid* indicates that originally it was situated in ar-Ruṣāfah, but that this section around it had fallen into ruin, so that it was presently (ca. 1300) half a *farsakh* from the houses of the town (*Muʿjam*, 4: 28; *Marāṣid*, 3: 385). Cf. also LeStrange, p. 205; Map V, ref. no. 51; Massignon, *Mission*, 2: 38; Canard, *Hamdanides*, 1: 163–64; Makdisi, *Topography*, pp. 289, 296, n. 3—citing Harawī *K. az-Ziyārāt* (ed. J. Sourdel-Thomine, *PIFD*, 1953), p. 74, who locates it near the Khayzurān Cemetery.
18. An abbreviated version of the following story is cited in Yāqūt, on the authority of at-Tanūkhī (*Muʿjam*, 4: 29).
19. S: *ʿUbaydallāh b. Muḥammad b. ʿUmar b. ʿAlī b. al-Ḥusayn b. ʿAlī b. Abī Ṭālib.* He is apparently not in Abū-l-Faraj al-Iṣfahānī's, *Maqātil aṭ-Ṭālibiyīn.* The closest one can get is Muḥammad b. ʿUmar b. Alī b. Abī Ṭālib.
20. Aḥmad b. 'Abdallāh al-Warrāq, d. 379/989 (*TB*, 4: 234).
    Muḥammad b. Hammām, d. 332/944 (*TB*, 3: 365).
    Muḥammad b. Mūsā al-Barbarī, d. 294/908 (*TB*, 3: 243).
    Sulaymān b. Abī Shaykh, d. 246/860–861 (*TB*, 9: 50).
21. S: *al-Ḥasan*; C: *al-Ḥusayn.*
22. Al-Ḥasan b. Zayd b. al-Ḥasan b. ʿAlī b. Abī Ṭālib d. 168/784–785 (*TB*, 7: 309 ff.).
    Hishām b. ʿUrwah (cf. Ibn Khallikān, *Wafayāt*, 2: 194–95; also text below).
23. Al-Ḥasan b. ʿAlī al-Jawharī, d. 454/1062 (*TB*, 7: 393).
    Muḥammad b. al-ʿAbbās al-Khazzāz, d. 382/992–993 (*TB*, 3: 121–22).
    Aḥmad b. Muḥammad b. Mūsā, d. 405/1014 (*TB*, 5: 94 ff.).
    Abū-l-Ḥusayn b. al-Munādī, d. 336/947 (*TB*, 4: 69 ff.).
24. Ḥamzah b. Muḥammad, d. 424/1033 (*TB*, 8: 184).
    Aḥmad b. ʿAbdallāh b. al-Khaḍir, d. 402/1012 (*TB*, 4: 237).
    Ibn al-Mubārak, d. 181/797 (cf. *GAL, Supplement*, 1: 256).

25. Abu Bakr al-Barqānī, d. 425/1034 (cf. *GAL, Supplement*, 1: 259).
'Abd ar-Raḥmān b. 'Umar, d. 397/1007 (*TB*, 10: 301).
Muḥammad b. Aḥmad, d. 331/942–943 (*TB*, 1: 373–75).
Ya'qūb b. Shaybah, d. 262/876 (*TB*, 14: 281–83).
26. Al-Ḥasan b. al-Ḥusayn, d. 431/1040 (*TB*, 7: 300–301).
Isḥāq b. Muḥammad, d. 369/979–980 (*TB*, 6: 400–1).
'Abdallāh b. Isḥāq, d. 311/924 (*TB*, 9: 413–14).
Qa'nab b. al-Muḥarraz: I can find no biographical entry for him, but he is mentioned as a teacher of Muḥammad b. al-Ḥusayn al-Qaṭā'i'ī, d. 320/932 (Ibn al-Jawzī, *Muntaẓam*, 6: 246).
'Abd al-Malik b. Abī Sulaymān (*TB*, 10: 393 ff.).
27. According to Yāqūt, it is situated in the vicinity of Qanṭarat Bāb Ḥarb (cf. *Mu'jam*, 4: 586). Cf. also LeStrange, p. 158; Map V, ref. no. 12—should be situated to the left of the high road as specified by Yāqūt.

Part II A

1. Situated midway between al-Kūfah and Baghdad (Yāqūt, *Mu'jam*, 4: 946—confuses with Madīnat b. Hubayrah; Iṣṭakhrī, p. 85; also Ibn Ḥawqal, p. 166; Muqaddasī, pp. 53, 115, 130). E. Reitemeyer, *Die Städtegründungen der Araber im Islam* (Leipzig, 1912), p. 49.
2. Presumably Madīnat b. Hubayrah which Ṭabarī and Yāqūt confuse with Qaṣr b. Hubayrah (cf. *Annales*, 3.1: 80, 183; *Mu'jam*, 1: p. 680; 3: 208; 4: 123, 946). Cf. also LeStrange, p. 6, n. 1.
3. Balādhurī, *Futūḥ*, p. 287.
4. Balādhurī, *Futūḥ*, p. 287; Ya'qūbī, *Historiae*, 2: 429; Ibn Rustah, p. 109 (n.d.); Ṭabarī, *Annales*, 3.1: 80. Al-Anbār was situated on the Euphrates 10 farsakh (60 km.) from Baghdad (cf. *EI*, *s.v.* al-Anbār).
5. Balādhurī, *Futūḥ*, p. 287; Ya'qūbī, *Historiae*, 2: 429–30; *Buldān*, p. 237; Ibn Quṭaybah, *K. al-ma'ārif*, p. 189; Dīnawarī, *Akhbār*, pp. 372–73; Ṭabarī, *Annales*, 3.1: 87; Mas'ūdī, *Tanbīh*, p. 339: also *K. al-'uyūn*, p. 211.
6. Ya'qūbī, *Historiae*, 2: 450; Ṭabarī, *Annales*, 3.1: 271, 272.
7. *Annales*, 3.1: 271, 319. Reitemeyer, *Städtegründungen*, pp. 41 ff.
8. Ṭabarī, *Annales*, 3.1: 129–33, 271, 318 ff.; also gives dates 136, 137; Yāqūt, *Mu'jam*, 1: 680.
9. Dīnawarī, *Akhbār*, p. 379; Ṭabarī, *Annales*, 3.1: 271.
10. Situated in Lower Nahrawān between Wāsiṭ and Baghdad (cf. Yāqūt, *Mu'jam*, 2: 54).
11. Ṭabarī, *Annales*, 3.1: 275; Yāqūt, *Mu'jam*, 1: 680.
12. Cf. Yāqūt, *Mu'jam*, 1: 464.
13. Ṭabarī, *Annales*, 3.1: 273, 276.
14. Ya'qūbī, *Buldān*, pp. 237–38; Ṭabarī, *Annales*, 1: 272.
15. On the date of construction, see Khaṭīb, 66–67.
16. Ṭabarī, *Annales*, 3.1: 272–73, 276; Khaṭīb, p. 66; Yāqūt, *Mu'jam*, 1: 680; Ibn aṭ-Ṭiqṭaqā, *Fakhrī*, pp. 217–18.
17. Khaṭīb reads *Niqlāṣ*. Note, however, the reading *Miqlāṣ* is preserved in two late (seventeenth century) MSS. of the Khaṭīb: Damad Ibrāhim 889, fol. 7b; Nuru Osmaniya 3093, fol. 17a. The name Miqlāṣ presumably refers to the Manichaean Imām who resided at Ctesiphon; see text below.
18. *Annales*, 3.1: 272.

19. One of the names used to indicate Baghdad. See Khaṭīb, p. 77.
20. Ṭabarī, *Annales*, 3.1 : 278, 281.
21. Balādhurī, *Futūḥ*, p. 295, Ibn Quṭaybah, *K. al-ma'ārif*, p. 192; Ṭabarī, *Annales*, 3.1 : 281, 319; Mas'ūdī, *Tanbih*, p. 360.
22. Balādhurī, *Futūḥ*, p. 287, Ya'qūbī, *Buldān*, p. 238; Ṭabarī, *Annales*, 3.1 : 276; Yāqūt, *Mu'jam*, 2 : 734–35. Note, however, Ya'qūbī, *Historiae*, 2 : 430, 445, who states that the city plan was traced during the reign of as-Saffāḥ.
23. Cf. *Fihrist*, p. 334.
24. Cf. for example Khaṭīb, p. 68.
25. Balādhurī, *Futūḥ*, p. 276; Ṭabarī, *Annales*, 3.1 : 274, 277; Muqaddasī, p. 113; Yāqūt, *Mu'jam*, 1,: 680.
26. Khaṭīb, p. 66.
27. Ya'qūbī, *Buldān*, pp. 237-38; Ṭabarī, *Annales*, pp. 272–73, 276–77; Muqaddasī, pp. 115–20; Yāqūt, *Mu'jam*, 1 : 680–81.
28. See, for example, T. Noeldeke, *Sketches from Eastern History*, (London, 1892), pp. 129–30; LeStrange, pp. 6–10; M. Streck, *Die alte Landschaft Babylonien*, p. 54; E. Reitemeyer, *Die Städtegründungen der Araber im Islam*, pp. 50–51; B. Lewis *The Arabs in History* (London, 1950), pp. 81–83.
29. *Baghdad*, pp. 7–8.
30. Yāqūt, *Mu'jam*, 3: 327; also see Ya'qūbī, *Buldān*, p. 242; Suhrāb, *'Ajā'ib*, pp. 123–24 = Ibn Serapion, pp. 14–15; Iṣṭakhrī, p. 84; Ibn Ḥawqal, p. 165; Khaṭīb, p. 122, based on Suhrāb.
31. *Buldān*, pp. 237–38. This passage in Ya'qūbī is also translated in Lewis, *The Arabs in History*, p. 82.
32. For a concise description of Baghdad in pre-Islamic times, see Duri, art. "Baghdad" in *EI*, 2nd edition, p. 895.
33. See *EI*, *s.v.*, al-Madā'in, the Arabic name for Ctesiphon.
34. Khaṭīb, pp. 127–30. Variants of this account are found in Ṭabarī, *Annales*, 3.1 : 320; Ibn aṭ-Ṭiqṭaqā, *Fakhri*, p. 212.
35. Ya'qūbī, *Historiae*, 2 : 437–39; Ṭabarī, *Annales*, 3.1 : 93–98.
36. Cf. J. Wellhausen, *The Arab Kingdom and Its Fall* (Calcutta, 1927), pp. 488 ff.; G. Van Vloten, *Recherches sur la Domination Arabe* (Amsterdam, 1894), pp. 65–70; R. N. Frye, "The Role of Abū Muslim in the 'Abbāsid Revolt," *Muslim World*, 37 (1947): 28–38; also Van Vloten, *De Opkomst der Abbasiden in Chorasan* (Leiden, 1890), pp. 70–131; S. Moscati, "Studi su Abu Muslim," *I–III*, *Rend. Linc.* (1949), pp. 323–35, 474–95, (1950), pp. 89–105.
37. Cf. I. Friedlander, "The Heterodoxies of the Shiites in the Presentation of Ibn Ḥazm," *JAOS*, 28 (1907): 36 ff.; commentary in 29 (cf. *Index*, p. 163).
38. Ya'qūbī, *Historiae*, 2: 440–41; Dīnawarī, *Akhbār*, pp. 376–78; Ṭabarī, *Annales*, 3.1 : 105–17.
39. Cf. B. Spuler, *Iran in früh-islamischer Zeit* (Wiesbaden, 1952), pp. 48 ff.; also Blochet, *Le Messianisme dans l'hétérodoxie musulmane* (Paris, 1903), pp. 40 ff.
40. Cf. Ṭabarī, *Annales*, 3.1 : 119 ff.
41. Ibid., p. 120.
42. Ed. & Tr. by C. Sheffer (Paris, 1893), pp. 266 ff. (trans.).
43. *Mu'jam*, *s.v.* al-Madā'in.
44. Cf. O. Grabar, "The Ceremonial Art of the Umayyads"—unpublished dissertation, Princeton University, 1955.

45. *Buldān*, pp. 239 ff.; Khaṭīb, pp. 69 ff.
46. K. A. C. Creswell, *Early Muslim Architecture* (Oxford, 1940), 2: 4 ff.; on prototypes, see pp. 18–21. Cf. also Part II B.
47. Ibid., p. 21.
48. O. Reuther, *Die Ausgrabungen der Deutschen Ktesiphon-Expedition im Winter* 1928/29, pp. 6–9.
49. O. Reuther, "Sassanian Architecture (City Planning)," in A. U. Pope, *Survey of Persian Art*, 1: 575.
50. M. ʿAlī Muṣṭafā, "At-Tanqīb fī-l-Kūfah," *Sumer*, 12 (1950): 3–32; "Taqrīr al-awwal," 16 (1954): 73–85; F. Safar, *Wāsiṭ, The Sixth Season's Excavation* (Cairo, 1945).
51. Ṭabarī, *Annales*, 1.3: 2491–92.
52. Creswell, 1: 31.
53. Ibid., 2: 3.
54. O. Grabar, "Al-Mushatta, Baghdad, and Wāsiṭ," *The World of Islam: Studies in Honor of Phillip K. Hitti* (London, 1959), pp. 99–108.
55. Khaṭīb, p. 73, 107–9; Balādhurī, *Futūḥ*, p. 290; *Muʿjam*, 4: 885.
56. Balādhurī, *Futūḥ*, p. 290, Ya qūbī, *Buldān*, p. 322; Ibn Rustah, p. 187.
57. See n. 52 above.
58. Grabar, *Studies*, p. 106; citing Ibn ʿAsākir, *Taʾrīkh Dimashq*, 3: 284.
59. Ṭabarī, *Annales*, 3.1: 418 ff.
60. Khaṭīb, p. 75.
61. Dīnawarī, *Akhbār*, pp. 367–72; Ṭabarī, *Annales*, 3.1: 61–66.

Part II B

1. For a general survey of the Islamic city, see G. Marçais, "La conception des villes dans l'Islam," *Revue D'Alger*, 2 (1945): 517–33.
2. Khaṭīb, p. 70; Ṭabarī, *Annales*, 3.1: 277; Yāqūt, *Muʿjam*, 1: 682.
3. See text of Khaṭīb, p. 67, n. 4.
4. Ibid, p. 70, n. 9, 11—indicating that production was halted during a Shīʿite revolt.
5. Ibid, p. 85; Yaʿqūbī, *Buldān*, p. 248.
6. LeStrange, Map III.
7. Khaṭīb, pp. 79–82.
8. See Introduction to the text.
9. Herzfeld, *Archäologische Reise*, 2: 103 ff.; Creswell, 2: 4 ff.
10. See Fig. 1.
11. See Introduction, p. 32.
11a. This is strikingly similar to W. Barthold's description of pre-Islamic cities in Iran and Turkestan. They comprised a citadel and the town proper. The market was outside the town proper in the suburbs (*berūn = ar-rabaḍ*), in some instances enclosed by a second wall. See W. Barthold, *Turkestan to the Mongol Invasion*, trans. H. A. R. Gibb (2nd ed., London, 1948), p. 78; also idem, *Mussulman Culture* (Calcutta, 1934), pp. 31–32, cited in G. Von Grunebaum, *Islam* (London, 1955), p. 148.
12. *Buldān*, p. 240. Yaʿqūbī indicates that in his time this portico was used as a place for prayer (*muṣallā*), thereby suggesting that it was in fact the Dār al-Qaṭṭān which is mentioned by the Khaṭīb, pp. 108–109. That is to say, when there was no longer sufficient room in the principal-mosque, the Dār al-Qaṭṭān was added to it in the year 260/873–

874 or 261/874–875. The structure of a portico (surrounding a court) would have been ideally suited for conversion into a place of prayer.

13. Ibid.
14. *Ḥawla-r-raḥbah kamā tadūrū.*
15. However, Creswell does mention this account in his text (p. 17).
16. See Maps II, III; text of LeStrange, pp. 30–31.
17. See my reconstruction Figs. 2, 3, and 9.
18. *Annales*, 3.1: 322–23.
19. Ibid, p. 323; Khaṭīb, p. 77 ff. The Khaṭīb confuses two accounts: one concerning Dāwūd b. ʿAlī, the other ʿAbd aṣ-Ṣamad. Note that Dāwūd b. ʿAlī is reported to have died in 133/750 before the city was built (Ṭabarī, 3.1: 73). The variant in Ṭabarī seems to clarify this confusion; the uncle was ʿĪsā b. ʿAlī who apparently suffered from the gout.
20. That is to say, the third *intervallum* of the city marking the limit of the residential section. See Figs. 3, 9.
21. Variants of this account are found in the Khaṭīb, pp. 78–79, 80; Ṭabarī, *Annales*, 3.1: 323, 324; Yāqūt, *Muʿjam*, 4: 254.
22. Khaṭīb, pp. 76, 77. Herzfeld (followed by Creswell) is of the opinion that the length indicated by the Khaṭīb does not leave sufficient room for the guards (1000 men). It is assumed that these guards were actually quartered in the flanking rooms. Consequently, a larger figure is arrived at by assuming that each room was eight cubits wide, with two cubits allowed for the partition walls. Cf. Herzfeld, p. 129; Creswell, p. 16; also Fig. 7.
23. Khaṭīb, p. 76. Yaʿqūbī does not mention this second series of arches.
24. Herzfeld, p. 129, Creswell, p. 16 ff. See Fig. 8.
25. According to Yaʿqūbī, it was a vaulted structure of burnt brick cemented by gypsum, and was protected by two iron doors (*Buldān*, p. 240). Wiet (LesPays, p. 15) incorrectly translates *waʿalayhi bābā ḥadīdin* as *fermé par un porte en fer a deux battants.* This is presumably based on the analogy of the outer gateways; cf. Khaṭīb, p. 75. No dimensions are given for the corridor in the Arabic text. I have chosen the dimensions 30 × 20 on the analogy of the first corridor of the city (Fig. 4), and have reconstructed the buildings of the inner ring as a series of courts flanked by chambers. See Fig. 9.
26. Yaʿqūbī, *Buldān*, p. 239.
27. Creswell, p. 17. See Fig. 8.
28. See Figs. 3, 9.
29. Yaʿqūbī, *Buldān*, p. 239; Khaṭīb, pp. 74–75.
30. Even after the markets were removed, al-Manṣūr, following the advice of Abān b. Ṣadaqah, left a grocer (*baqqāl*) in each of the city's quandrants. He was permitted to sell only vinegar and greens (cf. Ṭabarī, 3.1: 324–25).
31. The old market of the West Side (Sūq Baghdād) was situated in al-Karkh (Ṭabarī, 2.2: 910, 914). The position of this market is fixed by Balādhurī as somewhere near Qarn aṣ-Ṣarāt, the point at which the Ṣarāt Canal empties into the Tigris (*Futūḥ*, p. 246). For al-Karkh, see n. 32.
32. That is to say, the area comprised by al-Karkh, the southern suburb of the city; cf. LeStrange, Map I. The Caliph reportedly called for a wide garment and traced the plan of the markets on it. The butchers market (Sūq al-Qaṣṣābīn) was placed at the end for security reasons (Khaṭīb, p. 80). The development of al-Karkh is discussed in the Khaṭīb, p. 79 ff. A less convincing explanation is found in Yāqūt. He indicates that the Caliph moved the markets from the city because smoke from them caused the walls to blacken (*Muʿjam*, 4: 255). Note a similar explanation is found for the Caliph

al-Mu'taḍid's decision to abandon the construction of the Tāj Palace: cf. Ibn al-Jawzī, *Muntaẓam*, 5.2: 144.

33. This was particularly true of the Būyid period in the tenth and eleventh centuries.
34. Khaṭīb, p. 81.
35. Khaṭīb, p. 79 ff.; Ṭabarī, 3.1: 324.
36. That is to say, the two brothers who led revolts in al-Baṣrah and the Ḥijāz in 145/762; cf. Ṭabarī, 31: 278, 281.
37. Khaṭīb, pp. 75, 80, 92–93; Ya'qūbī, *Buldān*, p. 249.
38. Khaṭīb, p. 87; *Buldān*, p. 249.
39. The date for the beginning of construction as reported in Ya'qūbī (143/760–761) hardly seems possible since according to virtually all the authorities, the building of the Round City was not begun until 145/762; cf. *Buldān*, p. 251.
40. Ṭabarī, 3.1: 364 ff.; Khaṭīb, pp. 82–83; Yāqūt, *Mu'jam*, 2: 783. According to another report in Ṭabarī, 3.1: 460, the moat was not dug and the wall (*ḥā'iṭ*) not built until 159/775–776.
41. *Mu'jam*, 2: 783.
42. Balādhurī, *Futūḥ*, p. 295, Mas'ūdī, *Tanbīh*, p. 360 Khaṭīb, p. 83; *Mu'jam*, 3: 677.
43. Ṭabarī, 3.1: 365 ff.
44. Note Ya'qūbī, *Buldān*, p. 245. He indicates that original plans called for the creation of a palace complex south of the Round City. This area was known as ash-Sharqīyah. A principal mosque was located there, but later its minbar was removed.
45. Ṭabarī, op. cit., p. 380, Khaṭīb, p. 115.
46. Op. cit., p. 116.
47. *Buldān*, p. 249.
48. Ibid., p. 248.
49. Ibid., p. 246.
50. Ṭabarī, 3.1: 364; Khaṭīb, p. 82.
51. Ibid., p. 367.
52. For 'Īsā b. Mūsā, see Ṭabarī, *Index*. On the events leading to his deteriorating position, see Ṭabarī, 3.1: 331–52.
53. Ibid., p. 367.

Part II C

1. See Index to his *Opera Minora*, ed. Y. Moubarac (Beirut, 1963); and especially his *Mission*, pp. 66 ff.
2. *Mission*, pp. 90–92; also his "Les Corps de métiers et la cité Islamique," in *Opera Minora*, 2: 369 ff.
3. *Mission*, pp. 88–92, 93; LeStrange, *Baghdad*, pp. 217–18, 316–17, 323.
4. *Archäologische Reise*, 2: 147–48.
5. M. Canard, *Hamdanides*, 1: 158–63.
6. G. Makdisi, *Topography*, pp. 179, 298–302, 305–6
7. Art. "Baghdad" in *EI*, 2nd edition.
8. *Aṭlās Baghdād* (Baghdad, 1952).
9. See Chronological Map.
10. See Introduction, p. 32, Khaṭīb, pp. 118, 120 for statements on the size of the city. For a full discussion see J. Lassner "The *Ḥabl* of Baghdad and the Dimensions of the City: A Metrological Note," *JESHO*, 6 (1963): 228–29.

11. Iṣṭakhrī, p. 83 = Ibn Ḥawqal, p. 164.
12. For Constantinople see D. Jacoby, "La population de Constantinople," *Byzantion*, 31 (1961): 94 ff.; Note the excavations of Ctesiphon have never been completed. The site thus may be somewhat larger than the 540 ha. given by R. Adams, *Land Behind Baghdad* (Chicago 1965), pp. 62–63, 72.
13. Khaṭīb, pp. 79–80.
14. Ibid., p. 71.
15. *Buldān*, p. 248. In the time of Yāqūt (d. 1224) it was confined to the area of Bāb Ḥarb two *mil* (4 km.) distant from the actual city. The surrounding environs had fallen into ruin so that it gave the appearance of a separate town; see *Mu'jam*, 2: 234; also Le-Strange, *Index*, p. 365; Map V.
16. See Chronological Map.
17. Khaṭīb, p. 71.
18. Ibid.
19. See LeStrange, Maps V and VI.
20. *Buldān*, p. 251.
21. Ibn Ḥawqal, p. 164 = Iṣṭakhrī, p. 83; also *Buldān*, p. 254.
22. See Introduction, p. 38.
23. *'Uyūn al-anbā'*, 1: 221, 224, 310; also Ibn al-Athīr, *Kāmil*, 8: 85.
24. For example – Khaṭib, pp. 107–08; this figure is accepted by Duri in his article "Baghdad" in *EI*, 2nd edition.
25. Hilāl aṣ-Ṣābi', *Rusūm*, pp. 18 ff.
26. On the population of Constantinople, see D. Jacoby in *Byzantion*, 31: 81–105; esp. p. 83, n. 1. For a summary of many views, pp. 102 ff. Note that less conservative studies estimate a population as one million for various periods. The present estimate is based on the figures of Jacoby who claims for the time of Theodosius II, 150,000 for the inner city (700 ha.). Theodosius doubled the size of the city by adding a second wall but this area was sparsely populated, so that the greater city was about 180,000 or about 130 per ha. He estimates that a century later the population grew to about 360,000 for the city and 375,000 for the city and its suburbs.
27. *Land Behind Baghdad: A History of Settlement on the Diyala Plains* (Chicago, 1965).
28. Ibid., pp. 63, 75–76, 77.
29. Computed on the basis of Adams' tables 18 and 19, pp. 62, 72.
30. Ibid., p. 72.
31. Ibid., p. 74.
32. A paper on the ethnic occupation of Baghdad was given by S. al-Ali at a conference on the Islamic city in the summer of 1965 at Oxford University. The paper will appear when the proceedings of the conference are published.
33. See Part II A.
34. See Part II B.
35. *Rusūm*, pp. 8–9, Khaṭīb, pp. 100 ff.
36. *Buldān*, p. 246.
37. On the canals see Khaṭīb, pp. 79, 111–15.
38. *Buldān*, p. 251.
39. Ibid.
40. See LeStrange, Map V.
41. Khaṭīb, pp. 82, 115.
42. See Map; Khaṭīb, p. 93; *Buldān*, p. 252; *'Ajā'ib*, p. 130 = Ibn Serapion, p. 22; *Mu'jam*, 3:

194; *'Arib*, pp. 28–29; Ṣūlī, *Akhbār*, p. 90; Canard *Hamdanides*, p. 161—attempts to identify with Sūq a<u>th</u>-Thalā<u>th</u>ā' in keeping Massignon's Theory of Fixity, also Le-Strange, Map V.

43. *Buldān*, p. 242.
44. In Ibn al-Jawzī, *Manāqib Baghdād*, pp. 25–28; trans. and annot. in Makdisi, *Topography*, pp. 185–97.
45. LeStrange, Map V, ref. no. 59; *Mission*, pp. 88–91.
46. Ibid., <u>Kh</u>aṭīb, p. 116.
47. Makdisi, *Topography*, p. 186, n. 5.
48. Ibid., pp. 282–83, 298. The commercial enterprises of the upper West Side were situated quite a bit inland. The shore line had from the earliest period been reserved for palaces and exclusive residences. The fiefs occupying the shore are rarely if ever mentioned in the accounts of the eleventh century. One would have to assume that such areas would have declined somewhat earlier than the others. As such no pressing needs would have been fulfilled by the continued existence of the Bāb aṭ-Ṭāq bridge since it did not lead to a populated area. Some damage was also inflicted on the areas of the lower West Side in the last years of the Būyids. One year after Ṭu<u>gh</u>ril began construction of his city in al-Mu<u>kh</u>arrim, violent fires causing severe damage hit the lower West Side (*Muntaẓam*, 8: 181; *Topography*, p. 283). The reconstruction of al-Kar<u>kh</u> was not begun until 452/1060; however, these programs were limited to restoring the market. Streets, small shops, and residences were allowed to go unrepaired (*Muntaẓam*, 8: 212; Ibn al-A<u>th</u>īr, *Kāmil*, 10: 5; *Topography*, p. 285). In 455/1063 work started on the demolition of the remaining buildings along the right river bank by order of the Caliph al-Qā'im (*Muntaẓam*, 8: 232). Aside from the truncated market area of al-Kar<u>kh</u>, the remaining sections of the West Side probably became, more or less, self-contained units by the middle of the eleventh century. Thus, only one bridge was necessary to unite the markets of al-Kar<u>kh</u> with the East Side. Note that this bridge fell into disrepair in 450/1059–60, and was then returned to the moorings at Bāb aṭ-Ṭāq. This, however, does not seem to be a reflection of the city's needs, but rather those of the wazīr al-Basāsīrī, whose troops were stationed near Bāb aṭ-Ṭāq at Bustān az-Zāhir (<u>Kh</u>aṭīb, p. 116; *Muntaẓam*, 8: 132 *sub anno* 450). In any event, the bridge was later moved further south again.
49. D. 1065.
50. See the remarks accompanying Duri's map in his article on Baghdad in *EI*, 2nd edition.
51. *Muntaẓam*, 8: 68–69 quoted in *Topography*, p. 185, n. 4.
52. See for example <u>Kh</u>aṭīb, p. 100 ff.
53. *Muntaẓam*, 5: 70 quoted in *Topography*; p. 185, n. 4.
54. When Ṭu<u>gh</u>ril entered Baghdad there were 170 palaces along the river banks. These were reportedly all destroyed by 455. See *Muntaẓam*, 8, p. 232.
55. *Mu'jam*, 2: 234.
56. C. Cahen in *Baghdad 1962: Volume special publié à l'occasion du mille deux centième anniversaire de la fondation*, p. 295, published as *Arabica*, 9 (1962).

Appendix A

1. *Ta'rī<u>kh</u> Baghdād* (Cairo), pp. 132–33.
2. <u>Kh</u>aṭīb, p. 81.
3. See for example Ibn al-Jawzī, *Muntaẓam*, 7: 153, 174; Miskawayh, *Tajārib*, 3: 387; 4: 408; Ibn al-A<u>th</u>īr, *Kāmil*, 9: 74, 119.

4. Khaṭīb, p. 71.
5. Ibid., p. 110.
6. Ibid., pp. 75, 76.
7. See Part II C.
8. Oral communication of O. Grabar who has spent several recent campaigns excavating that site.
9. A discussion of these matters can be found in *K. al-fiqh ʿalā-l-madhāhib al-arbaʿah, qism al-ʿibādat*, 2nd edition, (Cairo, 1345/1931), pp. 346–48. I am indebted in this matter to Prof. J. Schacht for his advice.
10. Khaṭīb, pp. 109 ff..
11. For the judical authorities see the list compiled by L. Massignon in his "Cadis et Naqibs Baghdadiens," *Opera Minora*, 2: 258 ff.
12. Iṣṭakhrī, p. 84.
13. Khaṭīb, pp. 109–10.
14. See Le Strange, Map VI.
15. *Muʿjam*, 2: 234.

Appendix B

1. Khaṭīb, pp. 91 ff.
2. Ibid., pp. 79 ff.
3. Ṭabarī, *Annales*, 3.1: 323–24; Yaʿqūbī, *Historiae*, 2: 481; Balādhurī, *Futūḥ*, p. 295; Yāqūt, *Muʿjam*, 4: 254.
4. *Muʿjam*, 4: 254.
5. Yaʿqūbī, *Buldān*, p. 254.
6. See S. D. Goitein, "The Rise of the Near-Eastern Bourgeoisie," *Journal of World History*, 3 (1958): 583–604, esp. pp. 598 ff.
7. Oral communication of A. Udovitch of Cornell University who is preparing a major work on Islamic commercial law.
8. *Buldān*, p. 252.
9. Ibid., p. 259—for a similar situation at Sāmarrā.
10. *Muʿjam*, 6: 300–1.

Appendix C

1. See Fig. 1; Introduction, p. 32.
2. Khaṭīb, p. 107.
3. Ibid., pp. 107–8.
4. Ibid., p. 108.
5. Ibid.
6. *Archäologische Reise*, 2: 135 ff.
7. *Early Muslim Architecture*, 2: 32 ff.
8. See Part II B.
9. Khaṭīb, pp. 75, 80, 92–93; Yaʿqūbī, *Buldān*, p. 249.
10. Khaṭīb, pp. 80, 109, n. 9; LeStrange, Map III.
11. The previous construction was of mud brick and clay; cf. Khaṭīb, p. 107.
12. See Figs. 10, 11.
13. Assuming that the mosque was situated along the north wall of the palace; cf. below.

14. See Fig. 12. The assumption of Herzfeld and Creswell is that only the courts of the two mosques were of equal dimensions. The total area of ar-Rashīd's mosque and that of al-Mu'taḍid vary somewhat. Perhaps the Khaṭīb wishes to indicate that the two sections of the mosque were of equal size.
15. Khaṭīb, p. 108.
16. See Fig. 13.
17. Khaṭīb, p. 108.
18. Creswell, p. 32.
19. Ibid., p. 280, fig. 223.
20. Ibid., p. 46, fig. 33. The plan reveals only three aisles but the spacing clearly indicates room for five.
21. See n. 1 above.
22. Note that Ibn Ṭūlūn came from Sāmarrā.
23. See Fig. 13.
24. See Fig. 14.
25. Khaṭīb, p. 108; also Figs. 2, 11.
26. Creswell, p. 33.
27. Ibid, pp. 33, 34.
28. Italics mine.
29. Ya'qūbī, *Buldān*, p. 240.
30. Ibid.

Appendix H

86. The *isnād* is: Muḥammad b. 'Ali al-Warrāq and Aḥmad b. 'Alī al-Muḥtasib——— Muḥammad b. Ja'far an-Naḥwī———al-Ḥasan b. Muḥammad as-Sakūnī——— Muḥammad b. Khalaf.
87. The *isnād* is: Muḥammad b. 'Alī al-Warrāq and Aḥmad b. 'Alī al-Muḥtasib——— Muḥammad b. Ja'far an-Naḥwī———al-Ḥasan b. Muḥammad as-Sakūnī——— Muḥammad b. Khalaf Wakī'.
88. The *isnād* is: Abū 'Abdallāh al-Ḥusayn b. Muḥammad b. Ja'far al-Khāli'———'Alī b. Muḥammad b. as-Sarī al-Hamadhānī———al-Qāḍī Abū Bakr Muḥammad b. Khalaf.
89. The *isnād* is the same as in n. 88 above.
90. The *isnād* is: Abū-l-Qāsim al-Azharī———Aḥmad b. Ibrāhīm———Ibrāhīm b. Muḥammad b. 'Arafah.
91. Fl. ninth century; cf. *TB*, 11 : 373.
92. Fl. ninth century; cf. *TB*, 4: 131.
93. This entire chapter including the account credited to 'Abdallāh b. Muḥammad b. 'Alī al-Baghdādī, who was a direct authority of the Khaṭib, is virtually identical in content and language with Suhrāb, *'Ajā'ib al-aqālim as-sab'ah*. It can be assumed that Suhrāb was the source of this information.
94. Ed. Tr. M. Amar in *JA*, X, 19 (1912); cf. pp. 243 ff.
95. Cf. G. Makdisi, *Ibn 'Aqīl* (Damascus, 1963), *Index*.
96. D. 461/1068 (?), cf. *GAL*, 1 : 563—an abbreviated version of the Khaṭīb.
97. D. 562/1167; cf. *GAL*, *Supplement*, 1 : 564–65.
98. D. 597/1201; cf. *GAL*, *Supplement*, 2 : 548–49.
99. D. 637/1239; cf. *GAL*, *Supplement*, 1 : 565.
100. D. 634/1236–37; cf. Rosenthal, *Historiography*, p. 387, n. 1.

101. D. 643/1245; cf. *GAL, Supplement*, 1: 613.
102. D. 674/1275; cf. *GAL, Supplement*, 1: 596.
103. D. 748/1348; cf. *GAL, Supplement*, 2: 45-47.
104. D. 774/1372; cf. *GAL, Supplement*, 2: 30.
105. He is listed by Ḥajjī Khalīfah as the author of a *K. at-tibyān*; I can find no biographical information about him.
106. Described by Ḥajjī Khalīfah as a history (*ta'rīkh*) in twenty-seven volumes.

Selected Bibliography*

Arabic Texts

Abū-l-Fidā'. *Ta'rikh*, ed. J. Reiske. 5 vols. Copenhagen 1789–94.

'Arīb b. Sa'd al-Qurṭubī. *Ṣilat ta'rikh aṭ-Ṭabari*, ed. M. J. De Goeje. Leiden, 1897.

al-Balādhūrī, Aḥmad b. Yaḥyā, *K. futūḥ al-buldān*, ed. M. J. De Goeje. Leiden, 1866; trans. P. K. Hitti, *The Origins of the Islamic State*, New York, 1916, and F. C. Murgotten, New York, 1924.

Bar Hebraeus, Abū-l-Faraj Yuḥannā Gregorius Ibn al-'Ibrī. *Chronography* (Syr.), ed. and trans. A. W. Budge. 2 vols. Oxford, 1932.

———. *Dyanasties*, ed. and trans. E. Pococke. Oxford, 1663.

adh-Dhahabī, Muḥammad b. Aḥmad. *K. tadhkirat al-ḥuffāẓ*. 5 vols. Hyderabad, 1915–16.

ad-Dīnawarī, Aḥmad b. Dāwūd. *K. al-akhbār aṭ-ṭiwāl*, ed. V. Guirgass. Leiden, 1888; indices by I. Kratchkovsky (1912).

Elias of Nisibus. *Chronography*, ed. F. Baethgen as *Fragmente syrischer und arabischer Historiker*. In *Abhandlungen für die Kunde des Morgenlandes*, VIII (1884).

Eutychius (Sa'd Ibn al-Biṭrīq). *Annales*, ed. L. Cheikho. Beirut-Paris, 1906–9.

al-Hamadhānī, Muḥammad b. Abd al-Malik, *Takmilat ta'rīkh aṭ-Ṭabarī*, ed. A. J. Kannan. In *al-Mashriq* (1955), pp. 21–42, 149–73; (1957), pp. 185–216.

al-Ḥumaydī, Muḥammad b. Futūḥ. *Jadhwat al-muqtabis fī dhikr wulāt al-Andalus*. Cairo, 1952.

*Further entires can be found in the introduction to Makdisi's *Ibn 'Aqil*, and more particularly in the comprehensive *Bibliography of Baghdad* (Baghdad, 1962) compiled by G. 'Awād and 'Abdul-Hameed al-'Alouchi, which is extremely useful for recent Arabic publications. In some cases, there exist more recent editions which were not available to me and which, therefore, have not been listed here.

Ibn Abī Uṣaybi'ah, Aḥmad b. al-Qāsim. *'Uyūn al-anbā' fī ṭabaqāt al-aṭibbā'*, ed. A. Muller. Cairo–Königsberg, 1882–84.

Ibn al-Athīr, 'Alī b. Muḥammad. *Al-kāmil fī-t-ta'rīkh*, ed. C. J. Tornberg. 12 vols. Leiden, 1851–76.

———. *Al-lubāb fī tahdhīb al-ansāb*. 3 vols. Cairo, 1357/1938.

Ibn al-Faqīh, Aḥmad b. Muḥammad. *K. al-buldān*, ed. M. J. De Goeje. Leiden, 1855. *BGA* 5.

Ibn Ḥajar, Aḥmad b. 'Alī. *K. tahdhīb at-tahdhīb*. 12 vols. Hyderabad, 1907–9.

———. *Lisān al-mīzān*. 6 vols. Hyderabad, 1911–13.

Ibn Ḥawqal, Abū-l-Qāsim an-Naṣībī. *K. al-masālik wa-l-mamālik*, ed. M. J. De Goeje. Leiden, 1897. *BGA* 2.

Ibn al-Jawzī, 'Abd ar-Raḥman b. 'Alī. *Manāqib Baghdād*, ed. M. M. al-Atharī. Baghdad, 1923; partially trans. and annotated by G. Makdisi. *Arabica* 6 (1959): 185–95.

———. *Al-muntaẓam fī-t-ta'rīkh al-mulūk wa-l-umam*, ed. F. Krenkow. Vols. 5^2–10. Hyderabad, 1938–39.

Ibn Kathīr, Ismā'īl b. 'Umar. *Al-bidāyah wa-n-nihāyah*. 14 vols. Cairo, 1932–40.

Ibn Khallikān, Aḥmad b. Muḥammad. *K. wafayāt al-a'yān wa anbā' abnā' az-zamān*. Cairo, 1881; trans. M. G. DeSlane, *Ibn Khallikans Biographical Dictionary*. 4 vols. Paris–London, 1843–71.

Ibn Khurradādhbih, 'Ubaydallāh b. 'Abdallāh. *K. al-masālik wa-l-mamālik*, ed. and trans. M. J. De Goeje. Leiden, 1889. *BGA* 6.

Ibn Khurradādhbih, 'baydallāh b. 'Abdallāh. *K. al-masālik wa-l-mamālik*, ed. and trans. and D. S. Margoliouth, *The Eclipse of the Abbasid Caliphate*. 7 vols. London, 1920–21.

Ibn an-Nadīm, Muḥammad b. Isḥāq. *K. al-fihrist*, ed. G. Flügel. 2 vols. Leipzig, 1871–72.

Ibn Quṭaybah, 'Abdallāh b. Muslim. *K. al-ma'ārif*, ed. F. Wüstenfeld. Göttingen, 1850.

Ibn Rustah, Aḥmad b. 'Umar. *K. al-a'lāq an-nafīsah*, ed. M. J. De Goeje. Leiden, 1892. *BGA* 7; trans. G. Wiet, *Les Atours Précieux*. Cairo, 1955.

Ibn Taghrī Birdī, Yūsuf. *An-nujūm az-zāhirah fi mulūk Miṣr wa-l-Qāhirah*, ed. T. G. J. Juynbol' and B. F. Mathes. Vol. 1. Leiden, 1855–61.

Ibn Ṭayfūr, Aḥmad b. Abī Ṭāhir. *K. Baghdād*, ed. and trans. H. Kellert. 2 vols. Leipzig, 1908.

Ibn aṭ-Ṭiqṭaqā, Muḥammad b. 'Alī b. Ṭabāṭabā. *Al-kitāb al-fakhrī fi-l-adab as-sulṭānīyah wa-d-duwal al-islāmiyah*, ed. H. Derenbourg. Paris, 1895; trans. C. E. J. Whitting, *Al-Fakhri*. London, 1947; also E. Amar, *Histoire des dynasties musulmanes depuis la mort de Mahomet jusqu'à la chute du Khalifat 'Abbāside de Baghdadz*. Paris, 1910.

Ibn az-Zubayr, ar-Rashīd. *Al-Dhakhā'ir wa-t-tuhaf*, ed. Salāḥ ad-Dīn al-Munajjid. Beirut, 1959.

al-Iṣfahānī, Abū-l-Faraj 'Alī b. al-Ḥusayn. *K. al-aghānī*. 20 vols. Cairo, 1289/1868. Vol. 21 ed. R. Brünnow. Leiden, 1888.

al-Iṣfahānī, Ḥamzah b. al-Ḥasan. *Tawarīkh sini mulūk al-arḍ wa-l-anbiyā'*, ed. and trans. J. M. E. Gottwaldt. 2 vols. Leipzig, 1844, 1848.

al-Iṣṭakhrī, Ibrāhīm b. Muḥammad. *K. masālik al-mamālik*, ed. M. J. De Goeje. Leiden, 1870. *BGA* 1.

al-Khaṭīb al-Baghdādī. *Ta'rīkh Baghdād*. 14 vols. Cairo, 1931.

al-Khuwārizmī, Muḥammad b. Mūsā. *K. ṣurat al-arḍ*, ed. H. V. Mzik. Leipzig, 1926. *BAHG* 3.

K. al-ʿuyūn, ed. M. J. De Goeje. In *Fragmenta Historicorum Arabicorum*, I. Leiden, 1869.

Marāṣid al-iṭṭilāʿ ʿalā asmāʾ al-amkinah wa-l-biqāʿ, ed. T. G. S Juynboll. 6 vols. Leiden, 1852.

al-Masʿūdī, ʿAlī b. al-Ḥusayn. *Murūj adh-dhahab wa-maʿādin al-jawāhir*, ed. and trans. by C. Barbier de Meynard and Pavet de Courteille. *Les Prairies d'Or*. 9 vols. Paris, 1861–77.

———. *K. at-tanbīh wa-l-ishrāf*, ed. M. J. De Goeje. Leiden, 1894. *BGA* 8; trans. Carra de Vaux. *Le Livre de l'avertissement et de la revision*. Paris, 1896.

al-Muqaddasī, Muḥammad b. Aḥmad. *K. aḥsan at-taqāsim fī maʿrifat al-aqālīm*, ed. M. J. De Goeje, Leiden, 1877. *BGA* 3; trans. G. S. A. Ranking. In *Biblioteca Indica* 137 (1897).

Qazwīnī, Ḥamdallāh Mustawfī. *Nuzhat al-qulūb* (Pers.), ed. G. LeStrange. London, 1915, *GMS* 23; trans. LeStrange. *The Geographical Part of the Nuzhat al-Qulūb of Qazwīnī*. London, 1919.

al-Qifṭī, ʿAlī b. Yūsuf. *Taʾrīkh al-ḥukamāʾ*, ed. J. Lippert. Leipzig, 1903.

Qudāmah b. Jaʿfar. *K. al-kharāj*, ed. and trans. M. J. De Goeje. Leiden, 1889. *BGA* 6.

aṣ-Ṣābiʾ, Hilāl b. al-Muḥassin. *K. al-wuzarāʾ*, ed. H. F. Amedroz. Beirut, 1904.

———. *Rusūm Dār al-Khilāfah*, ed. M. ʿAwād. Cairo, 1963.

as-Sakhāwī, Muḥammad b. Aḥmad. *Al-iʿlān bi-t-tawbīkh liman dhamma ahl at-tawārīkh*; trans. F. Rosenthal. In *A History of Muslim Historiography*. Leiden, 1952.

as-Samʿānī, ʿAbd al-Karīm b. Muḥammad. *K. al-ansāb*, ed. D. S. Margoliouth. London, 1912. *GMS* 20.

ash-Shābushtī, ʿAlī b. Aḥmad. *K. ad-diyārāt*, ed. K. ʿAwād. Baghdad, 1951; trans. E. Sachau. *Vom Klosterbuch des Shābushtī*. Berlin, 1919.

Suhrāb. *ʿAjāʾib al-aqālīm as-sabʿah*, ed. H. V. Mžik. Leipzig, 1930. *BAHG* 5; section on hydrography = Ibn Serapion. *Description of Mesopotamia and Baghdad*, ed. and trans. G. LeStrange. London, 1895—originally in *JRAS* of that year.

aṣ-Ṣūlī, Muḥammad b. Yaḥyā. *Akhbār ar-Rāḍī wa-l-Muttaqī*, ed. J. H. Dunne. London, 1935; trans. M. Canard. Algiers, 1946, 1950. *PIEO* 10 and 12, 2 vols.

———. *Ashʿar awlād al-khulafāʾ*, ed. J. H. Dunne. Cairo, 1934.

Sūsah Aḥmad. *Aṭlas Baghdād*. Baghdad, 1952.

aṭ-Ṭabarī, Muḥammad b. Jarīr. *K. akhbār ar-rusul wa-l-mulūk* (*Annales*), ed. M. J. De Goeje and others. 13 vols. Leiden, 1879–1901.

at-Tanūkhī, Abū ʿAlī al-Muḥassin b. ʿAlī. *Nishwār al-muḥāḍarah wa-akhbār al-mudhākarah*, Part I: ed. and trans. D. S. Margoliouth. *The Table Talk of a Mesopotamian Judge*. London, 1921 (Oriental Trans. Fund, N. S. 27 and 28). Part II: text in *RAAD* 12 (1932), 13 (1933–35), and 17 (1942); trans. in *Islamic Culture* 5 (1931): 169–93, 352–71, 559–81; 6 (1932): 47–66, 184–205, 370–96. Part III: text in *RAAD* 9 (1930); trans. in *Islamic Culture* 3 (1929): 490–522; 4 (1930): 1–28, 223–28, 363–88, 531–57.

Wakīʿ, Muḥammad b. Khalaf. *Akhbār al-quḍāh*. 3 vols. Cairo, 1947–50.

al-Yaʿqūbī, Aḥmad b. Abī Yaʿqūb. *Taʾrīkh* (*Historiae*), ed. M. Th. Houtsma. Leiden, 1883.

———. *K. al-buldān*, ed. M. J. De Goeje. Leiden, 1892. *BGA* VII; trans. G. Wiet, *LesPays*. Cairo, 1937. *PIFAO* I.

Yāqūt, Yaʿqūb b. ʿAbdallāh. *Irshād al-arib ilā maʿrifat al-adīb* (*Muʿjam al-udabāʾ*), ed. D. S. Margoliouth. London, 1907–31. *GMS* VI.

———. *Mu'jam al-buldān*, ed. F. Wüstenfeld. 6 vols. Leipzig, 1866–73.

———. *Mushtarik*, ed. F. Wüstenfeld. Göttingen, 1846.

Western Sources

Amar, E. *Prolégomènes à l'étude des historiens arabes par* as-Safadī. In *JA* (1911–12).

Arabica.

Ars Islamica.

Ars Orientalis.

Ben Cheneb, M. *Abū Dolāma, Poète bouffon de la cour des premiers Califes abbasides.* Algiers, 1922.

Brockelmann, C. *Geschichte der Arabischen Literatur.* 2 vols. Weimar, 1898–1902; *Supplement.* 3 vols. Leiden, 1937–41; second edition. 2 vols. Leiden, 1943–49.

Bulletin of the School of Oriental and African Studies.

Byzantion.

Canard, M. *Histoire de la dynastie des Hamdanides de Jazira et de Syrie.* Vol. 1. Paris, 1953.

Cattenoz, H. G. *Table de Concordance des Ères Chrétienne et Hégirienne.* 2nd ed. Rabat, 1959.

Christensen, A. *L'Iran sous les Sassanides.* Paris, 1936.

Creswell, K. A. C. *Early Muslim Architecture.* 2 vols. Oxford, 1940.

Dennett, D. C. *Conversion and Poll Tax in Early Islam.* Harvard Hist. Monograph Series XXII. Cambridge, Mass., 1950.

Donaldson, D. M. *The Shi'ite Religion.* Mashad, 1933.

Dozy, R. *Dictionnaire détaillé des noms des vêtements chez les Arabes.* Amsterdam, 1895.

———. *Supplément aux dictionnaires Arabes.* 2nd ed. Leiden–Paris, 1927.

Dussaud, R. *Les Arabes en Syrie avant l'Islam.* Paris, 1907.

Encyclopedia of Islam.

Fraenkel, S. *Die aramäischen Fremdwörter im Arabischen.* Leiden, 1886.

Frye, R. N. *The History of Bukhara.* Cambridge, 1954.

Geographische Zeitschrift.

Grohmann, A. *Einführung und Chrestomathie zur arabischen Papyruskunde.* Vol. 1. Prague, 1954—.

Heer, F. J. *Die historischen und geographischen Quellen in Jāqūt's geographischen Wörterbuch.* Strassburg, 1898.

Herzfeld, E., and F. Sarre. *Archäologische Reise im Euphrat und Tigris Gebiet.* Vol. 2. Berlin, 1921.

Hinz, W. *Arabische Masse und Gewichte.* Leiden, 1955.

Der Islam.

Islamic Culture.

Journal Asiatique.

Journal of the American Oriental Society.

Journal of the Royal Asiatic Society.

Journal of World History.

Kramers, J. H. *Analecta Orientalia.* Vol. 1. Leiden, 1954.

Kritzeck, J., and R. Bayly Winder. *The World of Islam Studies in Honor of Philip K. Hitti.* New York, 1959.

La Voix, H. *Catalogue des monnaies musulmanes de la Bibliothèque Nationale*, I. Paris, 1887.

LeStrange, G. *Baghdad during the Abbasid Caliphate.* London, 1900.

———. *Lands of the Eastern Caliphate.* Cambridge, 1905.

Løkkegaard, F. *Islamic Taxation in the Classic Period*, Copenhagen, 1950.

L'Orange, H. P. *Studies in the Iconography of Cosmic Kingship in the Ancient World.* Cambridge, 1953.

Makdisi, G. *Ibn'Aqīl et la resurgence de l'Islam traditionaliste au XIe siècle.* Damascus, 1963.

Margoliouth, D. S. *Lectures on Arabic Historians.* Calcutta, 1930.

Massignon, L. *Mission en Mésopotamie (1907–1908).* Vol. 2. Cairo, 1912 (*MIFAO* 2).

———. *Opera Minora*, ed. Y. Moubarac. 3 vols. Beirut, 1963.

Miquel, A. *La Géographie humaine du monde musulman jusqu'au milieu du 11e siècle.* Paris, 1967.

Muslim World.

Noeldeke, T. *Sketches from Eastern History*, trans. J. S. Black. London, 1892.

Reitemeyer, E. *Die Städtegründungen der Araber im Islam.* Munich, 1912.

Revue des Études Islamiques.

Ritter, H. *Orientalia I (Istanbuler Mitteilungen I).* Istanbul, 1933.

Rivista degli Studi Orientali.

Rosenthal, F. *A History of Muslim Historiography.* Leiden, 1952.

Salmon, G. *L'Introduction topographique à l'histoire de Baghdadh.* Paris, 1904.

Sourdel, D. *Le Vizirat 'Abbāside.* 2 vols. Damascus, 1959–60.

Streck, M. *Die alte Landschaft Babylonien.* Leiden, 1900.

Sumer.

Syria.

Von Vloten, G. *Recherches sur la Domination Arabe.* Amsterdam, 1894.

Wellhausen, J. *The Arab Kingdom and its Fall*, trans. M. G. Weir. Calcutta, 1927.

Wensinck, A. J. *Concordance et indices de la tradition musulmane.* Leiden, 1936.

Wiener Zeitschrift für die Kunde des Morgenlandes.

Zambaur, E. de. *Manuel de généalogie et de chronologie pour l'histoire de l'Islam.* Hanover, 1927.

Zeitschrift der Deutschen Morganländischen Gesellschaft.

Index of Persons and Peoples

This index of persons and peoples contains all such names mentioned in the text and the bibliographical references in the footnotes. When a footnote contains an extended discussion of a western author's views, he is listed as well.

In the alphabetization, no distinction has been made between different Arabic sounds. Thus t and ṭ are treated as the same letter. The words b. (*ibn*), bt. (*bint*), and the definite article (al-) in all its forms are disregarded in the alphabetical order, as are the *'ayn* (') and *ḥamzah* ('). An attempt has been made to identify all individuals according to their Arabic proper names, even though they may be better known under their patronymic, genealogy, and/or professional background. Thus the jurist Abū Ḥanīfah is to be found under an-Nu'mān b. T̲h̲ābit, and the historian aṭ-Ṭabarī, under Muḥammad b. Jarīr. Where the Arabic proper name is not known, the individual is listed according to the form first mentioned.

Index of Places

This index contains all place names mentioned in the text and notes. Many Arabic terms may be variously translated into English, and moreover, specific monuments may in time lend their names to surrounding areas. Therefore it is often difficult and sometimes impossible to render precise English translations, or to know whether a particular architectural structure or a wider geographical locality is indicated. In this respect the translation lends itself to considerable interpretation, much of which is highly conjectural. The reader is therefore referred to the Arabic glossary of technical terms related to topography (Appendix F). An attempt has been made as well to cross-index various locations according to both English and Arabic names.

Since the text is confined specifically to the Early Middle Ages, and centers largely about the work of the Khaṭīb, the list of locations in the index is by no means all inclusive. Enquiries may be directed to the index of LeStrange, and the Arabic texts of Ya'qūbī and Yāqūt.

Jacob Lassner is associate professor of Near Eastern languages and literatures at Wayne State University. He received his B.A. from The University of Michigan (1955), his M.A. from Brandeis University (1957), and his Ph.D. from Yale University (1963). His *Caliphate at Samarra* is in press.

The manuscript was edited by Robert H. Tennenhouse. The book was designed by Richard Kinney. The type face for the text is Times Roman designed by Stanley Morison in 1931; and the display face is Legend designed by F. H. E. Schneidler for Bauer in 1937.

The book is printed on S. D. Warren's Olde Style Antique paper and bound in Columbia Mills Bayside Vellum cloth over boards. Manufactured in the United States of America.